A Collection of the
VERY FINEST
RECIPES
ever assembled into one Cookbook
CONVENTIONAL AND MICROWAVE

If additional copies of this book are desired, please send

$12.00

for each book ordered to:

BECKER PUBLICATIONS, INC.
Dept. SUP 1
680 Hegenberger Road
Oakland, Ca 94621

California residents please add appropriate sales tax.

ISBN No. 0-940115-00-X

Library of Congress Catalog
Card Number: 80-123367

Recipe for Cover Photo can be found on page 170.

RECIPE FOR HAPPINESS

Take: 2 Heaping Cups of Patience

1 Heartfull of Love

2 Handfuls of Generosity

Dash of Laughter

1 Headfull of Understanding

Sprinkle: generously with Kindness

Add: plenty of Faith and Hope

MIX WELL:

Spread over a period of a lifetime

Serve: generously to everyone you meet

GENERAL MICROWAVE USAGE INSTRUCTIONS

1. Power Levels and Wattage

Because there is no real standardization in the microwave oven industry, it makes cooking in your particular oven often difficult when following a recipe unless you are aware what the wattage was in the oven in which the recipe was tested. Microwave ovens will vary in wattage from 400 - 720 watts for home units. The wattage and the size of the cavity of the oven are always related. Small ovens have lower wattage and large ovens have higher wattage. A general rule is always undercook your food because you can always add time, you can't take it away. The cooking time for recipes in this book may vary depending on many things as in the starting temperature of the food, the container used and the wattage of the oven. Many microwave ovens have only one power level which makes them suitable for a limited amount of cooking and generally only reheating. Most microwave ovens have variable power levels ie, full power, medium-high, medium, simmer, low, warm. To obtain any real cooking functions the variable power levels are necessary. In following the microwave cooking instructions in these recipes, unless specifically noted, use the power setting equivelent to the conventional cooking temperature indicated.

2. Covering

Most foods when cooked in a microwave oven should be covered. Much of the outcome of the cooked food will depend on covering with the proper product. A heavy quality plastic wrap is used to entrap steam. This will be used over all vegetables and most reheating processes. Wax paper and paper towels are used to cover to prevent splattering and also to somewhat more evenly distribute heat over the food product.

3. Utensils

In many of these recipes a browning dish is used in lieu of a fry pan. The browning dish should always be preheated as per your instructions that come with the dish. A good general rule to follow when preheating the dish would be to preheat from 5-7 minutes on full power, depending on the wattage of your oven. The browning dish will give you the same pan fried effect of the fry pan. All oven tempered glass and corning glass cooking utensils are great in the microwave oven. Also, as a general rule, make sure all plastics are designated usable in the microwave. When a recipe makes reference to a saucepan, make sure you use either glass, corning, or plastic and NEVER metal.

MAIN DISHES

SWEDISH MEAT BALLS

¾ Lb. Lean Ground Beef
½ Lb. Ground Veal
¼ Lb. Ground Pork
1½ Cups Soft Bread Crumbs
1 Cup Light Cream or Half & Half
½ Cup Chopped Onion
1 Egg
¼ Cup Finely-chopped Parsley
1¼ Tsp. Salt
Dash of Ginger
Dash of Pepper
Dash of Nutmeg
2 Tbs. All-purpose Flour
½ Cup Canned Condensed Beef
   Broth
¾ Cup Cold Water
½ Tsp. Instant Coffee

Have meat ground together twice. Soak
bread in cream about 5 minutes. Cook
onion in 1 tbs. butter until tender. Combine meats, crumb mixture, onion, egg,
parsley and seasonings. Beat until fluffy,
about 5 minutes at medium speed on
electric mixer. Form into 1½" balls.
Brown in 2 tbs. butter; remove. [MW:
5-6 min. on full power] Make gravy.
Stir flour into drippings; add broth,
water and coffee. Heat and stir until
thickened. Return meat balls to gravy;
cover and cook slowly about 30 min.,
basting occasionally. Makes 2½ dozen
balls.

BARBECUED FLANK STEAK

½ Cup Soy Sauce
2 Tbs. Honey
2 Tbs. White Vinegar
1½ Tsp. Garlic Powder
1½ Tsp. Ginger Powder
½ Cup Finely-chopped Red Onion
¾ Cup Oil
2 to 4 Lbs. Flank Steak

Combine all ingredients for marinade. Add
flank steak and marinate overnight. Barbecue each side of flank steak 5 to 7 minutes
over hot coals. [MW: 4-5 min. on each side
in browning dish on full power]

FIVE—HOUR OVEN STEW

1½ Lbs. Boneless Stew Meat (or round),
   cut in 1" cubes
5 Medium Potatoes, pared and cut into
   eighths
2 Cups Cut-up Carrots, in 1" chunks
1 Cup Very Coarsely Chopped Onion
1 Cup Celery, cut in ½" pieces
2 - 14½ oz. Cans Stewed Tomatoes
2 Tbs. Quick Cooking Tapioca
1 Tbs. Sugar
½ Tsp. Salt
1/8 Tsp. Pepper

Combine all ingredients in large bowl, mix
gently but well. Turn into a 3 quart casserole; cover. Bake at 275 degrees for 5
hours. Let stand 5 minutes before serving.
[MW: full power for 30 min., reduce power
to low for another 60 min. Let stand for
20 minutes.] Makes 6 servings.

WORKPERSON'S ROAST

1 Roast (can be beef or pork, expensive
   cuts do not taste better than inexpensive ones; size is determined by need)
1 Pkg. Lipton's Onion Soup Mix
2 Tbs. Worcestershire Sauce
1 Can (8 Oz.) Cream of Mushroom Soup
1 Section Fresh Garlic

Place the roast in center of large sheet of
aluminum foil wrap [MW: 3-quart oblong
glass dish] ; cut slits in roast and push in cut
sections of fresh garlic. Pour mushroom
soup over roast; pour the Worcestershire
sauce over soup. Sprinkle dry soup over
that. Add seasoning salt & salt and pepper
to taste. Add meat tenderizer, depending
on cut of meat. Pull foil up and seal across
top and ends; be sure it is sealed tightly,
leaving space above and around roast.
Place in cake pan and put in oven at 250
degrees from 7 A.M. to 5 P.M. [MW: cover
with plastic wrap; cook 45-60 minutes on
medium power depending on size of roast]

POLYNESIAN MEAT LOAF

1 Lb. Hamburger, lean
½ Lb. Sausage
1 Can Pineapple (med.) Chunks or
  Crushed (drained)
½ Cup Quick Brown Rice OR
  ¾ Cup Cooked White Rice
1 Large Onion, chopped coarse
5 Stalks of Celery, chopped coarse
1/3 Cup Soy Sauce
1 Tsp. Fresh, Grated Ginger
3 Tbs. Sugar
2 Eggs
1 Can Water Chestnuts, drained
Garlic to taste
Salt and Pepper to taste

Mix hamburger and sausage; add salt and
pepper and garlic to taste. Add rest of the
ingredients and mix well. Put into baking
dish and bake at 350 degrees for 1 hour &
15 minutes, or longer. [MW: put into ring
mold or bundt dish, cook 15-17 min. on
full power. Let stand 10 minutes.] It will
be a real moist meat loaf. Mushrooms can
also be added.

TERIYAKI KABOBS

For Marinade:
½ Cup Soy Sauce
½ Cup Pineapple Juice
1/3 Cup Red Wine Vinegar
1/3 Cup Salad Oil
1 Clove Fresh Garlic, minced

For Kabobs:
1 Lb. Sirloin Steak, cubed
1 Large Yellow Onion, cut into bite-size
  pieces
1 Green Bell Pepper, cut into bite-size
  pieces
½ Cup Pineapple Chunks (canned in own
  juice)
6 Fresh, Large Mushrooms, halved
6 to 8 Wooden Skewers (available at
  supermarket in package of 100)
Hibachi or Barbecue Charcoal

Early Afternoon: Mix ingredients for teriyaki marinade in shallow bowl or cake pan.
Wash vegetables and cut into bite-size pieces.
Marinate steak chunks and vegetables in
teriyaki 2 to 4 hours, covered in refrigerator.

Later: Skewer steak chunks, pineapple chunks,
and vegetables on skewers while waiting for
coals to get hot in hibachi or barbecue. Place
skewers close above coals and turn over when
steak is well browned, about 4 to 5 min. Cook
on other side until done. [MW: use wood
skewers. Place skewers on roasting rack, cook
covered with wax paper 6-8 min. on full power.]
Serve with steaming hot seasoned brown rice.
Serves 2. No sugar, high fiber, and lots of
vitamins and minerals!

CHINESE BEEF AND PEA PODS

1½ Lbs. Sirloin Steak, ¾" thick
1 Tbs. Soy Sauce
1 Slice Fresh Ginger Root, crushed
1 Clove Garlic, crushed
1 Lb. Fresh Snow Peas
¼ Cup Salad Oil
½ Lb. Mushrooms, sliced
3 Stalks Chinese Cabbage, cut into
  ¼" slices
1 Med. Onion, sliced
1 - 8 Oz. Can Water Chestnuts,
  drained and sliced
1 - 8 Oz. Can Bamboo Shoots, drained
1 - 13¾ Oz. Can Chicken Broth, or
  1-2/3 Cups
3 Tbs. Cornstarch
2 Tbs. Soy Sauce
½ Tsp. Salt
¼ Tsp. Sugar
Chow Mein Noodles

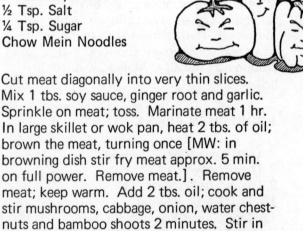

Cut meat diagonally into very thin slices.
Mix 1 tbs. soy sauce, ginger root and garlic.
Sprinkle on meat; toss. Marinate meat 1 hr.
In large skillet or wok pan, heat 2 tbs. of oil;
brown the meat, turning once [MW: in
browning dish stir fry meat approx. 5 min.
on full power. Remove meat.]. Remove
meat; keep warm. Add 2 tbs. oil; cook and
stir mushrooms, cabbage, onion, water chestnuts and bamboo shoots 2 minutes. Stir in
snow peas and 1 cup of the chicken broth.
Cover; cook 2 minutes. Mix the remaining
chicken broth, cornstarch, soy sauce, salt &
sugar; pour into skillet. Cook, stirring constantly, until mixture thickens and boils.
Boil and stir 1 minute. Add meat; heat
through. Serve over chow mein noodles.
Serves 5.

BEEF ENCHILADAS SUPREME

1 Lb. Lean Hamburger
2 Spanish Onions, chopped
1 Large Clove Garlic, minced
1 Tsp. Chili Powder
1 Tsp. Mexican Oregano Leaves
½ Tsp. Salt
½ Cup Enchilada Sauce
¼ Cup Water
1 Dozen Corn Tortillas
2 - 7 Oz. Cans Whole Ortega Chilies,
   cut into 2" wide strips (optional)
1 Lb. Medium-sharp Cheddar Cheese,
   grated
2 - 4 Oz. Cans Sliced Black Olives,
   drained
1 - 8 Oz. Can Whole Pitted Olives

Sauce:
½ Cup Butter
½ Cup Flour
1 - 10 Oz. Can Las Palmas Red Chili
   Sauce
3½ Cups Water
½ Tsp. Ground Oregano
¼ Tsp. Thyme
2 Tsp. Chili Powder
Garlic Salt to taste

Brown the hamburger, onions, garlic & oregano [MW: Cook hamburger, onions, garlic & oregano 4 min. on full power]. Add chili powder, salt, enchilada sauce and water. Cover and simmer for ½ hr. [MW: Cover and cook on medium power for 15 min. Brush tortillas with oil on one side only and heat for 1 min. on full power or until soft. Do not stack tortillas to heat - do them one at a time] Quickly fry 6 tortillas in small amount of oil until just soft; place each between paper towels. Lay a tortilla on a large plate, sprinkle grated cheese down center, cover with sliced olives, a strip or two of ortega chili and 1/3 cup of meat mixture. Roll up and place folded-side down in a greased 9" x 13" x 2" baking pan. These can be used immediately or covered and refrigerated (without sauce) until ready to use.

Cover with heated sauce, whole black olives and remaining grated cheese [MW: Cook covered with plastic wrap 5-10 min. on full power]. Bake at 350 degrees for 15 to 20 min. if enchiladas are warm (30 min. if refrigerated). This is a good recipe to use up left-over turkey. Chop up turkey and moisten with small amount of sauce and use in place of meat mixture.

Sauce Directions: Make a paste out of the oregano, thyme, chili powder and a little water; set aside. Melt the butter in a large heavy pan [MW: in mw dish 1 min. on full power]; add flour and cook about 3 min. [MW: 2 min. stirring every minute] - do not brown. Add chili sauce, water and spice paste. Cook over medium low heat until thickened, stirring constantly. Simmer on low for ½ hour, uncovered [MW: 5 min. on full power stirring every min.]. Garlic salt may be added to taste.

MUSHROOM STUFFED BEEF BIRDS

1 Round Steak, ½" thick (2½ to 3 Lbs.)
½ Lb. Fresh Mushrooms
½ Cup Parsley
½ Cup Chopped Onion
1 Cup Grated Sharp Cheddar Cheese
¼ Cup All-purpose Flour
1 Tsp. Salt
1 Tsp. Pepper
3 Tbs. Shortening or Drippings
1 - 10½ Oz. Can Condensed Consomme
½ Tsp. Dry Mustard

Cut steak in 6 portions with knife; pound steak to ¼" thickness. Remove mushroom caps from stems; chop parsley, onion and cheese in mixing bowl. Place approximately 3 tbs. mushroom mixture in center of each piece of steak, reserving remainder of mixture. Roll steak around stuffing and fasten with skewers. Tie with string. Combine flour, salt and pepper. Dredge meat in seasoned flour. Brown in shortening or drippings in large skillet. Pour off drippings. Combine consomme and dry mustard; add to steak rolls. Add mushroom caps; cover tightly and cook slowly over low heat 45 minutes. Add remainder of mushroom mixture and continue cooking 45 minutes, or until meat is tender [MW: cover tightly and cook 30 min. on full power. Add remaining mushroom mixture and continue cooking 20 min. on full power]. If gravy is desired, thicken. Serves 6. Serve on a bed of parsley spaghetti.

BOEUF BRAISE FLAMANDE
(Flemish Style Braised Beef)

3-3½ Lb. Round, Rump or Sirloin Tip
  of Beef
2 Tbs. Oil
2 Onions, sliced
2 Carrots, sliced
2 Stalks Celery, sliced
3 Leeks, sliced
1 Cup Ale
1 Cup Stock
Bouquet Garni
1 Clove Garlic, crushed
1 Tsp. Tomato Paste
2 Tbs. Butter kneaded with
1 Tbs. Flour
1 Tbs. Chopped Parsley

For Tomato Coulis:
4 Tomatoes, peeled, sliced and seeded
1 Tbs. Oil
1 Bermuda or Large Onion, sliced in rounds
Salt and Pepper

In deep flame-proof casserole heat the oil
and brown the meat thoroughly on all
sides. Remove meat. [MW: In large 3-4
quart deep casserole dish place meat,
vegetables, ale, stock, bouquet garni, garlic and tomatoe paste. Cover tightly
with plastic wrap and cook on simmer on
medium power for 45 min. or until meat
is tender. Take out the beef.] Add the
vegetables, turn down the heat, cover
and cook gently for 5-7 min. or until the
oil is absorbed. Replace the meat, add
the ale, stock, bouquet garni, garlic and
tomato paste. Cover tightly and braise
in a 325 degree oven (moderately low)
for 1½ to 2 hrs. or until the meat is
tender. Take out the beef and keep
warm. Strain the cooking liquid into a
pan, bring to a boil and whisk in the
kneaded butter, a piece at a time, to
thicken the sauce. Taste for seasoning.
To make the tomato coulis: Heat the oil
and fry the onion until browned. Add
the tomatoes, season, cover and cook 2-3
min. until the tomatoes are just soft.
[MW: Cook onion 5 min. on full power.
Add the tomatoes, season, cover and
cook 2 min. on full power until tomatoes
are just soft.] Spoon the coulis down
the center of a warm platter. Carve the
beef in 3/8" slices and arrange them, overlapping, on the tomato coulis. Spoon over
a little of the sauce and serve the rest separately. Sprinkle the dish with parsley and
serve with mashed potatoes.

HUNGARIAN BEEF GOULASH

2 Lbs. Boned Chuck or Round, cut into
  1½" pieces
1/3 Cup Flour
1 Tbs. Oil
1 Lb. White Onions, peeled and shredded
2 Tbs. Salt
1 Tbs. Sweet Paprika
Vinegar
1 Tbs. Tarragon Vinegar
1 Tsp. Marjoram
1 Tsp. Capers
2 Bay Leaves
2 Parsley Sprigs
1 Cup Dry White Wine
1 Tbs. Caraway Seeds

Cut beef into cubes and dredge with flour.
Heat oil and brown meat well [MW: use
browning dish]. Add onions and seasonings
and blend. Add wine. Put all in tightly
covered dutch oven and simmer 1 hour until
tender. [MW: Put in tightly covered casserole
dish and simmer 40 min. until tender.] Serve
goulash with broad cooked noodles or over
boiled potatoes.

FRIDADELLERS (Danish Meatballs)

1 Cup Soft Bread Crumbs
1 Egg, well beaten
1 Cup Applesauce
½ Cup Catsup
1 Tsp. Salt
¼ Tsp. Nutmeg
1/8 Tsp. Pepper
1½ Lbs. Ground Beef
¼ Cup Minced Onion
¼ Cup White Wine, or water

Mix thoroughly the bread crumbs, egg, ½
cup applesauce, ¼ cup catsup, seasonings;
blend in meat, onion. Form into 1" balls.
Bake in large, shallow pan 15 min. at 425
degrees. [MW: 7-9 min. in shallow baking
dish on full power]. Drain fat. Combine
remaining applesauce, catsup and wine.
Spoon over meatballs. Bake 10 minutes
longer. Makes 6 servings.

CALZONE

1 Pkg. Dry Yeast
¼ Cup Warm Water
¾ Cup Milk
1½ Tsp. Salt
¼ Cup Sugar
3½ Cups Flour
1/6 Cup Shortening
1 Egg

Meat Mixture:
1 Lb. Hamburger
1 Diced Bell Pepper
1 Diced Onion
Salt & Pepper to taste
1 Jar Ragu Sauce

Dissolve yeast in water and set aside. Scald the milk, salt and sugar. Stir until dissolved and let stand until it cools to lukewarm. Add yeast to milk mixture and half of the flour. Stir in shortening and unbeaten egg with the remaining flour. Mix well. Place in a greased bowl. Brush the top with shortening, cover with wax paper and put in the refrigerator for 2 hours. Remove from refrigerator and roll out into 8 circles. Fill with meat mixture. Add grated cheese to the meat mixture and bake at 375 degrees for 25 minutes.

MARINATED FLANK STEAK

1 Flank Steak

Marinade:
¼ Cup Oil
¼ Cup Wine Vinegar
¼ Cup Soy Sauce
½ Cup Chopped Onion
1 Tsp. Garlic Salt
1 Tsp. Basil
1 Tsp. Salt
1 Tsp. Pepper
½ Tsp. Ginger

Prepare marinade and pour over steak. Marinate for at least 4 hours. Turn and poke with fork. Broil or barbecue about 5 minutes on each side. [MW: Cook in browning dish on full power 3-4 min. per side.] Slice against the grain and serve. Delicious cold on sandwiches.

SPECIAL ENCHILADAS

Sauce:
1 Cup Shortening
2 Cups Flour
1 - 8 Oz. Can Tomato Sauce
2 Tbs. Garlic Salt
Liquid from Olives and Onion Juice, from filling ingredients (or substitute onion powder)
¼ Lb. Grated Tillamook Cheese
2 to 3 Oz. Chili Powder
3 Tbs. Cumin
Salt
2 Quarts Cold Water

Filling:
½ Lb. Ground Beef
3 Hard-boiled Eggs
1 to 2 Dry Onions
¾ Lb. Grated Tillamook Cheese
Parmesan Cheese (dry)
1 Small Can Chopped Black Olives
1 Small Can Spanish Olives (optional)
12 Flour Tortillas

Sauce: Heat shortening in large pan. Add flour, stirring. Add 2 quarts cold water, stirring constantly till smooth. Add tomato sauce, garlic salt, olive liquid, onion juice, cheese, chili powder, cumin and plenty of salt.

Filling: Brown ground beef. Drain off grease and set aside. In flat baking dish, grind hard-boiled eggs and onions (drain excess onion juice). Add chopped olives and hamburger; mix well.

Thin some of the sauce with water and dip tortillas in sauce. Place approximately 3 tbs. of the filling on each tortilla; sprinkle with some grated cheese and Parmesan cheese. Roll and place in baking dish. Pour sauce over enchiladas. (May save a little sauce to serve at the table.) Sprinkle remaining grated cheese and Parmesan over sauce. Bake at 350 degrees approximately 20 to 25 minutes, or until bubbling.

PARTY WON TON

1 Lb. Ground Chuck, lean
1 Bunch Parsley
1 Egg (optional)
2 Tbs. Soy Sauce
1 Tbs. Wine
7 - 8 Slices Salami, finely chopped
½ Tsp. M.S.G.
1 Tsp. Cornstarch
1 Pkg. Won Ton Skins
1/8 Tsp. Ginger
1 Tbs. Brown Sugar
2 Scallions, minced, 4" each

1. Place the beef in a large bowl; snip the parsley into bowl with beef.

2. Add all the remaining ingredients, except won ton skins; lightly blend or toss, using two forks.

3. Fill the skins, one at a time, with about 1 tsp. filling. As you work, be sure to keep won ton skins covered with a damp cloth so they don't dry out.

To fold, bring corners together to make a triangle; moisten with water and close; seal sides. Pull the two bottom edges together and pinch firmly to seal, using a little water if necessary. Continue till all filling is used. As you work, cover finished won tons with damp cloth to prevent them from drying out. Have guests fondue their own in oil, or make ahead and freeze individually on a cookie sheet; separate layers with wax paper. To freeze longer, put in plastic bags - keeps 2 weeks or more.

When ready to serve, fry them up quickly in the kitchen - no need to defrost - and serve hot with soy sauce, hot Chinese mustard and/or sweet and sour sauce.

Hot Mustard:
2 Tbs. Mustard
4 Tbs. Water
1 Tsp. Vinegar
Few Drops Oil
Few Grains Salt

Mix all ingredients; if too thin, add mustard or thin with water. Double recipe for party.

Sweet-Sour Sauce:
1 Tbs. Cornstarch
4 Oz. Tomato Sauce
4 Oz. Crushed Pineapple
2 Tbs. Soy Sauce
2 Tbs. Vinegar

Mix cornstarch and soy sauce in a custard cup. Combine rest of ingredients in saucepan and bring to a simmer; add cornstarch mixture and simmer till it thickens and clears, stirring constantly. If too thick, thin with a little pineapple juice.

MEATBALL STROGANOFF

1 Lb. Ground Beef
¾ Lb. Ground Pork
1 Cup Cracker Crumbs
2 Tsp. Salt
Dash of Pepper
Dash of Thyme
Dash of Oregano
½ Cup Milk
2 Eggs
2 Tbs. Fat
1½ Cups Dairy Sour Cream

½ Cup Dairy Sour Cream
1 - 6 Oz. Can Mushrooms, drained

Combine meats, crumbs, seasonings, milk and eggs; mix well. Form meat mixture into small balls, 1½" across, and brown in hot fat. [MW: Cook on full power 5 min.] Drain off excess fat. Add 1½ cups sour cream; cover and simmer for 1 hour. [MW: Cook 15 minutes on low power]

Remove meat balls to warm serving dish. Stir ½ cup sour cream into mixture in skillet; add mushrooms and heat to boiling point. Pour over meatballs. Serve with egg noodles or rice if you wish. Serves 6 to 8.

BARBECUED SHORT RIBS & BEANS

1 Lb. Pinto Beans, rinsed and picked over
6 Cups Water
4 Lbs. Beef Short Ribs
2 Tbs. Oil
4 Med. Onions, chopped
1 - 8 Oz. Can Tomato Sauce
¼ Cup Packed Brown Sugar
1 Tbs. Cider Vinegar
1 Tbs. Worcestershire Sauce
1 Tbs. Prepared Mustard
2 Tsp. Salt
2 Tsp. Chili Powder
2 Tsp. Liquid Smoke
Boiling Water (optional)

In Dutch oven [MW: 3-4 quart casserole],
soak beans overnight in 6 cups water or bring
to boil and boil 2 min., then cover and let
stand for 1 hr. Brown ribs well on both sides
in hot oil in skillet [MW: browning dish]; remove ribs and set aside. Saute' onions in pan
drippings [MW: browning dish] until tender;
stir into undrained beans with remaining ingredients, except boiling water. Top with ribs;
cover and simmer 3-4 hours [MW: 1-2 hours
on low power] or until beans are tender.
Check liquid level occasionally and, if necessary, add boiling water to keep moist but not
soupy. Makes 6 servings.

SWEET AND SOUR MEAT BALLS

1 Lb. Ground Round
1 Egg
2 Tbs. Flour
1 Cup Chicken Bouillon
Salt And Pepper
½ Cup Cooking Oil
2 Large Green Peppers, cut into small pieces
2 Slices Canned Pineapple, cut into pieces
3 Tbs. Cornstarch
 Tbs. Soy Sauce
½ Cup Vinegar
½ Cup Pineapple Juice
½ Cup Sugar

Shape meat into small balls. Combine egg,
flour, salt and pepper to make a smooth
batter. Heat oil in large skillet. Dip meat
balls in batter and fry until brown on all
sides. Remove meat balls from skillet and
keep warm. Pour out all but 1 tbs. fat
from skillet. Add ½ cup chicken bouillon,
ground pepper and pineapple pieces. Cover
and cook over medium heat for 10 min.
Blend remaining ingredients and add to
skillet. Cook, stirring constantly, until mixture comes to a boil and is thickened. Return meat balls to sauce and heat. Serve with
hot boiled rice. NOTE: You can increase
the first 5 ingredients without increasing the
rest of the recipe.

FIERY HONAN BEEF

1 Lb. Lean Beef, thinly sliced
¼ Cup Soy Sauce
2 Tbs. Sherry
1 Clove Garlic
3 Tbs. Oil
2 Bunches Scallions or Green
  Onion Tops, in 1" lengths
1 Cup Carrots, thinly sliced
2 Cups Celery, thinly sliced
½ Tsp. Ground Ginger
½ to 1 Tsp. Hot Pepper Flakes
  (optional)
2 - 6 Oz. Cans Button Mushrooms,
  whole
1 Tsp. Salt
¼ Cup Toasted, Blanched Almonds

Mix beef, soy sauce, sherry and garlic. Let
stand at room temperature for 1 hour. In
large skillet [MW: browning dish], heat oil
until it sizzles. Add beef mixture and stir-
fry until brown. Add 1 cup water; simmer
with lid on for 10-15 min. [MW: cook 5 min.
on low power] or until meat is tender. Add
remaining ingredients, except pepper flakes.
Cook until vegetables are tender but crisp.
Add pepper flakes until they are the way you
like it. They are very hot, so add a few at a
time. Serve over cooked rice. Enjoy!

BEEF WELLINGTON (Individual - 6)

1 Lb. Chopped Mushrooms
½ Onion, chopped
½ Cup Sherry
¼ Cup Butter
¼ Cup Fresh Parsley, snipped
6 Small Fillets of Beef Steaks
1 Pkg. Frozen Patty Shells

Sauce Bearnaise (Makes 1½ cups- enough
   for 3 steaks):
½ Cup White or Red Wine
2 Tbs. Tarragon Vinegar
1 Tbs. Finely Chopped Onion
2 Crushed Peppercorns
2 Sprigs Chopped Tarragon
1 Sprig Parsley, chopped
3 Egg Yolks
¾ Cup Melted Butter

Cook the first 5 ingredients in a frying
pan till all liquid is absorbed and mixture
resembles a paste. Cover tops of steaks.
Partially thaw patty shells and roll out
thin enough to cover top, sides and part
of the bottom of each steak. Cover with
plastic wrap and store in refrigerator till
serving time.

Sauce:
Cook over direct heat until reduced by
half, the first 6 ingredients. Strain mixture and cool. Before serving: in top
of double boiler over hot (not boiling)
water, beat in alternately the yolks and
the melted butter. Preheat oven to 425
degrees. Cook steaks on a rack, uncovered,
for 25 minutes. They will be rare but
will continue cooking while sauce is added
and dish is served.

Sounds complicated but most is done early
in the day and sauce takes about 5-10
minutes of last minute operation. Besides,
this is very elegant when served. It is
very rich, so plan menu accordingly.

WESTERN MEAL IN ONE

1 Lb. Ground Round
1 Tbs. Salad Oil
1 Clove Garlic, minced
1 Tsp. Salt
1 Large Onion, chopped
1 Green Pepper, chopped
1 Tsp. Chili Powder
1 No. 2 Can Tomatoes
1 No. 303 Can Kidney Beans
¾ Cup Uncooked Rice
¼ Cup Chopped Ripe Olives
1 Can Mushrooms (optional)
¾ Cup Grated Cheese

Brown meat in oil slightly. [MW: Cook 5 min.
on full power] Add garlic, salt, onion, pepper
and chili powder and saute' 5 minutes. [MW:
3 min. full power] Mix in remaining ingredients, except olives and cheese, and pour into a
2 quart casserole. Bake at 350 degrees for 45
minutes. [MW: 15-20 min. on full power]
Sprinkle olives and cheese on top and bake 15
min. longer [MW: 5 min.], or until cheese is
melted. Serves 8.

CANNELLONI

2/3 Cup Chopped Onion
2 Tbs. Oil
1 Tsp. Mixed Italian Herbs
4 Cups Ground or Finely Chopped Cooked
   Beef
1 Tsp. Salt
1 Pkg. Frozen Spinach
12 Crepes
1 Slice Monterey Jack Cheese
Tomato Sauce

Saute onion in oil with herbs until soft. [MW·
Cook beef 6 min. on full power] Brown beef,
add salt. Stir in enough tomato sauce to make
beef and onion mixture spreadable. Cook
frozen spinach, chop and add to beef and onion
mixture. Divide into 12 portions and roll a
crepe around each. Pour a thin layer of sauce
into a shallow baking dish. Place cannelloni,
seam side down in a single layer in the sauce.
Pour on remaining sauce. Cover each with a
slice of cheese about the same size. Bake in
350 degree oven 15 minutes. [MW: cover with
wax paper and cook 5-7 min. on full power]
Broil a minute or two to brown tops. Serves
6 with 12 crepes.

CHINESE PEPPER STEAK

1 Lb. Round Steak
¼ Cup Oil
1 Clove Garlic
½ Cup Coarsely-chopped Onion
2 Cups Bite-size Pieces Green Pepper
1 Tsp. Salt
¼ Tsp. Pepper
¼ Tsp. Ginger
1 Tbs. Cornstarch
1 Cup Stock or Bouillon
1 Tbs. Soy Sauce

Cut steak diagonally across grain into thin slices; cut into strips 2" long. Heat oil in skillet over medium heat [MW: use browning dish on medium power. Add garlic and meat and cook 5 min. on full power]; add garlic and remove after 3 min. Add meat and brown. Mix onion, green pepper, salt, pepper and ginger. Cook over medium heat, [MW: 3 min. on full power] stirring constantly, for 3 minutes, until just tender. Blend cornstarch with stock & soy sauce. Stir into mixture in skillet [MW: browning dish, cook 3-4 min. on full power]. Bring to boil and cook, stirring constantly, until liquid is thickened. Serve over rice. Yield 4 servings.

STUFFED FLANK STEAK

1 Large Flank Steak, tenderized
¾ Cup Burgundy or Rose' Wine
¼ Cup Olive Oil
1 Tsp. Garlic, puree
½ Tsp. Seasoned Salt
1 Tsp. Oregano
1 Lb. Mushrooms
1 Medium Onion
Pinch Garlic Powder
1 Tsp. Oregano
Dash Salt & Pepper
2 Drops Tabasco Sauce
1 Large Tomato, diced
½ Small Green Pepper, diced
3 Tbs. Butter

Marinate the steak for 24 hours in the first five ingredients. Marinate in refrigerator. Saute' the mushrooms, onions, and peppers in butter. Add seasoning when the vegetables are soft. Simmer mixture for 15 minutes. Spread stuffing mixture on meat roll and hold together with toothpicks. Broil for 8 minutes on each side. Serves 4.

SAVORY MEATBALL CASSEROLE
with CHILI CHEESE BISCUITS

1 Lb. Ground Beef
¼ Lb. Pork Sausage
½ Cup Dry Bread Crumbs
1/3 Cup Pet Milk
2 Tbs. Chopped Onion
1 Tsp. Chili Powder
1/8 Tsp. Pepper
1 Can Cream of Mushroom Soup
1 Can Cream of Celery Soup
1 Cup Pet Milk
½ Cup Water

Chili Cheese Biscuits:
1-1/3 Cups Sifted Flour
3 Tsp. Baking Powder
½ Tsp. Chili Powder
¼ Tsp. Salt
1/3 Cup Shortening
1 Egg, unbeaten
1/3 Cup Pet Milk
1½ Cups Shredded American Cheese
1 Tbs. Dried Parsley

Meatballs: Mix well the first 7 ingredients. Shape by tablespoonfuls into meatballs. Brown in skillet. Cover and cook 10 min. Place in 2½ quart casserole dish. In the same skillet, combine the next 4 ingredients. Heat until steaming. Pour over meatballs. Top with chili cheese biscuits. Bake at 400 degrees for 20 to 25 minutes. Serves 6 to 8 people.

Chili Cheese Biscuits: Sift together flour, chili powder, baking powder and salt. Cut in shortening until particles are fine. Combine unbeaten egg with Pet milk. Add to dry ingredients. Stir until dough clings together. Knead on floured surface 10 times. Roll out to a 12" square. Sprinkle with shredded cheese and parsley. Roll up and cut into eight slices. Place slices on top of meatballs and bake as directed.

SAUERBRATEN (Marinated Beef)

4 Lb. Cross Rib Roast (any beef pot roast)
2 Cups Vinegar
2 Cups Water
1 Large Onion, sliced
2 Tsp. Salt
10 Peppercorns
3 Whole Cloves
2 Bay Leaves
1 Lemon, rinsed and cut into ¼"
  slices

1. Wipe pot roast with a clean damp cloth and place in deep 3 or 4 quart bowl. Set aside.
2. Combine in saucepan and heat, [MW: use glass bowl] without boiling, the vinegar, water, onion, salt, peppercorns, cloves and bay leaves.
3. Pour mixture over meat in bowl and allow to cool. Add lemon slices.
4. Cover and set in refrigerator. Marinate for 4 days, turning meat once each day.
5. Set out 4 quart kettle or Dutch oven [MW: use 4-quart casserole] with tight fitting cover.
6. Remove meat from marinade and drain thoroughly. Strain and reserve marinade.
7. Heat 2 to 3 tbs. butter in kettle [MW: casserole] over low heat. Add pot roast and brown slowly on all sides over medium heat.
8. Slowly add 2 cups of the reserved marinade (reserve remaining marinade for gravy). Bring liquid to boiling.
9. Reduce heat; cover kettle tightly and simmer 2½ to 3 hours [MW: Cover casserole tightly and cook 1-1½ hours on medium power] or until meat is tender when pierced with a fork. Add more marinade if necessary. Liquid should at all times be simmering, not boiling.
10. Remove meat to warm platter; keep warm. Reserve cooking liquid.

Gravy:
1. Melt ¼ cup butter in kettle, [MW: use glass bowl] blend in ¼ cup flour. Heat until butter-flour mixture bubbles and is golden brown, stirring constantly. [MW: cook 2 min. on full power stirring constantly].
2. Add gradually, stirring constantly, 3 cups liquid. Add reserved marinade or hot water, if necessary, to equal 3 cups liquid. Bring to rapid boil, stirring constantly, until gravy thickens. Cook 1-2 minutes longer; lower heat.

3. Add ½ cup dark, seedless raisins. Cook 3-5 minutes - do not boil. [MW: 1-3 min. on full power].
Serve meat and gravy with potato pancakes.

ITALIAN MEAT ROLL

1:
1 Lb. Ground Beef
2 Tbs. Grated Romano Cheese
2 Tbs. Dry Bread Crumbs
½ Lb. Ground Pork
1/8 Tsp. Garlic Powder
1 Egg

2:
2 Tbs. Diced Romano Cheese
2 Sprigs Fresh Parsley
4 Slices Hard Salami
2 Hardboiled Eggs

3:
1 Sliced Onion
3 Carrots, sliced
1 Tsp. Basil
4 Stalks Celery
1 Green Pepper
3 - 8 Oz. Cans Spanish-style
  Tomato Sauce

4:
Green Noodles or Spaghetti, cooked

1: Combine ingredients of No. 1. Add salt and pepper to taste. Divide mixture in two; spread each half on a sheet of waxed paper.

2: On divided mixture, line up ingredients of No. 2 in lengthwise rows. With the aid of the wax paper, roll up mixture. Chill, then brown rolls in fat.

3: Simmer meat rolls in sauce of No. 3 ingredients for 1½ hrs. [MW: 45 min. on medium power].

4: Serve with noodles or spaghetti.

Ingredients can be frozen (except noodles or spaghetti).

BEEF STROGANOFF

2 Lbs. Filet of Beef or Flank
4 Tbs. Butter
1 Cup Chopped Onion
1 Clove Garlic
½ Lb. Fresh Mushrooms
3 Tbs. Flour
2 Tsp. Meat-Extract Paste
1 Tbs. Catsup
½ Tsp. Salt
1/8 Tsp. Pepper
1 Can Beef Bouillon
¼ Cup White Wine
1 Tbs. Fresh Dill or ¼ Tsp. Dried
1½ Cups Sour Cream

1. Trim fat from beef. Cut into ½" slices.
2. Over high heat and in 1 tbs. butter, sear beef quickly. [MW: in browning dish]
3. In 3 tbs. butter (same pan) saute' onion, garlic and mushrooms about 5 minutes. Remove from heat.
4. Stir in flour, meat extract paste, catsup, salt and pepper and stir until smooth.
5. Gradually add bouillon, stirring; bring to boiling. Reduce heat, simmer for 5 minutes.
6. Over low heat [MW: Medium], add wine, dill and sour cream. Add beef; simmer until beef is hot.
7. Serve over wild rice mixture. Serves 6.

SWISS MEAT LOAF

2 Lbs. Ground Chuck or Ground Round
1½ Cups Diced Swiss Cheese
2 Beaten Eggs
½ Cup Chopped Onion
½ Cup Chopped Green Pepper
1½ Tsp. Salt
½ Tsp. Pepper
1 Tsp. Celery Salt
½ Tsp. Paprika
2½ Cups Milk
1 Cup Dry Bread Crumbs

Mix all ingredients together in approximate order given. Press into one big greased loaf pan. Bake uncovered at 350 degrees for 1½ hours. [MW: full power 20-25 minutes, covered with wax paper] Serves 6 or 7.

BEEF BURGUNDY

16 Small White Onions, peeled (about 1 lb.)
6 Strips Lean Bacon, diced
¼ Cup (1/8 Lb.) Butter or Margarine
4 Lbs. Beef Chuck, cut into 1½" cubes
¼ Cup Brandy (optional)
1½ Tsp. Salt
¼ Tsp. Freshly-ground Pepper
2 Cups Burgundy or other dry red wine
2 Whole Cloves Garlic, peeled
2 Cups Small Whole or Sliced Fresh
  Mushrooms
1½ Cups Water
1 or 2 Sprigs Parsley
1 Celery Top
1 Carrot, quartered
1 Bay Leaf
1 Sprig Fresh Thyme, or 1 tsp.
  dried thyme
6 Tbs. Flour
½ Cup Cold Water

Brown onions with bacon and butter in a Dutch oven [MW: glass casserole]; remove onions and bacon with a slotted spoon and set aside. Add meat to pan and brown well on all sides. If desired, pour brandy over beef and set aflame, tilting pan to keep flame going as long as possible. Sprinkle meat with salt and pepper. Add burgundy, garlic, mushrooms, the 1½ cups water, onions and bacon. Make a bouquet garni by tying together in a piece of cheesecloth the parsley, celery top, carrot, bay leaf, and thyme (use a string so the bouquet can easily be removed from pan). Add bouquet garni. Cover and simmer for about 1½ hrs. [MW: 45 minutes on simmer], or until meat is tender.

Lift beef, mushrooms and onions out of the pan with a slotted spoon; arrange in a covered 3-quart casserole or baking dish. Strain the liquid through a sieve, discarding bouquet garni, garlic and bacon. Mix flour to a smooth paste with the ½ cup cold water; stir into meat stock and cook, stirring, until gravy is thick and smooth. Pour the gravy over meat and serve immediately, or refrigerate and reheat, covered in a moderate oven, 350 degrees, for about 35 min. [MW: 15 minutes on full power], or until hot and bubbly. Makes 8 to 10 servings.

BEEF ROAST with MUSHROOM STUFFING (German Dish)

½ Tsp. Salt
¼ Tsp. White Pepper
2 Lbs. Flank Steak
1 Tsp. Dijon-Style Mustard

Mushroom Stuffing:
2 Tbs. Vegetable Oil
1 Small Chopped Onion
4 Oz. Can Mushroom Pieces, drained
¼ Cup Dried Bread Crumbs
1 Tbs. Tomato Paste
2 Tbs. Chopped Chives
¼ Cup Chopped Parsley
¼ Tsp. Salt
¼ Tsp. Pepper
1 Tsp. Paprika

Lightly salt and pepper flank steak on both sides. Spread one side with mustard.

To prepare stuffing, heat vegetable oil in a frying pan; [MW: browning dish]; add onion and cook for 3 min., until lightly browned. Add mushroom pieces and cook for 5 min. [MW: 3 min.]. Stir in the parsley, chives, tomato paste and bread crumbs. Season with salt, pepper and paprika. Spread stuffing on mustard-side of flank steak; roll up jelly-roll fashion and tie with thread or string.

Gravy:
3 Strips Bacon, cubed
2 Small Onions, finely chopped
1 Cup Hot Beef Broth
1 Tsp. Dijon Mustard
2 Tbs. Tomato Catsup

To prepare gravy, cook bacon in Dutch oven [MW: glass casserole] until partially done. Add the meat roll and brown on all sides, approximately 10 minutes [MW: full power]. Add the onions and saute' for 5 minutes [MW: 3 min.]. Pour beef broth; cover and simmer for 1 hour [MW: 45 min. on simmer]. Remove meat to a preheated platter; season pan juices with mustard, salt and pepper to taste, stir in catsup. Serve the gravy separately. Makes 6 servings.

TALLARINES

1 Lb. Ground Round
½ Lb. Tillamook Cheese
4 Oz. Can Tomato Sauce
8 Oz. Can Whole Kernel Corn
1 Lb. Can Pitted Ripe Olives, undrained
    half cut-up, half whole
2 Onions, chopped
1 Green Pepper, chopped
2 (4 Oz.) Cans Mushrooms
8 Oz. or More Mushroom Sauce
½ Cup Olive Oil
1 Lb. Pkg. Noodles
Worcestershire Sauce
Salt & Pepper

Saute' onions, pepper and meat until brown. Add sauces, corn and olives, and about ½ of the juice from the olives. Add diced cheese, then noodles, salt, pepper and worcestershire sauce. May be topped with additional cheese, grated. Can be made ahead and frozen. Bake at 350 degrees for 1½ hours or longer. [MW: full power for 30-40 minutes]

TAMALE PIE

1 Lb. Lean Ground Beef
1 Med. Onion, chopped
2- 8 Oz. Cans Tomato Sauce
2- 8 Oz. Cans Water
1 Tbs. Chili Powder
12 Oz. Can Corn Niblets
1 Cup Olives, pitted
¾ Cup Yellow Corn Meal
2 Cups Milk
Salt to taste
Pepper to taste

In large frying pan [MW: browning dish]: Brown hamburger and onions, drain off excess fat. Add tomato sauce and water, chili powder, salt and the pepper. Simmer covered 45 min. [MW: simmer 15 min.] Stir in corn and olives. Add milk and corn meal, mix together. Cook 3 to 5 minutes [MW: 3 min.] until thickened. Pour into a 3 quart casserole. Bake 40 min. at 350 degrees or until almost dry [MW: 20 min. on full power or until almost dry].

PASTIE PIE (Main Dish Recipe)

2 Pie Crusts
1 Egg
7 Medium Potatoes, peeled & sliced
1 Large Onion, sliced
¼ Lb. Swiss Cheese, sliced
1 Lb. Round or Chuck Steak
¼ Cup Butter or Margarine

Preheat oven to 350 degrees. Cut steak in ½ inch cubes. Layer potatoes, meat, onions and cheese in crust, ending with the cheese. Drizzle melted butter over pie. Cover with top crust and prick. Baste top crust with egg. Bake in a 350 degree oven for 1½ hours. Take out and set on rack for 30 minutes. Serve with a green vegetable and salad.

HAWAIIAN HAMBURGERS

2 Lbs. Ground Beef
½ Cup Soy Sauce
1 Tbs. Sugar
1 Tsp. Salt
Dash Pepper
1 Tsp. Ginger
1 Clove Garlic, minced
¼ Can Bean Sprouts, rinsed & drained
1 - 5 Oz. Can Water Chestnuts, drained, rinsed & chopped
3 Green Onions, chopped fine

Combine meat with ½ cup soy sauce, sugar, salt, pepper, ginger and garlic; mix until well blended. Shape into 12 large, thin patties. Combine bean sprouts, water chestnuts and onions. Spread 2 to 3 tbs. of this mixture over 6 patties. Cover with the other 6 patties; pinch edges together. Brush with remaining soy sauce. Broil 3 to 4 minutes on each side, 4 inches from the flame, basting with soy sauce during cooking. [MW: preheat browning dish 7 min., cook patties 1 to 3 minutes on each side depending on doneness desired on full power] Makes 6 servings.

STUFFED FLANK STEAK

1½ - 2 Lbs. Flank Steak
1 Cup Dry Bread Cubes
½ Cup Chopped Celery
¼ Cup Chopped Onion
1 Tbs. Dry Parsley Flakes
½ Tsp. Salt
¼ Tsp. Pepper
1 + Tbs. Hot Water
4 Tbs. Butter
4 to 6 Large Mushrooms, scrubbed
4 to 6 Carrots, pared
4 Small Whole Onions, peeled
¾ Cup Burgundy Wine
Salt, Pepper and Paprika

Score flank steak on one side and place scored side down on chopping board. Rub top of steak with salt and pepper. Prepare stuffing from the next six ingredients as follows: Melt 2 tbs. butter in medium-size frying pan [MW: browning dish] over medium heat; saute' celery and onion until golden, then add parsley, salt and bread cubes. Toss lightly and add just enough water to moisten slightly. Spread evenly over steak. Roll steak lengthwise (like a jelly roll) and fasten with skewer. Tie with string in four or five places. Rub steak roll with paprika and brown on all sides in 2 tbs. butter in same frying pan [MW: browning dish]. Transfer to deep casserole. Saute' mushrooms, carrots and onions in pan, adding more butter if needed - then put vegetables around steak. Deglaze the pan with the wine and pour warmed wine and pan drippings over the steak and vegetables. Salt and pepper to taste. Cover tightly and put in 350 degree oven for 1½ hours [MW: 1 hour on medium power]. Check occasionally, adding more liquid if necessary. When meat is fork tender and vegetables are done, slice the meat roll in 1-1½" slices, surround with vegetables and serve with gravy made from the liquid in the casserole. Serves 4.

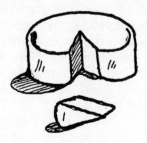

ROAST ORIENTAL

1 - 3 to 4 Lb. 7-Bone Roast
2/3 Cup Soy Sauce
1½ Cups Orange Juice
½ Cup Diced Raw Onion
½ Cup Oil
3 Tbs. Vinegar
½ Tsp. Pepper
¼ Tsp. Garlic Powder

Combine ingredients and marinate meat at least 4 hours. Skim off 2 tbs. oil into skillet. Dredge meat in flour. Brown meat on both sides. Add marinade and simmer slowly for 2 hours. [MW: once marinated cook immediately for 1 hour on medium power]. Remove meat and thicken marinade with:

2 Tbs. Cornstarch
¼ Cup Water

Serve with steamed rice.

CORN PONE PIE

1 Lb. Ground Beef
1 Medium Onion, sliced in circles
Salt & Pepper to taste
Garlic Powder to taste
1 - 15 Oz. Can Kidney Beans
1 - 15 Oz. Can Tomatoes

Corn Bread:
1 Cup Flour
1 Cup Corn Meal
1 Egg
1 Tsp. Salt
¾ Cup Shortening
1 Cup Milk
2 Tsp. Baking Powder

Brown the ground beef. Add the next 5 ingredients and let simmer while preparing the corn bread recipe. Mix all ingredients of corn bread recipe together. Pour meat mixture into a 2-quart glass casserole dish. Drop corn bread mixture by spoonfulls on top of the meat mixture. Bake in a 400 degree oven for 20 minutes [MW: 10 min. on full power] or until corn bread is done. This is a meal in itself. Serve with a vegetable and your favorite salad.

MAINE DYNAMITE

1 Large Bunch Celery (use all)
10 Large Onions
10 Green Peppers
1 Bunch Fresh Parsley
6 Cloves Garlic
2 Lbs. Ground Beef
2 No. 2½ Cans Italian Tomatoes
3 Large Cans Tomato Paste
1 Tsp. Rosemary
1 Tsp. Thyme
1 Tsp. or 3 Leaves Basil
1 Tsp. Oregano
1 Tsp. Dry Red Pepper
1 Tbs. (at least) Salt
1 Tsp. Coarse Ground Pepper

Brown ground beef in olive oil. Chop all vegetables to medium-size. Mix tomatoes and tomato paste with 2 cans water in large pot, add all spices at this time. Start heating over low flame [MW: low power]; add browned beef and vegetables. When boiling well, turn down and simmer at least 6 hours [MW: 2 hours]. If you want it very thick, simmer 12 hours [MW: 4 hrs]. It can serve a large crowd over rice, spaghetti, macaroni or on toast. Or it can be frozen in 2 cup containers and used any time. When mushrooms are in season, they are a delightful addition.

GOURMET CORNED BEEF

4 to 5 Lb. Round or Brisket
2½ Qts. Water
2 Cups White Wine
½ Cup CHopped Onion
1/8 Tsp. Garlic Powder
1 Tsp. Dill
2 Stalks Celery
2 Bay Leaves
1 Sliced Orange
1 Stick Cinnamon
3 Whole Cloves
2 to 3 Drops Tabasco

Place all ingredients in large kettle [MW: glass casserole]. Cover and simmer until tender, about 3 to 3½ hours [MW: 1 to 1½ hours]. Carrots, potatoes and cabbage can be added.

TAGLIARINI

1 Lb. Ground Beef
3 Tbs. Butter
1 Medium Onion
1 Can Tomato Sauce
1 Cup Water, or more
3 Cups Uncooked Egg Noodles
1 Can Corn
1 Can Ripe, Pitted Olives
1 Cup Grated American Cheese
Salt and Pepper to taste

Fry chopped onion in butter until browned. Add meat; stir and cook until browned. Add tomato sauce and water; stir. Add noodles; stir and cook until noodles are tender, about 20 min. [MW: 10 min.]. More water may be added. Season to taste. Add corn and olives; stir. Pour into large buttered casserole dish. Sprinkle with cheese. Bake 1 hour or less at 350 degrees [MW: 15 min. on full power].

BARBECUED BEEF SANDWICHES

4 - 5 Lbs. Boneless Roast, rolled and
   tied
2 Tbs. Salad Oil
2 Large Onions, chopped
1 Large Green Pepper, seeded and chopped
2 Stalks Celery, chopped
2 Large Cloves Garlic, minced or pressed
1 Cup Catsup
1 - 16 Oz. Can Stewed Tomatoes
¼ Cup Cider Vinegar
1/3 Cup Brown Sugar, packed
1 Tsp. Chili Powder
½ Tsp. Dry Basil
½ Tsp. Oregano Leaves
½ Tsp. Ground Cinnamon
½ Tsp. Salt
½ Tsp. Liquid Smoke

In 6 to 8 quart Dutch oven [MW: glass casserole], brown meat in salad oil over medium-high heat; remove from pan and set aside. Reduce to medium; add onion, celery, garlic. Saute' until onion is limp. Add catsup, tomatoes, vinegar, brown sugar and chili powder. Then stir in dry basil, oregano leaves,

ground cinnamon, salt and liquid smoke. Return meat to pan and spoon some of the sauce over it. Cover and bake in a 325 degree oven until meat is tender when pierced, about 3 hours 'MW: 1½ hours on medium power]. Let cool; cover and refrigerate up to 2 days.

To give yourself plenty of time, begin preparing meat about 2 hours before serving. Spoon off congealed fat and discard, then lift out meat and thinly slice. Return the sliced meat to the pan, layering it with sauce; cover and heat in a 350 degree oven until hot and bubbly, about 55 minutes [MW: 15-20 min.] Spoon meat and sauce onto buns to serve.

MEATLOAF RING

2 Lbs. Ground Beef
1 Pkg. Onion Soup Mix
½ Tsp. Garlic Powder
¼ Tsp. Salt
1/8 Tsp. Pepper
20 Saltine Cracker Squares, crumbed
2 Eggs
1 Tbs. Liquid Smoke
6 Medium-size Potatoes
¼ Cup Cheddar Cheese, shredded

Place all ingredients except potatoes and cheese in mixing bowl and mix well. Place meat mixture in an 8" or 9" jello ring mold [MW: glass or plastic] and put in freezer for 15 minutes (until mixture has set).

Remove from freezer and tip meatloaf onto cookie pan with edge and bake at 350 degrees for 45 minutes [MW: 15 min. on full power] Meanwhile peel, cube and boil potatoes until done. Shred cheese.

Remove meatloaf ring from oven; drain off excess fat and place on serving platter. Mash potatoes and place in center of ring; sprinkle cheese on top of potatoes. Return to oven [MW] until cheese is melted. Serve immediately. Serves 6.

TIJUANA TORTE

1 Lb. Ground Beef
1 Medium Onion, chopped
1 - 1 Lb. Can Stewed Tomatoes
1 - 8 Oz. Can Tomato Sauce
1 - 4 Oz. Can Diced Green Chilies
1 Pkg. Taco Seasoning
Flour Tortillas
1 Lb. Cheddar Cheese, grated

Brown beef and onion in pan; add other ingredients, (except cheese). Simmer 10-15 min. [MW: 5 to 10 min.] Place ¼ cup mixture in a 9" x 13" baking dish. Place a layer of tortillas on top; add more mixture, then cheese. Repeat same until finished. Bake at 350 degrees for 25 min., until cheese is bubbly [MW: 15 min. on full power]. Serves 4 to 6.

Optional: Before adding last layer of tortillas, spread 1 to 1½ cups sour cream over mixture. It is yummy!

BEEF BIRDS WITH OLIVE GRAVY

1 Lb. Round Steak, ½" thick
1 Tsp. Salt
¼ Tsp. Garlic Salt
¼ Tsp. Celery Salt
¼ Tsp. Pepper
2 Bouillon Cubes OR 2 Tsp. Meat
  Extract Paste
2 Cups Hot Water
2 Cups Fresh Bread Crumbs OR
  1 Cup Cooked Rice
¼ Cup Minced Onions
¼ Cup Thinly Sliced Celery
½ Cup All-purpose Flour
1 Tsp. Paprika
5 Tbs. Fat or Salad Oil
1/3 Cup Chopped Ripe Olives

Early in the day: With edge of heavy plate, pound both sides of meat. Cut meat into 3" squares; sprinkle with ½ tsp. salt, garlic and celery salts, and pepper. Pound again. Dissolve bouillon cubes in hot water. Mix bread or rice with onion and celery; add just enough bouillon to moisten slightly. Place about 2 tbs. stuffing on each meat square; roll up. Tie or skewer; refrigerate rolls, bouillon also.

About 1¾ hrs. before dinner. Combine flour ½ tsp. salt, paprika; use to coat stuffed meat rolls. Brown rolls in hot fat in Dutch oven [MW: browning dish] or electric combination fryer casserole. Add bouillon. Cook slowly, covered, about 1½ hrs. [MW: 45 min. on medium power], or until meat is very tender (add more water, if needed, so there will be about 1 cup thickened gravy left). Last 5 min. stir in olives. Serve birds with gravy. Makes 4 servings.

COUNTRY PIE WITH BEEF CRUST

The Crust:
½ of 8 Oz. Can Tomato Sauce
½ Cup Bread Crumbs
¼ Cup Finely-chopped Onion
Salt to taste
1/8 Tsp. Pepper
1 Lb. Ground Round
¼ Cup Finely-chopped Green Pepper
1/8 Tsp. Oregano (optional)

The Filling:
1-1/3 Cups Minute Rice
2 Cans Tomato Sauce
1 Cup Water
Salt to taste
1 Cup Grated Cheese

Combine all the ingredients for the crust; mix well. Place the mixture in a deep 10" glass pie pan and spread evenly over the pan, building up the edge around the pan to form the crust. Combine the ingredients for the filling, using only ¼ cup of the grated cheese. Mix well and pour into the crust. Cover with foil [MW: wax paper] and bake in a 350 degree oven for 60 min. [MW: 15 min. on full power]. Remove covering; sprinkle remaining cheese over the top; return to the oven [MW] for 15 to 20 min. [MW: 5 min.]. Served with buttered peas, tossed salad and hot garlic bread, makes a meal fit for a king!

OXTAIL STEW

2 Lb. Oxtail
½ Cup Flour
1 Tbs. Salt
½ Tsp. Pepper
2½ Cups Water
1 Cup Diced Onion
2 Cups Stewed Tomatoes
1 Clove Garlic
1 Tsp. Worcestershire Sauce
1 Cup Cut Celery
1 Bay Leaf
4 Carrots, cut in 1" pieces
4 Onions, quartered
4 Potatoes, quartered
2 Cups Canned Tomatoes

Boil oxtail in water; add salt, pepper, diced onion, tomatoes, garlic, bay leaf and celery. Cook 2 hours [MW: 1 hr. on medium power]; add more water if needed. Add cut carrots, onions and potatoes and tomatoes; cook 30 minutes longer [MW: 20 min. on full power]. To make thickening, stir ½ cup flour into 1 cup water; pour slowly into stew and cook 15 min. longer [MW: 5 min. on full power]. Serves 6.

PAN-FRIED BEEF RIBS
(In Barbecue Sauce)

10 to 12 Beef Ribs, meaty, English cut
Pepper
Lemon Juice

Sauce:
1 Cup Chutney
½ Cup Catsup or Tomato Sauce
1 Tbs. Brown Sugar
1 Tsp. Dry Mustard
¼ Tsp. Hot Sauce
Dash Cayenne Pepper
¼ Tsp. Garlic Powder
1 Medium Onion, minced
½ Cup Rum (optional)

Sprinkle pepper and lemon juice over ribs and let stand 30 minutes. Brown ribs in lightly greased skillet, spoon sauce over them. Brown at high heat. These cook like steak. Combine ingredients for sauce and cook until done and pour over the ribs.

$25,000 CALIFORNIA CASSEROLE

2 Lbs. Veal or Beef Round Steak
1/3 Cup Flour
1 Tsp. Paprika
¼ Cup Salad Oil
1¾ Cups Small Cooked Onions
1 Can Cream Of Chicken Soup
1 Can Water

DUMPLINGS:
1 Cup Flour
2 Tsp. Double-acting Baking Powder
¼ Tsp. Salt
½ Tsp. Poultry Seasoning
½ Tsp. Celery Salt
½ Tsp. Dry Onion Flakes
1/8 Cup Salad Oil
½ Cup Milk
1/8 Cup Melted Butter
½ Cup Crackers

Coat 2 lbs. of meat with mixture of 1/3 cup flour and 1 tsp. paprika. Pound mixture into meat, cut into 2 inch cubes. Brown thoroughly in oil. Put in a 9x13 inch pan and add can of onions. Combine chicken soup and water in skillet used for browning. Bring to boil and pour over meat. Bake in moderate oven, 350 degrees, for about 45 min. or until meat is tender. Add dumplings, increase temp. to 425 degrees, bake for 20 to 25 min. or until golden brown.

DUMPLINGS:
Sift together flour, baking powder, salt and poultry seasoning. Add celery salt, onion flakes, salad oil and milk. Drop rounded tbs. of dough into mixture of melted butter and broken up crackers. If more gravy is desired add another can of cream of chicken soup and 1 can water

POLLERINE

2 Lbs. Hamburger
2 Onions, chopped
4 Tbs. Chili Powder
1 or 2 Cans Creamed Corn
1 Can Pitted Olives
1 Can Whole Tomatoes
1 Can Tomato Paste
1 - 16 Oz. Can Tomato Sauce
1 Cup Grated Cheese
1 Pkg. Wide Egg Noodles
Salt & Pepper to taste

Cook egg noodles and set aside. Brown hamburger and onion; add salt and pepper to taste; stir in tomato sauce, tomato paste, corn and olives. Add rest of ingredients except grated cheese. Stir well. Reduce heat and sprinkle cheese on top. Cover and simmer 1 hour [MW: 15 min. on full power]. Serves 4 to 6.

MEXICAN BEEF SANDWICH ROLLS.

1 Can Sliced Olives, drained
1 - 7 Oz. Can Green Chili Salsa
¼ Tsp. Ground Cumin
¼ Tsp. Salt
½ Tsp. Chili Powder
6 Rectangular French Rolls
½ Lb. Lean Ground Beef
1 Onion, chopped
¼ Lb. Sliced Mushrooms
4 Oz. Cheddar Cheese, sliced
4 Oz. Jack Cheese, sliced
6 Slices Crisp Bacon

Cut rolls in half lengthwise; scoop out most of insides. Lightly toast cut sides; set aside. Crumble beef into frying pan over medium heat and brown [MW: in glass casserole for 4 min. on full power]; add onion and mushrooms and cook until limp. Stir in olives, chili salsa, cumin, salt and chili powder; simmer until liquid is absorbed. Arrange cheddar cheese on one half of each roll. Top each with 1 slice of bacon, 1/6 of meat mixture, and the jack cheese. Add to half of roll; wrap each sandwich in foil [MW: wax paper]. Chill if made ahead. Heat in 375 degree oven for 12-15 minutes (30 min. if chilled). [MW: 6-7 min. on full power]. Serves 6.

TAMALF LOAF

½ Cup Oil
1 Medium Onion, chopped
2 Lbs. Hamburger
1 Can Olives, pitted & drained
2 - 17 Oz. Cans Creamed Corn
2 - 16 Oz. Cans Stewed Tomatoes
2 Cups Corn Meal (Yellow)
2 to 3 Tsp. Chili Powder
1 Cup Milk
2 Eggs
2 Tsp. Catsup (optional)
2 Tsp. Worcestershire Sauce
Salt
Pepper

Cook onion in oil until transparent. Add hamburger and brown. Add salt and pepper to taste. Warm stewed tomatoes and creamed corn slowly in a large pan on low heat. Beat eggs slightly, add milk to eggs and when corn and tomato mixture is warmed well, add egg and milk mixture to corn meal, stirring just to mix and add this to corn and tomato mixture. Add chili to meat, stirring in thoroughly and combine with corn and tomatoes. Let this stand on low heat for a little while to set up. Place a layer of tamale loaf mixture in a well buttered casserole dish. Place a layer of olives and continue with the tamale mixture and olive layers, ending with a decorative arrangement of olives on top. Bake at 350 degrees for 1½ to 2 hours [MW: 15-30 min. on full power], if put in 1 large casserole dish. If you wish to divide in half, bake smaller casserole about 1 hr. [MW: 15 min.]. Knife inserted in center should come out clean when done. You can start without cover and as it browns cover then, or cover at beginning and remove last half hour or so. Serves 12 to 14 people. Also keeps well in warm oven, if necessary to hold up on serving. Can be made day before, stored in the refrigerator and baked on the day of serving.

FLORENTINE MEAT PIE

1 Cup Flour
1½ Tsp. Sugar
¼ Tsp. Salt
½ Cup Shortening
2 Tbl. Ice Water

FILLING

1 Lb. Lean Ground Beef
1 Pkg. (10 Oz.) Frozen Chopped
   Spinach, thawed and drained
1 Can (6 Oz.) Tomato Paste
¾ Cup Finely Crushed Saltine
   Cracker Crumbs
1 Tbl. Instant Onion Flakes
2 Large Eggs
1 Tsp. Salt
1 Tsp. Oregano
1 - 9 Inch Unbaked Pie Shell with
   High Fluted Rim
2 Tbl. Milk
½ Cup Grated Cheddar Cheese
4 Slices Bacon, halved crosswise
   and cooked until crisp for
   garnish if desired.

Add sugar and salt to flour. Cut in shortening till fine. Add water, stir with fork until mixture forms a ball. Roll out to fit 9 inch pie pan. Make high fluted rim. In a medium mixing bowl mix together well the beef, spinach, tomato paste, cracker crumbs, onion, 1 egg, salt and oregano. Press firmly into pie shell. Cover pie shell edge with 2 inch wide strip of foil to prevent excessive browning. Bake in a pre-heated 425° oven for 50 minutes. Remove foil strip. Beat remaining egg slightly and stir in milk and cheese; pour over top of pie (but not over pastry edge), spreading evenly. Reduce heat to 350 degrees and bake until topping sets. Remove from oven and let stand 10 minutes before cutting. Garnish with bacon, if desired. Makes 6 servings. This can be done ahead of time. Makes a super dish to take on a picnic. Served with a green salad, it makes a good main course for Sunday supper. Also warms up well in a micro-wave oven, if you use a glass dish.

STUFFED ROUND STEAK

1 Large, Tenderized Round Steak
2 Cups Bread Crumbs (cubes)
2 Carrots
1 Onion
1 Beef Bouillon Cube
½ Cup Water
1 Tsp. Sage
½ Tsp. Thyme
Dash of Salt
1 Can Mushroom Soup

Very lightly salt round steak or use seasoned tenderizer salt. Grate carrots; add to prepared bread cubes. Add sage, thyme and grated or chopped onion. Mix bouillon cube in water until dissolved. Add to the bread and carrots (dressing should be rather moist; if not, add a little more water). Put on round steak and roll and tie. Brown in electric skillet or regular skillet [MW: browning dish]. Cover with mushroom soup, undiluted. Cook in electric skillet at 300 degrees, or wrapped in foil in oven at 350 degrees for approximately 1½ hours [MW: 15-30 min. on full power], or until steak is tender.

CONNECTICUT SUPPER FOR 6

1 Lb. Beef Chuck Steak, cubed
2 Large Potatoes, sliced ½" thick
2 Large Onions, sliced
1 Can Cream of Mushroom Soup
1 Cup Sour Cream
1½ Cups Milk
1 Tsp. Salt
½ Tsp. Pepper
1 Cup Grated Cheddar Cheese
½ Cup Crushed Wheaties

Brown onions in 2 tbs. oil; add meat and 1 cup water. Simmer, covered for 50 min. [MW: 15 min.]. Pour into baking dish, 13" x 9" x 2". Place potato slices over meat. Blend soup, cream, milk, salt and pepper together. Pour over top; sprinkle with cheese and wheaties. Bake, uncovered, in 350 degree oven for 1½ hours, [MW: 30 min. on full power] or until done.

VIENNESE POT ROAST

3½ - 4 Lb. Chuck Roast - 1½" thick
2 Tbs. Brown Sugar
3 Tbs. Flour
½ Tsp. Salt
¼ Tsp. Pepper
¼ Tsp. Rosemary (Opt.)
½ Tsp. Dry Mustard
1 Bay Leaf
¾ Cup Catsup
1 Tbs. Worchestershire Sauce
1 Tbs. Vinegar

Double a 5 foot length piece of foil. Place on broiler pan. Place roast on foil and brown under broiler. (May also be browned in electric skillet.) Combine remaining ingredients. Spoon half of sauce under roast and remaining sauce on top. Seal foil. Roast at 325° for 1½ to 2 hours or until tender. Foil-wrapped roast may also be baked in outdoor electric barbecue with lid. I do the whole thing in the electric skillet without foil. If sauce gets too thick, add a little water.

HOT TEXAS RED CHILI

3 Lbs. Coarsely Ground Lean Beef (no veal)
¼ Cup Olive Oil
6 Tbs. Chili Powder
3 Tsp. Salt
1 Tbs. Sugar
10 Cloves Garlic, chopped or pressed
1 Tsp. Cumin
1 Tsp. Oregano
1 Tsp. Cayenne Red Pepper
3 Tbs. Paprika
3 Tbs. Flour
6 Tbs. Yellow Corn Meal

With olive oil hot in a large pot, add meat and sear over high heat, stirring constantly until meat is grey in color (not brown). Add 1 quart of water and cook at bubbling simmer about 1½ hours [MW: 20 min.]. Add all ingredients except flour and corn meal. Cook 30 minutes more [MW: 15 min. on full power]. Mix flour and corn meal in ½ cup water and add to mixture. Cook 5 minutes more to determine if more water is needed.

PIROZHKI
(Russian Meat-filled Pastries)

Filling:
1 Large Onion, chopped
1 Lb. Ground Beef
½ Cup Water
1 Tbs. Fat or Shortening
1 Tbs. Flour

Make filling first and let it cool while you prepare dough. Saute' onion in fat until pink, but not brown. Add ground beef, stirring with fork to prevent formation of chunks. Cook until no red is visible in the meat. Sprinkle with 1 tbs. flour; mix well and add ½ cup water, mixing all ingredients well. Cool. Use to fill Priozhki dough.

Dough:
2 Cups Scalded Milk, cooled to lukewarm
1/3 Cup Sugar
6 Tbs. Butter
6 Cups Sifted Flour (about)
1 Pkg. Dry Yeast*
2 Tsp. Salt
2 Eggs, slightly beaten

*Use 1 pkg. at 5,200 foot altitude; 1½ pkgs. should be used at sea level.

Add sugar and salt to milk; sprinkle with yeast and mix well. Add melted butter and the eggs and mix in. Gradually add flour, mixing and kneading about 5 min. on floured board as for bread dough. Form into ball; grease lightly; cover with a towel and let rise in a warm, draft-free place about 2 hours, until doubled. Punch dough down and let rise again for about 30 to 60 minutes, or until dough is puffy. Take pieces of dough (of the same size as for dinner rolls) and flatten. With a floured rolling pin on a floured board, roll each piece into an oval about 3" long and about ¼" thick. Put 1 tbs. of filling along the center of the oval. Close and seal edges of dough over filling. With sealed sides down, place Pirozhki on lightly greased, floured cookie sheet and bake in 375 degree oven about 20 minutes, or until nice and brown. Makes about 25 Pirozhki.

LASAGNA ROLLS

1 Lb. Lean Ground Beef
1 Cup Chopped Onion
1 Lg. Clove Garlic, minced
2 Tbs. Parsley Flakes
1 Tsp. Salt
¼ Cup Sliced Green Onion
½ Tsp Seasoned Salt
1 Tsp. Dried Basil
1 Tsp. Dried Oregano
1 - 16 Oz. Can Tomato Puree
1 - 16 Oz. Can Whole, Peeled Tomatoes, chopped
½ Tsp. Garlic Salt
4 Egg Yolks
½ Cup Dry Red Wine
1 Lb. Ricotta Cheese
½ Cup Shredded Cheddar Cheese
¾ Cup Shredded Mozzarella Cheese
½ Cup Grated Parmesan Cheese
Chopped Parsley

In a large skillet [MW: glass casserole] saute' beef, breaking it up as it cooks. Add onion and garlic; simmer 5 min., stirring occasionally. Add parsley flakes, salt, basil, oregano, tomato puree, tomatoes and juice, and wine. Simmer, stirring occasionally, for 45 minutes, [MW: 20 min.] or until sauce is desired thickness.

Meanwhile, combine ricotta, cheddar, ½ cup mozzarella and ¼ cup Parmesan cheese. Stir in green onion, seasoned salt, garlic salt & egg yolks, mixing well; set aside. Cook the lasagna as directed on package. Rinse with cold water; drain. Spread about ¼ cup of the cheese mixture on each lasagna; roll up jelly-roll style. Arrange rolls, seam-side down, in sauce. Spoon part of the sauce over rolls. Cover and simmer about 20 minutes [MW: 10 min.] Sprinkle remaining mozzarella and Parmesan cheese over rolls. Cover and simmer 5 minutes longer. Garnish with chopped parsley. Makes 12 servings.

OYSTER SAUCE BEEF

1 Lb. Beef, sliced thin
½ Cup Green Onions
¼ Tsp. Salt
½ Tbs. Soy Sauce
1 Tbs. Cornstarch
Dash of Sugar
2 Tbs. Oil
2 Tbs. Oyster Sauce
¼ Cup Chicken Stock
½ Tsp. MSG
1 Tbs. Cornstarch
1 Tbs. Water

Place in bowl salt, soy sauce, 1 tbs. cornstarch and sugar. Mix ingredients thoroughly and add beef; marinate 5 minutes. In a preheated skillet [MW: browning dish], place oil, sliced beef and green onions. Add oyster sauce. Cook on high heat 3 minutes. Add chicken stock, MSG, 1 tbs. cornstarch mixed with 1 tbs. water. Add bean sprouts, celery, snow peas, water chestnuts, fresh mushrooms as desired. Toss and mix until gravy thickens and coats the vegetables. Serve on steamed rice.

DAAL-GHOSH (Beef Stew - East Indian Style)

½ Cup Yellow Split Peas
1 Lb. Boneless Beef Stew
1 Medium Onion
1 Tsp. Salt
¼ Tsp. Paprika
¼ Tsp. Red Crushed Chili Pepper
½ Tsp. Ground Cumin
½ Tsp. Ground Coriander
½ Tsp. Italian Seasoning
1 Tbs. Oil
Optional: Few Boiling Onions, 2 Carrots, Big Pieces of Cut Green Beans

Heat 1 tbs. oil to smoking point; add chopped onion, stew pieces and brown meat until it loses its red color. Add spices and dal or split peas. Add 1 cup water and cook in a pressure cooker 15 minutes after pressure is built up. Serve over plain, steamed white rice, about 1 to 1½ cups. Serves 4 to 6 adults. If desired, add vegetables. Cook for 2 or 3 minutes.

MEXICALI CASSEROLE

2 Lbs. Ground Beef
½ Lb. Sausage
4 Tbs. Chopped Onion
2/3 Cup Evaporated Milk
2 Tbs. Chili Powder
¼ Tsp. Pepper
Salt to taste
1 Small Onion, chopped
1 - 7 Oz. Can Ortega Green Chili Pepper
2 Cans Cream of Mushroom Soup
2 Cups Milk
12 Corn Tortillas
2/3 Lb. Cheddar Cheese

Mix ground beef, sausage, chopped onion, evaporated milk, chili pepper, salt and pepper. Make into tbs. size balls and brown. Make sauce of 1 small onion, Ortega green chili pepper, mushroom soup and 2 cups milk. Layer with this mixture and cheddar cheese. Also layer 12 tortillas cut in strips. Use a 3 or 4 quart casserole dish. Bake at 350 degrees for 45 minutes. [MW: 15 min. on high power]

SATURDAY NIGHT PIZZA

1 Pkg. Active Dry Yeast
1-¼ Cups Warm Water
¼ Cup Vegetable Oil
4-½ Cups Flour, (Approximate)
½ Tsp. Salt
½ Tsp. Pepper
½ Lb. Mozzarella
½ Lb. Provolone
½ Lb. Pepperoni
½ Lb. Salami
½ Lb. Cooked Ground Beef
1 Cup Mushrooms.

Pizza Tomato Sauce:

1 Can (15 Oz.) Tomato Sauce
1 Tsp. Oregano Leaves
½ Tsp. Basil Leaves
½ Tsp. Sugar
2 Tsp. Water

In large bowl, sprinkle yeast over ¼ cup warm water. Stir to dissolve. Add remaining water and oil. With large spoon, beat in 1-½ cups flour until smooth, continue beating 2 minutes. Add salt, pepper and enough remaining flour to make a stiff dough. Turn out onto lightly floured board. Knead until smooth and elastic, about 5 to 8 minutes. Place in oiled bowl, turning to oil top. Cover and let rise in warm place, until doubled in bulk, about 1 hour. Punch dough down, divide in half. Press onto a lightly oiled pizza pan with ½ inch high borders. Preheat oven to 400 degrees and spread each with 1 cup tomato sauce, add toppings and bake 20 to 25 minutes, until crust is golden brown. Sauce: Combine all ingredients in small saucepan. Heat to boiling, reduce heat and simmer uncovered for 5 minutes. Makes 2 pizzas.

SILVER—PLATED POT ROAST

4 Lbs. Blade Bone Pot Roast, 1½" thick
Salt and Pepper
3 Tbs. Flour
1 Tbs. Brown Sugar
1 Tsp. Salt
Dash of Pepper
½ Tsp. Dry Mustard
¾ Cup Catsup
1½ Tbs. Worcestershire Sauce
1 Tbs. Vinegar
Aluminum Foil
1 or 2 Stalks Celery, sliced on bias
1 or 2 Carrots, sliced
1 Medium Onion, sliced

Brown roast slowly on grill over hot coals with hickory added (20 to 30 minutes). Season well with salt and pepper. Combine next 8 ingredients for sauce. Tear off a 5' length of household-weight foil; fold double (or use 2½ ft. of heavy-duty foil). Spoon half of sauce in center of foil; place meat atop and cover with vegetables and remaining sauce. Fold foil over and seal securely. Bake over slow coals (have a double thickness of extra foil on grill) for 1½ to 2 hrs., or until tender.

WAIKIKI MEAT BALLS

1½ Lbs. Ground Beef
2/3 Cup Cracker Crumbs
1/3 Cup Minced Onion
1 Egg
1½ Tsp. Salt
¼ Tsp. Ginger
¼ Cup Milk
1 Tbs. Shortening
2 Tbs. Cornstarch
½ Cup Brown Sugar, packed
1 - 13½ Oz. Can Pineapple Bits, drained
   (reserve syrup)
1/3 Cup Vinegar
1 Tbs. Soy Sauce
1/3 Cup Chopped Green Pepper

Mix meat, crumbs, onion, egg, salt, ginger and milk. Shape mixture into balls by rounded tablespoonful. Melt shortening in large skillet [MW: browning dish] ; brown and cook meatballs. Remove meat balls and keep warm. Pour fat from skillet [browning dish].

Mix cornstarch and sugar. Stir in reserved pineapple juice or syrup, vinegar and soy sauce until smooth. Pour into skillet [MW: growning dish] and cook over medium heat, stirring constantly, until mixture thickens and boils. Boil and stir 1 minute.

Add meat balls, pineapple tidbits and green pepper. Heat thoroughly. Makes 6 servings.

BEEF & BARLEY SOUP

3 Lbs. Lean Beef Short Ribs
2 Large Onions, chopped
¼ Cup Chopped Parsley
3 Cloves Garlic, minced or pressed
¾ Cup Each Split Peas and Dried Baby Limas
8 Cups Water
3 Beef Bouillon Cubes
1 Tbs. Dillweed
¼ Lb. Mushrooms, sliced
½ Cup Pearl Barley
8 Large Carrots, in 1 inch slices
Salt & Pepper to taste

In a 6 to 8-quart kettle [MW: glass casserole], brown meat on all sides. Add onion and saute' until limp. Stir in parsley, garlic, split peas, limas, water and bouillon cubes. Cover and simmer 2 hours [MW: 1 hr.] or until meat is tender when pierced. Lift out meat; skim and discard fat from broth. Whirl broth and vegetables a small amount at a time in blender until pureed. Return to kettle [casserole], stir in dill, mushrooms, barley and carrots. Discard bones and break meat into bite-size pieces. Stir into soup. Add salt and pepper to taste. Cover and simmer about 45 min. [MW: 15 min.] or until barley is tender. Makes 6 to 8 servings. Serve with French bread and a big green salad for a very hearty meal!

TACO BAKE

1½ to 2 Lbs. Ground Beef
1 Small Onion, finely chopped
1 Clove Garlic, chopped
3 - 8 Oz. Cans Tomato Sauce
1½ Cups Water
1 Small Can Sliced Olives, drained
2 Tbs. Flour
2 Tbs. Vinegar
2 Tbs. Chili Powder
1 Cup Grated Cheddar Cheese
1 Pkg. 12 Taco Shells

In small amount of oil, brown ground beef, onion and garlic; drain off fat and add tomato sauce, water, olives, flour, vinegar and chili powder. Simmer for 10 minutes [MW: 5 min.]. Butter an oblong baking dish and layer meat sauce and taco shells, beginning and ending with the meat sauce. Sprinkle grated cheese over top and bake in a 350 degree oven for 45 minutes [MW: 15 minutes on full power]. Let stand 10 minutes and serve. Serve with green salad and your favorite cheap red wine. Good company dish and a family favorite..

SIZZLING SHORT RIBS

5 Lbs. Beef Shortribs
Water
1½ Cups Catsup
½ Cup Wine (never cook with a wine you
  don't like to drink)
1/3 Cup Packed Brown Sugar
1 Tbs. Worcestershire Sauce
2 Tsp. Grated Lime Peel
1½ Tsp. Dry Mustard
¾ Tsp. Garlic Salt
¼ Tsp. Pepper

Early in the day or a day ahead: In an 8
quart dutch oven, cover the shortribs in water over high heat. Heat to boiling. Reduce
heat to low. Cover and simmer 2 hours or
until ribs are tender. Remove ribs to platter
and cover and refrigerate.

About 1 hour before serving: Prepare outdoor grill for barbecuing. Meanwhile, in a
small bowl, combine the catsup and remaining ingredients. Place cooked ribs on grill
over medium coals. Cook for 20 to 25 minutes until heated through, brushing occasionally with catsup mixture and turning often.
Can also be fixed in the oven. Makes 6 serv.

MEXICAN BEEF CASSEROLE SUPREME

2 Lbs. Ground Chuck
1 Medium Onion, chopped
1 Pkg. Taco Seasoning Mix
1 Cup Water
1 Bottle Taco Sauce (12 Oz.)
10 Corn Tortillas
2 Pkgs. Frozen Chopped Spinach, thawed
  and drained
3 Cups Grated Jack Cheese, about ¾ lb.
½ to ¼ Lb. Cooked Diced Pork or Ham
1½ Cups Sour Cream
Salt to taste
Black Olives, sliced
Green Olives, sliced

Combine beef and onions in large skillet.
[MW: glass casserole] Brown, stirring meat
to crumble. Salt to taste, about ½ tsp. and
stir in the taco seasoning mix and add water.

Cover and simmer 10 minutes [MW: 5 min.].
In a 13" x 9" x 2" baking dish, place 5
quartered tortillas, coated with taco sauce,
overlapping in two rows. In a wire strainer
press out most of the water from the spinach.
Stir half of the spinach into the beef mixture.

Spoon half of the beef-spinach mixture over
the tortillas in the casserole and sprinkle with
half the cheese. Cover with remaining tortillas coated with taco sauce and spread the
balance of taco-meat mixture on the tortillas.
Spread evenly the chopped pork or ham over
the tortilla meat mixture and spread on the
sour cream. Put remaining spinach over the
cream. Top evenly with remaining cheese.
Refrigerate several hours or overnight.

When ready to cook, take out of refrigerator
early enough so that it is almost at room
temperature. Bake at 375 degrees for 50
min. [MW: 20 min. on full power] , covered
for the first half of the cooking time. Before serving, garnish with sliced olives and
sliced green onions.

Note: If desired, bake in two 8" x 8" x 2"
casseroles. Fix one, freeze the other one
for a later dinner.

BEEF MARINADE

1 Cup Soy Sauce
2 Medium Onions
4 Cloves Garlic
½ Cup Kitchen Bouquet
4 Tsp. Beau Monde

Put soy sauce, onions and cloves of garlic
into blender and liquefy. Add Kitchen
Bouquet and Beau Monde to liquified mixture and blend. Marinate any meat.

SLIM MEATBALLS

Meatballs:
1 Lb. Lean Ground Beef
2 Tbs. Instant Minced Onion
½ Tsp. Garlic Salt
1 - 10 Oz. Pkg. Frozen, Chopped
   Spinach, thawed
1 Cup Lowfat Cottage Cheese
¼ Cup Diced Bread Crumbs
1 Egg
1 Tbs. Water

Lightly combine ground beef, onion, garlic
salt, spinach, cottage cheese and bread
crumbs in a large bowl. Beat egg with water
in a small bowl; blend into beef mixture..
Shape into balls, using a tbs. of meat mixture for each meatball. Broil just until brown
[MW: full power], turning once. Add
browned meatballs to 1 pint tomato sauce
(following). Simmer for 30 min. [MW: 15
min.]. Serves 5 at 243 calories per serving.
A ½ cup serving of tender, cooked spaghetti
adds 78 calories per serving.

Tomato Sauce:
4 Onions, chopped
3 Small Cloves Garlic, minced
3 Tbs. Oil
4 - 28 Oz. Cans Tomatoes
4 - 6 Oz. Cans Tomato Paste
½ Lb. Sliced Mushrooms
1 Cup Chopped Parsley (or 1/3
   cup dried Parsley Falkes)
3 Tbs. Sugar
1½ Tbs. Salt
4 Tsp. Oregano
2 Bay Leaves
4 Oz. Red Wine

Saute' onions and garlic in oil until limp.
Add remaining ingredients and simmer for
2 to 3½ hours [MW: 1½ to 2 hours]. Let
cool to room temperature. May be frozen
in pints and quarts and used for veal parmi-
giana, manicotti and other Italian dishes.

GREEK SARMA

½ Lb. Ground Beef
½ Lb. Ground Lamb
½ Cup Cooked Rice
1 Onion, finely chopped
1 Clove Garlic, finely minced
1 Tbs. Chopped Parsley
½ Tsp. Basil
Salt & Pepper to taste
1 Tsp. M.S.G.
½ Jar Grape Leaves
2 - 8 Oz. Cans Tomato Sauce

Mix meat, rice, onion, garlic and spices
together. Place a small amount in each
grape leaf, roll and arrange in single layer
in flat casserole dish, folds on bottom.
Cover with 2 cans tomato sauce. Cover
with foil [MW: plastic wrap] and bake
in a 350 degree oven for 1 hour [MW:
20 min. on full power]. Extra leaves
may be frozen.

HUNGARIAN GOULASH SOUP

4 Tbs. Butter
1 Lb. Veal, cubed
1 Lb. Lean Beef, cubed
2 Cups Chopped Onion
2 Tbs. Sweet Paprika
1 Cup Diced Green Pepper
1 Can Stewed Tomatoes
8 Cups Boiling Water
1½ Tsp. Salt
½ Tsp. Ground Pepper
3 Large Cubed Potatoes
½ Cup Red Burgundy Wine (optional)

Melt butter in large pot; add cubes (½"
size) veal and beef. Cook over medium
heat until browned [MW: full power].
Add onions and cook until soft. Stir
in paprika, salt and pepper. Add undrained stewed tomatoes, green peppers, boiling water and wine (optional).
Bring just to a boil, cover and simmer
over low heat for 1½ hours [MW: 40
min.]. Stir occasionally. Add cubed
potatoes. Cook for 20-30 minutes more
[MW: 15-20 min. on full power].
Serve in soup bowls with fresh French or
sourdough bread or rolls. With a green
salad, makes a total meal. Serves 6; keeps
well in refrigerator or may be frozen.

LAHMADJOUN
(Armenian Meat Pie, Pizza - Like)

5 Cups Sifted All-Purpose Flour
1 Pkg. Dry Yeast
2 Tsp. Salt
¼ Cup Vegetable Oil
1½ Cups Lukewarm Water (approx.)

Meat Filling:
2 Lbs. Ground Beef or Lamb
1 to 2 Green Peppers, finely chopped
1 Bunch Parsley, finely chopped
1 Onion, finely chopped
1 or 2 Cloves Garlic, crushed
2 Tsp. Salt
½ Tsp. Black Pepper
¼ Tsp. Cayenne Pepper
¼ Tsp. Allspice
1 Tsp. Paprika
4 Tbs. Tomato Paste (optional)
1 - 28 Oz. Can Whole Tomatoes, chopped
   (use the juice too)
1 or 2 Lemons (juice optional)

To Prepare Meat Filling: Chop all vegetables very fine, or put them through the medium blade of a meat grinder. Mix together meat, vegetables and seasonings, as well as tomato paste, whole tomatoes with juice and lemon juice. Blend well.

To Prepare Dough: Sift flour into large bowl. Dissolve yeast as directed on the package, using 1 cup of the lukewarm water in recipe. Combine dissolved yeast, remaining ½ cup water, oil and salt; stir and pour over flour. Blend well and knead dough into a soft smooth dough. Dough should be softer than bread dough. Cover; let stand 1 or 2 hours, until double in size. Punch down dough. Divide into 36 to 40 balls. Roll out each ball on a well-floured board into very thin 6 to 7 inch circles. Arrange on greased baking sheets. Spread evenly with the meat mixture, right to the edge of the circle, and press down lightly with fingers. Bake in a 500 degree oven for 6 to 8 minutes on a wire rack. Stack two together and cover pies to prevent from drying. Combine in this manner until dough and meat mixture is used. Serve hot with tossed salad.

PORTUGUESE SOPAS

1 - 3 Lb. Pot Roast
1 - 8 Oz. Can Tomato Sauce
1 Large Onion, diced
½ Tsp. Pepper
2 Tbs. Ground Cinnamon
1 Clove Garlic, diced
1 Cup Red Wine
1 Tsp. Cloves
2 Tsp. Ground Cumin
3 Bay Leaves
2 Tsp. Allspice
1 Cup Mint Leaves
2 Medium Heads Cabbage
1 Tsp. Salt
Water
1 Loaf French Bread

In a large pot combine the first 12 ingredients and salt. Cover with water. Cook at medium heat for 4 hours [MW: 1 hour]. Add more water if water cooks out. Quarter cabbage and add to the soup. Cook for 30 minutes [MW: 20 minutes] or until cabbage is tender. Serve over sliced french bread.

DANISH MEAT BALLS
(Frikadeller)

1½ Lbs. Ground Beef
½ Lb. Ground Pork
1 Small, Grated Onion
1 Egg
½ Cup Milk
½ Cup Flour
1 Tsp. Salt
½ Tsp. Pepper

Combine meat, egg, onion, salt and pepper in large mixing bowl. With wooden spoon, work in flour; add milk last, a little at a time. Mix thoroughly. Let stand about 10 minutes.

In heavy skillet [MW: browning dish], melt 3 tbs. butter or margarine; when light brown turn heat to low. Form meatballs, with large tablespoon, and brown on all sides. Fill pan and cook over medium heat for 15 min. [MW: 10 minutes], or bake in oven, 325 degrees, for 30 minutes [MW: 8-10 minutes on full power]. Very good served with creamed cabbage, creamed spinach and small, boiled potatoes.

STEAK, KIDNEY, MUSHROOM & OYSTER PIE

1½ Tbs. Margarine
1½ Tbs. Vegetable Oil
½ Lb. Onions, sliced thin
½ Lb. Mushrooms, washed
1½ Lbs. Steak
8 Lamb Kidneys
2 Dozen Oysters
1 Tbs. Corn Flour
½ Cup Milk or Water

Put in a frying pan and heat the margarine and vegetable oil. Add onions that have been sliced thin and cook until golden brown. Add mushrooms that have been washed but not peeled or broken. Cook for 3 minutes. Remove from pan. Cut up and roll in seasoned flour the steak and lamb kidneys. Brown in pan, using a little more oil if necessary. Combine the onions and mushrooms with the meat in a heavy casserole dish. Combine together with a bouquet garni or a sprinkle of herbs and add enough hot beef stock to comfortably cover them. Cook gently on top of stove or in a 300 degree oven until the meat is tender. Add the oysters that have been drained and the 1 tbs. corn flour that has been mixed with the cup of water or milk. Reheat. To avoid a pastry crust which is over-cooked, cook it separately and crown the pie with it five minutes before you take it out of the oven.

REUBEN BURGER PIE

Meat Pie Shell:
1 Lb. Ground Beef
2/3 Cup Quaker Oats (quick or old fashioned)
½ Cup Thousand Island Dressing
1 Egg
¾ Tsp. Salt
¼ Tsp. Pepper
1/8 Tsp. Garlic Powder

Combine all ingredients; mix well. Press onto bottom and sides of 9'' pie plate. Bake in preheated moderate oven, 350 degrees, for 15 min. [MW: 6 min. on full power]; drain.

Filling:
1 - 16 Oz. Can Sauerkraut, drained
2 Cups (8 Oz.) Shredded Swiss Cheese
1½ Tsp. Caraway Seeds

Combine all ingredients; toss lightly, mixing well. Spoon into partially-baked meat shell. Continue baking 10 to 12 minutes [MW: 5-7 min. full power], or until cheese is melted. Cut into wedges, serve with additional thousand island dressing, if desired. Makes 6 servings.

BRAISED SIRLOIN TIPS OVER RICE

2 Tbs. Wesson Oil
2 Lbs. Beef Sirloin or Round Sliced into 3 inch strips
2 Bouillon Cubes dissolved in water and Mushroom Juice to equal 10½ ozs.
1/3 Cup Burgundy or Cranberry Juice
2 Tbs. Soy Sauce
2 Cloves Garlic, minced
2 Tbs. Minced Onion
1 Can (4½ Oz.) Mushrooms
1 Can Sliced Water Chestnuts
1 Pkg. Chinese Pea Pods
2 Tbs. Cornstarch
¼ Cup Hot Water
4 Cups Hot Cooked Rice

Brown beef in hot oil [MW: browning dish]. Mix together and add bouillon, wine, garlic, onion, shoyu and mushrooms. Bring to a boil, reduce heat; cover and simmer 1 hr. [MW: 20-25 min.] or until meat is tender. Add in water chestnuts and pea pods. Blend cornstarch and water; stir in gradually into mixture of meat. Cook, stirring constantly, until mixture thickens and boils. Boil and stir 1 minute. Serve immediately over rice. 4-6 servings.

WINTER WEEKEND SOUP

2 Lbs. Beef Short Ribs
1 Large Beef Knuckle Bone, split
3 - 32 Oz. Cans Peeled Tomatoes
2 - 15 Oz. Cans Tomato Sauce
2 Quarts Water
2 Large Turnips
2 Large Bell Peppers
½ Stalk Celery
2 Large Onions
1 Small Red Cabbage
½ Lb. Green Beans
1 Bunch Turnip Greens
3 Large Carrots
2 Small Zucchini Squash
½ Tsp. Thyme
1 Bay Leaf
1 Oregano Leaf
2 Tbs. Sugar or Honey
Salt and Pepper to taste
1 Clove Garlic, if you like

Use large pot! Sear short ribs in pot; add tomatoes (squeeze through fingers to break up). Add tomato sauce and drop in the knuckle bone. Add seasonings and bring to a boil while you cut up vegetables into large pieces. Add 1 turnip, 1 bell pepper, ¼ stalk celery, 1 onion, ½ head cabbage and ½ bunch greens. Cook at slow boil for 2 hours [MW: 45 min. medium power]. Add carrots and green beans; allow to boil slowly for 30 min. [MW: 15 min. on medium power].

Add remaining cut up vegetables and cook for about 30 minutes more, or until these vegetables are cooked but firm. Start serving and relax for the weekend. The soup improves with age. This is a low-calorie soup, so enjoy!

LUMPIA

1 Lb. Ground Beef
½ Lb. Ground Pork or Sausage
4 Cups Thinly Sliced Cabbage
2 Cups Shredded Carrots
1-2 Onions, sliced thin
1 Cup Bean Sprouts
1 Bell Pepper (optional), sliced thin
Lumpia Wrappers (available at oriental food stores)

Brown ground beef and pork in Dutch oven. Add onion; cook till it is slightly limp. Add remaining ingredients and cook till tender. Season with salt and pepper. Remove from heat and drain, if needed; cool. Separate the lumpia wrappers. Place approximately 1-1½ tbs. of mixture in wrapper. Roll like an egg roll. Seal with a mixture of cornstarch and water. Deep fry lumpia until golden brown. Serve with sweet 'n sour sauce, or your favorite sauce.

CHOW MEIN

1 Flank Steak, cut in diagonal strips, then into 1" strips
1 Entire Stalk Celery, washed and cut in diagonal strips
2 Large Bell Peppers, cut into diagonal strips
2 or 3 Beef Bouillon Cubes, dissolved in 1 cup hot water
1 Tbs. Sugar
2 Tsp. Oil
¼ Cup Soy Sauce
2 Fresh Tomatoes, dipped in hot water, peeled and cut into eighths
1 Large Can Tomatoes
¼ Cup Cornstarch, dissolved in ½ cup cold water

In Dutch oven or large pan [MW: browning dish], saute' meat in oil until it loses its red color, remove meat. Add celery to pan and saute' on medium heat [MW: full power] until it starts to turn a little clear; add onions When onions also turn a little clear, add bell peppers and meat. Cook 2 or 3 minutes. Add bouillon, sugar, soy sauce and both kinds of tomatoes. Cook until heated through. Add cornstarch and water and cook until the juice turns a little clear. Serve over pan-fried noodles and pass the soy sauce.

Pan-Fried Noodles: Cook 1 pkg. Chinese noodles by directions. Pour into colander and rinse in cold water (wash hands well). Drop by handfuls into hot fat. Fry until brown and turn; brown other side. Drain on crumpled paper towels. Rinse noodles in cold water when needed to keep them from sticking together. The chow mein and noodles both freeze well.

CHILI EASTERN STYLE

1 Lb. Ground Beef, Cooked until
   Gray
2 Sm. or 1 Lg. Onion, Chopped Fine
1/2 Tsp. Garlic Salt
3/4 Tbs. Vinegar
1 Can 4 oz. Tomato Sauce
1 Tbs. Chili Powder
1/2 Tsp. Red Pepper
1 Dash Worcestershire Sauce
Salt and Pepper to taste
1/2 qt. Water
2 1/2 Bay Leaves
18 Allspice (whole)

Cook ground beef until gray then chop fine.
Add onion, chopped very fine. Then add
garlic, vinegar, tomato sauce, chili powder,
red pepper, worcestershire sauce, salt and
pepper, and water. Put bay leaves and allspice in spice cup. Cook over medium heat
for 3 hrs. [MW: 45 min. on medium power]
When finished remove spice cup with bay
leaves and allspice. Serve as plain chili or
on hot dogs with cheese or on top of spaghetti.

SPICED BEEF TONGUE

1 Fresh Beef Tongue
Salt
1 Tbs. Saucepan Drippings
1 Finely Chopped Onion
1 Tbs. Flour
2 Cups Liquid in which tongue was boiled
1 Lemon, in thin slices
4 Tbs. Chopped Blanched Almonds
1/3 Cup Seedless Raisins
Small Stick Cinnamon
3 Tbs. Molasses
2 Tbs. Brown Sugar
½ Tsp. Ground Cinnamon
2 Tbs. Vinegar
Cress, used as a garnish

Lay fresh beef tongue in cold water for 2 hrs.
Remove, wipe clean and place in pot with
enough water to barely cover, add salt. Closely
cover pot and boil for 3 hours [MW: 1 hour
on full power], or until fork can be run thru
thickest part. Pare off the thick skin from
tongue, slice and sprinkle each slice with a
little salt. Now make sauce by placing in
sauce pan 1 tbs. of drippings, 1 finely chopped onion and cook until onion is clear. Add
1 tbs. flour and stir in, gradually, 2 cups of
liquid in which the tongue was boiled. Cut
1 lemon in thin slices, remove seeds and add
to sauce with 4 tbs. chopped blanched almonds, 1/3 cup seedless raisins, a small
stick cinnamon, 3 tbs. molasses, 2 tbs. brown
sugar, ½ tsp. ground cinnamon and 2 tbs.
vinegar. Let this boil and lay in sliced tongue and boil 5 min. Serve with sauce and
garnish with cress.

ALMOND BEEF HAWAIIAN

3 Cups Water
1 Tbs. Chicken Seasoning Stock Base
1 Tsp. Butter
1½ Cups Long Grain White Rice
2 Tbs. Vegetable Oil
¼ Tsp. Garlic Powder
1 Lb. Sirloin, cut in ¼ inch thick strips
1 Cup Chopped Celery
1 Medium Onion, chopped or sliced
½ Tsp. Ground Ginger
1 Tsp. Mei Yen Seasoning
2 Tsp. Cornstarch
¼ Cup Soy Sauce
½ Cup Water
½ Cup Cubed Green Peppers
6 Cherry Tomatoes, halved
½ Cup Slivered Almonds

Bring water to a boil with chicken stock
base and butter. Stir in rice. Cover and
cook over low heat for 20 minutes or until rice is tender. Heat 2 tbs. oil and garlic powder in skillet. Stir in sirloin strips
and brown. Remove from pan and keep
warm. Add celery and onion, cover and
beat for 1 minute. Stir in ginger, Mei Yen
seasoning, cornstarch, soy sauce, ½ cup
water, beef, peppers, cherry tomatoes &
almonds. Heat, covered, for 1 minute.
Serve over rice. Serves 4.

MEAT LOAF in SOUR CREAM PASTRY
(Lihamarekepiiras)

Pastry:
2¼ Cups Flour
1 Egg
½ Cup Sour Cream
1 Tsp. Salt
12 Tbs. Unsalted Butter

Meat:
4 Tbs. Butter
¾ Cup Chopped Mushrooms
¼ Cup Chopped Parsley
3 Lbs. Meat
½ Cup Milk
1/3 Cup Chopped Onions
1 Cup Grated Cheese

Pastry:
Cut butter into ¼" bits. Sift flour and
salt into large chilled bowl and add
butter and rub together with hands
until it has the appearance of flakes of
coarse meal. In separate bowl, mix
together egg and sour cream and stir
this into the flour-butter mixture,
working with fingers into a soft, pliable
ball. Wrap in waxed paper and refrigerate
1 hour. Divide in half and roll each half
into rectangular 6" x 14" piece. Butter
bottom of jelly roll pan. Lift one rectangle onto pan.

Meat Filling:
Combine 1 egg with 2 tbs. milk. Meat
may be beef, pork, ham, lamb or veal
or a combination. Melt butter, cook
mushrooms over moderate heat 6 to 8
minutes. Add meat and cook until
meat sauce looses red color and liquid
has cooked away. Scrape into a large
mixing bowl and add next 4 ingredients.
Stir. Place meat mixture on pastry and
pat into a narrow loaf. Lift second
sheet of pastry on top of meat loaf,
press edges together and seal with a
fork after moistening edges with egg
and milk mixture. Prick top with
fork. Preheat oven 375 degrees,
brush with egg-milk mixture. Bake
45 minutes or till golden brown. Serve
thick slices with sour cream.

BEEF RAISIN ROAST

4 Lb. Chuck Roast
1 Tsp. Salt
1 Small Onion, chopped
¼ to ½ Cup Raisins
½ Cup Water
6 Potatoes

Rub meat with salt; brown in a little fat
in frying pan [MW: browning dish]. Place
in baking pan. Cover with chopped onion,
raisins and water. Bake at 325 degrees to
350 degrees for 2 hours [MW: 45 min. on
full power]. Add potatoes and bake 1½
hours more [MW: 45 min. more on medium power]. Serves 6.

STEAK DIANE

4 (4-6 Oz. Each) Beef Loin Tenderloin
  Steaks
2 Tbs. Flour
½ Tsp. Salt
1/8 Tsp. Ground Black Pepper
4 Tbs. Butter, divided
1½ Tbs. Dijon Mustard
2 Tsp. Lea & Perrins Worcestershire
  Sauce, divided
2 Cups Thinly-sliced Mushrooms
2 Tbs. Minced Onion
¼ Cup Brandy
½ Cup Beef Bouillon, or broth

Pound steaks between 2 pieces of waxed paper until ¼" thick. Dredge steaks in flour
mixed with salt and pepper. In large skillet
melt 1 tbs. butter. Add steaks; brown
about 1 minute on each side; remove steaks
to a platter. Spread both sides with mustard and sprinkle with 1 tsp. Lea & Perrins;
set aside. In same skillet, melt remaining
butter. Add mushrooms and onions. Saute'
for 2 minutes. Add brandy and flame. Stir
in bouillon and remaining Lea & Perrins.
Cook and stir until hot. Return steaks to
skillet and reheat for 2 minutes. Sprinkle
with parsley, if desired. Yield: 4 portions.

INSIDE-OUT RAVIOLI CASSEROLE

1 Lb. Ground Beef
1 Medium Onion, chopped
1 Clove Garlic, minced
1 Tbs. Salad Oil
1 (10 oz.) Pkg. Frozen Chopped Spinach
1 (1 lb.) Can Spaghetti Sauce w/Mushrooms
1 (8 oz.) Can Tomato Sauce
1 (6 oz.) Can Tomato Paste
½ Tsp. Salt
Dash Pepper
1 (7 oz.) Pkg. Shell or Elbow Macaroni
    Cooked
4 Oz. Sharp Processed American Cheese
    Shredded (1 cup)
½ Cup Soft Bread Crumbs
2 Well Beaten Eggs
¼ Cup Salad Oil

Brown first 3 ingredients in the 1 tablespoon salad oil. Cook spinach according to package directions. Drain, reserving liquid; add water to make 1 cup. Stir spinach liquid and next 5 ingredients into meat mixture. Simmer 10 minutes. Combine spinach with remaining ingredients; spread in 13" x 9" x 2" baking dish. Top with meat sauce. Bake at 350 degrees for 30 minutes [MW: 15 min. on full power]. Let stand 10 minutes before serving. Makes 8 to 10 servings.

YANKEE POT SOUP

2½ to 3 Lbs. Yankee Pot Roast
6 Carrots
1 Bunch of Broccoli
1 Small Head of Cauliflower
3 Large Zucchini
1 Onion
3 Potatoes
1 Bell Pepper
1 Large Can Tomatoes
¼ Cup Water
All Seasons, Lawry's
2 Tbs. Vegetable Oil

Cook roast in crock pot with ¼ cup water on high until tender [MW: medium power]. Boil potatoes in water with skins on. Slice all remaining vegetables into small slices. Pan fry with 2 tbs. vegetable oil in cast-iron skillet [MW: in browning dish on medium power] at medium temperature until good and hot through. Cover with tight lid; turn down heat to low and let cook until tender. [MW: cook similarly].

Cube potatoes, roast and tomatoes. Mix together with juices and vegetables. Sprinkle with All Seasons to taste. Add V-8 juice if more juice is needed. Serve with French bread, toasted, or crackers.

STEAK & SHRIMP TOSS

1 Lb. Boneless Beef Round Steak
2 Large Onions
8 Oz. Fresh Mushrooms
2 Sweet, Red or Green Peppers
1 Lb. Zucchini
2 Tbs. Oil
2 Tbs. Worcestershire Sauce
1 Tbs. Cornstarch
2 Tbs. Catsup
¼ Tsp. Crushed Red Pepper (optional)
½ Cup Beef Broth
½ Lb. Shelled, Frozen or Fresh Shrimp

Trim fat and cut meat across the grain into strips about ¼" thick, 1" wide, and 3" long. Peel and slice onions; wipe mushrooms clean with damp paper towel and slice lengthwise. Seed peppers and cut into strips; trim the zucchini and cut into 3" sticks. Heat oil in wok or large skillet [MW: browning dish]; stir toss meat strips to brown on both sides (1 or 2 minutes). Push to side of pan; add onions and mushrooms; stir each to glaze. Add pepper strips, zucchini; cook about 3 minutes, tossing occasionally. Add worcestershire sauce which has been stirred with cornstarch; then add catsup, crushed red pepper (if desired) and beef broth. Bring to a boil; add shrimp. Cover and cook until shrimp are pink and hot through (1 to 4 minutes). Stir lightly and serve. Makes 4 servings.

If chicken is used instead of beef, substitute chicken broth instead of beef broth. For vegetarians, use eggplant slices instead of meat, and use vegetable broth.

MEATBALLS & YORKSHIRE PUDDING

1½ Lbs. Ground Beef
1 Pkg. Onion Soup Mix
2 Tbs. Chopped Parsley
¼ Tsp. Pepper
¼ Tsp. Poultry Seasoning
¼ Cup Chili Sauce
1 Egg, slightly beaten
1 Tbs. Water
1½ Cups Sifted All-purpose Flour
1½ Tsp. Baking Powder
1 Tsp. Salt
4 Eggs
1½ Cups Milk
3 Tbs. Melted Butter or Margarine

Combine ground beef, soup mix, parsley, pepper, poultry seasoning and chili sauce. Blend egg with water; add to meat mixture. Mix thoroughly. Form into 24 balls. Place in well-greased 13 x 9 inch baking dish. Mix and sift flour, baking powder and salt. Beat remaining eggs until foamy. Add milk and butter; mix well. Add dry ingredients all at once to egg mixture. Beat with rotary beater (or low speed on mixer) until smooth and well blended. Pour batter over meat balls. Bake in moderate oven, 350 degrees, for 50 to 60 minutes or until golden brown. Serve hot, with packaged beef gravy if desired. Recipe serves 8 to 12 people. Excellent economic dish to serve to company.

CHINESE BEEF N' PEPPERS

1 Lb. Stew Meat, cut in strips
Salt
2 Onions, chopped
1 Cup Beef Broth
3 Tbs. Soy Sauce
1 Clove Garlic, minced
2 Green Peppers, cut in strips

Brown meat [MW: browning dish]; season with salt. Push to one side; add onion and cook until tender. Stir in broth, soy sauce and garlic. Simmer. Add green peppers and simmer. Serve over fluffy white rice.

ROLATINIS ON PASTA

1½ Lbs. Beef Top Round, thinly sliced
¼ Cup Olive Oil
1 Tbs. Fresh Basil, chopped
1 Clove Garlic, minced
1 Tsp. Oregano, crumbled
Generous Pinch of Salt and
 Freshly-ground Pepper
2 Oz. Thinly-sliced Proscuitto
2 Oz. Thinly-sliced Italian Fontina
1 Tbs. Butter + 3 Tbs. Olive Oil
Hot, Cooked Al Dente Noodles
½ Cup Parmesan, grated

Mushroom Tomato Sauce:
1 Onion, chopped
2 Tbs. Olive Oil
1 Lb. Tomatoes, peeled, seeded and
 chopped OR 1 Lb. Can Tomatoes
1 Clove Garlic, minced
Pinch of Sugar
1 Tbs. Fresh Basil, chopped
Salt and Freshly-ground Pepper
 to taste
½ Lb. Sliced, Sauteed Mushrooms
 (or more, if you prefer)

Blend ¼ cup olive oil with basil, garlic, oregano, salt and pepper. Spread half on beef. Top beef pieces with prosciutto and optional cheese. Roll up, enclosing prosciutto inside. Fasten with picks. Rub remaining herb oil mixture on outside of rolls. Heat 1 tbs. butter and 3 tbs. olive oil in heavy bottomed skillet over medium-high heat [MW: in browning dish on full power]. Add beef rolls. Brown, turning often for 3 to 6 minutes [MW: 3-4 min.] depending on thickness of meat and desired degree of doneness. Remove picks. To serve, place over noodles on heat-proof platter. Top with tomato sauce; sprinkle with Parmesan cheese and place briefly under broiler until cheese melts   Serves 4.

Mushroom Tomato Sauce: Cook onion in olive oil about 7 min. [MW: 4 min.], until translucent. Add tomatoes, garlic, sugar, bay leaf, basil, salt and pepper. Bring to a boil, then reduce heat and simmer for at least 30 minutes [MW: 15 min.], adding mushrooms during the last half of the cooking time. Remove bay leaf. Serve sauce over beef rolls.

BRAISED BEEF

1½ Lbs. Beef Sirloin Tip
1 Cup Flour
1 Tsp. Salt
2 to 4 Tbs. Butter or Margarine
½ Cup Chopped Onion
1 Clove Garlic, minced
½ Lb. Mushrooms, sliced
1 Cup Bouillon
1 Cup Red Wine
1 Tbs. Worcestershire Sauce

Cut meat into 1" cubes. Blend flour with salt and coat meat cubes with mixture. Melt butter in skillet; add meat and brown on all sides. Transfer meat to a 3-quart casserole. Add onion, garlic and mushrooms to butter in skillet; cook over medium heat until onion is soft but not brown, about 5 minutes. Add bouillon, wine and Worcestershire sauce to onion mixture, stirring to blend. Pour over meat in casserole. Cover and bake at 350 degrees for 1½ hours or until meat is tender [MW: 40 minutes on full power]. Thicken gravy with flour. Serve over boiled potatoes or rice. Serves 4.

STUFFED STEAK ROAST

2 Lb. Round Steak
1 Tsp. Salt
¼ Tsp. Pepper
2 Cups Seasoned Bread Crumbs
3 Tbs. Grated Onion
1 Tsp. Poultry Seasoning
1/3 Cup Milk
2 Tbs. Melted Butter
1 Egg, beaten

Season steak with salt and pepper. Combine remaining ingredients, spread evenly over steak. Roll as a jelly roll. Tie with string. Place open side down, uncovered in a roasting pan. Roast at 350 degrees for 45 minutes or until tender [MW: 20 min. on full power]. Baste with steak or bacon drippings.

MEON BURGERS

1 Lb. Hamburger
1 Tsp. Sage
¾ Cup Cheddar Cheese
½ Tsp. Salt
½ Tsp. Pepper
½ Tsp. Garlic Salt or Powder
1/8 Tsp. Oregano
½ Cup Onions (more or less, whichever is preferred)
1 Can of Beer

Combine all ingredients except beer; knead until all ingredients are blended. Shape into 4 patties. Place patties over hot coals and grill until desired doneness. Pour beer over patties while cooking - about a tbs. per patty.

MEATBALLS con QUESO

1½ Lbs. Ground Beef
1½ Cups Bread Crumbs
1/3 Cup Chopped Onions
1/3 Cup Milk
3 Tbs. Chopped Parsley
¼ Tsp. Pepper
1 Egg
3 Tbs. Salad Oil
16 Oz. Velveeta Cheese
1 - 4 Oz. Can Chopped Green Chilies
1 Pkg. Taco Seasoning Mix
Corn Bread

Mix first 7 ingredients and shape into 1" balls. Fry in oil [MW: browning dish]. Remove cooked meatballs from skillet [MW: browning dish]; in same pan, on low heat, stir in chilies, cheese, taco seasoning and ¾ cup water. Simmer till cheese is melted, stirring constantly.

Return meatballs to mixture in skillet [MW: dish]. Cover and simmer until completely heated throughout. Serve immediately with hot corn bread. A mouth-watering, tummy-warming delight.

BEERY BEEF STEW

¼ Cup Flour
1 Tsp. Salt
½ Tsp. Pepper
2 Lbs. Stew Meat, cubed
½ Cup Olive Oil
2 Lbs. Onions, peeled & sliced
1 Clove Garlic, crushed
1 Giant-size Can Beer
1 Tbs. Soy Sauce
1 Tbs. Worcestershire Sauce
1 Tbs. Steak Sauce
½ Tsp. Crumbled Bay Leaves
1 Tsp. Dried Thyme
2 Lbs. Potatoes, pared & quartered
4 Medium Carrots, in chunks
Boiling Water
Parsley

Coat the cubed meat in the flour which
has been mixed with salt and pepper;
set aside. In a large pot, heat ¼ cup of
the olive oil and saute' the onion and
garlic until tender, about 5 minutes.
Remove onion from pot; add the remaining oil. Heat and add the floured
meat, browning it well on all sides. Return the onion-garlic mixture along with
the beer, the 3 sauces, and the herbs. Mix
well; bring mixture to a boil. Reduce heat;
Cover and simmer for 1½ hours [MW: 40
minutes on simmer]. Add the pared,
quartered potatoes to the stew with just
enough boiling water to make enough
juice for them to cook in. After about 15
minutes [MW: 10 minutes], add the carrots.
In another 20 minutes or so [MW: 30 min.
or so], when potatoes are tender, you are
ready to serve. Sprinkle some parsley on
top just before carrying the pot to the
table. Makes 4 to 6 servings.

CHIVICHUNGAS

2 Lbs. Beef Stew Cubes, diced
1 Tsp. Garlic Powder
2 Tsp. Salt
Water, enough to cook
1 Medium Onion
1 Large Can Whole-pack Tomatoes
2 Fresh Green Chilies
2 Dozen Flour Tortillas (12 inch)
2 Tbs. Flour

Put beef that has been diced in 1" pieces
in water with garlic powder and salt added.
Cook, but do not overcook. Saute' diced
onion and green chilies in 2 tbs. lard. When
done, add whole-pack tomatoes. Add flour
to thicken. Add your beef stock which
has been put aside to cool. Add meat and
let cook for about 1 hour. Fill each tortilla with the mixture. Put toothpicks on
each end and deep fry.

SIMPLIFIED LAHMAJOUN

1 - 8 Oz. Pkg. Refrigerated Biscuits

Beef Filling:
1½ Lbs. Ground Beef
3 Chopped Green Onions
¼ Cup Chopped Parsley
1 Tsp. Salt
½ Tsp. Oregano
½ Can (8 Oz. size) Tomato Sauce
1 Cup Shredded Jack Cheese

Lamb Filling:
1½ Lbs. Ground Lean Lamb
3 Chopped Green Onions
2 Tbs. Chopped, Fresh Mint (or
    ½ tsp. dried mint)
1 Tsp. Salt
½ Can (8 Oz. size) Tomato Sauce
1 Cup Grated Jack Cheese

Roll out each biscuit on a lightly-floured
board to a thin round about 5" in diameter.
Arrange rounds slightly apart on two large,
greased baking sheets. Divide filling into
10 portions; spread evenly over surface of
each biscuit. Be sure to spread the meat
clear to the edge of the biscuit as the meat
will shrink while baking. Sprinkle cheese
over the meat.

Bake in 450 degree oven for 10 to 12 min.
or until meat is cooked and biscuits are
crisp. Serve hot as they are or rolled up
and fastened with wooden picks. Makes
10.

This is a middle eastern snack sold by the
street vendors. They shout "lahmajoun"
in much the same tone as Americans use
when they sell hot dogs at football games.
Great for after-game warm-ups or for a
super snack.

KOTLET (Persian Dish)

2 Lbs. Lean Ground Beef
1 Large Potato
2 Eggs
1 Oz. Flour

Grind the potato with medium grinder and put into bowl with meat. Mix this very well. Add the 2 eggs and mix again. Add spices (salt, pepper, onion powder and turmeric) and flour and mix it again very well. Add more flour if the mix is liquid.

Prepare pan. Have some oil in it and don't let it get too hot. Take half a handful of mix and put it on the palm of other hand and shape it as an ellipse (not very thick) and put it in the pan [MW: browning dish]. When both sides of it get brown, it's ready to eat. You should be able to make 15 to 18 of these Kotlets, which would serve 4 to 5 people.

Note: In Iran we eat this food with plain yogurt and radish and French fries, but salad, or any other stuff is okay.

CHOW MEIN

1 Lb. Round Steak, cut into
   1" pieces
2 Tbs. Soy Sauce
1 Can Beef Broth (bouillon)
1 Small Jar Mushrooms, sliced
1½ Cups Diagonally-sliced Celery
½ Cup Green Onions
1 Can Water Chestnuts, sliced
1 Lb. Bean Sprouts
2 Tbs. Cornstarch
½ Cup Water

Brown steak in oil; [MW: browning dish]; add soy sauce, mushrooms and beef broth. Simmer 30 min. [MW: 15 min.]. Add celery, onions and water chestnuts. Cook 20 minutes [MW: 10 min. on full power]. Add bean sprouts and bring to a boil. Mix water and cornstarch and stir into chow mein until thickened. Serve over rice with chow mein noodles.

ITALIAN STEAK SANDWICH

2 Sirloin Steaks, sliced thin, or your
   favorite steak
1 - 8 Oz. Can Mushrooms
4 Green Onions
2 Bell Peppers, sliced ¼"
2 or 3 Cloves of Garlic, sliced
2 - 7 Oz. Submarine Rolls
Parmesan Cheese
Butter or Margarine
Oregano
Garlic Powder (optional)
Oil
Chili Pepper (dried)
Cumin

Slice bread lengthwise; spread butter on both sides. Sprinkle heavily with Parmesan cheese. Add garlic powder and diced oregano. Set aside for now.

Remove stems, seeds and white inner membrane from bell pepper. Slice in ¼" slices. Clean onions and chop greens only.

Pour oil in frying pan; [MW: browning dish]; enough to cover bottom of pan. Cook peppers until browned, turning several times. Reduce heat and cover.

Prepare meat with salt and pepper; place in broiler. When peppers are tender, uncover and add onions and mushrooms. Season to taste with the following: black pepper, cumin, McCormick season-all seasoned salt, crushed whole chili peppers. Saute'.

Now place bread in oven until cheese is melted. Remove from oven. Steaks should be done by now. Place steaks on one side of bread, and peppers, mushrooms and onions on the other side. Pour any juice from steak over the meat. Serve with your favorite wine. Bon appetit!

PORCUPINES

Sauce:
4 Cups Tomato Juice
2 Tsp. Chili Powder
¼ Tsp. Allspice
½ Tsp. Celery Seed
1 Tsp. Worcestershire Sauce
1 Tsp. Brown Sugar

Porcupines:
1 Lb. Lean Ground Beef
½ Cup Uncooked Rice
½ Cup Chopped Green Pepper
½ Cup Finely-chopped Celery
1 Egg
2 Tsp. Prepared Mustard
1½ Tsp. Salt
¼ Tsp. Pepper

Combine all ingredients for sauce. Cover and simmer 10 minutes. Combine all ingredients for porcupines. Mix well and form into 1½" meat balls. Place in baking dish. Pour sauce over meat balls. Cover and bake at 350 degrees for 1 hr. [MW: 20 minutes on full power].

Serve with green salad, red wine and French bread. Makes a complete meal. Freezes nicely also. Makes 6 servings.

BEEF FILLETS WELLINGTON

8 - 5 Oz. Fillets of Beef
Cooking Oil
1 Lb. Ground Sirloin
1 Clove Garlic, crushed
1 Tbs. Snipped Parsley
8 Frozen Patty Shells, thawed
1 Slightly-beaten Egg White

Put fillets in freezer 20 minutes to chill. Take out & brush with cooking oil and sprinkle with salt and pepper. Sear in skillet for 5 minutes on each side; chill in refrigerator. Combine ground sirloin with ½ tsp. salt, dash of pepper, garlic & parsley. Divide into 8 portions; place a rounded portion on top of each fillet. Return the fillets to refrigerator.

Roll patty shells out to 9 x 5 inch rectangles, 1/8" thick. Place the steaks with sirloin down in the pastry rectangles. Turn in first one side, then end, then the other side, and finally the other end. Place them sealed-side down in shallow baking pan. Decorate with cutouts from an additional rolled out patty shell, if desired. Refrigerate till party time. Brush with beaten egg white. Bake in 450 degree oven 10 minutes for rare, 12 minutes for medium rare, and 15 minutes for medium. Serve immediately with tarragon sauce. Makes 8 servings.

HAWAIIAN SHORT RIBS

3 Tbs. Sesame Seeds
4 Lbs. Beef Short Ribs
1 Med. Onion, sliced
½ Cup Soy Sauce
¼ Cup Brown Sugar, firmly packed
1 Large Clove Garlic, minced
¼ Tsp. Ground Ginger
¼ Tsp. Pepper
2 Small, Dried Hot Chili Peppers, seeded and crushed
1½ Cups Water
1 Tsp. Cornstarch
1 Tsp. Water

Put the sesame seeds into a 4 or 5-quart kettle; place over medium heat until lightly browned, shaking pan often to toast evenly. Remove from heat & arrange ribs (which have been cut into two or three inch lengths) and onion on top of the sesame seeds.

Combine the soy sauce, brown sugar, garlic, ginger, pepper, chili peppers and water and pour over meat. Cover and bake in a 400 degree oven for 2½ hrs. [MW: cover in plastic wrap and cook 1 hr. on full power], or until meat is tender. Stir well occasionally.

Lift meat to warm platter; keep warm. Skim fat from pan juices. Combine cornstarch and water. Stir into pan juices and cook, stirring until thickened. Pass in a bowl. Serve over steamed rice. Makes 4 to 6 servings.

BEEF STEW ANDALUSIA

1½ Lbs. Stew Meat or Round Steak,
  cut into 1" cubes
2 Tbs. Margarine
1½ Tsp. Olive Oil
1 Tsp. Salt
½ Tsp. Pepper
½ Tsp. Thyme
1 Bay Leaf
1 Medium Onion, stuck with 2 cloves
3 Green Onions, cut into ½" lengths
2 Slices Bacon, cut into strips
2½ Cups Beef Bouillon, diluted, not
  condensed
2 Tbs. Dry Sherry
12 to 18 Mushroom Caps
½ Cup Sliced, Ripe Olives
1 Tbs. Lemon Juice
8 or 12 Oz. Pkg. Noodles

In a large skillet [MW: browning dish],
brown meat lightly in margarine and olive
oil for about 5 minutes; add beef bouillon,
salt, pepper, thyme, bay leaf, onion stuck
with cloves, 3 green onions and bacon.
Cover and simmer for 2 hours [MW: 1 hr.].
Add sherry, mushrooms, olives and lemon
juice and cook 30 minutes more [MW: 15
min. on full power]. Serve with cooked
noodles. Serves 4 to 6.

FOUR STAR CHEDDAR MEAT LOAF

3 Lbs. Lean Beef, ground
1½ Cups Rolled Oats
½ Cup Chopped Onions
½ Cup Chopped Green Peppers
1 Cup Grated Sharp Cheddar Cheese
2 Tsp. Salt
¼ Tsp. Pepper
2 Eggs
2 Cans Tomato Sauce (8 oz. each)
4 Slices American Cheese, optional

Combine all ingredients except sliced cheese.
Pack into 9" x 5" x 3" loaf pan. Bake at
350 degrees about 1½ hours [MW: 30 min.
on full power]. Let stand five minutes. If
desired, remove to shallow pan and place
cheese star cut-outs on top. Return to
400 degree oven for a few minutes until
cheese begins to melt and brown [MW: 5
minutes on full power to melt cheese].
Makes 8 to 18 servings.

ROPA VIEJA

2 Lbs. Rump Roast
2 Cups Water
1 Bay Leaf
½ Tsp. Coarse Black Pepper
2 Tsp. Salt
3 Tbs. Oil
1 Cup Chopped Onions
2 Green Peppers, chopped
3 Tomatoes, peeled and chopped
½ Tsp. Instant Garlic Powder
½ Tsp. Oregano Leaves

Put meat in saucepan [MW: glass dish]. Add
water, bay leaf, black pepper and 2 tsp. of
salt. Simmer until meat is very tender, about
3 hours [MW: 1 hour]. With a fork, pull
meat apart into strings. Heat oil, saute' onions
until golden. Add remaining ingredients, including meat, and ¾ tsp. salt. Simmer 30 min.
[MW: 15 min.], or until most of the moisture
is gone. Serve over fluffy rice. Serves 4 to 6.

BEEF MALAGA

Olive Oil
2 Lbs. Top Round Steak
1 Medium Onion
1½ Cups Red Table Wine
½ Can Mushroom Soup
½ Cup Grated Sharp Cheddar Cheese
1 Tsp. Salt
2 Pinches Oregano
1 Pinch Thyme
1 Small Clove Garlic, Minced
½ Lb. Fresh Mushrooms or 1 Lg. Can
  B & B Mushrooms
½ Pint Sour Cream

Cut round steak into ½" x ¼" x 1" pieces.
Brown a few chunks at a time in olive oil,
rapidly, so that they do not stew. Add
chopped onion and brown; add red table
wine, scraping bottom of pan well. Add
remaining ingredients, except mushrooms
and sour cream. Simmer for 2½ hrs. [MW:
1 hr.], covered. Add mushrooms. If
using fresh mushrooms, soak in 1 cup water,
slice and add water; if using canned, use
liquid also. Simmer 20 minutes longer
[MW: 15 min.]. Just before serving, add
sour cream. Stir to mix and warm. Serve
with rice.

STUFFED GRAPE LEAVES

50 Grape Leaves
1 Lb. Ground Beef or Lamb
1/2 Cup Rice (uncooked, soaked
   for 10 min.)
1 1/2 Tsp. Salt
1/2 Tsp. Pepper
1/2 Tsp. Cinnamon
1 1/2 Tsp. Allspice
1/4 Cup Lemon Juice and Water

Put bottled grape leaves in colander and wash with cold water. Fresh grape leaves should be washed with hot water and blanched for 30 secs. Mix the meat, rice and seasonings very well. Take a grape leaf and put vein side up, nip off the stem and put about 1 Tbs. meat mixture on leaf.

(Amount will vary according to size of leaf). Fold the stem end over the meat, then the 2 sides toward the center and roll up. Arrange the rolled leaves in layers in a 2 qt. casserole which has been lined with several unstuffed leaves. Pour in water and lemon juice just to cover leaves, and put a small plate over to hold leaves down. Cover. Bring to boiling and then immediately put to simmer or low, for 1-1½ hrs. [MW: 45 min. on full power] til tender. Delicious served with plain yogurt and tossed green salad.

STEAK ST. LOUIS

4 Lbs. Sirloin Steak, 2" thick
2 Small 4 Oz. Cans Mushrooms, drained
1 Large Purple Onion
1 Cup Catsup
1 Tbs. Lemon Juice
3 Tbs. Worcestershire Sauce
3 Tbs. Butter or Margarine, melted
Dash Garlic Salt

Mix together 1 can mushrooms, drained, 1 large onion, sliced thin, 1 cup catsup, 1 tbs. lemon juice, 3 tbs. Worcestershire sauce, melted butter and a dash of garlic salt. Brown steak in heavy skillet [omit for MW]. Place steak in a 9" x 13" oblong cake pan [MW: glass] or use broiler pan [omit broiler for MW]. Put on the above sauce, then top with onions and the remaining can of mushrooms (drained). Bake in a 350 degree oven for one hour. [MW: 20 minutes on full power]. Serves 6. Serve with baked potato, crisp green salad, hot vegetable and a light dessert. Note: Round steak may be substituted for meat.

TURNIP-STEAK SAUTE'

1 Lb. Round Steak
¾ Lb. Turnips
¼ Cup Cooking Oil
4 Green Onions (& some tops), thinly
   sliced
1 Small Clove Garlic, minced
1 Cup Beef Bouillon
½ Tsp. Pepper
2 Tsp. Soy Sauce
1 Tsp. Salt, (or to taste)
2 Tbs. Cornstarch
¼ Cup Water
Paprika

Put meat in freezer for a few minutes and then cut across the grain in about ¼ inch strips. Cut turnips in halves, then cut in fairly thin slices. Brown meat in oil, add onion and garlic and cook over moderate heat for about a half hour. Add turnips and bouillon. Bring to a boil, reduce heat, simmer for about 15 minutes or until turnips are done. Blend pepper, soy sauce and salt with cornstarch which has been dissolved in water. Pour over meat and turnips in pan and stir lightly. Remove meat and vegetable and make gravy from juices left. Sprinkle meat with paprika before serving. Takes approx. 1 hour to make and serves 4

LUMPIA (Chinese Egg Roll)

Filling:
10 Oz. Minced Pork
1 Onion, chopped
1 Clove Garlic, chopped
3 or 4 Leeks, chopped
Handful of Celery Leaves, chopped
¼ Cup Bean Sprouts, drained
A few Cabbage Leaves, shredded
Salt and Pepper
Pinch of Monosodium Glutamate
Few Drops of Ketchup
Oil

Covering:
3 Cups Flour
4 Eggs
¾ Cup Water
Salt
A Thin Mixture of Water & Flour

Start with the filling. Fry the chopped
onion and garlic in a little oil; add the
minced pork, loosely forked, and the
finely chopped vegetables. Fry together
for a few minutes, then add pepper, salt,
ketchup and monosodium glutamate and
cook the mixture for 8 to 10 minutes
longer, stirring constantly. The vegetables
should be cooked but still a little crisp
and most of the liquid should have
evaporated.

Make a pancake batter from the flour,
eggs, water and salt. In a large frying
pan make thin but firm pancakes, cooking them on one side only. When the
upper side is practically set, slide the
pancake onto a plate. Place a generous
amount of the filling in the center and
fold up the ends and then the sides,
making an oblong. Do this as quickly
as possible, while the pancakes are still
supple. Close the edges with the flour
and water mixture, making sure that the
filling will not drop out. Dip the oblongs
in the flour and water batter and deep
fry them in hot oil until crisp and golden
brown.

ORIENTAL PORK & CABBAGE

3 Pork Steaks
1 Medium Cabbage, shredded
1 White Onion
2 to 3 Tsp. Cooking Oil
6 Tbs. Water
9 Tbs. Soy Sauce
Salt & Pepper to taste
½ Lb. Mushrooms

Cut up the pork into bite-size pieces. Brown
pork in oil [MW: in browning dish on full
power], add the mushrooms and saute' until
partially done. Pour off oil and add shredded
cabbage. Just lay it over the meat. Slice the
onion and lay it over the cabbage. Add the
soy sauce, water, salt and pepper. Turn
down to simmer and cover. Simmer for
about 40 min. [MW: 20 min.] or until the
cabbage and onion are tender. Mix well
with the pork and sauce and serve. Serves 4.

CREPES ENSENADA

12 Thin Ham Slices
12 Flour Tortillas
1 Lb. Jack Cheese, cut into ½" strips
1 Can Green Chilies, cut into ¼" strips

Cheese Sauce:
¼ Lb. Butter
½ Cup Flour
1 Quart Milk
¾ Lb. Grated Cheddar Cheese
1 Tsp. Prepared Mustard
½ Tsp. Salt
½ Tsp. MSG (optional)
Dash Pepper
Paprika

Place 1 slice of ham on each tortilla; put 1
stick of cheese in the center of ham and top
with strip of chili. Roll tortilla and secure
with toothpick. Place rolled tortillas,
slightly separated, in greased 13" x 9" pan.
Pour cheese sauce over crepes to cover;
sprinkle with paprika and bake at 350 degrees for 45 minutes [MW: 15 minutes
on full power.

Cheese Sauce: Melt butter and blend in
flour. Add milk, grated cheese, mustard,
salt and pepper. Cook and stir until
smooth. Serves 6.

PRUNE STUFFED PORK

3-4 Lb. Boned Loin of Pork
12 Pitted Prunes
2 Tsp. Salt
1 Tsp. Ginger
½ Tsp. Pepper

Sauce:
1 Apple
1 Yellow Onion
4 Prunes
2 Cups of Water
2 Tbs. Soy Sauce
1 Tbs. Flour

1. Make a hole through the meat with the handle of a wooden spoon or ask your butcher to cut a jacket in the center along the length of the roast. Preheat the oven to 325 degrees.

2. Cover pitted prunes with boiling water and soak 30 minutes. Drain and stuff the prunes in the hole of the pork so that they are evenly distributed throughout.

3. Tie cotton string to one end of the loin and make loops along the horizontal surface.

4. Mix the seasonings and rub the meat with them. Cut apple, onion, prunes into pieces. Put meat thermometer in meat and place it in a roasting pan with fruits and onion around. Roast in 325 degree oven for about 45 min. per pound [MW: 8 min. per pound on full power] or until the thermometer registers 185 degrees. Add water and soy sauce.

5. Strain the liquid from the roasting pan into a saucepan. Beat in 1 tbs. flour and let boil for 5 minutes while the meat is cooling before being carved. Serve with boiled potatoes, sauce and pickled cucumber.

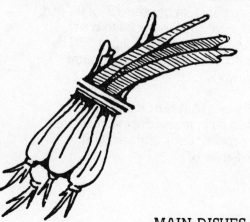

PANCIT - Philippine Shrimp & Pork Chops

4 Pork Steaks
½ Lb. Cooked Shrimp
1 Bell Pepper
2 Stalks Celery
2 Cups Cooked Noodles or Rice
1 Tbs. Salt
1 Clove Garlic
1 Small Onion
1 Can Sliced Mushrooms (black mushrooms, if preferred)
Dash Pepper
4 Tbs. Soy Sauce
¼ Cup Water

Cut pork steaks into bite size pieces and brown. Chop celery, bell pepper, onion and mushrooms and saute' in butter. Add garlic and soy sauce and season to taste. Add water and shrimp and simmer for 45 minutes [MW: 20 minutes]. Serve over cooked noodles or rice.

BRAISED SPANISH PORK CHOPS

5 Thick Rib Pork Chops (2 lbs.)
1 Tbs. Fat
1 Onion, sliced
2 Cups Canned or Diced Fresh Tomatoes
½ Tsp. Salt
¼ Tsp. Pepper
3 Tbs. Flour
3-4 Cups Hot Boiled Rice (1 cup raw)

Brown chops slowly on both sides in the fat in a heavy skillet [MW: browning dish] ; remove chops from pan. Saute' onion in same pan; add chops, tomatoes and seasonings. Cover and simmer for 45-60 min. [MW: 15-20 min.] or until tender.

Remove meat and thicken the tomato mixture with the flour mixed to a smooth paste with ¼ cup cold water; boil 2 to 3 minutes, stirring constantly. Place rice in center of platter; arrange chops around rice and pour tomato sauce over the chops. 5 servings.

PORK VINDALOO

1½ Lbs. Lean Pork
½ Cup Vinegar
2 Onions, chopped
1 Tsp. Minced Garlic
1½ Tsp. Powdered Ginger
1 Tbs. Mustard Seed
1 Tsp. Ground Turmeric
½ Tsp. Cayenne
¼ Cup Salad Oil
1 Can Chicken Broth
6 Medium Potatoes, peeled & quartered

Cut meat into 1 inch cubes. Place meat in a large bowl with the vinegar, onions, garlic, and spice. Let the mixture marinate for at least 2 hours. When ready to cook, place meat mixture in a Dutch oven or large saucepan [MW: glass casserole]. Add salad oil and chicken broth. Cook over medium heat for 20 min. [MW: 10 min. on full power]. Add potatoes and cook slowly, covered for about 45 min. [MW: 25 min. on medium power] or until potatoes are tender. Makes 4 servings.

PORK with WALDORF RICE

4 - ¾" Thick Slices of Fresh Pork
  (chops, steaks, or boneless cuts, 4 oz. ea.)
Salt and Pepper
2 Tsp. Instant Chicken Bouillon, or 2
  Chicken Bouillon Cubes
2 Cups Hot Water
½ Tsp. Ground Ginger
1/8 Tsp. Tabasco Sauce
¾ Cup Rice
1½ Cups Chopped Cooking Apples
1 Cup Diced Celery
¼ Cup Minced Onion

In non-stick skillet [MW: browning dish], slowly brown pork on both sides; season with salt and pepper and remove to plate. Meanwhile, dissolve the bouillon in hot water; add ginger, ½ tsp. salt and the tabasco sauce, mixing well.

Sprinkle rice in bottom of casserole, combine apple, celery and onion and sprinkle over rice. Place browned pork over all. Stir bouillon and pour over all; bake, covered, in a 350 degree oven for 45 min. [MW: 25 min. on full power]. If desired, garnish with orange sections.

CHILI VERDE

4 Pork Steaks
1 Onion, chopped
5 Tbs. Flour
4 Cups Water
¼ Tsp. Garlic
½ Tsp. Red Pepper
½ Tsp. Oregano
2/3 Tsp. Cumin (ground)
2 - 7 Oz. Cans Whole Green Chilies,
  chopped

Cut fat off steaks. Cut steaks into bite size pieces. Fry until well done [MW: in browning dish on full power]. Remove meat and cook onion until tender. Remove onion. Make gravy with drippings and flour and water. Return meat and onion to gravy with all other ingredients; simmer. Add 2 or 3 hot Fresno chilies if desired.

BARBECUED SPARERIBS, WESTERN STYLE

3-4 Lbs. Meaty Spareribs
Lemon Slices
Onion Slices

Sauce:
1 Cup Catsup
1/3 Cup Worcestershire Sauce
1 Tsp. Chili Powder
1 Tsp. Salt
3 Dashes Tabasco Sauce
2 Cups Water

Use kitchen scissors or sharp knife to cut meat in serving pieces; two ribs to each piece. Turn your oven on now to 450 degrees. With meaty side up, place ribs in shallow roasting pan and top each sparerib piece with a thin slice of onion and a slice of unpeeled lemon. Anchor with toothpicks. Roast the ribs in hot oven, 450 degrees, for 30 minutes while you make the barbecue sauce [MW: 20 min. on full power]. After this cooking time, reduce heat to 350 degrees, pour boiling sauce over ribs and bake for about 1 hr. [MW: 45 min. on full power] or until tender. Remove toothpicks and serve bubbling, tangy sauce. Eat 'em with your fingers if you like.

COUNTRY—SAUSAGE and OYSTER DRESSING

½ Cup Margarine
1 Pound Mushrooms, chopped
1 Cup Chopped Onion
1 Cup Chopped Celery
1 Pint Fresh Oysters, chopped
    (reserve liquid)
1 Quart White Bread Crumbs
1½ Quarts Corn Bread Crumbs
2 Tbs. Chopped Parsley
2 Tsp. Salt
3 Tbs. Sage (rubbed)
1 Lb. Country Sausage
1 Cup Chopped Olives
1 Cup Grated Carrot
4 Eggs, well beaten
2/3 Cup Oyster Liquid
2½ Cups Poultry Broth

Heat margarine in large skillet [MW: browning dish]; add the sausage and mushrooms. Add onion, celery and carrots. Cook 5-8 min. over medium heat [MW: 5-8 min. on full power], stirring occasionally. Mix all ingredients together in a large bowl. Stuffing for a 14 to 16 pound turkey.

ITALIAN SAUSAGE MEATLOAF

1½ Lbs. Mild Italian Sausage
2 Eggs, beaten well
¼ Lb. Sharp Process Cheese, cut in
    ¼ inch cubes
¾ Cup Fine, Dry Bread Crumbs
1/3 Cup Milk
¼ Cup Finely-Chopped Onion

Remove casing from sausage. In large mixing bowl, break sausage apart with a fork. Add remaining ingredients and mix well. Shape into a loaf. Bake at 350 degrees for about 1 hour, [MW: 15 minutes on full power] or until done. Serves 4. Leftover slices make excellent sandwiches.

SPICY ORIENTAL SPARERIBS

2½ to 2¾ Lbs. Pork Spareribs
1 Tbs. Chinese Black Bean Sauce
    With Chili
1 Tbs. Salad Oil
½ Tsp. Salt
1½ Cups Water
1 Tbs. Cornstarch
2 Green Peppers, sliced into chunks
1 Dry Onion, sliced

Cut ribs into bite-size pieces. Heat oil in pan [MW: browning dish] and saute' ribs until lightly browned. Add salt and chili sauce. Coat ribs well and cook 5 minutes, stirring often. Add water and reduce heat when it begins to boil and simmer for about 30 min. [MW: 15 min.]. Then add onion and green peppers. Add cornstarch dissolved in water and mix well until sauce thickens. Do not overcook the vegetables. Serve with hot rice.

CHERRY BAKED HAM

1 Can (3 - 4-½ Lb.) Ham
½ Cup Brown Sugar
½ Cup Honey

Cherry Sauce:
1-½ Tbs. Cornstarch
¼ Cup Sugar
¼ Tsp. Allspice
¼ Tsp. Ground Cloves
1 Can Red Sour Pitted Cherries

Remove ham from can. Place ham, fat side up, on shallow pan [MW: place fat side down on roasting rack]. Combine brown sugar and honey; spoon over ham. Bake in slow oven at 325 degrees 1¼-2 hours [MW: 1 hr. on medium power]. Baste occasionally with drippings.

Cherry Sauce: Combine dry ingredients. Slowly add juice from cherries. Cook until thick and clear. Add cherries and red food coloring. Serve hot, spooned over baked ham. Serves 4.

KOA-PAI-KU (Barbecued Spareribs, Chinese-Style)

2 Lbs. Spareribs, in 1 piece

Marinade:
¼ Cup Soy Sauce
2 Tbs. Honey
2 Tbs. Hoisin Sauce
2 Tbs. White Vinegar
1 Tbs. Chinese Rice Wine or Pale Dry
  Sherry
1 Tsp. Finely Chopped Garlic
1 Tsp. Sugar
2 Tbs. Chicken Stock, fresh or canned
1 Can Plum Sauce

Prepared Ahead: With a cleaver or large sharp knife, trim any excess fat from the spareribs. If breast bone is still attached, use a cleaver to chop it away from the ribs and discard it. Place ribs in a long, shallow dish, large enough to hold them comfortably. In a small bowl, combine the soy sauce, honey, hoisin sauce, vinegar, wine, garlic, sugar and chicken stock. Stir until they are well mixed. Pour sauce over the spareribs, baste them thoroughly and let them marinate for 3 hours at room temperature (6 hours in the refrigerator), turning them over in the sauce and basting them every hour or so.

To Cook: Preheat oven to 375 degrees. To catch the drippings of the spareribs as they roast and to prevent the oven from smoking as well, fill a large, shallow roasting pan or baking dish with water and place it on the lowest rack of the oven. Insert the curved tips of two or three S-shaped hooks (such as curtain hooks), or 5-inch lengths of heavy-duty wire or even unpainted coat hangers bent into shape at each end of the spareribs. As if hanging a hammock, use the curved ends of the hooks to suspend the ribs from uppermost rack of oven directly above pan of water. Roast ribs, undisturbed, for 45 minutes. Then raise oven temperature to 450 degrees and roast about 15 minutes longer, or until ribs are crisp and a deep golden brown. To serve, split into individual ribs. Serve hot or cold with plum sauce.

POLYNESIAN STYLE ISANDER RIBS

3 to 4 Lbs. Beef Short Ribs or English
  Cut
1½ Tsp. Salt
1 - 13½ Oz. Can Pineapple Tidbits
½ Cup Catsup
¼ Cup Vinegar
¼ Cup Water
¼ Cup Green Pepper, minced
½ Cup Onion, minced
3 Tbs. Brown Sugar
½ Tsp. Dry Mustard

Brown ribs in their own fat in Dutch oven [MW: browning dish]. Pour off drippings. Sprinkle ribs with 1 tbs. salt; cover and cook over very low heat for 1½ hours [MW: 45 min. on medium power]. Pour off drippings. Combine undrained pineapple, catsup, vinegar, water, onion, green pepper, brown sugar, dry mustard and remaining salt and pour over ribs. Cover and cook 30 min. longer [MW: 20 min. longer on medium power]. Serves 4-6 people Serve over rice. Excellent meal for company. The kitchen is clean and the fantastic aroma greets them at the door.

HOMEMADE SAUSAGE FROM MINNESOTA

2 Lbs. Lean Hamburger
1 Cup Water
1½ Tsp. Liquid Smoke
1/8 Tsp. Onion Powder
3 Tbs. Cure Salt OR Morton Tender
  Quick
1/8 Tsp. Mustard Seed
¼ Tsp. Garlic Powder
2 Tsp. Sugar

Mix all ingredients well and roll in 2 or 3 rolls as firmly as possible. Place on aluminum foil; put shiny side next to meat. Wrap so seam side is up. Allow to stand in the refrigerator for 24 hours. Punch holes in bottom of rolls. Place on rack in pan and bake at 325 degrees for 1½ hours. Chill before slicing. Comments: Easy & fun to make. Always a big hit.

BAKED STUFFED PORK CHOPS

4 Slices Day-Old Bread
¼ Cup Butter
½ Cup Finely-Chopped Onions
½ Cup Finely-Chopped Celery
2 Tbs. Finely-Chopped Parsley
½ Cup Dark Raisins
1½ Tsp. Salt
1 Tsp. Dried Marjoram Leaves
1/8 Tsp. Pepper
6 Rib Pork Chops (1½" thick each,
   about ¾ Lb. each)
¼ Cup All-Purpose Flour
1 Tsp. Salt
2 Tbs. Butter
1 Cup White Wine, Apple Juice or Cider

1. Make stuffing: trim some of the crust from the bread. Cut bread into ¼ inch cubes. In ¼ cup hot butter in skillet, saute' the onions and celery, stirring until the onion is golden, about 5 minutes. Add the bread crumbs. Stir to combine. Remove skillet from the heat.
2. Add parsley, raisins, 1½ tsp. salt, marjoram and the pepper. Toss lightly to combine. Preheat the oven to 350 degrees. Wipe pork chops with damp paper towels and trim off the excess fat. Reserve the fat. Cut a pocket in each chop all the way to the rib. Use a sharp paring knife to do this.
3. Fill each pocket with ¼ cup stuffing. Fasten together with two wooden picks. On a sheet of waxed paper, mix together the flour and 1 tsp. salt. Coat the pork chops on both sides with the flour mixture. Reserve the rest of the flour mixture to use in making the gravy.
4. Heat the butter and reserved pork fat in a large skillet [MW: browning dish]. Over low heat, brown the chops well on both sides. Turn with the tongs about 10 min. on each side. Cook 3 at a time. Remove, and brown the rest of the chops. Pour off the fat. Add wine, juice or cider to the pan.
5. Stir over medium heat to dissolve brown bits. Pour in the bottom of a 13 x 9 x 2 inch roasting pan [MW: glass casserole]. Stand chops in bottom of pan. Cover with foil. [MW: plastic wrap]. Bake for 1 hr. [MW: 20 min. on full power]. Remove from oven, discard wooden picks. Bake chops, uncovered, for 40 minutes] MW: 20 min. on full power]

until tender.
6. Remove chops to the platter. Keep warm. Make the gravy. Over medium heat, boil the drippings, uncovered, for 10 minutes [MW: 5 min. on full power]. Boil it until it is reduced to about 1 cup. Dissolve the reserved flour mixture in ½ cup water. Add to the drippings. Bring to a boil while stirring constantly. Simmer for 3 minutes and strain. Serves 6.

SWEET AND SOUR PORK

2-3 Lbs. Pork Meat (butt roast, pork
   chop, loin, or any kind)
1 Med. Bell Pepper, cubed
2 Med. Carrots, sliced
2 Stalks Celery, sliced
3-4 Green Onions, cut in 1" pieces (white
   part only)
1 Medium Onion, chopped or sliced
¼ Cup Soy Sauce
¼ Cup Vinegar
¼ Cup Sugar
2 Tbs. Lemon Juice
2 Tbs. Soy Sauce
1 Clove Garlic, smashed
1 Cup Water
Flour
Oil
1 Tsp. Accent or MSG
1 Big Tomato, sliced into wedges

Cut meat into serving pieces. Marinate meat with 2 tbs. lemon juice, 2 tbs. soy sauce & smashed garlic for 1 hour. While marinating the meat, prepare the vegetables and set aside. Coat meat with flour well; brown meat until golden. Drain on paper towel. Arrange fried meat in a 3 quart casserole dish and keep it warm. In the same pan, pour off some of the oil; leave about 3 tbs. Saute' onions until limp, then add all the vegetables and cook 5 minutes. Stir it once. Put all together the water, vinegar, soy sauce, sugar and accent. Put ¼ cup water in a cup and stir in 1 tbs. flour and add to the liquid mixture. Pour the liquid mixture into the vegetables, stirring constantly. Cook until the sauce thickens and is bubbly. Pour mixture on the meat. Makes 4 to 6 servings. Best served with fluffy white rice.

SAUSAGE RATATOUILLE

4 Large Italian Sausages
Yellow Crookneck Squash
Patty-Pan Squash
Chives
Tomatoes
Onions
Green Beans
Eggplant
Green Pepper
Zucchini
½ Tsp. Thyme
1 Tsp. Oregano
1 Tsp. Sugar
Salt & Pepper
1/8 Tsp. Garlic Powder
Butter
Cheese

Boil, slice and brown sausage. Layer in a
2 quart buttered casserole dish, sliced, halved
or whole: crookneck squash, patty-pan squash,
chives, tomatoes, onions, green beans, eggplant,
green pepper and zucchini. Put sausage layer on
top of this; sprinkle sausage with seasonings and
dot with butter. Pour in a glug of wine. Bake,
covered, at 350 degrees for 1 hour [MW: 15 min.
on full power]. Just before serving, sprinkle
with cheese and broil.

VIRGINIA BAKED SPARERIBS

6 Lbs. Spareribs, cut into 3 rib pieces
Sauce Ingredients:
½ Cup Chopped Onion
2 Garlic Cloves
¼ Cup Oil
2 Cups Tomato Puree
5 Tbs. Light Brown Sugar
¼ Cup Lemon Juice
¼ Cup Vinegar
2 Tsp. Tabasco
1½ Tsp. Dry Mustard
1½ Tsp. Salt
6 Bay Leaves

1/3 Cup Flour
3 Tbs. Light Brown Sugar

In a roasting pan [MW: glass casserole dish],
arrange spareribs in single layer, bake in a preheated oven at 325 degrees for 1 hour [MW:
15 min. on full power], turning to brown.
Make sauce by sauteing onion and garlic in oil
until soft. Stir in remaining ingredients and
bring to a boil. Drain most of the fat from the
roasting pan; baste spareribs with half of the
sauce and bake them for 1 hour; basting them
with the remaining sauce. In a dish, blend flour
and sugar. Sprinkle the spareribs with the mixture. Bake for an additional 30 minutes.

CALZONE (Main Dish)

3 Lbs. Frozen Bread Dough
10 Oz. Italian Sausage, sliced
1 Small Onion, diced
1 Clove Garlic, diced
1 Lb. Sliced Mushrooms
1 Carrot, grated
1 - 8 Oz. Can Tomato Sauce
1 - 2¼ Oz. Can Sliced Olives
1 Tsp. Dry Basil
½ Tsp. Oregano
½ Tsp. Sugar
2 Cups Grated Mozzarella Cheese
½ Cup Grated Parmesan Cheese
Salt and Pepper

Let frozen bread dough defrost (one or
two hours at room temperature). Brown
sausage. Add onion, garlic, mushrooms
and carrot. Cook until limp. Stir in
tomato sauce, olives, basil, oregano and
sugar. Simmer five minutes. Add the
two cheeses. Salt and pepper to taste.

Divide dough (each 1-pound loaf) into 3
sections. Pull or roll sections to make
circles with 6 to 8" diameters. Fill the
centers with approximately 2 to 3 tbs.
of filling. Fold dough over and pinch
sides together to close (shaped like a half
circle). Place on a greased cookie sheet.
Prick tops with fork. Can brush with
oil to promote browning. Bake at 475
degrees until browned (15 to 20 minutes).
To reheat, bake at 350 degrees until hot
(25 to 35 minutes).

HAM PATTIES

1 Tsp. Prepared Mustard
2 Cups Cooked Rice, cooled (not instant rice)
2 Egg Yolks
1 Tbs. Melted Margarine
2 Cups Chopped Ham
½ Cup Grated American Cheese

SAUCE:
2 Tbs. Margarine
2 Tbs. Flour
¼ Tsp. Salt
1 Cup Milk
1 Tbs. Chopped Onion
1 Small Can Peas, drained
1 Cup Shredded American Cheese OR
  Prepared Mustard To Taste

Combine first 6 ingredients. Make into
patties, 8 or 10. Dip in slightly-beaten
egg whites then into cracker crumbs. Refrigerate for a few hours. Fry in oil for
3 to 5 min. Serve with sauce: Melt
margarine, add flour and salt. Cook until
blended and add milk all at once. Cook
quickly, stirring until sauce boils and
thickens. Remove from heat and add
onion, peas and cheese OR mustard. Serve
over pattes.

SAUSAGE—BEAN CHOWDER

1 to 1½ Lbs. Bulk Pork Sausage
2 - 16 Oz. Cans Kidney Beans
1 - 1 Lb. 13 Oz. Can Tomatoes,
  broken
1 Quart Water
1 Large Onion, chopped
1 Bay Leaf
1½ Tsp. Seasoned Salt
½ Tsp. Garlic Salt
½ Tsp. Thyme
1/8 Tsp. Pepper
1 to 2 Cups Diced Potatoes
½ Green Pepper, chopped

In skillet [MW: browning dish], cook pork
until brown. Pour off fat. In a large kettle
[MW: casserole] combine kidney beans, tomatoes, water, onion, bay leaf, seasoned
salt, garlic salt, thyme & pepper. Add sausage; simmer, covered, for 1 hour. Add
potatoes and green pepper; cook 15 to 20
minutes [MW: 5-10 min. on full power],
until potatoes are tender. Remove bay leaf.

BLACK EYED PEAS and PORK

6 Cups Water
3 Cups Black Eyed Peas
¼ Cup Cooking Oil
1 Cup Chopped Onion
2/3 Cup Chopped Bell Pepper
1 Cup Chopped Mushrooms
3 Tbs. Salt
2 Tsp. Pepper
3 Stalks Celery
3 Bay Leaves
1 Tbs. Garlic (minced)
3 Chopped Pork Chops

Boil peas 5 minutes; throw in cooking
oil at this time. Turn fire down low for
3½ hours, really low. Go watch T.V. or
have a nice stiff drink. Red wine goes
good when you are ready to eat.

About 3 hours after you have turned the
fire down, throw in the remaining ingredients. Make sure the water doesn't boil
away. Add more, if needed. If you are
using a crock pot, these beans can cook
a long time - you can even go shopping.

After you have estimated about 3 hours,
turn fire to high for 30 to 40 minutes.
Depending on your appetites, you can eat
a couple of days. It is pretty cheap even
with the pork, but without it it only
costs about $4.00. Good deal, don't
you think.

The beans taste better the next day. Heat
them - throw them into a tortilla with
cheese. You can experiment if you want.

GALLETS (Gelled Pork)

1 - 4 to 5 Lb. Pork Roast
2 Pigs' Feet
1 Small Onion
5 or 6 Peppercorns
2 Bay Leaves
1 Tsp. Salt

Combine ingredients in large pot; cover with water and boil 2½ to 3 hours [MW: 1-2 hrs.], skimming foam from top as necessary.

When tender, remove roast and pigs' feet from broth. Strain broth into bowl and save. Remove meat from roast, excluding fat, gristle, and bone. Remove meat and skin from pigs' feet, excluding bone only.

Combine meat and put into two 2-quart casserole dishes. Pour broth over top of meat. Let cool at room temperature. Cover and refrigerate. Before serving, remove layer of fat from top surface. Serve with hot mustard and vinegar. Serves 4 to 6.

Hot Mustard:
1½ Tbs. Powdered Mustard
1 Tsp. Water
1 to 2 Tsp. Vinegar

Mix until smooth; let stand at room temp. approximately 6 hours, then refrigerate.

OVEN KALUA PORK

3 Tbs. Coarse Salt (Rock Salt)
2 Tbs. Monosodium Glutamate
¼ Cup Soy Sauce
1 Tsp. Worcestershire Sauce
1 Clove Garlic, crushed
1 Sm. Piece Ginger Root, crushed
12 Large Ti Leaves (can be obtained from florist) can be omitted
5 Lb. Pork Roast (Boneless Butt)
Few Drops Liquid Smoke
Aluminum Foil

In a small bowl combine salt, monosodium glutamate, soy sauce, worcestershire sauce, garlic and ginger. Rub roast with the sauce and a few drops of liquid smoke. Wrap roast and sauce in Ti-Leaves and Aluminum foil. (If Ti Leaves are used, remove fibrous part of leaves and wash). Put wrapped roast in pot. Seal with aluminum foil. Put foil over top of pot and crimp to the edges of the pan. Roast at 375° for five hours. Shred pork before serving. Serve with rice. Makes 6 servings. This oven Kalua Pork simulates the pig cooked in the pit at Hawaiian Luaus.

MARINATED PORK TENDERLOIN

½ Cup Red Wine
½ Cup Water
1 Onion, peeled and sliced
1 Whole Clove
½ Tsp. Ground Cinnamon
1 Small Bay Leaf
3 Parsley Sprigs
¼ Tsp. Salt
Pepper to taste
2 Lbs. Pork Tenderloin, in ½" slices
3 Tbs. Butter
3 Tbs. Oil
2 Tbs. Flour
½ Cup Chicken Stock

In a bowl, combine wine, water, onion, cinnamon, bay leaf, clove, parsley, salt and pepper. Arrange meat slices in 1 layer in a shallow dish and pour marinade over, turning to moisten. Marinate 2 hours, turning once.

Remove steaks from marinade and reserve marinade. Heat butter and oil in a large skillet until pork is done and browned on each side. Transfer to baking dish and set aside.

Add flour to fat in skillet and cook on low heat, mixing with wooden spoon until flour is lightly browned. Strain the marinade and add the chicken stock. Stir constantly with wire whisk and bring to a boil until sauce is smooth and slightly thickened. Taste for seasoning. Pour the sauce over steaks and bake for 10 minutes.

CHICKEN & RICE BALLS

½ Cup Chopped Celery
¼ Cup Sliced Green Onion
2 Tbs. Margarine
2 Tbs. All-purpose Flour
¼ Cup Chicken Broth
2 Cups Cooked Rice
1½ Cups Diced, Cooked Chicken
½ Cup Shredded American Cheese
1 Beaten Egg
½ Tsp. Salt
½ Tsp. Chili Powder
¼ Tsp. Poultry Seasoning
½ Cup Corn Flake Crumbs
1 Can Condensed Cream of Mushroom
   Soup
¼ Cup Milk
2 Tbs. Sliced Green Onion

Cook celery and ¼ cup onion in margarine till tender. Blend in flour; add broth and cook and stir till thick. Stir in rice, chicken, cheese, egg and seasonings. Form into small balls. Roll in corn flake crumbs. Bake in a 13" x 9" x 2" baking pan in 350 degree oven for 25-30 30 minutes [MW: 15-20 min. on full power]. Heat remaining ingredients and serve over balls. Serves 4.

Also very good if substitute ground beef for chicken, and beef broth for chicken broth.

PORTUGUESE CHICKEN
in CASSEROLE

1 - 2½ Lb. Fryer, cut up and
   skinned
½ Clove Garlic, crushed
Salt and Pepper to taste
Paprika to taste
1 Cup Orange Juice
½ Cup Tomato Puree
2 Tbs. Soy Sauce
2 to 3 Tsp. Prepared Mustard
1 Med. Green Pepper, chopped
2 Small Oranges, peeled and sectioned

Rub chicken with garlic and sprinkle with salt, pepper and paprika. Put in casserole.

Mix orange juice, puree, soy sauce and mustard. Add green pepper. Pour over chicken. Cover and bake in 350 degree oven 50 min. [MW: 25 min. on full power], or till tender. Add oranges; bake 5 to 10 minutes longer, [MW: 5 min. longer] until oranges are heated through. Makes 4 servings.

GOLDEN CORNISH HENS with
MUSHROOM STUFFING

Stuffing (for each game hen):
1/8 Cup Minced Onion
¼ Cup Chopped Celery (stalks and
   leaves)
3 Tbs. Butter or Margarine
¾ Cup Soft Bread Cubes
¼ Tsp. Salt
¼ Tsp. Crushed Sage Leaves
1/8 Tsp. Thyme Leaves
Dash of Pepper
Dash of Rosemary
¼ Cup Sliced Mushrooms, drained

Baste (for each game hen):
¼ Cup Butter or Margarine
¼ Tsp. Marjoram
¼ Tsp. Oregano
¼ Tsp. Pepper
¼ Tsp. Salt
1/8 Tsp. Ginger
¼ Cup Chablis Wine

Stuffing: in skillet [MW: browning dish] cook onion and celery in butter or margarine until onion is tender. Stir in ¼ to 1/3 of bread cubes. Turn into deep bowl; add remaining ingredients and toss until all cubes are well covered. Stuff Cornish hens just before roasting; do not pack.

Baste: Melt butter or margarine in saucepan; add all ingredients. Heat to simmer; keep warm.

After stuffing Cornish hen, tie legs together to hold in stuffing; place hen, breast-side up, upon rack in open, shallow pan. Roast at 325 to 350 degrees for 60 to 70 min. [MW: 30-40 min. on full power] Brush hen 3 or 4 times with baste.

CHICKEN LIVERS — CHOPPED

1 Tbs. Butter
2 Tbs. White Wine
2 Large Onions, chopped
3 Stalks Celery, chopped
1 Green Pepper, chopped
2 Lbs. Chicken Livers, halved
2 Tsp. Salt, or to taste
½ Tsp. Coarse Pepper
6 Hard-boiled Eggs, finely chopped
4 Tbs. Mayonnaise

Combine all ingredients, except eggs and mayonnaise, in non-stick skillet. Cover and simmer over moderate heat until onions are tender. Uncover and continue cooking until liquid evaporates. The livers and vegetables will begin to brown in the remaining fat; stir frequently. When the livers are done, remove and drain any excess liquid. Chop liver mixture very fine, or put through a food grinder or electric blender. Combine the liver mixture and chopped eggs with just enough mayonnaise to hold together. You may use a little sherry and less mayonnaise. Press mixture into mold; chill several hours. Unmold onto a bed of lettuce and serve with crackers.

KOTOPITS - CHICKEN IN FILO

8 Oz. Frozen Filo Dough or any Dinner
    Roll Dough
1 Cup Chopped Celery
¾ Cup Chopped Onion
1 Tbs. Butter or Margarine
2 Cups Chopped Cooked Chicken or
    Turkey
2 Tbs. Chicken Broth
2 Tsp. Dried Parsley Flakes
½ Tsp. Salt
½ Tsp. Ground Nutmeg
1/8 Tsp. Pepper
1 Beaten Egg
6 Tbs. Butter or Margarine, melted
4 Oz. Monterey Cheese
Hot Cooked Rice
Chicken or Turkey Gravy

Thaw dough for 2 hours at room temperature. In a covered skillet, cook celery and onion in the 1 tbs. of butter or margarine. Cook until vegetables are tender but not brown while stirring occasionally. Add the chicken or turkey and chicken broth. Cook and stir, uncovered, until all the broth is absorbed. Stir in the parsley, salt, nutmeg and pepper. Remove from the heat. Blend in the beaten egg. Set aside. For each of the chicken servings, roll out dough approx. 4 x 6 inches. Brush with melted butter or margarine. Spoon on some chicken mixture to within 1 inch of the edges. Place slices of cheese over the mixture. Fold dough over chicken, press seams. Slice each roll with 3 or 4 little air slots. Bake in a 350 degree oven for 40 minutes or until rolls are brown and crisp. Arrange on a platter with hot cooked rice. Spoon some gravy over the rolls, pass remaining sauce. Serves 4 people.

DEVILED CHICKEN

1 - 2 to 3 Lb. Chicken
¼ Cup Flour
½ Tsp. Salt
¼ Tsp. Chili Powder
1/8 Tsp. Pepper
3 Tbs. Shortening

In a paper or plastic bag, combine dry ingredients. Add chicken, 1 or 2 pieces at a time and shake. Brown chicken on all sides in shortening.

1/3 Cup Water
1/3 Cup Catsup
3 Tbs. Brown Sugar
3 Tbs. Vinegar
2 Tsp. Prepared Mustard
2 Tsp. Worcestershire Sauce
½ Tsp. Salt
Dash Pepper
1 Tsp. Lemon Juice
½ Medium Onion
4 Tbs. Margarine

Combine remaining ingredients in saucepan. Simmer, uncovered, for 20 minutes. Pour over chicken. Cover and simmer about 1½ hours. Baste frequently with sauce.

CHICKEN POT PIE

2 Broiler - Fryer Chickens, cut up in
   serving size pieces
3 Cups Water
2 Tsp. Salt
1 Tsp. Monosodium Glutamate
3 Sprigs Parsley
3 Celery Tops, with leaves
8 Peppercorns
1 Onion, sliced
1 Cup Sliced Carrots
1 - 10 Oz. Pkg. Thawed Frozen Peas
½ Cup Butter or Margarine
1 Small Onion, chopped
1 Cup Sliced Celery
½ Cup Flour
3 Cups Chicken Broth, from simmered
   chicken
1 Cup Milk
1 Tsp. Thyme
5 to 6 Cups Cut-up Cooked Chicken,
   from simmered chicken
1 - 8 Oz. Can Buttermilk Biscuits
½ Cup Shredded Cheddar Cheese

To Cook Chicken: Place chicken in kettle
with water and next 6 ingredients. Bring
to a boil. Reduce heat and cover tightly &
simmer for 1 hour or until tender. Remove
chicken to large platter, cover loosely and
place in refrigerator until cool enough to
handle. Remove meat from skin and bones
and cut into rather large chunks. Strain
broth and return to the kettle and boil rapidly, until reduced to 3 cups.

To Prepare Pot Pie: Place carrots in a saucepan with small amount of boiling salted water. Simmer covered for about 10 minutes.
Add peas and cook for 5 minutes longer.
Drain. Melt butter in a large saucepan. Add
onion and celery and cook until tender. Remove from heat and blend in flour. Gradually stir in chicken broth and milk. Add the
thyme. Cook, while stirring constantly, until
mixture thickens and comes to a boil. Remove from heat. Add chicken and drained
carrots. Then add the peas and mix well.
Turn into a 4 quart casserole dish. Top with
biscuits. Bake at 400 degrees for about 18
to 20 minutes until biscuits are browned.

NIPPONESE CHICKEN MANDARIN

¼ Cup Butter
6 Half Chicken Breasts or Parts
1 - 11 Oz. Can Mandarin Oranges
¼ Cup Soy Sauce
1 Tbs. Cornstarch
1 Tsp. Prepared Mustard
1 Tbs. Vinegar
¼ Cup Pineapple Preserves
¼ Tsp. Instant Garlic Powder
1 Tbs. Instant Minced Onion
½ Cup Diced Green Pepper

Melt ¼ cup butter in skillet [MW: browning
dish]. Saute' six half chickens, skin-side down,
until golden. Turn pieces. Drain juice from can
of mandarin oranges. Stir ½ cup mandarin syrup
and ¼ cup soy sauce into 1 tbs. cornstarch. When
smooth, add 1 tsp. prepared mustard, 1 tbs. vinegar, ¼ cup pineapple preserves, ¼ tsp. garlic powder and 1 tbs. minced onion. Pour sauce around
chicken. Cook, covered, about 15 minutes, stirring and basting occasionally. Add ¼ cup diced
green peppers and the drained mandarin oranges.
Cook for 5 minutes longer and serve. Serves 6.

CHICKEN BARBECUE SAUCE

½ Cup Oil
1½ to 2 Cups Chopped Onions (may
   use more if you like)
¾ Cup Tomato Catsup
¾ Cup Water
1/3 Cup Lemon Juice
3 Tbs. Sugar
3 Tbs. Worcestershire Sauce
2 Tbs. Prepared Mustard
2 Tbs. Salt (may use less if you like)
½ Tsp. Pepper

Cook onions in hot oil until soft. Add
remaining ingredients and simmer for 15
minutes. Makes enough sauce for basting
and serving with 2 chickens.

BOMBAY CHICKEN

8 Pieces Fryer Chicken
1/3 Cup Flour
1 Tsp. Paprika
1 Tsp. Salt
Butter
1 Medium Onion, thinly sliced
4 Chicken Bouillon Cubes
3½ Cups Boiling Water
1 Cup Uncooked Rice
1 Tsp. Salt
1 Cup Light Golden Raisins
½ Cup Coconut
1 Small Can Mandarin Oranges
1½ Tsp. Curry
¼ Cup, or more, Sliced Almonds

Coat chicken in 1/3 cup flour, paprika and salt. Brown in butter in a skillet. Remove chicken. Saute' onion in the skillet. Dissolve bouillon cubes in boiling water. Add to onions. Stir in 1 cup uncooked rice, salt, light golden raisins, coconut, mandarin oranges and curry. Turn into a 9" x 13" pan with chicken on top of rice mixture. Bake at 350 degrees, covered with foil, for 1¼ hours. During the last 15 minutes, sprinkle ¼ cup or more sliced almonds over all, or they can be put into the rice mixture beforehand. More raisins, coconut, oranges and almonds can be used according to taste, but don't overdo it!

CROCKPOT LEMON ROAST CHICKEN

1 - 3 Lb. or Larger Broiler-Fryer, Whole
  or Chicken Breasts
1 Tsp. Crumbled, dried Oregano
2 Cloves Garlic, minced
2 Tbs. Butter
¼ Cup Sherry or Water
3 Tbs. Lemon Juice
Salt and Pepper

Wash chicken and giblets. Pat dry. Season chicken with salt and pepper. Sprinkle half the oregano and garlic inside cavity. Melt butter in large frying pan. Brown chicken on all sides. Transfer to crock pot. Sprinkle with remaining oregano and garlic.

Add sherry (or water) to frying pan. Stir to loosen brown bits. Pour into crock pot. Cover. Cook on low (200°) 8 hours. Add lemon juice the last hour of cooking. Transfer chicken to carving board. Skim fat and pour juices into sauce bowl. Carve bird. Serve with some of juices spooned over chicken. Serves 6. Good with steamed zucchini sprinkled with Parmesan Cheese.

POLLO FLAUTA with GUACAMOLE SAUCE

6 Tbs. Butter
½ Cup Flour
½ Tsp. Salt
1 Cup Chicken Broth
1 Cup Half & Half
1 Tbs. Lemon Juice
2 Tbs. Minced Parsley
2 Tsp. Grated Onion
Dash Each of Paprika, Nutmeg
  and Pepper
1½ Cups Diced, Cooked Chicken
12 Corn Tortillas

Guacamole Sauce:
1 Avocado
½ Med. Onion, finely chopped
1 Ortega Chili, chopped fine
½ Tbs. Lemon Juice
½ Tsp. Salt
¼ Tsp. Pepper
1 Small Tomato, finely chopped
¼ Cup Mayonnaise

Melt butter; blend in flour and salt. Slowly add broth and half & half. Cook and stir till thickens and bubbles. Add lemon juice, parsley, onion, paprika, nutmeg and pepper. Add chicken and stir. Set aside. Soften tortillas in hot oil. Drain on paper towel. Then fill with 3 tbs. of chicken mixture. Roll each tortilla into a small tube and secure with a toothpick. Fry tortillas in about 2" of hot oil, turning until crispy all over. Drain; serve topped with your favorite guacamole recipe and/or sour cream.

Guacamole Sauce: Mash avocado; add onion, pepper, lemon juice, salt and pepper. Beat until creamy. Fold in tomato and mayonnaise.

POLLO EN JUGO DE NARANJA
(Chicken in Orange Juice)

1½ - 2 Lbs. Frying Chicken, cut in pieces
½ Cup Flour
1 Tbs. Salt
½ Tsp. Lemon Pepper
6 Oz. Can Frozen Orange Juice
1 - 8½ Oz. Can Crushed Pineapple
¾ Cup - 1 Cup Dry Sherry or any White
  Wine
½ Cup Raisins, preferably white
½ Cup Blanched Ground Almonds
¼ Tsp. Ground Cinnamon
1/8 Tsp. Ground Cloves
2 Tbs. Sugar, optional

Dredge chicken pieces in mixture of ½ cup flour, 1 tbs. salt and 1 tsp. lemon pepper. Brown them in hot oil and arrange the chicken in a shallow baking dish. Combine the frozen orange juice concentrate, crushed pineapple, dry sherry, raisins, ground almonds, cinnamon, cloves and if desired, the sugar. Pour the mixture over the chicken pieces. Bake 30 minutes at 325 degrees, basting several times. Increase temperature to 350 and bake 15 minutes longer but checking frequently to avoid over browning. [MW: 15-30 minutes on full power]. Serves 4 to 6.

TEN—MINUTE STIR—FRY
LEFTOVER CHICKEN

1 Egg White
2 Tsp. Cornstarch
2 Tsp. Dry White Wine
Leftover Chicken, cut into thin strips
2 Tbs. Peanut Oil
3 Slices Ginger Root, cut 1/8" thick
½ Cup Snow Peas*
½ Cup Bean Sprouts*
½ Cup Green Beans*
4 Water Chestnuts, sliced thin
1 Small Dried Hot Red Pepper (optional)
Walnut Halves
Soy Sauce

*Amounts of vegetables can be varied according to taste and what is on hand.

Combine egg white, cornstarch and wine.

Dip chicken in this and set aside. Place oil in wok or skillet at room temperature. Turn on heat; add ginger root. Stir-fry until oil is hot. Remove ginger; add walnuts. Stir-fry until brown; remove.

Add chicken; stir-fry until warm. Add vegetables and water chestnuts; stir-fry until tender but crunchy. Pour off excess oil. Add walnuts. When ready to serve, add a dash of soy sauce. Fast, easy and excellent. Serve with rice.

GOLDEN FRICASSEE OF CHICKEN

1 Fricassee Hen, 4 to 5 pounds
2 Cups Chablis, or other white table
  wine
1½ Cups Water
1½ Tsp. Salt
1 Carrot, sliced
2 Bay Leaves
1 Onion, sliced
2 Cloves Garlic, sliced
3 Stalks Celery, with tops (cut up)
Salt and White Pepper
3 Tbs. Flour
½ Cup Thin Cream
2 Egg Yolks, beaten
6 or 8 Sprigs of Parsley

Cut up the chicken and place in kettle [MW: casserole] with wine, water, salt, bay leaves, garlic, onion, parsley, carrot and celery. Cover and simmer slowly 2 hours or longer [MW: 1 hour or longer], until very tender. Take up chicken. Strain broth; skim off excess fat. Measure broth and add water and chablis wine, half and half, to make 3 cups liquid. Heat to boiling, adding salt & white pepper to taste. Mix flour, cream & beaten egg yolks; stir into hot broth and cook, stirring constantly, until smoothly thickened. Put the chicken back into the gravy to reheat. Arrange the pieces of chicken on a large platter and surround with a border of green rice - hot steamed rice mixed with enough chopped parsley to give a pretty green-and-white effect. Pour some of the golden gravy over the chicken. Serve the rest of the gravy separately in a sauceboat. Serves 5 or 6.

CHICKEN KIEV

4 Whole Chicken Breasts
12 Tbs. Butter
2 Eggs, beaten
Flour
2 Cups Fine Bread Crumbs
Vegetable Oil (for deep frying)
1 Tsp. Fresh Strained Lemon Juice
1 Tsp. Tarragon
1 Tsp. Chives
1 Tbs. Parsley, chopped
2 Tsp. Salt
Freshly Ground Black Pepper

Have butcher bone chicken. Skin the chicken breasts by starting at the pointed end of the breast, insert thumb under the skin and strip it off. If you decide to prepare the chicken breasts with the wing bone attached, cut off the wing tip and its adjacent bone, leaving the short leg-like bone attached to each breast. Place the 8 halved chicken breasts, smooth side down, on a cutting board. With a small sharp knife and your fingers, remove the small fillet from each breast. Cover the breasts with waxed paper and with the flat side of a cleaver, pound them to a thickness of 1/8 inch. If holes appear in the flesh, overlap the edges of the tear slightly, cover the patch with waxed paper and pound gently until the meat joins together. Cut the butter into 8 equal parts. Shape each piece of butter into a cylinder about ½ inch thick and 3 inches long. To assemble the cutlets, gently peel off the waxed paper. Sprinkle each chicken breast with ¼ tsp. salt, 1/8 tsp. tarragon, 1/8 tsp. chives, ½ tsp. chopped parsley, 1/8 tsp. strained lemon juice and freshly ground black pepper. Wrap the chicken breasts around the butter fingers, completely sealing in the seasonings and the butter. Dip the cutlets first in flour, then in the beaten eggs, making sure the entire surface is coated. Now, roll the cutlets into the fine bread crumbs until thoroughly coated. Arrange all 8 cutlets on a platter and refrigerate for 2 to 6 hours before frying. Deep fry the cutlets at 360 degrees for approximately 5 minutes, or until golden brown. Drain and serve immediately. Serves 4.

CASHEW CHICKEN

1 - 5 Oz. Can Chow Mein Noodles
2 Cups Diced, Cooked Chicken
¾ Cup Chopped Celery
½ Cup Chopped Green Onions
1 Can Cream of Mushroom Soup
1 Cup Cashew Nuts
¾ Cup Chicken Broth

Boil chicken and save broth. Set aside ½ cup crisp noodles. Combine remaining ingredients and place in a greased casserole - 2 quart. Sprinkle reserved noodles over top. Bake at 325 degrees for 30 minutes. [MW: 15 min. on full power].

MICROWAVE - FIESTA CHICKEN KIEV

4 Whole Chicken Breasts, halved, boned
    and skinned
3 Tbs. Butter or Margarine
3 Tbs. Old English-Style Sharp Cheese
    Spread
2 Tsp. Instant Minced Onion
1 Tsp. Salt
1 Tsp. Monosodium Glutamate
2 Tbs. Chopped Green Chilies
¼ Cup Butter, melted
1 Cup Cheddar Cheese Crackers, crushed
1½ Tbs. Taco Seasoning Mix

Pound each raw chicken breast with a mallet to flatten and tenderize. Beat together butter and cheese spread until well blended. Mix in onion, salt, M.S.G. and chilies. Divide mixture equally among the 8 chicken pieces, placing a portion towards 1 end of each piece. Roll up each piece, tucking in ends to completely enclose filling. Fasten rolls with toothpicks. Dip each roll in melted butter to cover, then coat with mixture of cheese crackers and taco seasoning mix. Arrange rolls in a 12 x 7 x 2 inch glass baking dish. Cover with wax paper. Place in microwave oven and microwave with full power (high) for 12 to 15 minutes. Serve chicken kiev on 2 beds of shredded lettuce with olives and tomato wedges. Serves 4 to 8.

CHICKEN AND ARTICHOKE CASSEROLE

1 to 2 Sprigs Parsley
1 Celery Top
1 Carrot, quartered
1 Bay Leaf
1 Sprig Fresh Thyme or 1 Tsp. Dried Thyme
2 Broiler-Fryers (3 lbs. ea.), cut in pieces
1 Tbs. Salt
¼ Tsp. Ground Pepper
2 Cups Water
2 Pkgs. (10 Oz. ea.) Frozen Artichoke
   Hearts, thawed
¼ Cup Butter or Margarine
¼ Cup Flour
3 Cups Shredded Mild Cheddar Cheese
½ Tsp. Nutmeg
½ Cup Fine Dry Bread Crumbs
1 Tsp. Savory
1 Tsp Thyme
2 Tbs. Butter

Make a bouquet garni by tying together in a piece of cheese cloth the parsley, celery top, carrot, bay leaf and thyme (use a long string so bouquet can be easily removed from pan.) Place chicken pieces, bouquet garni, salt, pepper and water in a large pan. Cover and simmer about 1 hour [MW: 25 min.] or until chicken is tender. Cool chicken in stock. Then remove meat from bones in good-sized pieces and arrange in 3-quart casserole along with artichoke hearts; reserve stock. To make cheese sauce, melt butter and blend in flour until smooth. Gradually add 2 cups of the chicken stock. Cook, stirring constantly, until thick and smooth. Then stir in cheese and nutmeg. Pour sauce over chicken and artichoke hearts. Sprinkle with bread crumbs, savory and thyme; dot with butter. At this point you may refrigerate the casserole, covered, until you are ready to heat it for serving. Bake uncovered in a moderate oven (350) for 30 minutes or until golden brown. [MW: 15 min. on full power]. Makes 8 servings.

ROAST DUCK in MUSHROOM SAUCE

2- 2½ to 3 Lb. Ducks
2 Cans Cream of Mushroom Soup
1 Cup Red Claret Wine
½ Cup Onion, chopped
4 Carrots
2 Celery Stalks
Salt and Pepper
Parsley

Combine in a roasting pan [MW: casserole] the soup, wine and chopped onions. Wash the ducks and stuff with carrots and celery Sprinkle with salt and pepper. Put ducks in pan and coat with the sauce. Cover with aluminum tent [MW: plastic or wax peper] Roast in oven for 1½ to 2 hours at 325 degrees [MW: 1-1½ hours on full power]. Serve on platter with wild rice bordering them. Use sauce over the rice. Garnish with parsley.

CHICKEN MADRAS

1½ Lbs. Boned Chicken Meat
1½ Tbs. Cornstarch
1 Tbs. Curry Powder
1½ Cups Chicken Broth
¼ Cup Catsup
¼ Cup Orange Marmalade
2 Tbs. Lemon Juice
1 Cup Celery, cut in 1 inch cubes
1 Large Green Pepper
1 Large Onion, sliced and separated into
   rings

Cut chicken into bite size pieces, season with salt and pepper and brown lightly in butter. Blend cornstarch, curry powder, broth, catsup, marmalade and lemon juice. Pour over chicken. Cook for 15 minutes, stirring often, or until the chicken is tender. Add onion, celery and green pepper. Cover and cook 5 minutes. Vegetables should be crisp and chicken glazed. Serve over bed of rice. Serves 4 people. [MW: instructions are the same.]

TERIYAKI ROCK CORNISH GAME HEN

3 Rock Cornish Hens Thawed
5 Tbs. Sugar
1 Cup Soy Sauce
1/2 Cup Orange Juice
1/3 Cup Sake (Japanese rice spirit)
    or Sherry (or any kind of white wine)
2 Tbs. Grated Ginger

Combine all ingredients except hens. Stir well until all sugar is dissolved. Remove giblets from hens and split hens into two halves. Marinate hen halves in the sauce 4-6 hrs. Turn occasionally. Arrange the marinated hen halves skin side down on pre-heated broiler about 5 in. from source of heat or on broiler-pan rack in the hottest oven (over 500 degrees). Broil about 15 min. Turn and broil skin side up another 15 min. Makes 6 servings.

PEANUT CHICKEN WITH SWEET AND SOUR SAUCE

1 Chicken
1/3 Tsp. Salt
Dash Fresh or Ground Pepper
1 Large Clove Garlic
½ Cup or so of Soy Sauce
Dash M.S.G. (optional)
2 Eggs
Cornstarch, as needed

Sauce:
1 Rounded Tbs. Cornstarch
½ Cup Cold Water
1/3 Cup Sugar
½ Tsp. Salt
½ Tsp. M.S.G. (optional)
2 Tbs. Vinegar
2 Tbs. Catsup

½ Head Lettuce (approximately)
1 to 1½ Cups Fresh Pineapple Chunks or
    Unsweetened Canned Chunks
1/8 Cup or so of Chopped Green Onion
½ Cup Chopped Peanuts, or more if you
    desire

Bone and skin an uncooked chicken. Cut into bite size pieces. Soak in salt, ginger, soy sauce, chopped garlic and M.S.G. for a few hours. Dip chicken into beaten eggs. Coat with cornstarch. Fry in deep fat or oil until done and golden brown.

Sauce: Dissolve cornstarch in water in a small pan. Add remaining ingredients and stir until thickened. Now add the pineapple juice and some pineapple chunks.

The platter can be arranged with sliced lettuce. Place chicken pieces over the lettuce and pour sweet and sour sauce over the chicken. Garnish with remaining pineapple, the peanuts and green onion. Serve with rice, tea or white wine. Guaranteed to please.

PHEASANT - ALL DRUNK & SPUNKY

2 Large Pheasants
Salt and Pepper to taste
1 Med. Orange, quartered
2 Celery Stalks, halved
1 Cup Apricot-pineapple Preserves
½ Cup Apricot Brandy
4 Strips of Bacon

Stuff 2 pieces of orange and 2 pieces of celery into cavity of birds. Tie legs closed with kitchen thread. Place in large roasting pan. Heat broiler to 400 degrees.

Heat mixture carefully in saucepan until preserves are melted. Spoon some of the mixture over the pheasants to glaze. Place pan with birds in broiler for 7 to 10 min., until birds are beautifully browned. Remove and spoon additional sauce over birds. Place 2 strips of bacon over each bird and roast at 400 degrees for ½ hour. After ½ hour, reduce heat to 350 degrees for 45 minutes, basting every 10 minutes with glaze. Remove and discard orange and celery and serve.

Note: Five minutes before serving, you may pour one-third cup of brandy over birds.

CHICKEN CHOWDER

¼ Cup Chopped Onion
½ Tsp. Curry Powder
2 Tbs. Oil
2 Tbs. Flour
4 Cups Chicken Broth
2 Tomatoes, chopped
2 Apples, pared and chopped
½ Cup Carrots, sliced
¼ Cup Green Pepper, chopped
2 Tbs. Parsley
1 Tbs. Lemon Juice
1 Tsp. Sugar
Dash of Pepper
1½ Cups Yellow Squash, pared and
  chopped
1 Cup Diced, Cooked Chicken

In large saucepan, cook onion and curry powder in hot oil till onion is tender but not brown. Blend in flour. Stir in the chicken broth, tomatoes, apples, carrots, green pepper, parsley, lemon juice, sugar, salt and pepper; bring mixture to boiling, stirring occasionally. Lower heat; cover and simmer 15 minutes. Stir in squash and chicken; simmer 15 minutes more, or till squash is tender. Serve over rice. Serves 6 to 8 people. It's fantastic!

CHICKEN BASQUE

6 Whole Chicken Breasts or 3 Whole
  Chicken Breasts & 6 Thighs for those
  who like dark meat
1 Lb. Small Boiling Onions (white), peeled
  and left whole
1 Large Eggplant, peeled and cut in fingers
2 Green Peppers, seeded and cut in fingers
1 Lb. Fresh Mushrooms, quartered
1 Bunch Green Salad Onions, bottoms, too,
  chopped
6 Cloves Garlic, pressed
28 Oz. Can Whole Tomatoes, drained and
  chopped
1 Tsp. Dry Thyme, Basil, Pepper, Salt &
  2 Bay Leaves
1¾ Cup Sauterne Wine
6 Strips Bacon, chopped

Chop bacon and fry in large frying pan, spoon out into 5 qt. Dutch oven. In bacon grease, brown chicken well on all sides; spoon out into Dutch oven. Add boiling onions and tomatoes in drippings from chicken. Saute' green salad onions, mushrooms and peppers (if there is not enough bacon grease, you can add a little butter at this point); spoon out into Dutch oven after sauteing for about 10 minutes. In all the juices from above, saute' the eggplant for 10 minutes. Spoon out into Dutch oven. Add the wine to the frying pan, garlic, thyme, salt, pepper, basil and bay leaves. Stir till pan comes clean and pour into Dutch oven. Cover and bake at 350· degrees for 45 minutes. Serve with rice, green salad and French rolls. Note: This can be made 1 day ahead of time and this will also freeze well.

CORNISH HENS WITH BREAD STUFFING

4 Cornish Hens
1 Loaf Frozen White Bread, cut into cubes
2 Eggs
¼ Cup Minced Onions
1/8 Cup Grated Parmesan Cheese
4 Cubes Chicken Bouillon, melted in 2 cups
  hot water
½ Tsp. Garlic Powder
¼ Cup Parsley Flakes
Salt and Pepper to taste
Lawry Season Salt

Wash Cornish hens and drain. For stuffing: In large bowl, to fit all the bread that is cubed, add all other ingredients, reserving 1 cup bouillon. Stir together until all is coated. Stuff Cornish hens firmly with the stuffing mixture until all stuffing is used. Lay stuffed hens in pan large enough to hold 4 stuffed hens. Sprinkle with Lawry season salt; pour on the remaining bouillon. Bake at 350 degrees for 2 hours [MW: 1 hr. on full power]. When pan dries, just add water to pan 1 cup at a time. Make brown chicken gravy with remaining juices in pan. Serves 6 to 8.

BAKED GOOSE

1 - 8 to 10 Lb. Goose
¾ Cup Flour
1 Lb. Salt Pork
2 Cups Chopped Onion
1 Tbs. Salt
1 Tsp. Black Pepper
2 Cups Good Wine
8 Oz. Egg Noodles
6 Cups Shredded Cabbage

Remove all skins and fat from goose and save. Cut up goose in small serving pieces, flour, salt and pepper. Cook fat and skins in pan. Brown goose in the fat oil and set aside. Cut salt pork in small even cubes and brown in roaster. Drain and pour in the onions. Then brown the goose. Pour 2 cups of good wine and bake 2 to 3 hours at 325 degrees. Cook egg noodles as directed on package. Add butter. Cook cabbage for 6 minutes in a covered pan. On a platter put cooked buttered noodles, cabbage and goose with sauce. Serve hot.

SAVORY CRESCENT TURKEY SQUARES

3 oz. Pkg. Philadelphia Brand Cream Cheese
  Softened
3 Tbs. Parkay Margarine, Melted
2 Cups Cooked Cubed Turkey
1/4 Tsp. Salt
1/8 Tsp. Pepper
2 Tbs. Milk
1 Tbs. Chopped Chives or Onion
1 Tbs. Chopped Pimento (if desired)
8 Oz. Can Pillsbury Refrigerated Quick
  Crescent or Italian Flavor Crescent Dinner
  Rolls
1 Cup Seasoned Croutons, crushed

Preheat oven to 350°. In medium bowl, blend cream cheese and 2 Tbs. margarine (reserve 1 Tbs.) until smooth. Add the next 6 ingredients. Mix well. Separate crescent dough into 4 rectangles; press perforations firmly to seal. Spoon ½ c. meat mixture onto center of each rectangle. Pull 4 corners of dough to top center and twist slightly and seal edges. Brush tops with reserved 1 tbs. margarine, dip in crouton crumbs. Bake on ungreased cookie sheet 20-25 minutes until golden brown. Makes 4 servings.

CHICKEN BREASTS IN ORANGE SAUCE

½ Cup Regular Flour
½ Tsp. Salt
½ Tsp. Paprika
Dash Pepper
Dash Garlic Powder
6 Halved Chicken Breasts
6 Tbs. Olive Oil or Salad Oil
1 - 3 or 4 Oz. Can Mushrooms
1 - 10½ Oz. Can Cream of Mushroom Soup
½ Cup Chicken Broth
½ Cup Orange Juice
½ Cup Dry White Wine
¼ Tsp. Nutmeg
2 Tsp. Brown Sugar
2 Cups Diagonally-Sliced Carrots (about ½ in.)

Blend flour, salt, paprika, pepper and garlic powder. Coat the chicken with flour mixture. Heat oil in an electric frying pan. Brown chicken breasts well on both sides in hot oil. Drain mushrooms, reserving the liquid. Scatter mushrooms over the chicken. Blend soup, reserved mushroom liquid, chicken broth, orange juice, wine, nutmeg and brown sugar until smooth. Pour soup mixture over chicken. Cover and cook at 225 degrees (or simmer in a regular pan over low heat) about 30 minutes or until chicken is tender. About 15 minutes before chicken is done, stir in carrots and continue cooking until tender. Makes 6 servings.

BUTTERMILK FRIED CHICKEN

1 (3 Lb.) Chicken, cut up
1 Cup Buttermilk
1 Cup Flour
2 Tbs. Cornmeal
4 Tsp. Seasoned Salt
1/4 Tsp. Black Pepper
3-4 Cups Oil

Dip chicken in buttermilk. Combine flour, cornmeal, salt and pepper in a grocery sack. Place chicken in bag 3 pieces at a time and shake till well coated. Do an hour ahead if possible, so coating can set. Heat oil in large frying pan (or wok). Fry chicken about 30-40 min. in frying pan (15-20 min. in wok) or till done. Handle chicken as little as possible while frying.

CHICKEN CREPES

Crepes:
1¼ Cups Flour
3 Eggs
1 Cup Milk
¼ Cup Water
½ Tsp. Salt
3 Tbs. Melted Butter
3 Tbs. Vegetable Oil

Filling:
1 Large Frying Chicken
2 Stalks Celery, chopped
1 Onion, chopped
1 Bay Leaf
3 Bunches Green Onions, chopped
½ Lb. Fresh Mushrooms, chopped
¼ Cup Butter
1 - 10 Oz. Pkg. Frozen Spinach,
   cooked and drained
1 - 10 Oz. Can Cream of Chicken Soup
½ Tsp. Nutmeg
1½ Tsp. Salt
1 Tsp. White Pepper
1 Tsp. Dry Mustard
2 Tbs. Sherry

Sauce:
½ Cup Butter
1 Cup Flour
4 Cups Milk
2 Lbs. Velveeta Cheese
1 - 12 Oz. Can Beer
2 Tbs. Sherry

Crepes: Combine all ingredients, except butter and oil. Whip in blender until smooth; chill, covered, for at least 1 hour. Heat a 6" crepe pan; brush with butter combined with oil. Pour in 2 tbs. batter; roll quickly to spread over pan. Cook until edges brown. Turn and brown other side. Refrigerate or freeze, tightly covered, for at least 1 day before using.

Filling: Simmer chicken with celery, onion, bay leaf and enough water to cover; bone and chop. Saute' green onions and mushrooms in butter until tender. Add spinach, soup (undiluted), chicken and all remaining ingredients. Mix well. Place a heaping spoonful of filling in center of each crepe. Roll one turn. Fold edges in and roll until tight; place in a flat oven-proof dish, seam-side down. Cover with mornay sauce and bake at 350 degrees until hot, about 20 to 30 minutes. Serve with extra sauce. Crepes can be made, filled and frozen. Keep separated until they are frozen; remove and place in plastic bags. Sauce cannot be frozen.

Sauce: Melt butter; add flour and cook until bubbly. Add milk slowly and cook until smooth. Boil 1 minute. Cut cheese into small chunks and beat into hot sauce. Using electric mixer, beat 15 minutes. Add beer, a little at a time, until sauce reaches desired consistency. Do not over-beat after adding beer. Add sherry. If stored for a few days, beat again to restore lightness. Serves 8. Two per person. If you do not wish a lot of sauce, cut the recipe in half.

FOIL—BAKED TURKEY (Serves 6)

1 Half Turkey Breast or Whole Turkey
   Thigh (2-3 lbs.)
Salt
2 Tbs. Butter
2 Tbs. Grated Parmesan Cheese
2 Tsp. Flour
¼ Tsp. Dill Weed
¼ Tsp. Crumbled Basil
1/8 Tsp. Pepper

Sprinkle underside of turkey lightly with salt. Cream butter, cheese, flour, herbs, ½ tsp. salt and pepper together. Spread over skin of turkey. Place on sheet of heavy foil and bring edges together up over meat and fold over twice. Fold ends twice to seal. Place packet in a shallow baking pan and roast in a 350 degree oven for about 1 hr. 50 minutes. Open foil carefully and pour off juices. Slice meat and serve with juices.

CHICKEN WAIKIKI BEACH

2 Whole Chicken Legs
2 Whole Chicken Breasts
½ Cup Flour
1/3 Cup Salad Oil or Shortening
1 Tsp. Salt
¼ Tsp. Pepper

Sauce:
1 - 1 Lb. 4 Oz. Can Sliced Pineapple
1 Cup Sugar
2 Tbs. Cornstarch
¾ Cup Cider Vinegar
1 Tbs. Soy Sauce
¼ Tsp. Ginger
1 Chicken Bouillon Cube
1 Large Green Pepper, cut cross-wise in
    ¼ inch circles

Wash chicken. Pat dry with paper towels. Coat chicken with flour. Heat oil in a large skillet [MW: browning dish]. Add chicken, a few pieces at a time, and brown on all sides. Remove as browned to shallow roasting pan, arranging pieces, skin-side up. Sprinkle with salt and pepper. Meanwhile, preheat oven to 350 degrees. Make sauce. Drain pineapple, pouring syrup into a 2-cup measure. Add water to make 1¼ cups. In a medium sauce-pan, combine sugar, cornstarch, pineapple syrup, vinegar, soy sauce, ginger & bouillon cube. Bring to boiling, stirring constantly. Boil for 4 minutes. Pour over chicken. Bake uncovered, 30 minutes [MW: 15 min. on full power]. Add pineapple slices and green pep-per. Bake for 30 minutes [MW: 15 min.] or until chicken is tender. Serve with white rice. Makes 4 servings.

BUSY DAY CHICKEN AND RICE

1 Cup Uncooked Rice
1 Chicken, cut-up
¼ Lb. Butter, 1 stick
1 Pkg. Dry Onion Soup
4 Cups Boiling Water
Salt and Pepper to taste

Preheat oven to 350 degrees. Grease bottom of 13x9½x2 inch pan. Cover bottom evenly with rice. Arrange chicken pieces on rice,

dot with butter. Sprinkle dry onion soup over all. Salt and pepper to taste. Pour boiling water into pan. Bake for about 1 hr. If browner chicken is desired, brown before placing on rice.

DRUNK CHICKEN

1 3 Lb. Fryer, cut up
3 Thighs or 2 Chicken Breasts, skin
    removed
¼ Cup Olive Oil
3 Cloves Garlic
½ Tsp. Salt
¼ Tsp. Seasoned Pepper
1 Large Yellow Onion
2 Lemons
1 Large Orange
1 Fifth Chablis Wine
1 Cup White Vinegar
¾ to 1 Lb. Spaghettini (small)
1 Can Sliced Water Chestnuts
1 Can Artichoke Hearts, quartered
    and drained
1 Can Garbanzo Beans, drained
¼ Cup Parmesan Cheese
¼ Cup Romano Cheese

Remove skin from chicken. Salt & pepper the chicken. Heat garlic cloves in oil. Add chicken and brown 20 to 30 minutes [MW: in browning dish for 15-20 min. on full power]. Layer in deep casserole, starting with the chicken. Place slices of onion, lemon, orange on next; repeat until ingre-dients are used. Add chablis and vinegar to cover.

Simmer until tender, about 30 to 40 min. [MW· 15-25 min. on full power] Meanwhile, boil spaghettini until not quite done. Rinse and drain. Add to chicken until hot or may sit with chicken to flavor. Add remaining ingredients at the same time. Serve with cheeses on top. Can thicken if desired. Serves 6.

CALCUTTA CURRY

2 Chicken Breasts, chopped
4 Onions, 2 mulched, 2 pureed, in blender
4 Cloves Garlic
1 Cube Butter, melted
Salt & Pepper
1 Can Evaporated Milk
2 Cups Coconut
2 Tsp. Brown Sugar
2 to 4 Tsp. Mint Flakes
2 to 4 Tsp. Cinnamon
Juice of 1 Lemon with Peel
Chicken Stock
2 Tsp. Ginger
2 Tsp. Fenugrek
2 Tsp. Cardomon
2 Tsp. Corriander
2 Tsp. Curry Paste
2 Tsp. Curry Powder
¼ to ½ Tsp. Turmeric or Saffron
¼ to ½ Tsp. Chili Powder
¼ to ½ Tsp. Ground Cloves
¼ to ½ Tsp. Fennel
1 to 2 Bay Leaves

Melt butter in frying pan [MW: browning dish] ; add chicken breats, onions and garlic; salt and pepper to taste; cook until done. Add evaporated milk, coconut, brown sugar, mint flakes, cinnamon and lemon juice and peel. Add chicken stock, then the rest of the spices. Most of these spices can be found in the Spice Island rack in Safeway. Add more chicken stock and eat it! This is an authentic recipe from India.

CREAMY CHICKEN SOUP

6 Cups Chicken Broth (see below)
1 Cup Half & Half
1 Cup Milk
½ Cup Flour
2 Tsp. Snipped Chives
2 Tsp. Dried Tarragon Leaves, crumbled
½ Cup Softened Margarine
3 Cups Cooked Chicken, cubed
½ Cup Cooked Peas
½ Cup Cooked Carrots, cut small

Make broth (see below). Place broth, Half & Half, milk, chives and tarragon in 5-quart Dutch oven [MW: casserole] ; heat to boiling. Combine flour and margarine to form a smooth paste. Stir in about 1 cup hot broth into flour mixture; stir gradually into other. Heat to boiling. Simmer, stirring occasionally, until mixture thickens slightly, about 10 minutes. Add chicken, carrots and peas. Bring to a boil. Top with cheese.

Broth:
1 Cut up Fryer
1 Sliced Onion
¾ Cup Sliced Carrots
2 Stalks Celery with leaves
6 Peppercorns
1 Tbs. Salt
1 Tbs. Parsley Flakes
¼ Tsp. Marjoram, crumbled
¼ Tsp. Thyme, crumbled
5 Cups Water

Heat ingredients to boiling, reduce heat and cover. Simmer 1 hour [MW: 40 min.] Remove chicken and bone it. Cube meat. Strain and discard vegetables.

CHICKEN CACCIATORE

1 Cut-Up Fryer
½ Cup Flour
1 Tsp. Salt
1/8 Tsp. Pepper
½ Cup Oil
2 Medium Onions, chopped
1 - 16 Oz. Can Tomatoes
2 Small Cans Tomato Paste
4 Cloves Garlic, crushed
½ Tsp. Oregano
1 Tsp. Celery Seed
1 Tsp. Salt
½ Tsp. Pepper

Brown chicken in flour, spices and oil. Remove and add onions to frying pan, let cook until soft, then add remaining ingredients. Cover and let simmer for 30 minutes [MW: 20 minutes]. Add chicken and let simmer for 30 minutes [MW: 20 minutes] or until the chicken is tender.

CASHEW CHICKEN

3 Whole Chicken Breasts
½ Lb. Edible Pod Peas or 2 Pkgs. Frozen
   Pods, partially thawed
½ Lb. Mushrooms
4 Green Onions
1 - 8 Oz. Can Bamboo Shoots, drained
1 Tbs. Chicken Stock Base, dissolved
   in 1 cup water or 1 Cup Regular
   Strength Chicken Broth
¼ Cup Soy Sauce
2 Tbs. Cornstarch
½ Tsp. Sugar
½ Tsp. Salt
¼ Tsp. Grated Ginger Root
1/3 Cup Salad Oil
1 - 4 Oz. Pkg. Cashew Nuts

Bone chicken breasts and remove skin. Slice horizontally in 1/8" thick slices, then cut in 1" squares. Arrange on a tray. Remove the ends and strings from fresh pea pods. Wash and slice mushrooms. Cut the green part of the onions into 1" lengths and then slash both ends several times making small fans, slice the white part ¼" thick. Slice bamboo shoots. Arrange all the vegetables on tray. Pour chicken broth into small pitcher. Mix together soy sauce, cornstarch, sugar and ginger root and salt, pour into a small pitcher. Place oil and nuts in containers. Arrange at the table with electric frying pan. To cook, heat 1 tbs. oil over 350 degree heat [MW: browning dish] add nuts all at once and cook 1 minute, shaking pan until lightly toasted. Remove from pan and set aside. Add remaining oil to pan, add chicken, cook quickly, turning until it turns opaque. Add peas and mushrooms, pour in broth and cover and simmer for 2 minutes. Add bamboo shoots. Stir the soy sauce mixture into the pan juices and cook until sauce is thickened, stirring constantly, then simmer 1 minute, uncovered. Mix in green onions, sprinkle with nuts. Serve over rice or chow mein noodles.

CHICKEN KIEV

4-6 Boned Chicken Breasts
1 Pkg. Boiled Ham
1 Pkg. Swiss Cheese
2 Eggs
1 Tbs. Milk
Butter
Parsley

Pound the boned chicken breasts until very thin. Salt & pepper the chicken. Put a small chunk of butter, a strip of ham and a strip of swiss cheese, a sprinkle of parsley on each piece of chicken. Roll (fold in sides and roll like a jelly roll). Dust with flour, dip in beaten egg and roll in cracker crumbs. Set in the refrigerator for at least 1 hr before cooking. Fry (just to brown) Bake in medium oven (325-350) for 1 hour. Serve with hollandaise sauce.

CRAB-STUFFED CHICKEN BREASTS

6 Chicken Breasts, skinned, boned &
   pounded flat
½ Cup Chopped Onion
½ Cup Chopped Celery
3 Tbs. Dry White Wine
3 Tbs. Butter or Margarine
1 - 7 Oz. Can Crabmeat, drained & flaked
½ Cup Herb-Seasoned Stuffing Mix

Cook onion and celery in butter or margarine until tender. Add wine and crabmeat and toss. Add stuffing mix and mix together well. Sprinkle chicken breasts with salt and pepper. Divide stuffing between breasts, roll and secure with toothpicks or skewers. Coat with 2 tbs. flour mixed with ½ tsp. paprika. Place in an 11¾ x 7½ x 1¾ inch baking dish. Drizzle with 2 tbs. melted butter. Bake uncovered, for 1 hr. in a 375 degree oven. [MW: 25 minutes on full power]. Serve with Hollandaise sauce mix, or make your own, blended with ¾ cup milk. Cook, stirring until thick. Add 2 tbs. dry white wine and ½ cup 2 oz.) shredded process Swiss cheese. Stir until cheese melts. Pour some over chicken on serving platter, pass remainder. Serves 6.

MANDARIN CHICKEN

2 Cups Pineapple Juice
½ Cup Mandarin Orange Juice
½ Cup Pineapple Juice, drained
  from pineapple
1 Tbs. Orange Marmalade
3 Tbs. Soy Sauce
1 Tsp. Ginger
2 Tbs. Lemon Juice
2 Tbs. Brown Sugar
3 Tbs. Cornstarch
1 Egg, beaten
1 Cup Flour
1 Cup Milk
1 Tbs. Wesson Oil
1 Tsp. Salt
¼ Tsp. White Pepper
3 Double Chicken Breasts or
  6 Halves, de-boned
1 Can Pineapple Chunks or Tid-Bits
1 Can Mandarin Oranges
1 Small Jar Maraschino Cherries

Mix together and boil for 2-3 minutes until thickened: pineapple juice, orange juice, soy sauce, ginger, lemon juice, sugar and cornstarch. Set aside. Dip deboned chicken into batter of egg, flour, milk, oil, salt and white pepper. Drop in oil and deep fry at 360 degrees until crisp. Drain off oil and keep warm. Place in baking dish and put pineapple sections and orange sections over it. Pour sauce over chicken and bake at 400 degrees for 15 minutes. Put cherries on and bake about 5 more minutes, until bubbly. Bell peppers and tomatoes may be used in place of cherries.

CHICKEN TAMALE PIE

1 Cup Corn Meal
2 Cups Canned Stewed Tomatoes
1 Cup Milk
1 Can Whole Kernel Corn
3 Eggs, beaten
1 Small Onion, chopped
2 Cups Cooked Chicken Breast, chopped
1 Tsp. Salt
2 Tsp. Chili Powder, or to taste
1 Can Sliced Olives

1. Mix corn meal, tomatoes and milk in top of double boiler.
2. Saute' onion in small amount of butter with chicken.
3. Add onions and corn to double boiler, along with the chicken.
4. Over medium heat, thoroughly cook the above until mixture becomes thick.
5. Add beaten eggs and olives and place in greased baking dish.
6. Bake 40 min. in 300-325 degree oven. [MW: 20 min. on full power].

PAELLA

1/3 Cup Oil
2 Whole Chicken Breasts
4 Chicken Legs
1 Cup Chopped Onion
1 Clove Garlic, pressed
2 - 14 Oz. Cans Chicken Broth
1 Tsp. Pepper
3½ Tsp. Salt
½ Tsp. Tarragon
½ Tsp. Paprika
1 Tsp. Saffron
2 Cups Rice
1 Large Can Whole Tomatoes
3 Chorizos (Spanish sausage)
1½ Lbs. Shrimp
12 Clams, in the shell
6 Mussels, in the shell
½ Pkg. Frozen Peas
1 Can Artichoke Hearts

Cook grease out of chorizos and strain. Put aside to cool. Saute' chicken in oil. Brown onion and garlic. Add broth, pepper, salt, tarragon, paprika and saffron. Bring to a boil. Add rice. Cook, covered, for 10 to 12 min. Add tomatoes, peas, ground sausage, shrimp and chicken; simmer 30 min. [MW: 15 min.]. Add clams and mussels, cover & steam until shells open. Add artichokes and serve. Serves 4 to 6.

SOUTH AMERICAN CHICKEN AND RICE

1 Cup Raw Rice, not Minute Rice
1 Cup Chopped Onion
1 Cup Chopped Celery
½ Cup Sliced Green Stuffed Olives
½ Cup Chopped Green Pepper
1 Clove Garlic, chopped
2½ Cups Chicken Broth
1 ½ Cups Cooked Diced Chicken
¼ Cup Olive Oil
Salt and Pepper to taste
Mushrooms, optional
1 Cup Cooked Peas, add last on top
   after cooked

Heat oil; put rice, onion, celery and garlic in hot oil. Keep turning. Add remaining ingredients, except peas. Put into covered roaster and cook for 1 hour and 15 min. in a 300 degree oven [MW: 15-25 min. on full power]. When done, add peas on top and serve with a salad and bread sticks for a beautiful one-dish meal. Serves 4, or may be doubled or tripled to serve company.

ORIENTAL STYLE LEMON CHICKEN

¾ Lb. Chicken Breast, deboned
Marinate:
½ Tsp. Salt
½ Tbs. Wine
½ Tbs. Light Soya Sauce
1 Tbs. Cornstarch
1 Tbs. Cold Water
1 Egg Yolk
1/8 Tsp. Pepper

8 Cups Oil
3 Drops Yellow Food Coloring

Seasoning Sauce:
3 Tbs. Fresh Lemon Juice
3 Tbs. Sugar
3 Tbs. Soupstock or Chicken Bouillon
½ Tsp. Salt
2 Tsp. Cornstarch
1 Tsp. Sesame Oil

To Coat Chicken:
6 Tbs. Cornstarch
3 Tbs. Flour

Remove chicken skin; cut the deboned meat into 1½" cubes, marinate in marinade 15-20 minutes. Mix seasoning sauce in small bowl and set aside. Coat chicken with flour and cornstarch mixture. Deep fry chicken over medium heat for 1 minute then remove. Then heat oil very hot, deep fry again for 30 seconds, remove and let chicken drain on platter or colander. Heat 1 Tbs. oil in fry pan and stir in seasoning sauce until thickened, add three drops yellow food coloring and cold water for desired consistency. Splash 1 tbs. hot oil to make sauce shine. Then return chicken to the pan and stir until chicken is covered with sauce. Garnish with fresh slices of lemon and parsley.

CHICKEN & MACARONI STEW

1 - 3 Lb. Fryer, cut up
¼ Cup Flour
2 Tsp. Paprika
½ Tsp. Pepper
2 Tsp. Salt
¼ Cup Salad Oil
2 Medium Onions, thickly sliced
1 - 28 Oz. Can Tomatoes
¼ Bunch Parsley
2 Tsp. Poultry Seasoning
2 Cloves Garlic, whole
1 - 10 Oz. Pkg. Peas, frozen
2 Cups Elbow Macaroni
1 Cup Water
2 Tsp. Salt

Two hours before serving, on wax paper combine flour, paprika, salt and pepper. Coat chicken. In Dutch oven, brown the chicken over medium-high heat in hot oil. Remove chicken; add onions and cook till tender. Add chicken, tomatoes, parsley (tied), 2 tsp. salt, poultry seasoning, garlic and 1 cup water. Cook, covered, over low heat about 1½ hrs. [MW: 30-40 min. on medium power]. Remove from heat; discard parsley and garlic cloves and skim fat. Add macaroni and cook over medium-high heat about 10 min. Add peas and cook, covered, over low heat about 15 min. more [MW: 10 min. more]. Serves 6.

SPECIAL STUFFED CHICKEN

4 Chicken Breasts
¼ Cup Flour
½ Tsp. Salt
¼ Tsp. Paprika
2 Cups Dry Bread Crumbs
1 Tbs. Chopped Onion
½ Tsp. Salt
¼ Tsp. Poultry Seasoning
Dash Pepper
2 Tbs. Melted Butter
¼ Cup Hot Water
½ Cup Butter, melted

Mushroom Sauce:
½ Lb. Fresh Mushrooms, cut in half
¼ Cup Minced Onion
2 Tbs. Butter
1 to 2 Tbs. Flour
½ Cup Heavy Cream
½ Cup Sour Cream
½ Tsp. Salt
¼ Tsp. Pepper

Split chicken breasts, just enough to fold. Combine flour, salt, paprika and dash of pepper in a paper bag. Add chicken, shake the bag to coat.

Stuffing:
Combine bread cubes, onion, ½ tsp. salt, poultry seasoning and pepper. Add 2 tbs. butter and hot water. Toss gently to moisten. Fill cavity of each piece of chicken with stuffing. Use toothpicks to hold stuffing in. Dip chicken in ½ cup melted butter. Place in baking dish, bake in 325 degree oven for 45 minutes [MW: 25 min. on full power], or until tender. Sprinkle with chopped parsley. Serve with mushroom sauce. Serves 4.

Sauce:
Cook mushrooms and onion lightly in butter until tender, not brown. Cover and cook 10 min. over low heat. Push mushrooms to one side and stir flour into butter; add heavy cream, sour cream and seasonings. Heat slowly, stirring constantly, almost to boiling point. Makes about 1½ cups sauce.

ARROZ CON POLLO
(Chicken with Rice)

1 Frying Chicken, (2½ lbs.) cut-up
Salt
3 Tbs. Olive Oil
1 Large Onion, chopped
1 Clove Garlic
1 Medium Green Pepper, chopped
1 (19oz.) Can Tomatoes
1/3 Cup Sherry
¼ Tsp. Pepper
Pinch Saffron
½ Tsp. Paprika
2 Whole Cloves
1 Bay Leaf
1¼ Cups Uncooked Long Grain Rice
1 Cup Cooked Peas
1 Pimiento, cut-up

Season chicken with salt. Brown in oil [MW: browning dish]. Add onion, garlic and green pepper. Brown about 5 minutes. Add next 7 ingredients and 1 cup water. Cover and simmer about 30 min. [MW: 20 min.]. Garnish with peas and pimento. Serves 4 to 6.

CREAM OF CHICKEN SOUP

1 Chicken (3 Lbs.)
3 Diced Carrots
2 Onions, Chopped
½ Cup Chopped Parsley
1-½ Cups Celery
Water to cover
Salt and Pepper to taste
3 Cups Milk
½ Cup Margarine
½ Cup Flour

Bring to boil in large covered pot. Skim off foam, cover and simmer until tender. Remove chicken and vegetables. Boil remaining liquid down to 3 cups. Stir in milk. Make a paste of the margarine and flour. Drop by spoonfuls into the soup. Stir over low heat until it bubbles and thickens. Skin, bone, and cut up the chicken into big chunks. Put chicken and vegetables back into broth. Reheat and season to taste. Can add garlic salt and MSG. Serve with rolls and salad.

SQUABS WITH DRESSING

4 - 14 to 15 Oz. Squabs
1 Cup Chopped Pipin Apples
1 Cup Raw or Frozen Cranberries
¼ Cup Diced Celery
1 Tbs. Parsley
¼ Cup Butter
¼ Cup Sugar
6 Cups Dried Diced Bread, broken
  into small pieces
1 Tsp. Salt
Pinch of Pepper
Poultry Seasoning to taste (optional)
3 or 4 Chicken Bouillon Cubes, in
  hot water, to taste

Dice apples into small pieces. Chop
cranberries into small pieces or use fine
knife food chopper. Dice celery and
parsley. Dry bread in oven until hard
but not brown. Melt butter and sugar
and add apples, cranberries. Cook 5 to
10 minutes on low heat. Remove from
heat. Add crumbs and seasoning and
mix well. Add chicken bouillon cubes
to mixture to soften bread crumbs. Stuff
each squab and bake in 325 degree oven
for 1 hour.

If you like the apple taste, use more
apples; if you like the tartness of the
cranberries, use a little more. The use
of more cranberries makes for better
taste with dark meat.

TURKEY GOBBLE—UPS

2 Large Avocados
½ Cup Mayonnaise
½ Medium Onion, diced fine
6 English Muffins
12 Slices Monterey Jack Cheese
2 Large Tomatoes, sliced
3 Cups Sliced or Diced Turkey Meat
Butter
Salt
Pepper

Split muffins and butter, place on cookie
sheet under broiler to toast. Mash both
avocados in a mixing bowl, add mayonnaise
and onion, salt and pepper to taste. Spread
avocado paste on each muffin half, add a
slice of tomato and diced or sliced turkey
meat; top with Monterey Jack cheese. Return to oven, set at 400 for 5 to 10 minutes. Turn to broil until cheese bubbles.
Serve piping hot. Variation: Add crisp
crumbled bacon on top of cheese.

CHICKEN TIVOLI

4 Large Chicken Breasts, boned
Salt and Pepper
Flour
Butter

Topping:
¼ Cup Butter
½ Cup Diced Onion
1 Clove Garlic
8 Small Mushrooms, diced
2 Ripe Avocados, peeled and mashed
2 Tbs. Flour
1 Tsp. Celery Salt
½ Tsp. White Pepper
½ Cup Chicken Stock
½ Cup White Wine
2 Egg Yolks, slightly beaten
1¼ Cups Shredded Havarti, Samsoe or
  Jarlsberger Cheese

Salt and pepper halved, boned chicken breasts.
Dredge in flour. Melt ½ cup of butter in large
skillet [MW: browning dish]. Brown breasts
quickly on both sides. Set aside while preparing topping. Melt butter in large saucepan.
Saute' onion, garlic and mushrooms until
onion bits are clear. Discard garlic. Add avocado. Blend all ingredients well, adding flour,
celery salt, shite pepper, chicken stock and
wine. Cook over low heat for 10 min. [MW:
5 min. on low power]. Add 2 tbs. of mixture to egg yolks. Then add eggs to avocado
mixture and let thicken over VERY low heat
3 to 5 minutes [MW: 3 minutes, whisking
every minute], stirring constantly. Remove
from heat and add ½ cup cheese; blend well.
Arrange cooked chicken breasts in baking pan.
Divide hot avocado topping evenly over chicken.
Top with remaining cheese. Place in a 375 degree oven for a few minutes [MW: 5 min. on
full power] until piping hot and cheese is
melted. Excellent with a Riesling or Chablis.

CHICKEN CURRY

2-2½ Lbs. Skinned Chicken Legs and
  Thighs and Boned, Skinned, Split
  Chicken Breasts
3 Tsp. Salt
½ Cup Vegetable Oil
1½ Tsp. Scraped, Finely Chopped Fresh
  Ginger Root
1½ Cups Finely Chopped Onions
1 Tsp. Turmeric
1 Tsp. Ground Cumin
1 Tbs. Finely Chopped Garlic
1 Tsp. Ground Coriander
1 Tsp. (or less) Ground Hot Red Pepper
¼ Tsp. Ground Fennel, or fennel seeds
  pulverized with a mortar and pestle
½ Cup Water
1 Cup Finely Chopped Fresh Tomatoes
  OR 1 Cup Chopped, Drained Canned
  Tomatoes
2 Tbs. Finely Chopped Fresh Coriander
½ Cup Unflavored Yogurt
1 Tsp. Curry Powder
1 Tbs. Fresh Lemon Juice

Pat the chicken pieces dry with paper towels
and sprinkle them with 2 tsp. of salt, In a
heavy 10" to 12" skillet [MW: browning dish],
heat the oil over high heat [MW: full power]
until a drop of water flicked into it sputters
instantly. Add the chicken and fry for 3 to 4
minutes, turning the pieces with a spoon until
they are white and somewhat firm. Transfer
the chicken to a plate.

Add the onions, garlic and ginger to the oil
remaining in the skillet [MW: browning dish]
and, stirring constantly, fry for 7 to 8 min.
[MW: 3-4 min. on full power], or until the
onions are soft and golden brown. Reduce
the heat to low; add the cumin, turmeric,
ground coriander, red pepper, fennel and 1
tbs. water and, stirring constantly, fry for a
minute or so. Stir in the tomatoes, 1 tbs. of
the fresh coriander, the yogurt and the remaining tsp. of salt.

Increase the heat to moderate [MW: medium
power] and add the chicken and any juice
that has accumulated in the plate. Pour in the
remaining water; bring to a boil; meanwhile,
turn the chicken about in the sauce to coat
the pieces evenly. Sprinkle the top with the
curry powder and the remaining tbs. of fresh

coriander; reduce the heat to low. Cover
tightly and simmer for 20 min. [MW: 10 min.],
or until the chicken is tender but not falling
apart.

To serve, arrange the chicken attractively on
a heated platter; pour the sauce remaining in
the skillet over it, & sprinkle with the lemon
juice.

NAPA VALLEY BARBECUED CHICKEN

1 - 3 Lb. Broiler Fryer
Seasoned Flour
¼ Cup Butter or Margarine
1 Cup Catsup
½ Cup Sherry
1/3 Cup Water
2 Tbs. Lemon Juice
1 Medium Onion, minced
1 Tbs. Worcestershire Sauce
2 Tbs. Butter
1 Tbs. Brown Sugar

Coat chicken with seasoned flour. Cook in
hot melted butter in a large skillet [MW:
browning dish] until evenly brown. Remove
to a 2 quart casserole dish. Start heating oven
to 325 degrees. In saucepan, combine catsup
and the next 7 ingredients; bring to a boil.
Pour over chicken. Bake, covered, for 1¼ hrs.
[MW: 30 min. on full power] or until tender.
Serves 4.

WAHENEE CHICKEN

1 Fryer, cut up
1 Pkg. Dry Onion Soup
1 Bottle French Dressing
Pineapple-Apricot Preserves
Pineapple Cubes (optional)
Mushrooms (optional)

Put chicken parts in baking dish; sprinkle dry
onion soup on top. Pour dressing over pieces;
dot with preserves. Marinate at least 2 or 3
hours. Bake in a 300 degree oven for 1 to 1½
hours [MW: 40 min. on full power], depending on how tender the chicken is. Also, baste
occasionally and turn when one side is brown.
Serve on bed of rice or noodles.

ROAST CHICKEN STUFFED WITH SPINACH AND CHEESE

Spinach-Cheese Stuffing:
½ Lb. Fresh Spinach, brown leaves
  and stems removed*
1 Cup Cottage Cheese
1 Egg
¼ Cup Grated Parmesan Cheese
1 Tsp. Salt
Dash Pepper
½ Tsp. Garlic Powder
1 Broiler-Fryer Chicken, about 3 lbs.
2 Tbs. Olive Oil
¼ Tsp. Ground Oregano
¼ Tsp. Ground Thyme
¼ Tsp. Rosemary
½ Tsp. Salt

Place spinach, with just the water which clings to leaves after washing, in saucepan; cover. Cook until soft and done, about 8 min. [MW: 3 min. on full power]. Cool slightly. Squeeze with hands until dry. Chop finely in blender or food mill; set aside. Sieve cottage cheese. Mix cottage cheese, egg, Parmesan cheese, salt, pepper and garlic powder. Stir spinach into egg-cheese mixture. Set aside. Heat oven to 375 degrees. Cut chicken completely down front, splitting breast bone. Remove neck bones. Place chicken skin-side up. Press down with palm of hand to "pop" bones so that chicken will lie flat. Use sharp knife and fingers to loosen skin on chicken to form a pocket between skin and chicken; start from neck edge, making sure skin is never broken or torn. Do not loosen skin covering wings or drumsticks. Place chicken skin-side up in a shallow roasting pan. Stuff pocket formed between skin and body with the spinach-cheese mixture. Press down to distribute evenly. Fold neck skin down to cover the stuffing. Tuck wings under body. Brush chicken with oil; sprinkle with herbs and salt. Roast about 1¼ hrs., [MW: 30 minutes on full power] until skin is crispy brown. Cut chicken lengthwise, then crosswise into fourths to serve.

* 1 - 10 Oz. Pkg. Frozen Spinach may be substituted for the fresh spinach. Cook as directed on package. Makes 4 servings.

PHEASANT and GRAVY

2 - 3 Lb. Pheasants, cut into serving
  pieces
5 Tbs. Olive Oil and Bacon Drippings,
  mixed
1 Large Onion, chopped
2 Tsp. Minced Garlic
1 Can Mushrooms, sliced
1 Can Mushroom Soup
1 Bunch Parsley
4 - 10½ Oz. Cans Bouillon
1 Bay Leaf
½ Cup Flour
½ Cup Water
1 Jar Currant Jelly
Salt and Pepper to taste

Brown pheasants well in oil and bacon drippings in heavy skillet or Dutch oven; add onion and garlic and saute' slightly. Add mushrooms, soup, parsley, bouillon and bay leaf; cover and cook, stirring occasionally, for 2 hours and 30 min., or until pheasant is tender. Combine flour, water and jelly; add to pheasant. Add salt and pepper to taste. Cook until thickened. Yield: 6 to 8 servings.

CURRIED CHICKEN

1 Cup Chopped Onion
1 Cup Chopped Green Pepper
¼ Cup Butter
1 Clove Garlic, crushed
2 Cans Cream of Celery Soup
1 Large Can Evaporated Milk
2 Tsp. Worcestershire Sauce
1 Tbs. Curry Powder
1 Tbs. Finely Chopped Ginger, crystallized
1 Tsp. Salt
2 Tbs. Chopped Pimento
4 Cups Cooked, Cubed Chicken

Saute onion, green pepper and garlic in butter. Stir in soup and evaporated milk until blended. Add remaining ingredients. Cook over low heat, stirring constantly for 15 minutes [MW: use medium power] or until thoroughly heated. Serve over rice with condiments: chutney, crumbled bacon, chopped peanuts, etc. Serves 8.

ROAST CHICKEN WITH WALNUT STUFFING

2 Oz. Butter
1 Onion, grated or finely chopped
2 Sticks Celery, finely chopped
½ Dessert Apple, peeled, cored or chopped
3 Oz. Walnuts, chopped
3 Oz. Fresh White Bread Crumbs
1 Tbs. Worcestershire Sauce
2 Tbs. Chopped Parsley
Salt & Pepper to taste
4½ Lbs. Oven Ready Chicken
¼ Pt. Chicken Stock
2 Tsp. Worcestershire Sauce

Stuffing: Melt butter in pan [MW: casserole] and fry [MW: cook] onion and celery gently for 5 minutes [MW: on low power]. Add apple and fry [MW: cook] for further 3 min. [MW: low power]. Stir in remaining ingredients and season to taste. Use to stuff chest cavity of chicken. Place chicken in roasting pan with stock and Worcestershire sauce. Roast at 400 degrees for 1 hour and 15 min. [MW: 25 min. on full power], or until chicken is cooked. Use juices from roasting pan to make gravy. Serves 4 to 6 people.

CHICKEN SAUTEED IN RIESLING

1-2½ to 3 Lb. Broiler Fryer Chicken, cut-up
Salt and Pepper
2 Tbs. Butter
1 Med. Onion
1 Clove Garlic
1 Bay Leaf
2 Whole Cloves
1 Cup Riesling
½ Cup Water
1 Cup Whipping Cream
2 Tbs. Flour
3 Beaten Egg Yolks
Dash Ground Nutmeg
Salt and Pepper
Hot Cooked Noodles

Sprinkle chicken pieces with salt and pepper. In large 12" skillet [MW: browning dish], slowly brown chicken in the 2 tbs butter for about 10 min. Add onion, garlic, bay leaf, cloves, wine, and water. Bring to boil; reduce heat. Cover and cimmer till chicken is tender, about 30 min. [MW: 20 min. on full power] Remove chicken pieces to platter; keep warm. Discard bay leaf and cloves. Skim excess fat from pan juices. Quickly boil pan juices and onion, uncovered, till reduced to 1¼ cups. Strain juices, discard onion pieces; set aside. Shake together whipping cream and flour. In saucepan, combine whipping cream mixture, pan juices, egg yolks, and nutmeg; cook and stir until thickened but do not boil. Season to taste with salt and pepper. Serve chicken and sauce over hot noodles. Makes 4 servings.

CHICKEN STUFFING CASSEROLE

5 Cups Dressing Cubes
1 Cup Chopped Celery
3 Cups Cooked Chicken, cut up
1 Tbs. Minced Dry Onion
6 Eggs
3 Cans Cream of Chicken Soup
2 Cups Milk
1 Tsp. Poultry Seasoning
½ Cup Flour
¼ Cup Grated Parmesan Cheese
¼ Cup Butter

Combine bread cubes and celery in a greased 9" x 13" baking dish. Place chicken over the above. Sprinkle with onion. Combine eggs, soup, milk, salt, poultry seasoning and pepper in a bowl. Beat eggs slightly with a fork. Pour over chicken, etc., in dish. Combine flour, cheese, and cut in butter; sprinkle over the above. Top with slivered almonds. Bake at 375 degrees for 35 to 40 min. [MW: 15-20 min. on full power], or until knife inserted comes out clean. Makes one 3-quart oblong casserole.

Note: You may choose to use seasoned dressing cubes and omit the poultry seasoning.

RISOTTO

2 Tbs. Oil
2 Tbs. Butter
1 Small Onion, chopped fine
½ Cup Mushrooms, chopped
1 Small Can Tomato Sauce
1 Cup Rice, washed
2½ Cups Chicken Bouillon
½ Cup Grated Parmesan Cheese
½ Tsp. Salt
¼ Tsp. Pepper
¼ Tsp. Nutmeg

Saute' onions and mushrooms in butter and oil until clear, not brown. Add tomato sauce, cook 2 minutes, stirring often. Add rice, cook 2 to 3 minutes, until rice begins to get reddish in color. Add 1 cup bouillon and cook 2 to 3 minutes, stirring constantly, or rice will stick. Add salt, pepper and nutmeg. Add remainder of bouillon and cook 2 minutes. Place in a lightly greased casserole dish. Cover and bake in a 350 degree oven for 30 minutes. Uncover, sprinkle with grated cheese and bake uncovered for 10 more minutes. Makes 4 to 6 servings. A great replacement for potatoes.

ONION DIP CHICKEN

1 Pkg. Dry Onion Dip
2 Cups Rice Krispies, or Corn Flakes
½ Cup Water
2 Tbs. Margarine
Salt to taste
2½ to 3 Lbs. Whole Chicken

Preheat oven to 375 degrees. Mix dry onion dip with ½ cup water to thin gravy consistency. Add more water if too thick. Brush chicken cavity with sauce.

Blend 2 cups corn flakes (or rice krispies) in large bowl with enough of the sauce to moisten.

Melt 2 tbs. butter or margarine and coat outside of chicken. Use remaining butter to cover the bottom of a shallow baking dish.

Stuff chicken with corn flakes and sauce mix. Place chicken in baking dish. Pour remaining onion sauce mix over the chicken. Bake at 375 degrees for 1 hour, or until tender.

For extra flavor, saute' one-half onion, diced, and one-half cup diced celery and add to stuffing. Onion or mushroom gravy may be substituted for dip mix.

GOURMET DUCK (Wild Duck)

1 Duck Breast
1 Small Can Pearl Onions or 1 Medium Onion, diced
½ Lb. Fresh Mushrooms or 1 Medium Can Mushrooms
2 Cubes Butter
Salt, Pepper & Garlic Salt
Dash Cinnamon
1 Tbs. Sugar or less
1 Tbs. Lea & Perrin Sauce
1 Cup Red Wine or Cream Sherry
Cooking Oil (to brown duck slices)

Bone out the breast of the duck with a sharp knife, remove all fatty tissue. (Don't cook the whole breast or it will roll up). Slice in thin slices; pat dry Sprinkle slices with garlic salt, salt and pepper; dust with flour. Sear onion in butter; add mushrooms, until golden brown. Brown duck in oil at high heat, five minutes on each side of slice. Add duck slices to onion and mushrooms. Add dash cinnamon, sugar, Lea & Perrin sauce and wine. Cover and simmer 15 minutes. Serve with rice, green beans and orange and avocado salad, or one of your own choice. Serves 4.

PHEASANT WITH GREEN APPLES AND COINTREAU

1 Pheasant
¼ Lb. Smoked Pork, cut into cubes
1 Small Onion, chopped
1 Garlic Clove, crushed
2 Tbs. Olive Oil
2 Tbs. Butter
5 Green Apples, peeled, cored & cut up
2 or 3 Ounces Cointreau
1 Cup Fresh Table Cream
Salt and Pepper to taste

Saute' the smoked pork, onion and garlic in a heavy frying pan in the butter and oil. When they are well done, remove them and put them to one side. In the same pan, brown the pheasant. Remove from pan and keep warm. Sprinkle apples with cointreau and brown them in the same way. Remove the apples from the pan. Spoon off excess fat from the sauce remaining in the pan; place the pheasant back in the pan, surrounded with the diced pork, apples, garlic and onion. Cook over a very low heat for a few minutes, then add the cream & season with salt and pepper. Bake in a 325 degree oven for 2 hours, or until meat is tender. Strain the sauce, which is quite thick by now, and pour it over the pheasant before serving. Serves 3 to 4.

HIGHLAND CHICKEN

2 Roasting Chickens
1 Cup Drambuie
¼ Cup Lemon Juice
Grated Rind of 1 Lemon
¼ Lb. Margarine, melted
2 Tbs. Soy Sauce
¼ Tsp. Salt
Dash of Pepper

Wash chicken and pat dry. Combine Drambuie, lemon juice, rind, butter, soy sauce & seasonings. Roast chicken at 375 degrees for 3 hours, or until tender and browned. Baste with Drambuie sauce every 15 minutes. Or place chicken on rotisserie. Cook over low speed, basting every 15 minutes, for 2 hours. Makes 12 portions.

CHICKEN PAPRIKA with DROP NOODLES

1 - 2 to 3 Lb. Frying Chicken
1 Quart Water
3 Parsley Sprigs
1 Bay Leaf
2 Large Onions
2 Tbs. Paprika Powder
Salt to taste
1 Cup Sour Cream
1 Clove Garlic
1 Fresh Green Pepper
2 Small Tomatoes

Noodles:
2 Quarts Water, boiling
2 Tsp. Salt
2-1/3 Cups Sifted Flour
1 Egg, slightly beaten
1 Cup Water

Fry the sliced onions with paprika powder, garlic and salt until golden brown. Add the sliced pepper and the sliced tomatoes with the cut-up chicken, bay leaf and hot water. Cover the pan; reduce heat and let it simmer for 45 minutes. Mix 1 tbs. flour and sour cream, then blend in the chicken and sauce. Stir it well. Serve with drop noodles.

Noodles: Bring 2 quarts water and 2 tsp. salt to boil. Sift flour and salt together. Combine in a bowl and mix 1 egg and 1 cup water. Gradually add flour mixture to egg mixture, stirring until it is smooth. Batter should be very thick and break from a spoon. Spoon batter into the boiling water by half teaspoonfuls, dipping spoon into water each time. Cook only one layer of noodles at one time. After noodles rise to the surface, boil gently 5 to 8 minutes. Remove from water with slotted spoon, draining over water for a second & place into a warm bowl. Toss noodles lightly with butter. Place chicken onto a platter and put noodles on, too. Cover with sauce. Sprinkle with paprika and garnish with parsley. Try it with a glass of gray risling wine mixed with sparkling soda, makes a delicious evening at home.

SCALLOPS NEWBURG

1 Lb. Scallops
3 Tbs. Butter
1 Tsp. Lemon Juice
1 Tsp. Flour
½ Cup Cream
2 Egg Yolks
2 Tbs. Sherry
½ Lb. Mushrooms
Salt
Cayenne

Slice mushrooms and clean scallops and cut in half. Cook 3 minutes with 2 tbs. butter; add 1 tsp. lemon juice. Cook 1 minute and set aside. Blend 1 tbs. butter, 1 tsp. flour and ½ cup cream in a sauce pan over low heat. Stir constantly over low to medium heat and bring to boiling point. Add 2 egg yolks, slightly beaten, & 2 tbs. sherry; add the scallops and mushrooms. Reduce heat & stir well. If the mixture curdles from over-cooking, add a little milk & stir till smooth again. Season to taste with salt and cayenne. Serve over rice. Serves 2 generously.

LOBSTER BISQUE DELUXE

2 Cups Brown Stock, Canned Consomme'
  or Water
¼ Cup Rice
2 Tbs. Butter or Olive Oil
1 Carrot, sliced
1 Onion, sliced
1 Bit of Bay Leaf
½ Tsp. Thyme
1½ Lbs. Fresh Lobster, or 2 small ones
1 Tsp. Salt
¼ Tsp. Pepper
1 Cup Dry White Wine, or
  ½ Cup Sherry
2 Cups Chicken Stock or Canned Chicken
  Broth
1 Tbs. Tomato Paste
1 Cup Cream
Croutons or Parsley

Put into a deep kettle the 2 cups of brown stock. Cook rice until very soft. Do not drain. In another pan put butter or olive oil. Put in 1 carrot and 1 onion and cook slowly 5 minutes; add bay leaf and thyme. Add lobster; cover and cook until lobster shells are red. Add salt, pepper and wine. Cook slowly 15 minutes; add 2 cups of chicken stock. Remove the lobster; strain the broth. Take lobster out of shells and set a-side. Scrape the shells and break them up to get out all the meat. Put shells and strained broth into a pan; cover and simmer 1 hr., or 10 minutes in a pressure pan [MW: 45 min. on full power]. Strain and add to the rice. Add the lobster meat, cut small, and 2 cups chicken broth. Put in a small pan 1 tbs. butter or olive oil, 1 tbs. tomato paste, lobster liver (if any); stir over low heat until smooth. Add slowly to the soup. Heat just before serving and add 1 cup cream. Season. Sprinkle with croutons or chopped parsley. Serves 8 to 10.

LOUISIANA SHRIMP BAKE

1 Cup Sliced Celery
1 Medium Sliced Onion
½ Cup Chopped Green Pepper
¼ Cup Butter or Margarine
¼ Cup All-Purpose Flour
½ Tsp. Salt
1 - 1 Lb. Can Tomatoes, cut up
7 Oz. Fresh or Frozen Shrimp
¼ Cup Cooking Sherry
1¼ Cups Cheddar Cheese, shredded
4 Hard-Cooked Eggs
3 Cups Rice

Saute' the celery, onion, green pepper and the butter in a medium saucepan [MW: glass] for about 5 minutes. Blend in the flour and salt. Cook until bubbly. Stir in tomatoes, shrimp and sherry. Bring to a boil and simmer covered for 10 minutes. Stir in ½ cup of cheddar cheese and the eggs (crumbled or sliced). Pour into a 2-quart casserole dish. Top with rice and sprinkle with the remaining 1 cup cheese. Bake at 375 degrees for 20 to 30 minutes [MW: 10-15 min. on full power]. Serves 6 to 8 people.

BUDIN DE CENTOLLA (Crab Pudding)

3 Tbs. Butter
1 Tbs. Finely Chopped Shallots or Onions
¼ Cup Flour
2 Cups Light Cream
2 Egg Yolks
12 Oz. Fresh, Canned or Frozen Crab Meat, picked over to remove all bits of shell and cartilage
1/8 Tsp. Ground Nutmeg
Pinch of Cayenne Pepper
½ Lb. Thinly Sliced Muenster Cheese
3 Egg Whites
1 Tsp. Salt
¼ Tsp. White Pepper
2 Tbs. Freshly Grated Parmesan Cheese

Preheat oven to 350 degrees. In a 2 to 3 qt. enameled or stainless steel saucepan, melt the butter over moderate heat. When the foam subsides, stir in the shallots or onions and cook for several minutes. Do not let them brown. Stir in the flour and cook, stirring constantly, for a minute or two. Slowly pour in the cream, stirring constantly with a whisk. Then over high heat, cook, stirring, until the sauce thickens and comes to a boil; reduce the heat and simmer slowly for 2 minutes to remove any taste of raw flour. One at a time, beat the egg yolks into the sauce. Then bring the sauce to a boil, stirring constantly, and boil for 30 seconds. Remove from heat, stir in the crab meat, nutmeg & cayenne. Lightly butter the bottom & sides of a 2 quart casserole or souffle dish, and spoon in half the crab mixture. Spread with half the cheese slices, then spoon in the rest of the crab mixture and cover with the remaining cheese.

In a large bowl, beat the egg whites, salt & pepper with a whisk or a rotary or electric beater until they form unwavering peaks on the beater when it is lifted out of the bowl. Gently spread the whites over the sliced cheese and sprinkle the top with the grated cheese. Bake in the middle of the oven for 25 minutes, or until the meringue is golden. Serve at once. Serves 4.

SHRIMP TEMPURA

1 Lb. Shrimp, large
Batter:
1 Cup Flour
1 Cup Corn Starch
1 2/3 Cup Cold Water
1 Egg
Salt to taste
¼ Tsp. Baking Powder

Butterfly Shrimp: Leave tails on, peel shell off, make knife cut from tail to mid-section. Open and flatten with knife. Mix ingredients for batter. Let stand 10 minutes. Dip shrimp in batter and fry in ½" hot oil. To make lacy tempura, use fingers to spray batter on top of shrimp in oil. Turn after 3 minutes. Serve on shredded lettuce with fresh lemon. This is a favorite island recipe from home-Hawaii!

SALMON, COLD BOILED

3 Lbs. Fresh Salmon
1 Quart Court* Bouillon
1 Cup Mayonnaise
½ Tsp. Curry Powder

*For "Bouillon"
1 Quart Water
2 Medium Onions
1 Small Carrot
2 Leaves from Celery Stalk Tops
½ Tsp. Pepper
2 Tsp. Salt
1 Pinch Rosemary, Marjoram, Tarragon and Basil
1 Bay Leaf

Boil all bouillon ingredients together for 20 minutes. Then add whatever fish you want to boil.

Place salmon in kettle [MW: casserole] and cover with court bouillon. Bring to a boil and reduce flame. Simmer for 15 to 20 min. [MW: 5-10 min.], or until flesh is firm but leaves the bones. Remove and chill. When cold, place in refrigerator for at least 2 hours; serve with mayonnaise mixed with curry powder.

This is particularly good on hot days when you can't bear to eat hot foods or be in the kitchen for longer than is absolutely necessary.

NEW ENGLAND CLAM CHOWDER

2 - 3 Slices Salt Pork
4 Potatoes
1 Small Onion
1 Pt. Clams
1½ Cups Evaporated Milk
Walnut-size Butter

Fry out bacon or salt pork and add potatoes cut in small cubes. Add onion if desired, salt and pepper; add clams. Add water to cover. Let cook until tender. Add butter and evaporated milk. Same recipe can be used substituting scallops for clams.

WILD RICE SHRIMP BAYOU

1 - 6 Oz. Pkg. Uncle Ben's Long
   Grain & Wild Rice
1 - 6½ Oz. Can Sliced Mushrooms
1 Tbs. Butter or Margarine
1 Tbs. Flour
¼ Tsp. Salt
¼ Tsp. Pepper
¾ Cup Milk
1 - 3 Oz. Pkg. Cream Cheese,
   softened
1 - 6½ Oz. Can Medium Shrimp,
   drained
1 - 15 Oz. Can Asparagus Spears,
   drained OR 1 Bunch Fresh Asparagus
   Spears, cooked till tender

Cook rice according to package instructions. Meanwhile, make sauce by melting butter over low heat. Mix in flour, salt and pepper; when bubbly, remove from heat. Stir in milk. Cook over medium heat [MW: medium power]; stirring constantly, until thickened. Cook 1 min. longer. Add cream cheese; stir with wire whip until smooth. Arrange asparagus spears on bottom of 2½ quart casserole. Mix shrimp and mushrooms with rice and spoon over asparagus. Top with sauce. Bake at 350 degrees for 10 minutes [MW: 7 min. on full power]. Makes 4 to 6 servings.

FRENCH FRIED SHRIMP

First Mixture:
½ Cup Flour
½ Tsp. Paprika
½ Tsp. Salt
½ Tsp. Black Pepper

Second Mixture:
½ Cup Pancake Flour
¼ Tsp. Cayenne Pepper
½ Tsp. Cinnamon
½ Tsp. Allspice

1 Lb. Large Shrimp or Prawns

Add all ingredients for the first mixture in a paper bag and shake well. Devein and split shrimp down center back, not cutting completely through the skin.

Prepare second mixture by adding enough water to form a medium mixture. First shake the shrimp in dry mixture, then in the batter and fry in deep, hot oil until nicely brown.

"ABALONE RELLENOS"

1 Abalone, sliced & pounded
3 Beaten Eggs
½ Can Beer
Cracker Meal or Dried French Bread
   Crumbs
1 Can Ortega Sauce, mild (Green Chile
   Salsa)
½ to 1 Lb. Mozzarella Cheese, shredded
Onions, chopped

Mix beer into beaten eggs. Put sliced abalone into beer mixture. Put cracker meal on both sides. Lay abalone flat & fill across center with spoonfuls of Ortega sauce, onions and cheese. Roll up abalone and seal closed with a toothpick. Fry in ½ to 1 inch of oil [MW: cook in browning dish]. Make sure oil is real hot. Fry abalone just until browned on all sides. Then remove and place them into a casserole dish as they come out of the oil. Keep them warm in oven set on low until they are browned enough for whatever size serving you need for your meal. Happy Eating!

CRAB CREPES LOUIS

1 Lb. Crabmeat
15 Water Chestnuts (chopped)
4 Tbs. Butter
1 Medium Onion
3 Tbs. Chopped Chives
5 Tbs. Chopped Parsley
1 Clove Garlic, minced
2½ Tsp. Salt
3 Tbs. Catsup
2 Cups Milk
1 Tsp. Black Pepper
Few Drops Tabasco Sauce to taste

Cheese Sauce:
5 Tbs. Butter
5 Tbs. Flour
1½ Cups Milk
½ Cup Sherry

Crepes:
4 Eggs
¼ Tsp. Salt
2 Cups Flour
2¼ Cups Milk
¼ Cup Melted Butter

Saute garlic, onion and chestnuts in butter. Add remaining ingredients. Bring to a boil: Add 4 tbs. cornstarch mixed with ¼ c. sherry. Cook until thick and bubbling. Cool. Fill crepes with cold filling. Put thin layer of sauce in casserole, then crepes, remainder of sauce and sprinkle with Parmesan, cover and bake 45 minutes at 400 degrees. Remove cover and put under broiler to brown.

Cheese Sauce: After cheese sauce is cooked, add 2 well beaten egg yolks, 4 ozs. Gruyere cheese, small pieces, 5 tbs. Parmesan cheese, 1 tsp. salt and ½ tsp. pepper.

Crepes: Combine ingredients in blender jar. Blend for about 1 minute, scrape down sides with rubber spatula and blend for another 15 seconds until smooth. Refrigerate batter for at least one hour.

Crepes: It is not necessary to grease pans having non-stick coating, others should be brushed with oil or butter. Heat pan over medium-high heat. With one hand pour in 2 or 3 tbs. batter. At same time, lift pan above heating unit with other hand. Immediately tilt pan in all directions, swirling batter to cover bottom in thin layer. Return to heating unit and cook over medium heat until bottom is browned. Turn with plastic spatula, cook a few seconds, stack on plate. May be made ahead and frozen. Separate with wax paper. Use upside down or traditional pan.

DEVILED EGG—STUFFED FLOUNDER ROLLS

4 Fresh or Frozen Flounder Fillets
 (about 16 oz.)
Salt and Pepper
3 Hard-cooked Eggs, chopped
2 Tbs. Snipped Parsley
2 Tbs. Mayonnaise
1½ Tsp. Dijon-style Mustard
1 - 10 Oz. Pkg. Frozen, Chopped
 Broccoli, thawed
2 Cups Cooked Long-grain Rice
1 Can Condensed Cream of Shrimp
 Soup
½ Cup Dry White Wine

Thaw fillets, if frozen. Sprinkle each fillet with salt and pepper. Combine chopped egg, parsley, mayonnaise and mustard. Spoon 3 to 4 tbs. of the egg mixture atop each fillet. Roll up lengthwise. If necessary, secure with wooden picks. Combine broccoli and rice. In bowl, stir together soup and wine. Stir 1 cup of the soup mixture into rice mixture. Turn rice mixture into 1½-quart round au gratin dish or a 10″ x 6″ x 2″ baking dish. Place fish rolls atop rice. Pour remaining soup mixture over rolls. Cover with foil [MW: plastic wrap]; bake in 375 degree oven for 25 minutes [MW: 12 minutes on full power]. Uncover; bake 20 to 25 minutes more [MW: 10 min. on full power], or till fish flakes easily. Makes 4 servings.

CRABMEAT & MUSHROOM BISQUE

6 Tbs. Butter or Margarine
4 Tbs. Finely Chopped Onion
4 Tbs. Finely Chopped Green Pepper
1 Scallion, finely chopped
2 Tbs. Chopped Parsley
1 Cup Sliced Fresh Mushrooms
2 Tbs. Flour
1½ Cups Milk
1 Tsp. Salt
1/8 Tsp. Pepper
¼ Tsp. Ground Mace
Dash Tabasco
1 Cup Half & Half
1½ Cups Cooked Crabmeat, or 2 - 6 Oz.
  Pkgs. Frozen Crabmeat, thawed
3 Tbs. Dry Sherry

In medium skillet [MW: glass casserole], heat 4 tbs. butter. Add the onion, green pepper, scallion, parsley & the mushrooms. Saute' until soft but not brown; set aside. In large saucepan, heat remaining 2 tbs. butter, remove from heat. Stir in the flour and gradually add milk. Cook, stirring constantly, until thickened and smooth. Stir in salt, pepper, mace and tabasco. Add sauteed' vegetables and Half & Half. Bring to boiling, stirring constantly. Reduce heat and add crabmeat. Simmer, uncovered, 5 min. [MW: 3 min. on low power, stir once or twice]. Just before serving, stir in sherry. Makes 4 servings.

HALIBUT PARMIGIANA

2 Eggs, beaten
¾ Tsp. Salt
Pepper
¾ Cup Bread Crumbs
1/3 Cup Grated Parmesan Cheese
2 Lbs. Halibut Steaks
1/3 Cup Olive Oil
1 - 8 Oz. Can Tomato Sauce
2 Tbs. Dry Red Wine
¼ Cup Sliced Olives
¼ Tsp. Basil
1 Clove Garlic, crushed
Sliced Mozzarella Cheese

Beat eggs with ½ tsp. salt and ¼ tsp. pepper. Combine bread crumbs and Parmesan cheese. Dip halibut steaks in egg mixture; drain slightly, then dip in crumb mixture. Heat olive oil in skillet [MW: browning dish] ; add halibut steaks & cook until browned on each side. Remove to a shallow baking dish. Combine tomato sauce, wine, olives, basil, ¼ tsp. salt, garlic and a dash of pepper. Spoon over halibut. Place triangles of mozzarella cheese on top. Place under broiler until cheese is melted and bubbly. [MW; until cheese is melted however cheese will not brown]. Makes 6 servings.

SEAFOOD THERMIDOR

1 Lb. Fresh or Frozen Cod Fillets
1 Small Onion, quartered
1 Lemon Slice
1 Can Condensed Cream of Shrimp Soup
3 Tbs. All-Purpose Flour
¼ Cup Milk
¼ Cup Dry White Wine
¼ Cup Shredded Mozzarella Cheese
2 Tbs. Snipped Parsley
½ Cup Soft Bread Crumbs
2 Tbs. Grated Parmesan Cheese
2 Tsp. Butter or Margarine
½ Tsp. Paprika

Thaw frozen fish; skin if necessary. Cut into ½ inch cubes. Place fish, onion and lemon in greased skillet [MW: prepare fish in browning dish and follow directions making sure to stir often]. Add water to cover. Bring to boiling; reduce heat and simmer, covered, 5 to 6 min., or until fish flakes easily. Meanwhile, in a small saucepan, blend soup and flour; gradually stir in milk and wine. Cook and stir until thickened and bubbly. Stir in the mozzarella cheese and parsley. Heat through. Carefully drain fish well; fold into sauce. Spoon into 4 coquille shells or if you prefer, a medium casserole dish. Combine bread crumbs, parmesan cheese, butter or margarine and paprika. Sprinkle over sauce. Broil 1 to 2 minutes. Makes 4 servings.

P.S. Sometimes I add thawed frozen crabmeat to this dish. This gives it even more of a rich flavor.

FILLET OF SOLE

6 Fillets of Sole (½ Lb. ea.)
1 Lb. Butter
3 Shallots, finely chopped
1 Tbs. Parsley, chopped
1 Tsp. Tarragon, crushed
1 Cup of Fresh, Fine Bread Crumbs
¼ Tsp. Salt
White Pepper to taste
1½ Cups Dry Vermouth
½ Lemon
½ Lb. Sliced Mushrooms
2 Tbs. Sliced Toasted Almonds

Rinse fillets of sole under cold running water and pan dry on paper towels. In a large ovenware dish, melt ¾ cup butter in a 300 degree oven. Remove dish from oven and sprinkle shallots and herbs over the bottom. Meanwhile increase oven temperature to 425 degrees. In a separate shallow skillet, melt ½ cup butter. Dip one side of each fillet into the melted butter and then into bread crumbs. Place sole, breaded-side up, in the hot ovenware dish. Season with salt and pepper. Add enough dry vermouth to half submerge the fish without wetting the crumb topping. Dribble another ½ cup melted butter over the fillets. Place in a hot 425 degree oven and cook until brown, about 30 minutes. While fillets are cooking, saute' the ½ pound of sliced mushrooms in a little of the extra melted butter. Remove fillets from oven and place on a hot serving dish. Garnish with a bit of chopped parsley and the toasted almonds. Reduce the juice in the pan the fillets were cooked in, to about 4 to 5 tbs. over medium-high heat. Remove from heat and stir in remaining ¼ cup butter, swirling pan to obtain a light, frothy sauce. Add a squeeze of lemon. Check seasonings. Add sauteéd mushrooms to sauce. Pour some sauce around the fillets and serve the additional sauce in a warmed gravy boat for those who would like more sauce.

Note: One pound of butter is the correct amount. The large quantity of butter keeps the fish moist and gives the sauce the desired consistency. Enjoy!

SEAFOOD BAKE

1 Can Cream of Mushroom Soup
1/3 Cup Mayonnaise
1/3 Cup Milk
6 Oz. Can Drained Shrimp
7 Oz. Can Drained Crab
5 Oz. Can Drained Water Chestnuts
1 Cup Diced Celery
2 Tsp. Grated Onion
1 Tbs. Monosodium Glutamate
2 Cups Cooked Rice
1½ Cups Fresh Bread Crumbs
3 Tbs. Melted Butter

Combine all in a 2 qt. casserole. Combine bread crumbs and melted butter. Sprinkle on top. Bake at 350 for 1 hr. [MW: 15 min. on full power].

OVEN—FRIED OYSTERS with TARTAR SAUCE

1 Dozen Oysters
1 Cup Flour
1 Tsp. Salt
¼ Tsp. Pepper
1 or 2 Eggs
Bread Crumbs
Salad Oil

Tartar Sauce:
1 Cup Mayonnaise
1 Tsp. Scraped Onion
1 Tsp. Minced Parsley
1 Tbs. Minced Dill Pickle
1 Tsp. Chopped Pimiento

Blend the flour, salt and pepper together. Roll the oysters in the flour mixture then dip them in the slightly-beaten egg. Roll the oysters in bread crumbs. Place in a shallow pan, having sprinkled both sides of oysters with salad oil. Bake in 400 degree oven until browned, about 15 min.

Tartar Sauce: Combine mayonnaise, scraped onion (or green onions or chives), minced parsley, minced dill pickle and chopped pimiento. Can delete parsley and pimiento when not available.

LOBSTER DESIREE'

1 Cup Packed, Chopped Parsley
1 Medium-size Onion, chopped
3 Tbs. Olive Oil or Salad Oil
1 Clove Garlic, mashed
2 - 8 Oz. Cans Tomato Sauce
2 - 6 Oz. Cans Tomato Paste
1 - 1 Lb. 12 Oz. Can Pear-shaped
   Italian Tomatoes
½ Cup Dry Red Wine
½ Tsp. Salt
1 Tsp. Oregano Leaves
1 Tsp. Basil Leaves
1 Tsp. Rosemary
½ Tsp. Pepper
½ Tsp. Sugar
1 Lb. Fresh Mushrooms, sliced
¾ Lb. Teleme Cheese
4 Large, Cooked Lobster Tails,
   cut into bite-size pieces

In large saucepan, heat oil and add parsley, onion and garlic. Cook, stirring, until onions are soft. Stir in tomato sauce, tomato paste and tomatoes, breaking up tomatoes with fork. Add also the tomato liquid, wine, salt, oregano, basil, rosemary, pepper, sugar and mushrooms. Cook over low heat, stirring occasionally, for 1½ hrs.

In bottom of casserole, cover with sauce. Alternate sauce, lobster pieces and teleme cheese, ending with teleme cheese. Bake in 450 degree oven for 7-10 min. [MW: 4-5 min. on full power] or until cheese melts. Serve at once. Makes 4 servings.

LOUISIANA GUMBO

2 Whole Crabs, cooked and cracked
1 Cup Shrimp
2 Dozen Oysters
1 Lb. Smoked Sausage
1/3 Cup Vegetable Oil
1 Cup Flour
1 Onion
1 Bay Leaf
2 Quarts Water
Gumbo Fillet, optional

Make gravy, brown flour lightly in salad oil. Add minced onions and saute' until tender, add water slowly and stir until smooth. Cut sausage into small pieces. Break crab into small pieces. Add sausage, crab and shrimp, also bay leaf. Season to taste with salt and pepper. Add oysters and cook until edges of oysters curl. Add gumbo fillet if used. Makes 1 gallon.

CIOPPINO

4 Dungeness or Rock Crabs
12 to 18 Clams, in the shell
1 - 2 Lbs. Fish Fillets
1 - 2 Lbs. Shrimp, peeled
1 Lb. Scallops
1 Lb. Oysters
Squid, Abalone and assorted
   seafood

1 Cup Onion, chopped coarsely
1 Cup Parsley
1 Cup Green Pepper Pieces
2 Garlic Cloves, chopped
½ Cup Olive Oil
1 Can Tomatoes, No. 2½ size
6 Cans Tomato Sauce
2 Cups Wine (dry white or red)
1 Tsp. Italian Seasoning
½ Tsp. Oregano, crushed
Salt and Pepper to taste

In a large, deep pot cook onion, parsley, green pepper and garlic in olive oil for a few minutes. Add tomatoes, tomato sauce, Italian seasoning, oregano, salt & pepper and simmer 30 minutes, with lid on. Add crab, broken into sections; clams, cut-up fish fillets; scallops and assorted shellfish and wine. Cover and simmer for 15 to 20 minutes. If too tomatoey, add a cup or two of water. Serve in large soup bowls with warm sourdough bread. Serves 6.

OLD WORLD CIOPPINO

1 Large Onion, sliced
1 Bunch Green Onions, sliced
1 Diced Green Pepper, seeded
½ Cup Chopped Parsley
4 Minced Cloves Garlic
1 Cup Chopped Celery
1/3 Cup Olive oil
1 Can (1 Lb.) Tomato Puree
1 Can (8 Oz.) Tomato Sauce
1 Cup Water
2 Cups White or Red Wine
½ Tsp. Sugar
1 Bay Leaf
3 Tbs. Salt
½ Tsp. Pepper
¼ Tsp. Tabasco
¼ Tsp. Rosemary
¼ Tsp. Thyme
2 Dungeness Crabs
12 Large Shrimp
12 Clams, in shell
12 Oysters, in shell
2 Lobster Tails
White Fish, if available

In Dutch oven saute onion, green pepper, garlic and celery in olive oil for 5 minutes. Add remaining ingredients, simmer for 1 hour. In bottom of large kettle place 2 cracked Dungeness crabs, shrimp, clams, oysters, lobster tails and white fish. Pour on hot prepared sauce. Cover and simmer until clams and oyster shells open, 10 to 15 minutes. Serve with green salad, bread and wine.

STUFFED SOLE

2 Tbs. Butter
½ Tsp. Seasoned Salt
1 Tsp. Lemon Juice
¼ Tsp. Horseradish
5 Drops Tabasco Sauce
1/3 Cup Heavy Whipping Cream
1 Can Crab OR ½ Lb. Fresh Crab
4 Fillet of Sole

Melt butter; add salt, lemon juice, Tabasco and horseradish. Blend in cream. Bring to a boil; cook and stir. Remove from heat; add crab. Butter a baking dish; layer fillet of sole, then crab mixture. Top with sole. Pour topping of parsley, melted butter and lemon over fish. Refrigerate before cooking. Bake at 350 degrees for 30 minutes [MW: 7 to 10 minutes on full power].

FINNAN HADDIE NILETA

1½ Lbs. Finnan Haddie
½ Pkg. (5 Oz.) Macaroni Bow Ties
1½ Cups Grated Sharp Cheddar Cheese
1 Large Onion, sliced thin
½ Cup Celery, sliced thin
½ Cup Green Pepper, sliced thin
4 Cloves Garlic, minced
2 Cups Milk
½ Cup Butter or Margarine
¼ Cup Flour

1. Place finnan haddie in pan and cover with boiling water. Let sit while you are preparing sauce.

2. Saute' onion, celery, green pepper in the butter until soft but not brown.

3. Add garlic and saute' ½ minute more.

4. Add flour and mix thoroughly.

5. Add milk gradually to make a thick sauce.

6. Add cheese and remove from heat.

7. Cook and drain the macaroni.

8. Break fish into bite-size pieces, removing any bones; discard liquid.

9. Combine the sauce, macaroni, fish in 3-quart casserole. Sprinkle with additional grated cheese. Bake in 350 degree oven for 20 min. to ½ hr. [MW: 5-6 min. on full power] until bubbly. Serves 4.

FISHERMAN'S PRAWNS

2½ Lbs. Raw Jumbo Prawns
¼ Cup Olive Oil
1 Tsp. Salt
1 Tsp. Leaf Oregano
1 Clove Garlic, finely chopped
1/3 Cup Prepared Horseradish
¾ Cup Dry White Wine
3 Oz. Lemon Juice
½ Cup Orange Marmalade

Shell, clean and devein prawns. Rinse well, drain on paper towels. Combine remaining ingredients, place prawns in a 13 x 9 inch pyrex dish, cover with marinade, refrigerate 2 or more hours. Preheat a large shallow casserole with enough of the marinade to cover the bottom of dish. Add prawns. Broil for 3 or 4 min. or until prawns are tender. [MW: when recipe says broil use microwave for 5-7 minutes and stir prawns to rearrange for even cooking - will not get a crispy brown]. Do not overcook. Serves 8. Serve with buttered rice, green salad, sourdough French bread and your favorate wine.

RED SNAPPER VICTORIA

1½ to 2 Lbs. Red Snapper Filets
1 - 15 Oz. Can Tomato Sauce
1 - 16 Oz. Can Stewed Tomatoes
1 Medium Onion, chopped
2 Stalks Celery, sliced
1 Bell Pepper, chopped
2 Carrots, sliced
1 Tsp. Oregano
1 Tsp. Garlic Salt
½ Tsp. Basil
Salt and Pepper to taste
2 Tbs. Oil (olive or vegetable)
1 Clove Garlic, pressed

Saute' garlic lightly in oil; add vegetables and saute' until onion is tender. Add tomato sauce and stewed tomatoes; sprinkle all with seasonings. Cover and simmer for 10 min. [MW: 5 min.] to blend flavors. Add snapper fillets, cut into serving-size portions. Bring to boil; lower heat and simmer for 15 min. [MW: 7 min.] or until fish is firm and flakes with a fork. Serves 4 generously. Good with Victoria's Cheese Bread and a green salad.

Victoria's Cheese Bread: Simply spread 1 loaf French bread (split lengthwise) with 1 cube soft butter, blended with 2 cloves pressed garlic. Top with 1 cup shredded Mozzarella cheese, 1 cup shredded cheddar cheese, 3 green onions (chopped fine) and a generous sprinkling of Parmesan cheese. Broil 4 to 6 inches from heat until cheese bubbles and browns slightly.

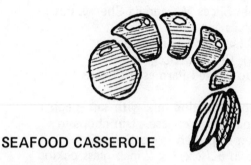

SEAFOOD CASSEROLE

6 Oz. Firm White Fish
6 Oz. Scallops
6 Oz. Green Shrimp, uncooked
1 Clove Garlic
2 Tbs. Clarified Butter
2 Tbs. Olive Oil
½ Cup Chablis (white)
½ Cup 100% Cream
2 Tsp. Dijon Mustard
1 Tbs. Fresh Lemon Juice
2 Tbs. Parsley
2 Tbs. Arrowroot or Cornstarch
Dill
Cayenne
Salt and Pepper

Slice white fish into slivers; cut shrimp into pieces and scallops into halves. Peel garlic clove. Measure in butter, chablis, cream and lemon juice. Mix arrowroot with a little white wine and the dijon mustard. Now assemble.

1. Place clarified butter and olive oil in pan and, when hot, add fish, shrimp & scallops. Fry quickly; cover and simmer 5 minutes.

2. Add crushed garlic, chablis and lemon juice. Stir to combine. Add arrowroot mixture to thicken the sauce and then add the parsley. Season. Add the cream and then sprinkle with dill and cayenne. Delicious!

MICROWAVE VEAL PARMIGIANO

1 - 2 Oz. Pkg. Coating Mixture For
    Pork
1 Tsp. Salt
¼ Tsp. Pepper
¼ Cup Grated Parmesan Cheese
6 Small Veal Loin Chops, ¾ inch
    thick
1 Egg, beaten
3 Thin Slices Mozzarella Cheese, cut in
    halves
2 - 8 Oz. Cans Tomato Sauce
1 Tsp. Crushed Oregano
¼ Cup Grated Parmesan Cheese

Combine coating mix with salt, pepper
and parmesan cheese. Dip chops in
beaten egg, then in coating mixture.
Place in a 12 x 7 x 2 inch glass baking
dish. Cover with wax paper. Place in
microwave oven and bake at full power
for 10 minutes. Place half-slice of
mozzarella cheese on each chop. Blend
tomato sauce and oregano, pour over
chops. Sprinkle with parmesan cheese.
Recover with wax paper and continue to
bake for 6 to 9 more minutes. Makes 6
servings.

VEAL CHOPS MONARGUE

4 Loin or Rib Veal Chops
¼ Cup Clarified Butter
1 Cup (¼ lb.) Mushrooms, finely chopped
½ Cup Grated Gruyere Cheese
Salt
Black Pepper, freshly ground
½ Cup Stock
½ Pkg. (½ lb.) Conchiglie (small pasta shells)
1 Tbs. Butter
2 Slices of cooked Ham, cut in strips
¼ Cup Port

Set the oven at hot (400° F). In a skillet or
shallow flameproof casserole heat 2 tbs.
clarified butter and fry the chops slowly on
1 side only until golden brown; take from
the pan. Add the mushrooms and cook over
high heat until all the moisture is evaporated.
Take from heat and stir in the cheese.

Season to taste and spread this mixture on
the browned side of the chops. Melt the remaining clarified butter in the pan, replace
the chops and brown the uncooked sides for
2-3 minutes. Pour in the stock and cover;
transfer pan to heated oven and bake the
chops for 15-20 minutes or until they are
tender.

Cook the conchiglie in plenty of simmering
salted water for the time stated on the
package or until almost tender ('al dente').
Drain them, rinse with cold water and reheat
them with 1 tbs. butter, the strips of ham
and plenty of pepper, tossing to mix well.
Take out the chops, arrange in a serving dish
and keep warm. Add the port to the pan and
bring to a boil, stirring to dissolve the pan
juices. Boil until well reduced. Strain the
sauce over the chops and garnish the platter
with ham and conchiglie.

VEAL JULIENNE

1½ Lbs. Veal, cut in Julienne strips
4 Tbs. Margarine
½ Cup Water
1 Tsp. Basil
1 Cup Thinly-Sliced Onions
1 - 6 Oz. Can Drained Mushrooms or
    Fresh Mushrooms
1 - 15 Oz. Can Special Tomato Sauce
1 Tsp. Worcestershire Sauce
Few Drops Hot Pepper Sauce
½ Cup Dry Sherry
1 Cup Sour Cream
1 Medium Green Pepper, diced
Salt & Pepper

In 2 tbs. margarine, brown meat; stir
often to prevent burning. Add water
and basil; simmer 20 minutes. Meanwhile, cook pepper and onion in remaining 2 tbs. margarine until soft, but not
brown; add to meat with mushrooms
and tomato sauce; mix well. Simmer 15
minutes longer. Stir in hot pepper sauce,
salt, pepper and sherry. Simmer 5 minutes at low heat. Stir in sour cream
slowly. Serve with cooked rice. Makes
6 servings.

SHISK KEBOB

¼ Cup Lemon Juice
¼ Cup Vinegar
1½ Tsp. Salt
1 Tsp. Pepper
2 - 3 Bay Leaves
Pinch of Oregano
½ Tsp. Sage
½ Tsp. Rosemary
½ Tsp. Thyme
3 Cloves Garlic, pressed
¼ - ½ Cup Oil
2 - 3 Cups Red Wine
5 - 6 Lbs. Lean Lamb, cut in 2" cubes
1 Large Onion, chopped
Small Onions
Cherry Tomatoes
1 Bell Pepper, cut in 1" Squares
Mushrooms, fresh if possible

Mix lemon juice, vinegar, salt, pepper, bay leaves, oregano, sage, rosemary, thyme, garlic, oil, and wine. Bring to a quick boil and simmer 2 min. Pour mixture over lamb, onion, and pressed barlic. Leave overnight to marinate. Skewer meat and vegetables separately as meat will require a bit more cooking. Baste frequently with marinade. For best results, barbecue or broiler can be used. 8 to 10 min. on each side. Vegetables should be cooked but not over done. Serve with pilaf, green beans, and salad.

LIVER SURPRISE

1 Lb. Liver
1 Can Applesauce
1 Tsp. Cinnamon

Sear liver on both sides in hot pan or a cast iron skillet. Place liver in a greased baking dish and pour applesauce over the top. Sprinkle with cinnamon and bake ½ hr. at 350 degrees [MW: 7-10 minutes]. Simple but tasty.

LAMB LOAF ALA GREQUE

1 Lb. Ground Lamb
2 Eggs, lightly beaten
1 Medium Zucchini, chopped
2 Cups Eggplant, chopped
1 Medium Tomato, chopped
½ Cup Bread Crumbs
1 Tbs. Lemon Juice
1 Tbs. Rosemary, ground
1 Clove Garlic, minced
Salt & Pepper
Parmesan Cheese, grated
Butter
Paprika

Combine the ground lamb, beaten eggs, zucchini, eggplant, tomato, bread crumbs, lemon juice, rosemary, garlic, salt and pepper in a mixing bowl. Blend thoroughly with a fork. Place in a lightly greased baking dish or loaf pan and top with a generous layer of grated parmesan cheese. Dot with butter. Sprinkle with paprika. Bake in a 350 degree oven for 45 minutes to 1 hour [MW: 10-12 min. on full power]. Serves 4.

VEAL SCALLOPINI

1½ to 2 Lbs. Veal Steak
2-3 Tbs. Butter
1 Clove Garlic
1½ to 2 Tbs. Flour
1-1½ Tsp. Salt
1 to 2 Medium Onions, sliced thin
½ to ¾ Cup Sauterne or Sherry Wine
Pinch of Fresh-ground Pepper
Pinch of Sage
Pinch of Nutmeg
1-1½ Small Cans Tomato Sauce
¾ Lb. Cooked Spaghetti

Melt butter [MW: browning dish] ; saute' garlic until brown then discard garlic. Brown veal strips in butter. Combine flour, salt, pepper, sage and nutmeg. When meat is golden brown, add flour mixture, stirring to coat each piece with flour. Add onions, wine and tomato sauce. Cover and simmer for 20 to 25 minutes, until meat is tender. Remove meat from pan and mix in cooked spaghetti.

VEAL CASSEROLE and DUMPLING TOPPING

2 Lbs. Veal Cutlets
Flour
Paprika
2¾ Cups Water
¼ Cup Shortening
1 Can Cream of Chicken Soup
1 Lb. Can Onions
Salt and Pepper

Butter-Crumb Dumplings:
2 Cups Flour
4 Tsp. Baking Powder
½ Tsp. Salt
1 Tsp. Poultry Seasoning
1 Tsp. Celery Salt
1 Tbs. Poppy Seeds
¼ Cup Salad Oil
1 Cup Milk
¼ Cup Melted Butter
1 Cup Bread Crumbs

Cream Sauce Topping:
1 Cup Sour Cream
1 Cup Cream of Chicken Soup
Pimento

Cube 2 lbs. veal cutlets. Roll in flour and paprika. Brown thoroughly in ¼ cup of shortening. Add salt and pepper and a cup of water; simmer for 30 minutes. Pour into a casserole dish. Heat 1 can of cream of chicken soup and 1¾ cups of water in the meat skillet. Stir constantly and bring to a boil; pour over the veal. Drain the 1 lb. can of small onions and pour the onions over the veal. Dot with butter-crumb dumplings.

Dumplings: Sift together the flour, baking powder, salt, poultry seasoning, celery salt and poppy seeds. After sifting together, add ¼ cup of salad oil and 1 cup milk; stir until moist. Drop by spoonful into mixture of ¼ cup melted butter and 1 cup bread crumbs.

Place dumplings on top of casserole & bake in oven. When ready to serve, pour over the individual servings a cream sauce made by adding 1 cup of sour cream to 1 cup of cream of chicken soup. Garnish with pimento.

EASTER LEG OF LAMB

5 or 6 Lbs. Leg of Lamb
3 Cloves Garlic
Salt and Pepper
¼ Cup Olive Oil
1-½ Cups Chablis Wine
¼ Cup Butter
½ Lb. Italian Sausage
3 or 6 Chicken Livers, cut up
½ Tsp. Mint Leaves
½ Tsp. Sweet Basil
1 Lb. Potatoes Cut into rounds or cubes
1 Lb. Small White Onions

Have butcher remove bone from leg of lamb. Wipe with damp cloth. Remove casing from sausage and crumble meat. Saute sausage meat lightly in a little butter, add chicken livers and continue sauteeing until livers are tender. Blend in mint and sweet basil. Stuff lamb cavity with this mixture. Sew or skewer opening. Rub leg with garlic and insert slivers of garlic into meat, here and there. Rub leg with salt and pepper and place olive oil, butter and lamb in roasting pan and sear in a hot 450 degree oven, turn on all sides until well browned. Moisten with wine, reduce temperature to 350 degrees and roast 20 min. per pound. Baste frequently with liquid from pan. 1 hour before roast is done, add potatoes and onions to pan and continue cooking until meat and vegetables are done. Arrange leg of lamb on platter, surround lamb with potatoes and onions, serve with rich gravy from pan.

STUFFED ZUCCHINI BOATS
(Main Dish)

4 Tbs. Olive Oil
½ Onion, chopped
1 Clove Garlic, finely chopped
¼ Lb. Ground Veal
¼ Lb. Ground Pork
½ Cup + 1 or 2 Tbs. Bread Crumbs
1 Egg Yolk
3 Tbs. Chopped Dill
2 Tbs. Chopped Parsley
1 or 2 Tbs. Parmesan Cheese

Sauce:
2 Cans Tomato Sauce
1 Tbs. Butter
½ Cup Chopped Onion
1 Clove Garlic
½ Tbs. Dried Thyme
1 Bay Leaf
Salt and Pepper

Split the six 8" zucchini lengthwise; scoop out seeds and fill with ingredients as follows: Heat 2 tbs. olive oil in large saucepan; [MW: glass pan] add meat, garlic and onion and cook until meat is done. Add zucchini pulp and seeds; cook about 3 min. Add ½ cup crumbs, salt and pepper, egg yolk, dill and parsley. Stir until mixture is slightly thickened; take care or egg will curdle.

Fill zuchini shell and cover with remaining crumbs and cheese. Dribble remaining oil over it and bake at 375 degrees for 45 min. [MW: 15 min. on full power].

Combine sauce ingredients, cook for 10 min. [MW: 6 min. on full power] and pour over zucchini boats and serve.

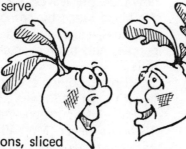

PICKLED BEETS

2 Medium-size Onions, sliced
2 to 3 Fresh Beets
2 Cups Sugar, or little less
1 Cup Water
1 Lemon, sliced thin
½ Tbs. Cinnamon
1 Cup Vinegar
½ Tsp. Cloves
½ Tsp. Allspice

Take fresh beets and trim off leaves, leaving about 2" stems on beets and tapered roots (prevents some bleeding). Wash, cover with water and boil until tender. Slip off skins and trim ends, then slice into a big bowl. Slice onions into rings and lay over beets.

Pickling Syrup: Mix the rest of the ingredients and boil together for 10 min. Pour while boiling hot over pickles. Either fill sterilized jars and cap airtight, or pack in containers when cool and refrigerate.

ITALIAN GNOCCHI (Nioki)

Gnocchi:
6 Potatoes
1 Egg
Flour
½ Tsp. Salt
Dash Pepper
Milk

Butter Sauce:
½ Cup Butter
Rosemary
1 Clove Garlic
Grated Parmesan Cheese

Boil and mash potatoes with a small amount of milk the day before; cover and refrigerate for 24 hours. Remove mashed potatoes; add egg, salt and pepper. Add flour as needed to make a dough. Knead dough for 5 minutes. Roll pieces of dough on floured surface into ¾ inch strips; cut strips into ½ inch pieces. Continue until the dough is finished; place small pieces 1 inch apart on a floured surface. Boil large pan of salted water. When fully boiling, add gnocchi, a few at a time. When they rise to the top, remove with a slotted spoon and place on platter. Continue to do so with all gnocchi. To make sauce, melt butter, rosemary and garlic in a small saucepan; strain onto gnocchi. Add parmesan cheese and serve. Also can be served with meat sauce. Serves 4 to 6.

HOLIDAY YAMS

4 Lbs. Yams
1 Tsp. Salt
1 Cup Brown Sugar
½ Cup Melted Butter
2 Tsp. Grated Orange Rind
2 Tbs. Lemon Juice
¼ Cup Orange Juice
½ Cup Chopped Nuts
¼ Tsp. Cinnamon
Dash of Mace
1 Cup Grated Coconut
Miniature Marshmallows

Cover yams with water; add salt and cook until tender. Peel yams and mash until smooth. Add remaining ingredients, except ½ cup coconut and marshmallows. Mix thoroughly. Place in a greased 2-quart casserole. Bake at 350 degrees for 30 min. [MW: 15 min. covered with plastic wrap]. Sprinkle with enough marshmallows to cover; top with coconut. Brown lightly before serving.

MOM'S BEST ZUCCHINI FRITTERS

5 Tbs. Bisquick
½ Cup Parmesan Cheese
¼ Tsp. Salt
1/8 Tsp. Pepper
2 Eggs
2 Tbs. Butter
2 Cups Zucchini

Blend the Bisquick, Parmesan cheese, salt and pepper; add the 2 eggs. Grate the zucchini and add to the above mixture, making a batter.

Melt 2 tbs. butter over medium heat and pour batter into pan/griddle into pancakes. Fry 3 minutes on each side.

Serve while warm. They are a delicious new way of serving a vegetable. Makes 8 to 10 fritters.

SWEET AND SOUR STUFFED CABBAGE ROLLS

1 Large Head Cabbage
1 Lb. Ground Beef
½ Cup Raw White Rice
1 Small Onion, diced
2 Eggs, beaten
1 Tsp. Salt
¼ Tsp. Pepper
1 Large Onion, sliced

Sauce:
2 - 8 Oz. Cans Tomato Sauce
1 - 1 Lb. 12 Oz. Can Tomatoes
1/3 Cup Lemon Juice
1 Tsp. Salt
1/8 Tsp. Pepper
¼ Cup Light Brown Sugar

1. In large kettle, bring 3 quarts water to boiling. Add cabbage; simmer 2 to 3 min. or until leaves are pliable. Remove cabbage and drain.
2. Carefully remove 12 large leaves from cabbage; trim thick rib if leaves are not soft enough to roll. Return to boiling water for 1 minute.
3. Preheat oven to 375 degrees.
4. In large bowl, combine beef, rice, diced onion, eggs, salt and pepper; mix well.
5. Place about ¼ cup meat mixture in the center of each of the 12 cabbage leaves. Fold sides of leaf over stuffing, roll up from thick end of leaf.
6. In Dutch oven, place a few of the remaining leaves, arrange rolls with seam side down on the leaves; top with onion slices.
7. Make sauce by combining tomato sauce, tomatoes, lemon juice, ¼ cup water, salt & pepper, and pour over cabbage leaves and rolls.
8. Bring to boiling over medium heat. Sprinkle with sugar and cover. Place in oven.
9. Bake 1½ hours, covered. Uncover and bake 1½ hours longer [MW: 45 min. only covered with plastic wrap on full power]. 6-8 servings.

HALUSHKE (Czechoslovakian Dish)
(Potato Dumplings & Cabbage)

5 Potatoes, grated
1 Tbs. Salt
3 Eggs, beaten
3 Cups Flour
2 Onions, sliced
1 Head Cabbage, shredded
½ Cup Butter

Add 3 cups flour to grated potatoes, enough to make a soft dough. Have a pot of water boiling as for spaghetti. Dip spoon into boiling water and drop dough by small spoonfuls into the water. If spoon is dipped the dough will not stick to the spoon. Cook 10 minutes, drain and rinse with hot water. Saute' two sliced onions in ½ cup butter until golden brown. Add shredded cabbage and cook until tender, about ½ hour. Add salt to Halushke, then mix cabbage and Halushke together and serve hot. Heat any leftovers in a frying pan for next meal.

PARAGUAY CORN PIE
(Chipa Guazu)

2 Onions, chopped
½ Cup Cooking Oil
2 Tomatoes, peeled and sliced
1 Can Creamed Corn
½ Pkg. Corn Muffin Mix (or small pkg. Jiffy)
3 Egg Yolks
½ Lb. Soft Cheese, coarsely grated Monterey
3 Egg Whites
½ Cup Ripe Olives (pitted) sliced

Saute' chopped onions in oil slowly until onion is soft. Add sliced tomatoes and cook 5 minutes. Mix creamed corn and muffin mix. Add to this: egg yolks, fried onion and tomato mixture, olives and then the cheese. Beat egg whites stiff and fold in. Turn into a greased shallow baking dish and bake in a slow 300 degree oven about 1 hr. or until firm [MW: 15 min. on full power covered with wax paper]. Serve immediately. Serves 8.

BORSCHT (Russian Soup)

4 Quarts Water
2 Pkgs. Chicken Necks and Backs or
  1 Pkg. Beef Short Ribs and 2 to 3 Bones
2 Large Potatoes
3 Cups Celery, including leaves
2 Cups Bell Pepper
3 or 4 Large Carrots, grated
1 - 8 Oz. Can Sauerkraut
½ Pkg. Frozen Lima Beans
4 Cups Cabbage, chopped or grated
1 Medium Onion, chopped
1 - 16 Oz. Can Whole Tomatoes
1 - 8 Oz. Can Tomato Sauce
Salt and Pepper to taste
Accent

Boil chicken necks and backs (or short ribs and bones) with peeled potatoes in water for 1 hour to make broth. While that is in process, chop celery, bell peppers, cabbage and onion. Grate carrots. Put in broth (take bones out). If using beef ribs, tear meat off and put in also. Put in sauerkraut, tomato sauce and whole tomatoes. Squash whole tomatoes in hand over broth so that it breaks it up into small pieces. Salt and pepper to taste. Sprinkle in accent, about 2 tsp. Let cook on low for about 3 hours. Take out potatoes and chop or squash into small pieces; put in lima beans and boil for 20 minutes. Ready to serve. Makes quite a bit; good for freezing.

CARROT LOAF - A MEAT SUBSTITUTE

2 Cups Cooked Rice
1 Cup Peanut Butter
2 Eggs
1 Medium Onion, grated
2 Tsp. Salt
3 Cups Grated Carrots
2 Cups Milk
2 Tsp. Butter
½ Tsp. Sage

Mix all together, bake in loaf pan until carrots are cooked through.

MATAR ALU SAMOSA
(Pastry Stuffed with Peas and Potatoes)

Pastry:
8 Oz. Flour
5 Tsp. Water
2 Oz. Butter
Pinch of Salt

Filling:
1 Oz. Butter
1 Oz. Ginger
8 Oz. Potatoes
¾ Tsp. Allspice
1 Tsp. Salt
2 Oz. Onions
6 Oz. Peas
¾ Tsp. Red Pepper
1 Dessert Spoonful Lemon Juice
2 Green Chilies
Oil, for frying

Pastry: Sieve together the flour and salt. Rub the oleo into it until mixture resembles fine bread crumbs. Add water & mix it to a smooth dough. Knead for 10 min. and leave it covered with wet cloth until needed.

Filling: Boil the potatoes, dip them in cold water, peel and cut into small cubes. Chop finely the onions, ginger and green chilies. Heat the oleo and fry the onions. Add the ginger, green chilies, peas, salt and red pepper. Fry for 2 to 3 min. Mix 4 tbs. of water and cook on slow heat until the peas are soft. Then add the cooked potatoes, allspice and lemon juice. Stir for 4 to 5 minutes; remove from fire and cool.

Samosa: Divide the dough into 24 equal pieces. Shape them into balls. Dredge with the dry flour and roll them into rounds as thin as possible. Cut each one of these into two halves. Moisten the edges of the semi-circles formed. Hold one of these from its two extremes, keeping the arc of the circle downwards, and fold it over so that they meat each other and form a join opposite the center of the arc. Seal the edge with a little paste made from flour and water. Fill the cone, thus formed, with a tbs. of the stuffing. Seal the top with the same flour paste. Pinch the edge thus formed and decorate with very small scallops. Fry in hot oil until crisp and golden in color. Serve hot with catsup.

AVOCADOS on the HALF SHELL

4 Large Avocados
½ Cup Sunflower Seeds
¼ Cup Nutritional Food Yeast
6 Oz. Tofu, cubed
1 Med. Onion
½ Cup Chopped Celery
½ Green or Red Pepper
2 Cloves Garlic
1 Tsp. Cayenne
1 Tsp. Vege Sal
1 Tsp. Lemon Juice
Sprigs of Parsley

Preheat oven to 350 degrees. Choose the largest, thick-skinned avocados - one for each person. They should be "just ripe" and just yield to thumb pressure. Cut each one in half. Scoop out pulp and save one of the halves from each for the salad.

Dice the other half; cover with lemon and set aside. Meanwhile, saute' or lightly steam medium-chopped vegetables and tofu (if it's the soft variety; don't cook it if it's cheese-like). In the blender, combine the sunflower seeds, nutritional yeast and spices and blend until a fine powder, then combine the sliced avocados, the steamed or sauteed vegetables and tofu, and mix in the seeds and yeast. Spoon the mixture into the avocado shells and place on a baking sheet. Put into the oven till warmed through - 10 minutes or so. Put parsley on top to garnish and serve hot.

"BIRD SEED" STUFFED PEPPERS

1 Cup Whole Millet
3 Cups Water
Sea Salt to taste
4 Medium Green Peppers, halved
    lengthwise and seeded
1/3 Cup Oil
1½ Cups Chopped Onions
1 Clove Garlic, chopped
½ Cup Sliced Mushrooms
3 Tbs. Parsley, chopped
1 Tsp. Basil
½ Tsp. Oregano
1 Tsp. Soy Sauce
2 Lightly-Beaten Eggs
½ Cup Cottage Cheese
Grated Cheddar Cheese

Put millet, water and salt in saucepan, bring to a boil and simmer, covered, until tender, about 30 minutes; drain. Steam the pepper halves over boiling water for 5 minutes. Preheat oven to 350 degrees. In a large skillet, heat oil and saute' the onions and garlic in it until tender. Add mushrooms and cook for 2 minutes longer. Stir in parsley, oregano, basil and soy sauce. Add cooked millet, the eggs and cottage cheese. Cook, stirring gently a minute or two. Fill pepper halves with millet mixture. Set in a baking dish with ½ inch hot water in the bottom. Top each pepper half with grated cheese. Bake for 25 to 30 minutes. Yield: 4 servings. Many people do not realize the wonderful flavor and high nutritional value millet possesses. It is the only alkaline grain, is easy to prepare, versatile and inexpensive. This dish can be used as a vegetarian main dish or a complement to a meal with meat.

GINGER SNAPS + YAMS

1 No. 2½ Can Yams
2 Tbs. Lemon Juice
2 Tbs. Butter
1 Cup Brown Sugar
12 Ginger Snaps
1 Tsp. Baking Powder
½ Tsp. Salt

Drain syrup off yams and save. Place yams in casserole dish and dot butter over them. Add lemon juice and brown sugar. Roll ginger snaps with rolling pin to small crumbs and then add to syrup you saved from the yams. Add baking powder and salt. Stir well and pour over yams. Cover and bake approximately 30 min. at 350 degrees. [MW: cover with plastic wrap and cook 10-12 min. on full power].

BAKED ACORN SQUASH

4 Medium Acorn Squash
4 Tbs. Margarine or Butter
8 Tbs. Brown Sugar
4 Tbs. Dark Karo Syrup, optional

Cut acorns in half. Remove seeds from each piece. Place in shallow pan, cut side up. Spread 1 heaping tablespoon margarine or butter in each half. Add 2 heaping tablespoons brown sugar to each half. Add 1 tablespoon dark Karo syrup, if desired for more sweetness, to each half. Bake in 350 degree oven for 1 hour [MW: 15 min. on full power covered with plastic wrap]. Serves 4.

ITALIAN GREEN BEANS

2 Cans Green Beans
1 Medium Onion
1 Can Stewed Tomatoes or Tomato
    Sauce
1 Tbs. Margarine or Bacon Drippings
Bacon, fried crisp and crumbled in mixture

Put all above in stew kettle; boil until juice boils down very low. If you desire a hotter taste, cook some hot peppers in mixture or add tabasco sauce. Good to take to pot luck dinners. They are always eaten up.

SWISS CHARD TORTA

1 Large Carton Cottage Cheese
2 Cups Swiss Chard, cooked and chopped
1/3 Cup Evaporated Milk
1 Tsp. Salt
¼ Tsp. Pepper
Dash of Accent
Dash of Garlic Salt
¼ Cup Fine Bread Crumbs
½ Cup Grated Parmesan Cheese
4 Eggs well beaten

Butter an 8 x 8 inch pan, then spread a thin layer of oil over and sprinkle with fine bread crumbs. Pour above mixture in, spreading evenly. Spread a tablespoon of evaporated milk over top and top with crumbs and bits of butter. Bake 30 min. in 475 degree oven [MW: 30 min. on medium power covered with wax paper]. Wonderful way to use cottage cheese that has passed the code date for freshness - the older the cottage cheese, the better.

ARTICHOKE HEARTS AU GRATIN

2 - 9 Oz. Pkgs. Frozen Artichoke Hearts
¼ Cup Butter or Margarine
¾ Tsp. Salt
Dash of Pepper
1 Tsp. Onion Salt
¼ Tsp. Dry Mustard
1/3 Cup All-Purpose Flour
1½ Cups Milk
1 Egg, slightly beaten
½ Cup Grated Swiss Cheese
1 Tbs. Fine Dry Bread Crumbs
Paprika

Cook artichokes as directed on the package. Drain. Reserve ½ cup liquid. Melt butter in saucepan. Stir in seasonings and flour. Gradually stir in artichoke liquid and milk. Cook over low heat, stirring constantly, until thickened. Remove from heat. Stir hot sauce gradually into egg and half of cheese. Blend well. Put artichokes in a layer in shallow baking dish. Cover with sauce. Sprinkle with remaining cheese, the crumbs and paprika. Bake in a preheated very hot oven of 450 degrees for about 15 min. [MW: 7-10 minutes on full power covered with wax paper]. Serves 6.

ZIPPY GLAZED CARROTS

2 Tbs. Butter or Margarine
¼ Cup Brown Sugar
2 Tbs. Prepared Mustard
¼ Tsp. Salt
3 Cups Sliced Carrots, cooked and drained
1 Tbs. Snipped Parsley

Melt butter in skillet [MW: browning dish]. Stir in brown sugar, mustard and salt. Add cooked carrots, heat, stirring constantly, until carrots are nicely glazed, about 5 min. [MW: 3 min. on full power]. Sprinkle with parsley. Serves 4.

SEATTLE GOURMET BROCCOLI

3 Lbs. Fresh Broccoli, or 3 - 10 Oz.
 Pkgs. Frozen, Chopped Broccoli
¼ Cup Butter or Margarine
¼ Cup Flour
1½ Tbs. Chicken Seasoned Stock Base
½ Tsp. Salt
2 Cups Milk
6 Tbs. Butter
2/3 Cup Hot Water
2/3 (8 Oz.) Pkg. Herb-seasoned Stuffing
 Mix
2/3 Cup Coarsely-chopped Walnuts or
 Slivered Almonds

Cook fresh broccoli in boiling salted water until tender-crisp; drain and chop coarsely. (Cook frozen broccoli as directed on package, then drain.) Make white sauce by blending ¼ cup butter, flour, chicken stock base and salt; add milk and cook until thickened. Meanwhile, melt 6 tbs. butter in hot water; pour over stuffing mix. Add nuts and toss together. Turn broccoli into greased 2-quart casserole [MW: do not grease]. Pour the white sauce over and top with stuffing; press down slightly. Bake in hot oven, 400 degrees, for 20 to 25 minutes [MW: 10 min. on full power covered tightly with plastic wrap]. Makes 8 to 10 servings.

LA—BO (Spanish String Beans)

1 Clove Garlic, chopped fine
¼ to ½ Lb. Bacon
1 Large Spanish Onion, chopped
1 - 28 Oz. Can Solid Pack Tomatoes
2 - 16 Oz. Cans French-cut String
  Beans
1 Cup Celery, chopped
Pinch of Salt
Pinch of Pepper
Pinch of Comino
Pinch of Oregano

In a pot, on low flame [MW: low power], combine bacon and garlic. Fry [MW] till you have some bacon drippings. Stir with wooden spoon. Add spices; stir. Turn fire up to medium-high to fry onions and celery, about 2 minutes [MW: 2 min. on full power]. Add French-cut beans (drain liquid); stir in a few at a time. You can use fresh French-cut string beans. Chop up the tomatoes and add to mixture. Cover. Let simmer on low flame for one-half hour [MW: 15 min. on full power covered with plastic wrap]. If you use fresh beans, simmer until they are done.

"POPEYE PIES"

2 - 10 Oz. Pkgs. Chopped Frozen
  Spinach
1 Cup Melted Butter
¾ Cup Minced Onion
3 Eggs, beaten
1/8 Tsp. Nutmeg
½ Tsp. Salt
¼ Tsp. Pepper
½ Cup Mozzarella Cheese, shredded
½ Cup Jack Cheese, shredded
½ Cup Blue Cheese, crumbled
8 Oz. Parmesan Cheese
¼ Cup Bread Crumbs
½ Lb. Filo Pastry Leaves

Thaw spinach then squeeze to remove excess water. Saute' onion in butter; add spinach and cook 5 minutes, or until most of the moisture evaporates. Remove skillet from heat and stir in eggs, salt, pepper, nutmeg, cheeses and bread crumbs.

Cut pastry leaves lengthwise into 5" strips and keep covered with a damp tea towel. Heat oven to 425 degrees. Take a strip, brush lightly with melted butter. Place 1 heaping tablespoon of spinach mixture in right hand corner and fold up like a flag into triangles. Place on cooky sheets, brush with butter and bake 15 to 20 minutes, or until golden. Very good!

EGGPLANT SUPREME

1 Large Eggplant
1 Large Egg
2 Tbs. Milk
¾ Cup Fine Cracker Crumbs
½ Lb. American Cheese Slices
1 - 10 Oz. Can Mushroom Soup
2 Tbs. Vegetable Oil, for frying

1. Peel the eggplant and slice in ¼ inch thick slices.
2. Mix the milk and egg. Beat slightly with a fork.
3. Dip eggplant slices in egg mixture & the cracker crumbs.
4. Fry at medium heat until lightly brown. Salt lightly.
5. Arrange browned slices in a 2 or 3 quart casserole dish.
6. Cut cheese slices in quarters and arrange them on top of the eggplant slices.
7. Spoon ½ of undiluted mushroom soup on top of the cheese.
8. Repeat the same thing for the next layer finishing with a few cracker crumbs for the topping.
9. Bake in a 350 degree oven for 20 to 30 minutes.
10. This dish may be made earlier in the day and refrigerated. In this case, reheat at 325 degrees for 45 minutes to 1 hour before serving.

CRAB-CHOKES

6 to 8 Medium Artichokes
1 Can Crab or 1 Fresh Crab, shredded
½ Cup Mayonnaise
1 Onion, diced
½ Cup Cheddar Cheese
½ Cup Swiss Cheese
½ Cup Mozzarella Cheese
Salt & Pepper
Italian Seasoning
Garlic Salt

Take raw fresh artichokes; wash and core center. Break middle, remove, leaving cup-like artichoke. Set aside. Mix together thoroughly the shredded crab, diced onion and the cheese. Mix to consistency with mayonnaise. Add salt, pepper, Italian seasoning and garlic salt to taste. Mix well, to consistency of salad dressing. Stuff center of artichokes with mixture. Set in deep baking dish. Fill ½ of the way with water. Cover and bake for 1 hour or until tender. [MW: do not add water, cover with plastic wrap and cook 20 minutes]. Remove and serve hot. Pull leaves off artichoke, dip in melted center and enjoy!

EGGPLANT CREOLE

1 Large Eggplant
2 Tbs. Flour
2 Tbs. Butter
1 Can Tomato Sauce
1 Can Water
1 Clove
2 Bay Leaves
1 Bell Pepper, chopped
1 Onion, chopped
1 Tsp. Salt
½ Cup Grated Cheese
½ Cup Bread Crumbs

Cut eggplant in cubes; cook in boiling water for 8 minutes; drain. Place butter and flour in skillet; when blended, add tomato sauce and water; stir until smooth. Add clove, bay leaves, bell pepper, onion and salt. When sauce thickens, fold in eggplant and sprinkle with cheese and bread crumbs. Bake for ½ hour at 350 degrees. [MW: 7-10 min. covered with plastic wrap on full power].

CARROT-CHEESE CASSEROLE

12 Medium Carrots
1 Small Onion, minced
¼ Cup Butter
1 Tsp. Salt
¼ Tsp. Dry Mustard
¼ Cup Flour
2 Cups Milk
1/8 Tsp. Pepper
¼ Tsp. Celery Salt
½ Lb. (or more) Velveeta Cheese
3 Cups Butter Fresh Bread Crumbs

Pare and slice carrots, cook carrots in boiling, salted water, covered, until barely tender. Drain. In saucepan, gently cook onions in butter for 2 to 3 minutes. Stir in flour, salt, mustard and milk. Cook, stirring until smooth. Add pepper and celery salt. In a 2 qt. casserole, arrange layers of carrots, cheese, carrots, etc. Pour on mustard sauce, top with bread crumbs. Can be refrigerated until ready to bake. Bake in a 350 degree oven for 30 to 40 min. [MW: 10 min. on full power covered with plastic wrap].

POTATO WEDGES

¼ Cup Butter or Margarine, melted
¼ Cup Catsup
1 Tsp. Prepared Mustard
½ Tsp. Paprika
¼ Tsp. Salt
3 Large Potatoes, unpeeled
¼ Cup Bread Crumbs (optional)

About 45 minutes before serving, preheat oven to 425 degrees. In a small saucepan, over low heat, melt butter, remove from heat; stir in catsup, mustard, paprika and salt until well mixed. Cut each potato into 4 wedges; slash each wedge crosswise at ¼" intervals, but do not cut through skin. Place potatoes skin-side down on cookie sheet; brush potatoes with 1/3 of butter mixture. Bake for 35 minutes, or until potatoes are fork tender. Brush potatoes occasionally with remaining butter mixture during baking. If you like, after last brushing with butter mixture, sprinkle with bread crumbs. Makes 4 servings.

MOQUESHOU (Smothered Corn)

1 Chicken, cut up
6 to 8 Ears of Fresh Corn
2 Medium Size Tomatoes
1 Medium Size Onion, chopped
½ Cup Flour
¼ Cup Cooking Oil
2 Tbs. Butter
Salt and Pepper to taste
Tabasco Sauce to taste

With a sharp knife, slice the very tops of the kernels off the corn into a bowl. Then bring the back of the knife across the cob so that the pulp and juice of corn is squeezed out. Do not cut too deeply into the cob or you will get the tough part of the kernel. Set aside.

Cut up chicken to frying size pieces and salt and pepper to taste. Dredge in flour. Brown lightly in oil and set aside. Pour out any excess oil and replace with butter. Saute' chopped onion in butter then add chicken, corn pulp and tomatoes, peeled and diced. Season with salt, pepper and tabasco; cover and simmer slowly until chicken is tender. If it appears too dry, you may add a little whole milk.

ORIENTAL GREEN BEANS

2 Cans French-Style Green Beans
1 Can Bean Sprouts
2 Small Cans Water Chestnuts, sliced
1/3 Cup Minced Onion (boil first)
1½ Cans Cream of Mushroom Soup, undiluted
1 Small Pkg. Frozen French-Fried Onions
1 Cup Grated Mild Cheddar Cheese

Mix together beans, bean sprouts, onion and mushroom soup. Place in casserole dish. Sprinkle grated cheese on top. Lay French-fried onions on top of cheese. Bake at 350 degrees until cheese is melted and rest is well heated. [MW: 10-15 min. on full power covered with plastic wrap.]

PENNSYLVANIA DUTCH POTATO FILLING

2 Cups Hot Mashed Potatoes
1 Egg, well beaten
4 Cups Cubed Dry Bread
1 Tsp. Salt
Pepper to taste
1 Tsp. Poultry Seasoning
1 Cup Diced Celery
1 Cup Minced Onion
1 Tbs. Parsley
2 Tbs. Butter

Mix together the potatoes and egg. Saute' onion, celery and parsley in butter until soft. Soak bread in cold water and squeeze dry. Fluff bread and mix gently with the potato mixture. Blend in the remaining ingredients and mix well. Use for stuffing a 6 to 8 pound bird. Or, can be baked in a greased casserole dish in a 325 to 350 degree oven and served as a side dish to compliment any roasted, baked or fried poultry main course.

DANISH RED CABBAGE

1 Med. Head Red Cabbage, finely cut or sliced
2 Tart Green Apples, peeled and cut up
2 Tbs. Butter
1 Med. Onion, sliced
1 Qt. Water
½ Cup Red Wine Vinegar
½ Cup Sugar
½ Tsp. Salt
¼ Tsp. Pepper
2 Cloves
1 Bay Leaf
Juice of ½ Lemon

Heat butter in large saucepan; saute' onion and apples for 3 to 4 minutes. Add water, vinegar and seasonings; bring to a boil and add cabbage Cover and simmer for 45 minutes, [MW: 20 min. on simmer] or until tender. Use a slotted spoon to serve.

ONION—CAULIFLOWER BAKE

1 - 16 Oz. Pkg. Frozen Cauliflower, thawed
2 - 9 Oz. Pkg. Frozen Onions with Cream Sauce
1½ Cups Water
2 Tbs. Butter
¾ Cup Shredded American Cheese
¼ Cup Toasted, Slivered Almonds
1 Tbs. Snipped Parsley
½ Cup Canned French-fried Onions

Cut up any large pieces of cauliflower; set aside. In a saucepan, combine frozen onions, water and butter. Cover; bring to a boil. Reduce heat and simmer for 4 minutes, stirring occasionally. Remove from heat; stir till sauce is smooth. Stir in cauliflower, cheese, almonds and parsley. Turn mixture into a 1½-quart casserole. Bake, uncovered, at 350 degrees till bubbly - about 35 min. [MW: 10-12 minutes on full power covered with plastic wrap]. Top with crumbled French-fried onions; bake, uncovered, 5 min. longer [MW: uncovered, 3 min. longer]. Makes 8 servings.

SPINACH RICOTTA TART

½ Pkg. Pie Crust Mix
2 - 10 Oz. Pkgs. Frozen Chopped Spinach
1 Small Onion, minced (¼ cup)
3 Tbs. Butter or Margarine
½ Tsp. Salt
¼ Tsp. Ground Nutmeg
Dash Black Pepper
15 Oz. Ricotta Cheese
1 Cup Light Cream, or Half & Half
½ Cup Freshly Grated Parmesan Cheese
3 Eggs, slightly beaten

1. Prepare pie crust mix, following label directions for one-crust pie. Line a 9 in. pie plate with pastry; flute edge, making a high rim to hold all the filling. Prick bottom and sides with fork to keep the pastry flat while baking. Fit a piece of wax paper in bottom; add a layer of rice or beans to weigh down.

2. Bake in a hot oven, 400 degrees, for 5 minutes. Remove paper and rice and let pastry brown about 6 to 8 minutes longer. Remove to wire rack,
3. Cook spinach following package directions; drain in a large strainer. Squeeze out liquid by pressing spinach against the sides of the strainer with a wooden spoon. Set aside.
4. Saute' onion in butter until transparent; stir in spinach, salt, nutmeg and pepper.
5. In a large mixing bowl, combine the Ricotta cheese, cream, Parmesan cheese & eggs; mix thoroughly. Stir in spinach mixture.
6. Pour into baked pastry shell. Bake in a moderate oven (350°) for 50 minutes, or until custard is set and top is lightly browned. Garnish with parsley and cherry tomatoes, if you wish. Serve hot or warm with a tossed salad and a square of corn bread.

CHEESE—SCALLOPED POTATOES AND CARROTS

2 Cups Boiling Water
2 Tsp. Salt
5 Cups Potatoes, peeled and thinly sliced
1½ Cups Chopped Onion
2 Cups Carrots, peeled and sliced diagonally

Cheese Sauce:
3 Tbs. Margarine or Butter
2 Tbs. Flour
1 Tsp. Salt
Pepper
Dash of Cayenne
1½ Cups Milk
1½ Cups Grated Cheddar Cheese

Cook all vegetables in the 2 cups of boiling water for 5 minutes. Drain. Make cheese sauce using 1 cup of cheddar cheese. Alternate layers of vegetables and sauce, using the remaining ½ cup of cheddar cheese on top. Bake 1 hour in 375 degree oven. Remove cover last 10 min. to brown top if desired. [MW: 15 min. on full power covered with plastic wrap].

CORN FRITATTA

2 Cups Cooked Rice
Slices of Velveeta Cheese, or any
  cheddar
1 - 17 Oz. Can Creamed Corn
2 Cups Shredded Swiss Cheese
6 Eggs
1 Pkg. Pressed Ham Slices, diced

Put 2 cups cooked rice in baking dish. Cover with slices of Velveeta cheese. Combine corn, Swiss cheese, eggs and diced ham. Pour over rice. Cover with grated cheddar cheese. Bake for 30 min. at 350 degrees. [MW: 15-20 min. on medium power, covered with wax paper]. Serves 12.

SALINAS VALLEY SPECIAL

2 Jars Marinated Artichoke Hearts,
  chopped (reserve liquid from 1 jar
  and discard the other)
¼ Cup Crumbs
1 - 8 Oz. Pkg. Sharp Tillamook or
  Cheddar Cheese, grated
4 Eggs
2 Tbs. Minced Parsley
1 Clove Garlic, minced
1 Small Onion, chopped
¼ Tsp. Tabasco
½ Tsp. Salt
½ Tsp. Pepper
½ Tsp. Oregano

Pour reserved artichoke liquid from 1 jar into skillet and saute: garlic and onion until soft but not brown. Beat eggs, add bread crumbs, garlic, onion, seasonings and parsley. Stir in cheese and chopped artichokes. Pour mixture in a greased 7 x 11 inch pan and bake at 325 degrees for 30 minutes [MW: 15-20 min. on medium power covered with wax paper]. If done ahead, all may be combined except the eggs. The eggs can be added as much as 2 hours ahead. Cut this delicious appetizer into cubes and serve warm. Guaranteed to be devoured and have no leftovers and hardly a chance to cool.

CREAM OF BROCCOLI SOUP

1 Bunch Broccoli
¼ Cup Butter
2 Onions
2 Cups Chopped Celery
1 Clove Garlic, chopped
½ Cup Flour
4 Cups Milk
4 Cups Chicken Broth
½ Tsp. Thyme
½ Tsp. Marjoram
Salt and Pepper to taste

Topping:
Sliced Almonds
Chopped Tomato

Trim broccoli and cut into ½" thick slices. Steam in salted water until tender. In large saucepan, melt butter and saute' onions, celery and garlic until brown. Stir in flour gradually. Add milk, chicken broth and herbs. Stir over low heat until soup thickens and boils. Add broccoli, salt and pepper. Serve hot. Sprinkle with almonds and chopped tomato. This is a great MW recipe - a helpful hint would be to puree broccoli after steaming in MW.

CANDIED YAMS

4 Medium-size Yams
¾ Cup Granulated Sugar
¼ Cup Light Brown Sugar
Dash of Salt
1 Tsp. Cinnamon
1 Stick Butter or Margarine
2 Slices Lemon
1 Tbs. Flour
½ Can Crushed Pineapple (small can)
1 Cup Water

Peel and cut yams as for French fries. Place in 8" x 12" x 2" baking dish. Combine the sugars, salt, cinnamon and flour and sprinkle over potatoes. Slice butter and place over this. Twist slices of lemon over this & place peel in with potatoes. Distribute the crushed pineapple over this. Now add water & cover with foil. Bake in 400 degree oven for 1 hr. or until potatoes are done [MW; 15-20 min. on full power, covered with plastic wrap].

CHINESE VEGETABLES and NOODLES

½ Cup Green Onions, sliced
½ Lb. Mushrooms, sliced
½ Small Can Water Chestnuts, rinsed,
  drained and sliced
½ Can Bamboo Shoots, rinsed, drained
  and sliced
1½ Tsp. Minced Fresh Ginger
½ Cup Soy Sauce
1 Lb. Spinach, coarsely chopped
1½ Lbs. Chinese Cabbage, coarsely
  chopped
1 Tbs. Cornstarch
1 Envelope Instant Vegetable Broth,
  in ½ cup water
½ Lb. Vermicelli Noodles, cooked
  according to package directions
2 Tbs. Sesame Seeds

Combine green onions, mushrooms, water
chestnuts, bamboo shoots, ginger and ¼
cup soy sauce in a 4-quart saucepan; cook,
uncovered, for 5 to 10 minutes. Add cabbage and spinach to saucepan; cover and
steam for 2 minutes.

Combine ¼ cup soy sauce, cornstarch and
broth. Add to vegetables and cook over high
heat until thickened, about 2 min. Add
cooked noodles to vegetables; mix well.
Sprinkle with sesame seeds. This recipe is
to be prepared as is in MW.

SHERRIED CREAMED ONIONS

12 Small Winter White Onions
3 Tbs. Butter
¼ Tsp. Salt
2 Tbs. Flour
1 Cup Milk
¼ Cup Sherry Wine
¼ Cup Blanched Almonds

Peel onions. Cut into thick slices. Melt
butter; add onions and salt. Cover and cook
until onions are tender (approximately 20
min.). Sprinkle with flour, stirring carefully. Add milk and cook gently until sauce
is thickened. Add sherry and almonds.
Serves 3 or 4. This recipe can be prepared
"as is" in MW.

This recipe can be doubled and is especially nice at holiday time with turkey
or ?

STUFFED MUSHROOM THOMAS

2 Pkgs. Frozen Chopped Spinach
1 Cup Sour Cream
1 Lb. Ground Chuck
12 Large Mushrooms
¼ Cup Each Green Onion Tops and
  Bottoms
1 Cup Grated Cheddar Cheese
1 Cup Grated Monterey Jack Cheese
½ Cup Parmesan Cheese
1½ Tsp. Salt
1 Tsp. Italian Seasoning or Oregano
Nutmeg

Cook 2 pkgs. chopped spinach according
to directions, drain. Mix 1 cup sour
cream with spinach. Add ½ cup grated
cheddar, monterey jack, parmesan and
¼ cup chopped green onion tops. Also
add ½ tsp. salt and 1 tsp. oregano or
Italian seasoning. Arrange mixture
around edges of two 9 x 13 inch baking
dishes. Arrange the washed mushrooms,
with stems removed and saved, in the
middle of baking dishes.

Filling For Mushrooms: Saute' 1 lb. ground
chuck. Add sliced mushroom stems, ¼ cup
sliced green onion bottoms and 1 tsp. salt.
Spoon over mushrooms. Top with ½ cup
grated cheddar and jack cheeses. Sprinkle
with nutmeg. Cover with foil [MW: wax
paper]. Bake at 350 degrees for 35 minutes.
[MW: 10-12 min. on full power]. Serves 4
to 6. Delicious!

VEGETABLE DINNER

4 Celery Stalks, sliced diagonally
2 Carrots, sliced diagonally
1 Zucchini Squash
¼ Medium Head Cauliflower, sliced
  thin
¼ Medium Bell Pepper, sliced
6 Green Onions, sliced
1 Cup Fresh Mushrooms
½ Cube Butter
1 Beef Bouillon Cube
2 Tbs. Water

Prepare vegetables in large bowl. Melt butter in large skillet. Saute' vegetables for 5 minutes, stirring occasionally. Add bouillon cube, water and mushrooms. Cover and simmer for 2 minutes. Stir and serve. This recipe can be prepared in MW.

EGGPLANT PARMIGIANA

1 Med. Eggplant, sliced thick
Flour
1 Egg, beaten with some milk
Dried Bread Crumbs, Wheat Germ
  or Cracker Meal
Olive Oil
½ Lb. Swiss or Mozzarella Cheese,
  sliced
6 Oz. Tomato Paste
White or Red Wine, as needed
Pinch of Oregano
Clove of Garlic
Salt and Pepper
1 Cup Fresh, Grated Parmesan
  Cheese

Wash the eggplant and, without peeling it, slice it about ¾" thick. Dip these slices first in flour, then into egg, then into the bread crumbs so they are well coated. Saute' them in a little olive oil, a few at a time, until they are browned on both sides. Tend them carefully and add oil if needed.

When they are crisp and brown, arrange them in a baking dish and put a slice or two of Swiss or mozzarella cheese on

each one. Make a thick tomato sauce by diluting the tomato paste with wine. Mix the tomato sauce with the oregano, salt, pepper and crushed garlic clove; spread 2 to 3 tbs. on each slice. Finally, sprinkle the grated Parmesan cheese on top of it all. Bake at 400 degrees for about 15 minutes and serve steaming hot. [MW: 10 minutes on full power, covered with plastic wrap].

MINESTRONE SOUP

½ Lb. Italian Sweet Sausage
1 Tbs. Olive Oil, or regular vegetable oil
1 Cup Diced Onion
1 Clove Garlic, minced
1 Cup Diced Carrots
1 Tsp. Basil
2 Small Zucchini, sliced
1 - 1 Lb. Can Italian Tomatoes
2 - 10 Oz. Cans Beef Bouillon
2 Cups Finely-shredded Cabbage
1 - 1 Lb. Can White Kidney Beans
½ Cup Rice
½ Cup Red Wine
Grated Parmesan Cheese
Chopped Fresh Parsley
Salt and Pepper to taste

1. Slice sausage crosswise; brown in olive oil in deep saucepan.
2. Add onion, garlic, carrots and basil and cook 5 minutes.
3. Add zucchini, tomatoes with liquid, bouillon, cabbage, salt and pepper. Bring soup to a boil; reduce heat and simmer, covered, for one hour.
4. Add beans, with liquid; rice and wine. Cook another 20 minutes, until rice is done. Cool and refrigerate.
5. Twenty minutes before serving, reheat soup and check seasonings; add salt and pepper if desired.
6. Serve in favorite bowls, topped with grated cheese and chopped parsley. Enjoy! OK to MW

HOW DANES ROLL CABBAGE

1 Large Cabbage
½ Tsp. Salt
Boiling Water
2 Tbs. Butter or Margarine
½ Cup Chopped Onion
¾ Cup Chopped Celery
1 Coarsely Shredded Carrot
1 Lb. Lean Ground Beef
¾ Lb. Danish Cheese, Harvarti or Tilston, can
   be found at deli
½ Cup Bottled Chili Sauce
1 Cup Beer, at room temperature

Rinse 1 medium-size cabbage & remove any outer marred leaves. Cut ½" slice off bottom to make separating leaves easy. Place cabbage in large kettle. Add ½ tsp. salt & boiling water to cover half way. Bring to a boil, cooking and lifting cabbage out of the water to remove leaves. Continue until all leaves are separated. Cut off heavy ribs with a sharp knife. Arrange large leaves and place smaller leaves on top.

Prepare the stuffing. Melt butter or margarine in a skillet. Add finely-chopped onion, finely-diced celery and coarsely-shredded carrot. Saute' until onion is golden; push to one side of pan and add 1 lb. lean ground beef. Cook, uncovered, stirring occasionally, until meat is no longer red, about 5 minutes. Mix in the saute'ed vegetables; season with salt and pepper to taste. Sprinkle a little less than ½ lb. Danish Harvarti or Tilston cheese on cabbage leaves. Fill center of each cabbage serving with ½ cup or a little more of the meat mixture. Fold 2 sides over stuffing and, starting at stem end, roll up. Arrange the cabbage rolls in baking dish, seam-side down. Pour in ¾ to 1 cup beer. Cover dish tightly with lid or aluminum foil [MW: plastic wrap]. Bake at 350 degrees for 30 min. [MW: 15 min. on full power].

Remove cover and spoon beer over the rolls. Blend ½ cup chili sauce and ½ cup shredded cheese. Spoon over top of each roll. Return to oven and bake about 10 minutes, [MW: 5 min. on full power] until cheese melts. Ingredients depend on number of people to be served. One cabbage and one pound of beef should feed 6 people.

Note: This is a great recipe to make a day or two ahead. Store the wrapped cabbage rolls in refrigerator and assemble in casserole several hours before cooking. The intermingling of flavors of vegetables, cheese and beer is unusually delightful.

CELERY ALMONDINE

1 Cup Blanched Whole Almonds
2 Tbs. Butter
4 Cups Sliced Celery
1 Chicken Bouillon Cube, crumbled
1 Tbs. Minced Onion
1 Tsp. Monosodium Glutamate
½ Tsp. Sugar
1/8 Tsp. Garlic Powder
1/8 Tsp. Ground Ginger

Saute' almonds in butter until lightly browned; add celery, bouillon cube, onion, monosodium glutamate, sugar, garlic powder and ginger. Mix well. Cover and cook, stirring occasionally, for 10 minutes or until celery is tender. Yield: 5 servings. This recipe can be prepared in MW.

SIMPLE VEGETABLE SOUFFLE'

¼ Cup Flour
¼ Tsp. Salt
¼ Tsp. Pepper
½ Cup Best Food Mayonnaise
¼ Cup Milk
1 Cup Cooked & Finely Chopped Vegetables (Carrots, Peas, Corn, Beets, Summer Squash), well drained
Always use Green Pepper
4 Egg Whites

Very gently stir flour, salt and pepper into mayonnaise. Do not over mix. Stir in milk slowly. Stir in vegetables. Beat egg whites until stiff, gently fold into mayonnaise mixture until well blended. Pour into a greased souffle' or Corning Ware casserole dish that is 1½ qt. size. Bake on 325 degrees for 40 minutes. Important: Serve immediately!

CANTONESE VEGETABLES

12 to 14 Small, Young Carrots, peeled
3 Stalks Celery
½ Med.-size Green Pepper, cored and
    seeded
2 Tbs. Peanut Oil, or other cooking oil
1 Scallion, chopped fine (include tops)
Pinch of Monosodium Glutamate

Cut carrots on the bias into diagonal
slices, about ¼" thick. Cut celery the
same way, making slices 1/8" thick. Cut
green peppers into matchstick strips.

Heat oil in large, heavy skillet over moderately low heat 1 minute. Add carrots
and celery and stir fry 4 minutes. Add
green peppers and scallions and stir fry 5
minutes, or until carrots are crisp tender.
Sprinkle vegetables with monosodium
glutamate; toss and serve. About 105
calories per serving. Makes 4 servings.

FRENCH ONION SOUP

5 Small Onions, thinly sliced crosswise
2 Tbs. Butter or Margarine
3 - 10½ Oz. Cans Beef Consomme
2 - 10½ Oz. Cans Water
1 Tbs. Worcestershire Sauce
½ Tsp. Salt
1/8 Tsp. Pepper
8 Slices French Bread, cut ¾" thick
3 Tbs. Butter or Margarine
1/3 Cup Grated Parmesan Cheese

Separate onions into rings and cook in
melted butter or margarine until glossy.
Add consomme, water, Worcestershire
sauce, salt and pepper. Bring to a boil.
Cover tightly and cook over low heat for
15 minutes.

Spread butter or margarine on one side of
each slice of bread. Sprinkle with Parmesan
cheese. Place slices under broiler until slightly
browned. Serve a bread slice atop each serving
of onion soup. Yield: Makes 6-8 servings.
This recipe can be prepared in MW.

POTATO CASSEROLE

8 Medium Potatoes, unpared
1 Bay Leaf
¼ Cup (½ stick) Butter, melted
1 Can Cream of Chicken Soup,
    undiluted
1½ Cups Dairy Sour Cream
½ Tsp. Salt
¼ Tsp. Pepper
3 Green Garden Onions (including
    tops), chopped
2 Cups (½ lb.) Grated Sharp Cheddar
    Cheese
½ Cup Crushed Corn Flakes

Cook potatoes in jackets with the bay leaf in
boiling salted water until barely tender. Cool.
Peel and grate coarsely. Add butter to soup;
stir till smooth. Blend in sour cream, salt,
pepper, green onions and 1½ cups of the
grated cheese. Pour over potatoes and stir
gently until blended. Spoon into buttered 2½
quart casserole; bake uncovered in moderate
oven, 350 degrees, for 30 min. [MW: 10 min.
on full power covered with plastic wrap].
Combine remaining ½ cup of cheese with corn
flake crumbs and sprinkle over casserole; bake
10 to 15 min. longer [MW: 5 min. longer on
full power].

GREEN & GOLD SQUASH SCALLOP

4 Cups Zucchini, Patty Pan and Yellow
    Crookneck Squash
1 Cup Crumbled Crackers (crumbs)
1 Cup Grated Cheddar Cheese
1 Medium Onion, chopped
3 Eggs
2 Tbs. Chopped Parsley
1 Tsp. Salt
½ Tsp. Pepper
2 Tbs. Salad Oil

Grate the squash. Crumble cracker crumbs.
Saute' onion in salad oil until soft. Beat eggs
with seasonings and combine with grated
squash. Grease a 10" square casserole. Add
squash to casserole, then grated cheese; top
with cracker crumbs. Bake at 325 degrees
about 45 min. [MW: 20 min. on full power
covered with plastic wrap], or until set and
top is golden.

GLAZED CARROTS & BANANAS

2½ Cups Diagonally-sliced, Pared
  Carrots
½ Cup Water
2 Tbs. Butter or Margarine
3 Tbs. Sugar or Corn Syrup
1 Tbs. Lemon Juice
½ Tsp. Salt
¼ Cup Chopped Parsley
2 Bananas, sliced in ¼" slices

1. Put carrots and water in a large skillet
and bring to boiling; cover, reduce heat &
boil gently for 15 minutes or until tender.
Drain carrots and put in bowl.

2. Melt butter in skillet; add syrup, lemon
juice and salt. Stir until glaze is dissolved
and well blended. Add carrots and parsley.
Cook, stirring occasionally, until carrots
are glazed.

3. Peel bananas, chop into ¼" crosswise slices
and add to skillet. Heat and serve. Makes 4
servings. This recipe can be prepared in MW.

POTATO BHUJIA (A Favorite from India)

¼ Tsp. Mustard Seeds
3 Tbs. Vegetable Oil
1 Large Onion
1 Fresh or Pickled Green Chili, small
  variety, finely chopped
½ Tsp. Grated Ginger
½ Tsp. Turmeric Powder
4 Large Potatoes, cubed
1 Medium Tomato, chopped
1 Tsp. Salt

Fry mustard seeds in hot oil until they
crackle. Add onions and saute: until golden
brown. Add chili pepper, ginger and turmeric
and fry for 1 or 2 minutes. Put in potatoes
and stir well. Add water occasionally to prevent sticking and to form a thick sauce. Simmer until potatoes are tender. Add tomatoes
and salt and cook another 5 to 10 minutes.
Serve hot with chappatis and your favorite
curry. [MW: use browning dish in lieu of fry
pan, follow times as above.]

PEAS AND LINGUICA

2 Cans Peas
1 Cup Onion
3 Sticks Linguica
1 - 8 Oz. Can Tomato Sauce
½ Tsp. Cumin Seed
¼ Tsp. Pepper
Salt to taste

Chop onion fine. Chop linguica into thin
rings. Saute' onion and linguica together
until onion is tender. Add the peas, tomato
sauce, cumin seed, pepper and salt. Boil at
low heat for 10 min. This recipe can be prepared in MW.

ZUCCHINI WITH MEAT

3 Tbs. Oil
1 Medium Onion, thinly sliced
1 Lb. Ground Beef
3 (8 Oz.) Cans Tomato Sauce
1 Cup Dry Red Wine
1 Tsp. Italian Seasoning
Dash Garlic Salt
1 Tbs. Sugar
½ Tsp. Salt
Pepper
2 Lbs. Zucchini
Grated Parmesan Cheese

Heat oil in skillet, add onion and beef and cook
until meat is lightly browned, stirring to keep
meat crumbly. Stir in tomato sauce, wine,
seasonings, garlic salt, sugar and salt and pepper
to taste. Cover and simmer for 1 hour [MW:
15 min.], stirring occasionally. Wash zucchini,
trim off ends and cook whole in boiling water,
salted. Boil 10 to 15 min. or until just tender.
Drain and when cool enough to handle, cut
in halves lengthwise. Arrange in a single layer,
cut-side up, in a greased and shallow baking
dish. Pour sauce over zucchini and bake at
350 degrees for 45 min. [MW: 15 min. on full
power, covered with plastic wrap]. Sprinkle
with Parmesan cheese. Makes 5 to 6 servings.

WILD RICE CASSEROLE

1 Lb. Pork Sausage
1 Lb. Fresh Mushrooms
2 Med. Large Onions
8 Oz. Wild Rice
¼ Cup Flour
½ Cup Heavy Cream
2½ Cups Chicken Broth
1 Tsp. Monosodium Glutamate
1 Pinch Oregano
1 Pinch Thyme
1 Pinch Marjoram
Salt and Pepper to taste
½ Cup Toasted Almonds

Pour boiling water to cover over wild rice. Let stand until cold. Drain and repeat two more times; set aside.

Saute sausage; drain on paper. Break up into small pieces. Reserve sausage fat.

Slice mushrooms and saute' in sausage fat along with chopped onions. Mix flour with heavy cream until smooth. Add chicken broth to flour-cream mixture and cook until thickened. Season with oregano, thyme, marjoram, salt & pepper.

Combine above "custard" with wild rice, sausage and vegetables. Mix well. Stir in toasted almonds. Pour into greased casserole and bake at 350 degrees for 25-30 min. [MW: 10-15 min. on full power]. Ready to serve when bubbly.

Special note: If mixed ahead and allowed to stand, liquid will be absorbed. In this case, mix in more chicken broth. It is preferable to add the "custard" mixture just before baking. Good with wild game birds, chicken or turkey.

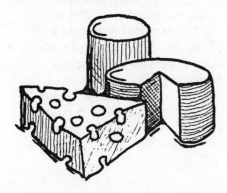

BULGAR PILAF

3 Stalks Green Onions
¼ Cup Cooking Oil
2 Tbs. Butter
1 Glass Bulgar
2 Glasses Water
1 Tsp. Salt

Brown cut-up green onions in ¼ cup cooking oil combined with 2 tbs. butter until degree of browning is satisfactory. Add 1 glass of bulgar and two glasses of water and 1 tsp. salt. Bring to a boil; lower heat to medium. Cover and cook the grain until water is absorbed. Turn off the heat and let it sit for 5 min. [MW: covered with plastic wrap], then serve with lamb shish kebob.

MONTEREY SUNDAY SUPPER

1 Cup Cooked Rice
1 - 7 Oz. Can Green Chilies
3 Zucchini
1 Large Tomato
1 Lb. Monterey Jack Cheese
2 Cups Sour Cream
1 Tsp. Garlic Salt
1 Tbs. Chopped Green Pepper
2 Tbs. Chopped Green Onion
1 Tbs. Parsley
Salt and Pepper to taste
1 Tsp. Oregano

Cook rice until tender. Slice and parboil zucchini. Slice chilies and remove seeds. Cut cheese in narrow strips and insert into half-cut chilies. In a well-buttered casserole dish, place rice, then a layer of cheese-filled chilies, then a layer of the zucchini and tomato slices. Mix the sour cream with the spices, pepper and onions and pour over vegetables. Grate the remaining cheese over the mixture. Sprinkle with parsley and bake in 350 degree oven for 30 min. [MW: 15 min. on full power, covered with plastic wrap].

This dish can be made ahead of time and kept in the refrigerator until 30 minutes before you are ready to eat.

SOUR CREAM RICE

1 Cup Raw Rice
1 Small Can Ortega Chiles, diced
½ Lb. Jack Cheese
2 Cups Sour Cream
4 Tbs. Butter
Salt and Pepper to Taste

Cook rice according to directions on package.
To the cooked rice, add the chiles, grated
cheese, and sour cream. Add salt and pepper.
Butter casserole, put rice mixture in casserole,
sprinkle cheese on top. Dot with butter. Bake
at 350 degrees for 30 min. [MW: 8 min. on full
power, covered with plastic wrap].

ALMOND BACON BROWN RICE

1 Cup Brown Rice
Boiling Water
6 Slices Bacon
¼ Cup Slivered Almonds
½ Cup Sliced Green Onion
1 Cup Sliced Mushrooms
1 to 2 Tbs. Soy Sauce
¾ Cup Thinly Sliced Celery

Cook the rice in boiling water according
to the package directions. Meanwhile,
in a large frying pan, fry the bacon until crisp, lift from pan, drain well, crumble
and set aside. Reserve the bacon drippings.
Heat 2 tbs. of the reserved drippings in
the frying pan over medium-high heat.
Add the nuts, about 6 tbs. of the onion,
celery and mushrooms. Cook, stirring
often, until almonds are toasted, about
5 minutes. Set vegetable mixture aside.
To the pan, add 2 more tbs. drippings,
stir in the cooked rice and cook, stirring,
until rice is lightly toasted. Add more
drippings of necessary to keep the rice
from sticking. Return vegetables to pan,
stir in soy sauce and heat through. Transfer to serving dish and top with bacon &
remaining onion. Serves 4 to 6.

BOSTON LINKED BEANS

1 Lb. White Navy Beans
½ Tsp. Dry Mustard
1 Tsp. Lemon Juice or Vinegar
¼ Cup Molasses
2 or 3 Grated Raw Carrots
¼ Cup Grated Celery
2 Finely Chopped Tomatoes, about
    1½ cups
1 Small Onion, finely chopped
Salt & Pepper to taste
1 Lb. Pork Link Sausages

Soak the beans overnight. In the morning,
boil until the skins are tender but not broken. Mix in all ingredients except for the
pork sausages. Place mixed ingredients in
a crockery casserole and top with the pork
link sausages. Place casserole in a pan of
water in the oven and simmer slowly at 250
degrees for about six hours. They can be
eaten in as short a time as three hours but
the longer this dish is simmered, the more
delicious it becomes. Should it become a
little dry as it simmers, water may be added
from time to time. Serve very hot with a
tangy green salad.

BROCCOLI SPAGHETTI

1 Bunch Fresh Broccoli or 2 Pkgs. Frozen
    Broccoli
1 Lb. Spaghetti
2 Cloves Garlic, sliced
Parmesan Cheese
1 Cube Butter, melted
Salt & Pepper to taste

Heat to boiling in a large saucepan, 4
quarts water and 2 tsp. salt. Add spaghetti and cook for 2 minutes. Cut up
broccoli into 1 inch pieces, then add to
spaghetti. Cook for 8 minutes and drain
into colander. Brown garlic in melted
butter and remove garlic. Pour over
broccoli spaghetti and sprinkle generously with grated parmesan cheese to your
taste. Serve immediately. Makes about
6 servings.

HOMINY CASSEROLE

1 - 16 Oz. Can White Hominy
1 - 16 Oz. Can Yellow Hominy
½ Lb. Grated Jack Cheese
¾ Cup Sour Cream
1 - 4 Oz. Can Diced Ortega Chilies

Mix white hominy, yellow hominy, sour cream and diced chilies in a bowl. Lightly grease, or even better spray with Pam, a 9" x 13" pan. Pour mixture into sprayed or greased pan and cover with the grated cheese. Bake at 350 degrees for 45 min. or until a nice dark golden brown. [MW: 15 min. on full power, covered with plastic wrap].

CUBAN—STYLE BLACK BEANS

1 Lb. Black Dried Kidney Beans
4 Cups Water
1/3 Lb. Salt Pork, diced
3 Cloves Garlic, minced or mashed
1 Med. Onion, chopped
1 Med. Green Pepper, chopped
½ Cup Celery, chopped
¼ Cup Honey
¼ Cup Prepared Mustard
2 Tsp. Paprika
1 Tsp. Chili Powder
1 Tsp. Oregano
¼ Tsp. Pepper

3 Cups Cooked Rice
Limes
Green Onions, chopped

Rinse and sort black beans. In a Dutch oven, combine beans and water. Bring to boiling and boil for 2 minutes. Remove from heat, cover and let stand 1 hour. Without draining beans, add remaining ingredients, stirring to blend. Cover and simmer for about 3 hours, or until tender, adding more water if needed to keep the beans moist. Add salt to taste. To serve, spoon over hot rice, top with green onions and a squeeze of lime. Mix beans and rice as eaten. Makes 8 to 10 servings. May be made ahead of time and reheated.

STUFFED MANICOTTI

1 Lb. Veal, ground twice
2 Fresh, Italian Pork Sausages (salsiccie), casings removed
4 Tbs. Olive Oil
2 Tsp. Minced Parsley
1 Clove Garlic, minced or mashed
2 Bunches Spinach, cooked, drained and finely chopped
1½ Cups Dry French Bread, grated
1½ Cups Grated Parmesan Cheese
5 Eggs
1 Pkg. (8 Oz.) Manicotti, cooked until barely tender
Italian Mushroom Sauce
Grated Parmesan Cheese

Grind together the veal and sausage; lightly brown in oil. Add parsley and garlic and simmer about 3 minutes more. Combine meat, spinach, crumbs and cheese. Let stand for 10 minutes. Vigorously beat in eggs.

Pipe mixture into manicotti tubes. Pour a little sauce into a large, shallow casserole. Arrange stuffed manicotti in a single layer; spoon sauce over each tube. Bake in a moderately slow oven, 325 degrees, until hot, about 45 minutes [MW: 15 min. on full power, covered with plastic wrap]. Sprinkle with cheese and serve with remaining sauce that has been heated. Makes 8 servings.

STUFFED ITALIAN SHELLS

½ Pkg. Jumbo Shells
3 Tsp. Butter
½ Lb. Ground Pork
1 Lb. Ground Beef
1/3 Cup Minced Onion
¼ Cup Minced Celery
1 Clove Garlic, minced
½ Lb. Ricotta Cheese
¼ Lb. Shredded Mozzarella Cheese
1/3 Cup Parmesan Grated Cheese
¼ Cup Chopped Parsley
1 Tsp. Salt
½ Cup Dry Bread Crumbs
2 Pt. Jars Spaghetti Sauce

Cook shells in 2 qts. boiling water to which
1 tbs. salt has been added. Boil for 20 to
25 minutes, drain and cool. Melt butter in
a large frying pan, add pork and beef, cook
until lightly browned. Add onion, garlic and
celery. Cover and cook for 10 to 15 min.
until celery is tender. Remove from heat and
stir in all grated cheeses, salt, bread crumbs
and parsley. Stuff each shell with slightly
cooled mixture and close. Pour one jar of
meatless spaghetti sauce into a shallow casserole dish. Arrange stuffed shells in the casserole and top with rest of sauce. Cover and
bake at 375 degrees for 35 to 40 minutes.
[MW: 10-12 min. on full power, covered with
plastic wrap]. Adequately serves 6.

MEATLESS PROTEIN LOAF

1 Cup Cooked Rice
½ Cup Wheat Germ
1 Cup Chopped Pecans
1 Onion, chopped
½ Cup Mushrooms, diced
¾ Lb. Sharp Cheddar Cheese, shredded
½ Tsp. Garlic Powder
¼ Tsp. Salt
4 Eggs, well beaten

Mix all ingredients well. Pour into a well-oiled
loaf pan. Bake at 350 degrees for about an hour.
[MW: 15 minutes on full power].

CLAM SPAGHETTI

¼ Cup Olive Oil
¼ Cup Margarine
½ Cup Chopped Onion
3 Large Cloves, chopped
1 Tsp. Parsley
1 Cup Water
1 Cup Canned Tomatoes, chopped
1 Cup Tomato Sauce
¼ Tsp. Oregano
¼ Tsp. Thyme
1 Tsp. Salt
1 Tsp. Pepper
½ Tsp. Paprika
2 Cans Chopped Clams

Simmer onions and garlic in oil-margarine
mixture; add remaining ingredients (except
clams) and simmer for one hour. Add
drained clams and simmer an additional
15 minutes. Serve over cooked spaghetti.
This recipe can be prepared in MW.

CHILI BEAN - NOODLE CASSEROLE

1 - 1 Lb. Pkg. Narrow Noodles
2 Lbs. Ground Beef
1 Large Can Chili Beans
1 Tsp. Salt
½ Tsp. Pepper
½ Tsp. Mixed Herbs
4 Tbs. Minced Dried Onions
½ Tsp. Garlic Powder
1 Medium Can Stewed Tomatoes
½ Cup Burgundy Wine
1 Small Can Chopped Olives (optional)
1½ Cups Mild or Medium Cheddar Cheese,
   grated

Cook noodles according to directions on pkg
While noodles are cooking, brown beef in a
little oil and add the next 9 ingredients. Simmer about ½ hour. Put meat mixture into
noodles and pour into a greased 2 qt. casserole dish. Top with cheese and bake at 350
degrees for 30 to 45 min. [MW: 12 min. on
full power, covered with plastic wrap] Serves
16. Excellent when served with toasted garlic bread, tossed lettuce salad, carrot & celery
sticks, a light dessert and coffee.

MOCK RAVIOLI

½ Lb. Bow Knot Macaroni
1 Pkg. Frozen Spinach
¾ Cup Spinach Water
2 Tbs. Crisco
1 Can Tomato Sauce
1 Onion, diced
2 Cloves Garlic
Salt & Pepper to taste
1 Lb. Ground Beef
1/3 Tsp. Ground Oregano
1/3 Tsp. Basil
1/3 Tsp. Rosemary
½ Cup Bread Crumbs
1 Cup Grated Cheese
1 Can Mushroom Sauce
1 Can Tomato Paste
½ Cup Oil
2 Eggs, beaten

Cook macaroni in salted water until tender. Cook spinach as the pkg. directs, saving water. Saute: onion and garlic in melted shortening. Add meat and cook until brown. Add ¾ cup spinach water, tomato paste, sauce, herbs, salt and pepper. Simmer 20 minutes. Meanwhile, chop spinach, then add bread and other garlic clove. Add cheese, oil and eggs. Mix well. Butter a baking dish and alternate layers of macaroni, spinach mixture and meat sauce. Sprinkle cheese on top. Let stand a few hours, or overnight in the refrigerator. Pour mushroom sauce over all. Bake in a 350 degree oven for 30 minutes [MW: 10-12 min. on full power, covered with plastic wrap]. Serves 5 to 6 people.

SOUR CREAM NOODLE BAKE

4 Cups Medium Egg Noodles
1 Lb. Ground Beef
1 Tbs. Butter
1 - 8 Oz. Can Tomato Sauce
1 Tsp. Salt
¼ Tsp. Garlic Salt
1/8 Tsp. Pepper
2 Cups Sour Cream
1 Cup Thinly-sliced Green Onions
1 Cup Shredded Cheddar Cheese

Cook noodles as directed on package. Drain. Brown beef in butter; stir in tomato sauce, salt, garlic salt and pepper. Simmer, uncovered, 5 minutes.

Mix together sour cream, onions and noodles. In buttered 2-quart casserole, alternate layers of noodle and meat mixtures, beginning with noodles and ending with meat. Sprinkle with cheese. Bake in 350 degree oven for 20 to 25 minutes, or until cheese is lightly browned. [MW: 10 min. on full power]. Serves 6.

SONORA RICE

3 Tbs. Oil
1 Cup MJB Rice
1 Onion, chopped
1 Clove Garlic, pressed
3 Stalks Celery, chopped
1 Can Tomatoes, cut up without juice
1 Can Beef Consomme' and enough water
   to make 2 cups liquid
Salt and Pepper

Brown the rice in oil; add all other ingredients, bring to a boil. Cover and simmer for 20 minutes.

OKLAHOMA FRIED RICE

½ Cup Green Onions, chopped
1½ Cups Ham, chopped
4 Eggs
2½ Cups Minute Rice, uncooked
Soy Sauce (Chun King)

Put rice on to cook. Lightly grease a large frying pan. Cook ham slowly. In small frying pan, scramble eggs until well done. When eggs are cooked, mix them in with ham and chopped onions. Rice should be done. Mix rice in the large frying pan with ham. Stir for a few minutes and season with soy sauce to taste. Serve as whole meal or with meat dish. Serves 4 easily.

MARINATED SMALL WHITE BEANS

1 Lb. Small White Beans
1 Bunch Green Onions
½ Cup Celery
½ Cup Bell Pepper (optional)
1½ Tsp. Salt
1½ Tsp. Coarse Ground Pepper
½ Tsp. Celery Salt
½ Tsp. Garlic Salt
1 Cup Salad Oil
1¼ Cups Vinegar

Cook beans until tender; drain and let cool. Dice green onions, celery and bell pepper. Add to beans and toss. Combine other ingredients and toss well. Marinate overnight. OK to MW. Nice for picnics and barbecues.

BASIL & BEAN SOUP

½ Lb. Dried White Beans, navy or kidney
1½ Lbs. Zucchini
3 Med. White Turnips
1 Large Potato
6 Med. Carrots
2 Celery Stalks, with leaves
2 Red Onions
1 Red Onion, studded with 4 cloves
1 Whole Bay Leaf
1 - 1 Lb. 1 Oz. Can Whole Tomatoes, undrained
1 Tbs. Dried Basil Leaves
1/8 Tsp. Dried Hot Red Pepper
1½ Tbs. Salt
2 Tbs. Salad Oil
2 Tbs. Chopped Parsley

1. Day before serving, soak beans overnight in cold water to cover.
2. The next day, drain beans in colander; rinse under cold water.
3. Prepare vegetables; dice zucchini, pare and dice turnips and potato; pare carrots and slice thinly; slice celery; coarsely chop 2 onions.
4. Turn beans into 6-quart Dutch oven with 6 cups of water. Bring to boil over medium heat.
5. Add prepared vegetables and rest of ingredients, except oil and parsley. Return to boiling; reduce heat and simmer, covered,

2½ hours, or until beans are tender.
6. To serve, remove and discard clove-studded onion and bay leaf. Stir in oil. Taste for seasoning. Sprinkle with parsley. Makes 4½ quarts.

HOMEMADE EGG NOODLES in CHICKEN BROTH

3 Cups Flour
½ Tsp. Salt
4 Eggs, at room temperature
1/3 Cup Water

Broth:
1 Boiling Chicken
4 Quarts Water
2 Chicken Bouillon Cubes
1 Tbs. Worcestershire Sauce
1 Tsp. Liquid Smoke
1 Tsp. Garlic Salt
½ Tsp. Celery Seed
1 Cup Chopped Onions
Salt and Pepper to taste

Egg Noodles: Put flour, salt and eggs in a bowl. Using your hand, mix together, adding 1 tbs. of water at a time and mixing until dough forms a ball.

Place dough on a well-floured board and knead until smooth and elastic, about 8 to 10 minutes. Cover and let set for 15 minutes.

Cut dough into 4 equal parts; keep covered. Roll 1 part of dough at a time until desired thickness is reached (about 1/16th of an inch). Roll around rolling pin and slip out. Cut in ½" to 1/8" strips and shake out on a towel to dry, for about 2 hours. Cook in 3 quarts of chicken broth.

Chicken Broth: Boil chicken in water. Remove chicken when done and remove the bones and skin. Put the chicken back into the broth and place all the other ingredients in pot; boil for 10 minutes. Place egg noodles in broth and boil for 10 to 15 minutes. Serve with chopped green onions on top.

FLORENTINE RICE QUICHE

4 Eggs
2 Cups Cooked Rice
2/3 Cup Finely Grated Swiss Cheese
1-10 Oz. Pkg. Chopped Spinach
2 Tbs. Butter or Margarine
½ Tsp. Salt
½ Pint Cottage Cheese
¼ Cup Grated Parmesan Cheese
6 Tbs. Heavy Cream or Evaporated Milk
3 Drops Hot Pepper Sauce
¼ Tsp. Nutmeg
Garlic Powder

Preheat oven to 350 degrees. Generously grease 9 inch pie pan. Beat 1 egg, add rice and Swiss cheese to egg. Mix well, add garlic powder. Spread evenly in pie pan making a crust. Refrigerate until ready to fill and bake. Cook spinach as directed. Pour into strainer and press out all liquids. Add butter to drained spinach and set aside. In medium bowl beat remaining 3 eggs, stir in salt, cottage cheese, parmesan cheese, heavy cream, hot pepper sauce and nutmeg. When well blended stir in spinach. Pour filling into rice crust. Bake 30 to 35 minutes, or until firm and knife inserted in center comes out clean. To serve cut into wedges.

FETTUCINI

1 Cup Chopped Green Onions, including tops
2 Cloves Garlic, minced
6 Tbs. Butter
3 to 4 Cups Hot, Cooked, Drained Vegetable Noodles
1 Cup Fresh Whipping Cream
1 to 2 Cups Grated Parmesan Cheese
Salt & Pepper

Cook green onion and garlic in butter until onion is limp. Set aside and keep warm. Just before serving, place hot, cooked noodles and cream in an attractive frying pan or other serving dish that can be used over direct heat. Stir mixture over heat until the cream reaches the boiling point. Immediately add onion butter to the noodles.

With 2 forks, toss noodles vigorously and sprinkle in 1 cup of the parmesan cheese. Continue lifting and mixing the noodles until well coated with cheese. Season with salt & pepper. Pass additional parmesan cheese to sprinkle over individual portions. OK to MW.

RICE CAKE

2 Cups Cooked Rice
1 Pkg. Frozen Spinach, cooked
1 Cup Milk
6 Eggs
¼ Cup Olive Oil
¾ Cup Parmesan Cheese
1 Tsp. Italian Seasoning
¼ Tsp. Garlic Salt
Salt
Pepper

Add milk to cooked rice; mix. Add cooked and drained spinach, beaten eggs, Parmesan cheese, olive oil and the rest of the seasonings. Mix. Pour into a 13" x 9" pan and bake for 30 min. at 325 degrees. [MW: 10 min. on full power, covered with wax paper]. Cut into serving pieces when ready to serve. Can be served hot or cold.

TAGLIARINI

2 Tbs. Cooking Oil
1 Green Pepper, chopped
1 Lb. Ground Beef
½ Lb. Sharp Cheddar Cheese, shredded
1 Clove Garlic, minced
1 Small Onion, minced
½ Cup Sliced Olives
¼ Cup Water
4 Oz. Egg Noodles, cooked
1 - 12 Oz. Can Whole Kernel Corn
1 - 1 Lb. Can Tomatoes
½ Tsp. Salt
¼ Tsp. Pepper

Heat oil. Add meat and green pepper. Cook, stirring until meat loses red color. Stir in cheese, garlic, onion and olives. Mix in remaining ingredients. Turn into a greased 2½ quart casserole. Bake in a 350 degree oven for 45 min. [MW: 10-12 min. on full power].

BAKED LENTILS WITH CHEESE

12 Oz. Lentils, rinsed
2 Cups Water
1 Whole Bay Leaf
2 Tsp. Salt
¼ Tsp. Pepper
1/8 Tsp. Marjoram
1/8 Tsp. Whole Sage, crumbled
1/8 Tsp. Whole Thyme, crumbled
2 Large Onions, chopped
2 Cloves Garlic, minced
1 - 1 Lb. Can Tomatoes
2 Large Carrots, sliced 1/8" thick
½ Cup Thinly-sliced Celery
1 Green Pepper, chopped
2 Tbs. Finely Chopped Parsley
3 Cups Shredded Sharp Cheddar Cheese

In a shallow baking dish (about 9x3"), mix the lentils, water, bay leaf, salt, pepper, marjoram, sage, thyme, onions, garlic and tomatoes. Then cover tightly with foil and bake in 375 degree oven for 30 minutes. Uncover; stir in carrots and celery. Bake, covered, for 40 minutes more, or until vegetables are tender. Stir in green pepper and parsley. Sprinkle cheese on top; bake, uncovered, for 5 minutes or until cheese melts. Makes 6 servings. This is an excellent meatless dish; high in protein and very tasty.

FRIED RICE YANG CHOW

4 Cups Cooked Rice
½ Cup Green Peas, frozen
¼ Cup Green Pepper
3 Eggs, beaten
½ Cup Chicken Meat, cooked
½ Cup Canned Shrimp
½ Cup Roast Pork or Ham, diced
¼ Cup Chopped Onion
Garlic Clove, if desired

Heat 2 tbs. oil in large skillet. Fry beaten eggs; break into small pieces and remove to plate. Add 2 more tbs. oil to skillet, saute' peas, peppers, onions and meats slightly. Add 9 tbs. oil and ¼ cup boiling water to skillet. Add rice, soy sauce, pepper and salt to taste; heat thoroughly, stirring constantly over low heat. At last, stir in the eggs. Shredded lettuce can be added at this point also.

Note: You may use only one kind of meat if preferred. It is even good without meat.

NOODLES NAPOLI

1 Med. Onion
1 Garlic Clove, minced
2 Tbs. Salad or Olive Oil
1 Lb. Ground Beef
1 (8oz.) Tomato Sauce
1 Can Tomato Paste
2 Tsp. Salt
1 Tsp. Oregano
2 Eggs
1 Pkg. 8 oz. Wide Noodles, cooked and drained
1 Cup Cream Cottage Cheese
1/3 Cup Parmesan Cheese, grated
Sliced Process American Cheese (about 8 slices from pkg.)
1 Pkg. Frozen Chopped Spinach, thawed and drained
1 Cup Chopped Fresh Mushrooms

Brown onion and garlic lightly in 1 Tbs. oil; add beef; cook and stir until brown. Stir in mushrooms and liquid, tomato sauce, tomato paste, 1 Tsp. salt and oregano. Simmer 15 min. Beat 1 egg slightly and pour over noodles; mix well. Beat 2nd egg. Add spinach, 1 Tbs. oil, cottage cheese, parmesan cheese and salt. Pour half tomato mixture into shallow oblong baking dish; layer of noodles on top. Spread with all of spinach mixture. Repeat noodle layer. Top with remaining tomato mixture. Cover with foil paper [MW: plastic wrap]. Bake at 350 degrees for 45 min. [MW: 10 min. on full power] Remove covering. Arrange strips of processed cheese on top. Bake 5 min. longer [MW: same]. Use 13" x 8¾" x 1¾" baking dish.

GOLDEN BEAN BAKE

1 - 3 Oz. Pkg. Cream Cheese
½ Cup Cottage Cheese
½ Cup Sour Cream
3 Green Onions and Tops, chopped
1 - 4 Oz. Can Chopped Green Chilies
1 - 15 Oz. Can Chili With Beans
½ Tsp. Garlic Powder
½ Cup Sliced Ripe Olives
¼ Tsp. Chili Powder
3 Tbs. Olive Oil
6 Corn Tortillas
1 - 29 Oz. Can Cling Peach Halves
½ Cup Shredded Cheddar Cheese
Paprika

Mix softened cream cheese until smooth. Stir in cottage cheese, sour cream and onions. Salt and pepper to taste. In a separate bowl, mix green chilies, chili, garlic powder, olives and chili powder. In frying pan, heat oil and fry tortillas. Drain. Layer 3 tortillas in bottom of a 1½ quart baker. Spoon cheese mixture evenly over tortillas. Layer 3 more tortillas and top with chili mixture. Bake at 350 degrees for 35 min. [MW: 10 min. on full power]. Press drained peaches on top. Sprinkle with cheese and paprika. Return to oven for 5 minutes..

ESAU'S POTTAGE
(Vegetarian, Low Cost & Delicious)

½ Lb. Dry Lentils
¼ Lb. Dry Barley
¼ Lb. Dry Short Grain Rice, or
  Brown Rice
1 Tsp. Salt
4 Tbs. Brewer's Yeast
2 Tsp. Soy Sauce or Maggi
1 Can Stewing Tomatoes, broken
  into small pieces
½ Tsp. Onion Powder

Wash the lentils thoroughly. Add lentils, barley, rice and salt to a large pan and cover with plenty of water. Cook on low heat until done. Delicious cooked in a crock pot for several hours. (Can cook while you work.) When done, add brewer's yeast, Maggi or soy sauce, stew-ing tomatoes and onion powder. Pottage should be moist. May bake in a 9" x 12" dish if desired. Bake, covered, for 35 min. at 350 degrees or may be eaten as is [MW: 10-12 min. on full power, covered with plastic wrap]. Note: High protein when served with 100% whole wheat bread and served with a fruit dish.

SCANDINAVIAN BEANS

2 Lbs. Pinto Beans
12 Cups Water
½ Tsp. Baking Soda
4 Tsp. Salt
4 Tbs. Cooking Oil
3 Slices Bacon, cut up
¼ Cup Diced Onion
1 Medium Clove Garlic
¼ Tsp. Black Pepper
¼ Cup Light Molasses
1 Cup Catsup
Tabasco Sauce to taste
1 Tsp. Worcestershire Sauce
1½ Cups Brown Sugar
½ Cup Cider Vinegar
¼ Tsp. Dry Mustard

Place washed beans in large kettle, add water and bring to boiling. Boil for 2 minutes only. Remove from heat, add baking soda to cut down cooking time. Cover. Let stand 1 hour or soak beans with baking soda in measured amount of water overnight. To cook, put kettle of beans with soaking water on high heat. Add salt and oil to keep down the foam, when boiling, reduce heat to simmer. Cover tightly and cook 2 hours or until tender. Mix together all remaining ingredients. Add to the cooked beans, stirring carefully with a wooden spoon to avoid breaking beans. Cook slowly, covered, on surface unit for 30 minutes or so, or place in a 325 degree oven for 1½ hours. Taste really improves with standing and reheating.

APPLE OMELET

¼ Cup Packed Brown Sugar
1 Tbs. Cornstarch
2/3 Cup Cold Water
2 Tsp. Lemon Juice
3 Apples, peeled, cored and cut
  into ½" thick wedges
2 Tbs. Butter or Margarine
3 Fully-cooked Smoked Sausage
  Links, sliced diagonally (optional)
4 Egg Whites
2 Tbs. Water
¼ Tsp. Salt
4 Egg Yolks
1 Tbs. Butter or Margarine

To prepare sauce, combine brown sugar
and cornstarch in saucepan. Stir in the
2/3 cup cold water and lemon juice.
Cook quickly, stirring constantly, till
thickened and bubbly. Add apples;
stir gently. Cover and simmer gently
for 3 to 5 minutes, or till apples are
tender. Add the 2 tbs. butter and sausage,
if desired. Stir till butter melts and the
sausage is hot; keep warm.

To prepare omelet, beat egg whites until
frothy; add water and salt. Beat egg whites
until stiff peaks form. Beat egg yolks till
very thick and lemon colored. Gently fold
yolks into whites.

Heat the 1 tbs. butter in a 10" ovenproof
skillet till a drop of water sizzles when
dropped atop. Pour in egg mixture and
spread evenly with spatula, mounding
higher at sides. Cook over low heat for
8 to 10 minutes, or till lightly browned.
Bake in 325 degree oven for 8 to 10 min.,
or till knife inserted near center comes out
clean. Loosen sides of omelet with spatula.
Make a shallow cut across omelet, cutting
slightly off-center so that the two portions
are unequal. Fold smaller portion over
larger portion. Using spatula, slip omelet
onto hot serving platter.

Set aside ½ cup of the apple mixture.
Unfold omelet and spoon remaining apple
mixture across center. Refold. Pour the
reserved apple mixture atop. Serves 4.

YORKSHIRE PUDDING

1 Cup Flour
½ Cup Milk Powder
¾ Tsp. Salt
2 Eggs
1 Cup Water

Combine ingredients. Beat until smooth.
Pour into a jar and let stand 1 hour. Put
1 tbs. drippings (from your favorite roast
beef) into muffin tins. Place in 450 degree oven until very hot (almost smoking).
Shake batter and pour into tins. Bake in
450 degree oven until big and brown.

To prepare delicious and moist beef roast,
wipe with damp cloth and rub with salt
and freshly-ground pepper. Place in rack
in roasting pan in a 300 degree preheated
oven. Do not baste. Use thermometer or
following timetable:

Rare:	18 to 20 min. a lb.
Medium Rare:	20 to 22 min. a lb.
Medium	22 to 25 min. a lb.
Well Done	27 to 30 min. a lb.

CHEESE STRATA

8 Slices Bread or Toast
¼ Cup Soft Butter or Margarine
2½ Cups Diced Sharp Process
  American Cheese
4 Eggs, slightly beaten
2½ Cups Milk
1 Tsp. Salt
¼ Tsp. Dry Mustard

Trim crust from bread, if desired. Butter
bread. Alternate layers of bread & cheese
in 11½" x 7½" x ½" baking dish, ending
with cheese on top. Mix eggs, milk and
seasonings; pour over layers and bake in
slow oven, 325 degrees, about 45 minutes
or until firm. Let stand a few minutes;
cut into squares and serve. Makes 6 servings. This is great as a brunch dish or
lunch. Serve with mix of fresh fruit.

WIENIE-LOTTAS

10 Tortillas
2 - 10½ Oz. Cans Chili Without Beans
1 Tbs. Chopped Onion
6 to 8 Drops Hot Sauce
1 Pkg. Frankfurters
1 - 8 Oz. Can Tomato Sauce
¼ Cup Seeded and Chopped Green
   Chili Peppers
1 Cup Shredded Cheddar Cheese

Cook tortillas according to package directions. Combine chili, onion and hot pepper sauce. Place a frank on each tortilla; top each with 2 tbs. chili mixture; roll tortilla around frank. Arrange, seam side down, in a 12 x 7½ x 2 inch baking dish. Combine remaining chili mixture and tomato sauce; pour over tortillas. Sprinkle with chopped chili peppers. Bake in a moderate 350 degree oven for 25 to 30 minutes. [MW: 10-12 min. on full power, covered with plastic wrap.] Top with shredded cheese. Makes 5 to 6 servings.

CHINESE EGGROLLS

1 Pkg. Eggroll Skins
½ Head Cabbage, shredded
½ Head Lettuce, shredded
1 Can Water Chestnuts
1 Small Onion, chopped
½ Cup Celery, chopped
½ Cup Bell Pepper, chopped
½ Lb. Shrimp, cooked
½ Lb. Pork Cubes, cooked
½ Lb. Bean Sprouts
1 Egg Yolk, beaten

Steam cabbage, lettuce, onion, celery and bell pepper until soft but not mushy. In a deep skillet, stiry-fry in ¼ cup oil the shrimp and pork for 3 minutes. Add water chestnuts and cook for 5 minutes. Add cabbage mixture and stir, then add bean sprouts and cook until soft. Place a small amount of this mixture onto eggroll skin. Fold envelope-style (corners together) and seal with a slight amount of egg yolk. Deep fry until brown or fry in ½ inch of oil until brown on each side.

FRIED WON TONS

2 Pkgs. Won Ton Skins
1 Lb. Hamburger
1 Lb. Ground Pork
3 Green Onions, chopped
2 Tbs. Minced Parsley
6 Canned Water Chestnuts, chopped
1 Tbs. Soy Sauce
1 Tbs. Salad Oil
1 Tsp. Cornstarch
¼ Tsp. Salt
1/8 Tsp. Pepper
1 Bottle Peanut Oil

Heat oil in wok to 350 degrees. Brush cornstarch from each won ton skin; cover with a towel until ready to use.

Mix all ingredients, except skins and oil, until well mixed. Place 1 tsp. meat mixture in center of skin, then spread over half of the skin making a triangle. Fold in half, then wet one side with water and fold again to form a triangle.

Cook in hot oil, turning once, about 1 or 2 minutes or till lightly browned. Drain and serve with sweet and sour sauce. Makes approximately 100 won tons.

HASENPFEFFER

Cut one 2½ to 3 pound dressed rabbit into serving pieces. Cover with equal amounts of vinegar and water (2 to 3 cups); add ½ cup sugar and 1 medium onion, sliced. Season with 2 tsp. salt, ¼ tsp. pepper and 1 tsp. pickling spices. Let stand in the refrigerator for 2 days.

Remove rabbit; dry. Dip into flour and brown in hot fat. Gradually add 1 cup of the vinegar water; cover and simmer 1 hour, or till tender. Remove meat to hot platter. Thicken liquid for gravy if desired. Makes 4 servings.

109 MAIN DISHES (MISCELLANEOUS)

SPANISH PAELLA

1 Quart Chicken Broth
¾ Cup Olive Oil
½ Lb. Boneless Pork, cut into ½" cubes
3 Chorizos, or hot Italian Sausage, cut into ½" slices
1 - 2½ Lb. Chicken, cut up
½ Tsp. Crumbled Thyme
2 Garlic Cloves, mashed
2 Med. Onions, chopped
1 - 4 Oz. Can Pimiento, drained and chopped
2 Cups Long Grain Rice
1 Small Tomato, chopped
1 Tsp. Whole Saffron Fibers or ¼ Tsp. Saffron Powder
2 Tbs. Lemon Juice
Salt and Pepper
1 Lb. Raw Shrimp, shelled & deveined
3 - 6 Oz. Frozen Rock Lobsters, cut in 1" slices, tails and all
1 - 10 Oz. Pkg. Frozen Peas
1 - 9 Oz. Pkg. Frozen Artichoke Hearts
16 Well-scrubbed Mussels
16 Well-scrubbed Clams

Heat olive oil in a large skillet. Brown pork and sausage pieces. As pieces brown, remove to a large (3-quart) casserole or roasting pan. Rub chicken with thyme and garlic. Brown on all sides in oil; remove chicken to casserole. Add onion & pimiento to pan drippings; saute' until onions are golden. Add rice, tomato and saffron and stir until rice is well coated.

Sprinkle rice mixture over chicken. Pour chicken broth and lemon juice over casserole contents. Add salt and pepper to taste. Put uncovered casserole in preheated 350 degree oven for 15 minutes. Put shrimp and lobster into casserole, pushing pieces down into liquid. Continue baking until rice is almost done - about 15 minutes.

At this time the liquid should be almost absorbed. Thaw peas and artichoke hearts and separate. Add to casserole and stir to distribute through rice mixture. Push mussels and clams into rice. Bake 5 minutes, or until clams and mussels open. Add more broth if nec-essary to keep moist. To keep warm and prevent over cooking, cover and lower heat to 250 degrees. Everything can be increased to serve more. This serves 6 to 8. Has always been a hit at pot lucks & family get-togethers.

CALZONE
(Italian Pizza Turnovers)

Dough Ingredients:
1 Pkg. Yeast
1 Cup Warm Water
½ Tsp. Salt
2 Tsp. Olive Oil
2½ to 3 Cups Flour

Filling Ingredients:
3 Italian Sausages
1 Small Onion, chopped
1 Clove Garlic, minced or pressed
1 Chopped Pepper (red ripe or green)
½ to 1 Cup Chopped Mushrooms
2½ Cups Grated Jack Cheese
¼ to ½ Cup Romano or Parmesan Cheese, grated
1 Cup or more Favorite Italian Sauce

Dough Directions: Dissolve yeast in water. Add salt, oil and part of flour. Beat well. Add rest of flour, mixing or kneading till smooth and satiny. Let rise in greased bowl in warm place till doubled. (May use your favorite pizza dough recipe.)

Filling: Skin and break apart sausages. Cook gently over medium heat. Add garlic, chopped onion and green or red bell pepper and saute' till limp. Drain well. Season to taste and allow to cool. Have sausage mixture, cheeses and sauce ready in separate containers. Grease two cookie sheets.

Assembly: Punch down dough. Divide in 4 parts. Roll or pat out to 8 inches across (one at a time). Put ¼ of sausage mixture, ¼ of cheese, 3 or 4 tbs. of sauce in center of dough. Fold over and seal with a fork. Prick top with fork. Brush with olive oil if desired. Bake at 475 degrees 10 to 20 minutes, until browned on outside and bubbly on inside.

GAZPACHO

3 Cloves Garlic, peeled
¼ Small Green Bell Pepper
¼ Onion, chopped
1 Cucumber
1 Large Ripe Tomato
4 Tbs. Olive Oil
3 Tbs. Wine Vinegar
2 - 6 Oz. Cans V-8 Vegetable Juice
   Cocktail or Tomato Juice, ice cold
¼ Tsp. Cumin Powder Seasoning
Salt & Pepper to taste

Chop and mash together all but liquid ingredients. Add liquid ingredients and blend on low speed of electric blender for only a moment. Serve in chilled soup bowls.

Note: Diced cucumber, pepper, chopped tomato, hard-boiled egg, cubed French bread or croutons may be served apart for each person to garnish his cold soup. This Spanish cold soup is most refreshing in summer as a first course or instead of a salad. In addition to putting hair on your chest, it's good for you!

VENISON STEAK

4 Venison Loin Steaks
1 Onion, chopped
1 Clove Garlic
½ Cup Lemon Juice
1 Tbs. Parsley
1 Tbs. Worcestershire Sauce
6 Tbs. Blue Cheese
6 Tbs. Butter

Mix the onion, garlic, lemon juice, parsley & Worcestershire sauce. Then mix the blue cheese and butter. Broil steaks until brown, 7 to 10 minutes on one side. Turn steaks over and pour all ingredients over them. Put them back into the oven until cheese and butter are melted, about 3 to 5 minutes.

MUSHROOM ROLL SUPREME

4 Tbs. Chopped Parsley
2 Lbs. Mushrooms
2 Cloves Garlic
1½ Sticks Butter
¼ Cup Dry Sherry
½ Tsp. Salt
1/8 Tsp. Pepper
4 Tbs. Fresh or Frozen Dried Chive
1 Cup Dairy Sour Cream
1 Lb. Sweet Butter
Bread Crumbs
1 Pkg. Strudel Dough or Filo
   (available at bakery)

1. Chop parsley; reserve.
2. Saute' finely-chopped mushrooms, cloves of garlic (mashed) in 1½ sticks of butter in large skillet for 3 minutes. (Mushrooms can be chopped in food processor, being careful not to pureé them.)
3. Add sherry, continue cooking, stirring constantly, until liquid has evaporated. Add salt and pepper, parsley and chopped chives. Remove from heat; add sour cream. Cover skillet; reserve.
4. Melt 1 lb. butter in a small saucepan.
5. Heat oven to 375 degrees.
6. Lay a dampened towel on the table. Remove plastic envelopes of strudel leaves; working quickly put 1 leaf on towel. Liberally spread with melted butter; repeat with second and third sheet, buttering last sheet. Sprinkle with 3 or 4 tbs. dry bread crumbs. Repeat above twice more as the sheets are very thin.
7. Leaving 2'' margins on sides, pile one-quarter of mushroom mixture along bottom edge.
8. Fold in margins. Holding the lower corners of towel taut, flip roll over and over until you are almost at end. Paint edge with butter; seal and complete rolling. Lift strudel roll onto buttered rimmed baking pan.
9. Cover loosely with waxed paper while making remaining bars. Remove waxed paper. Bake at 375 degrees for 20 min. or until golden; serve warm. Absolutely delicious!

GREEN ENCHILADAS with SOUR CREAM

2 Cups Cottage Cheese
1 Lb. Cheddar Cheese
¼ Cup Chopped, Cooked Onions
¼ Cup Crushed Tostadas
2 Tbs. Chopped Olives
2 Tbs. Chopped Jalapeno Chilies
1 Tsp. Salt
12 Tortillas
Oil

Green Enchilada Sauce:
2 Cans Cream of Mushroom Soup
  (Campbell's)
1 - 3½ Oz. Can Ortega Chilies
1 Large Onion, chopped
1 Clove Garlic, minced
1 Can Chicken Broth
½ Cup Raw Puréed Spinach
½ Tsp. Salt
2 Tbs. Flour
Sour Cream

Cheese Enchiladas: Mix cheeses, onions, tostadas, olives and chilies; add salt. Fry tortillas in oil until soft and pliable - not crisp. Drain and dip into Green Enchilada Sauce, coating both sides. Place filling in center of tortillas and roll. Place in greased baking dish with overlapped edges down. Pour remaining sauce over rolled enchiladas and bake in moderate oven, 350 degrees, until piping hot. Top with sour cream after removing enchiladas from oven.

Green Enchilada Sauce: Puree' mushroom soup, chilies, onion and garlic in blender. Add to chicken broth and bring to boil; add pureed spinach and salt and simmer 10 to 15 minutes. Thicken with flour mixed with a little cold water. Stir into sauce & bring to a boil. Reduce heat and stir constantly to avoid lumping.

FRANK & CORN CROWN

½ Cup Chopped Green Pepper
¼ Cup Chopped Onion
¼ Cup Butter or Margarine
2 Cups Soft Bread Crumbs
1 - 17 Oz. Can Cream Corn
1 - 12 Oz. Can Whole Kernel
  Corn, drained
2 Beaten Eggs
¼ Cup Fine, Dry Bread Crumbs
1 Tbs. Butter, melted
1 Lb. (8 to 10) Frankfurters, cut
  in half lengthwise

Cook green pepper and onion in ¼ cup butter till tender but not brown. Add next 4 ingredients and 1 tsp. salt; mix lightly. Spoon into an 8" x 1½" round baking dish (square will do also)

Combine dry bread crumbs and melted butter; sprinkle over corn mixture. Bake uncovered at 350 degrees for 30 min. [MW: 10 min. on full power]. Stand franks, cut end down, in crown around edge of stuffing. Bake 15 min longer. Serves 5 or 6.

MUSHROOM SOUP

1 Large Clove Garlic
2 Oz. Melted Butter
2 Oz. Olive Oil
1 Onion
1 Lb. Fresh Mushrooms, sliced
3 Cups Chicken Stock
2 Tbs. Tomato Paste
2 Oz. White Port
3 Egg Yolks
2 Oz. Parmesan Cheese, grated
½ Cup Parsley, minced
Salt and Pepper to taste

Saute' garlic and onion in butter and oil Add mushrooms. Cover and cook on medium heat until mushrooms are about 1/3 of their original size. Add chicken stock, tomato paste and wine. Salt and pepper to taste. Simmer for 10 min Mix in 3 beaten egg yolks, Parmesan cheese and parsley. Simmer for 5 min. Serve with garlic bread. This recipe can be prepared in the MW

BEEROCKS

Dough:
1 Cake Yeast
1 Cup Lukewarm Mashed Potatoes
1½ Cups Potato Water
2/3 Cup Sugar
1 Tsp. Salt
2 Eggs, well beaten
7 to 7½ Cups Sifted Flour
2/3 Cup Melted Shortening, cooled

Beerock Filling:
¼ Cup Shortening
1 Cup Sliced Onions
4 Cups Shredded Cabbage
2 Cups Cooked Roast Beef,
  shredded (or 1½ Lbs. Hamburger)
Salt and Pepper to taste

Dough: Crumble yeast into mixing bowl and add lukewarm potato water and mashed potato. Add sugar and salt; stir. Let stand until thoroughly dissolved, about 5 minutes. Add eggs and mix. Add about half of the flour. Beat with spoon until smooth and elastic so that batter will fall from spoon in sheets. Beat in cooled shortening. Add most of the remaining flour and knead well until dough is easy to handle. Turn dough onto lightly-floured bread board, cover and let stand 10 minutes to tighten up, then knead until smooth and elastic. Put into large greased bowl. Grease top, cover and store in refrigerator until ready to use. An hour before ready to use, remove from refrigerator. Makes about 15 Beerocks.

Filling: Melt shortening in Dutch oven; add cabbage and onions; steam them, stirring so they will not overcook. Add meat and mix well; add salt and pepper. Cool. Roll refrigerated dough on floured board about ½" thick. Cut into 5" squares and place a heaping tablespoon of filling on each square. Bring 4 corners together on cut edges. Place on greased baking sheet. Set in warm place to rise for 15 to 20 minutes. Filling for 15 Beerocks. Bake at 350 degrees for 20 minutes, or until golden brown.

"AFTER THE GAME" HOT DOGS

3 Tbs. Margarine
1 Tsp. Salt
1/8 Tsp. Paprika
½ Tsp. Worcestershire Sauce
½ Cup Grated Cheese
¼ Cup Flour
1/8 Tsp. Pepper
½ Tsp. Mustard
1 Can Tomato Soup
1 Cup Celery, diced
¾ Lb. Wieners, ground
10 Hot Dog Buns

Cook above ingredients together to heat through and melt cheese. Cool. Put into buns, wrap separately in aluminum foil, store in refrigerator until used. Then heat at 350 degrees until warmed through. Serve in foil wrapping. This is a recipe from the 1940's and was popular for easy serving after football games or occasions calling for easy snacks.

24—HOUR OMELETTE

8 Slices White Sandwich Bread
1 Lb. Longhorn Cheese, grated
8 Eggs
¾ Tsp. Salt
3 Cups Milk
¾ Tsp. Dry Mustard
Dash Cayenne Pepper
Green Onions
Fresh Mushrooms

Butter bread and cut into 1" cubes; place in greased 9 x 13" pan. Sprinkle grated cheese over bread cubes. Top with a layer of sliced onions and fresh mushrooms. Beat eggs, milk and spices together and pour over. Refrigerate overnight, or a minimum of 6 hours. Bake, covered, at 350 degrees for 1 hour; [MW: 40 min. on medium power, covered with wax paper] uncover to brown (about 5 min.). Serves approximately 8. Super brunch dish.

LASAGNA BREAD
(Looks Beautiful & Tastes Great)

½ Lb. Sausage
½ Lb. Hamburger
¾ Cup Chopped Onion
½ Clove Garlic, minced
1 Tbs. Parsley Flakes
½ Tsp. Leaf Basil
½ Tsp. Leaf Oregano
½ Tsp. Salt
Dash Pepper
1 Can Tomato Paste
1 Cup Creamed Cottage Cheese
1 Egg
¼ Cup Grated Parmesan Cheese
2 Cans Crescent Rolls
2 - 7 x 4 Inch Pieces Mozzarella Cheese
1 Tbs. Milk
1 Tbs. Sesame Seed

Meat Mixture: Brown meat, add all seasonings, onion and paste and simmer for 5 minutes.

Cheese Mixture: Combine cottage cheese, egg and parmesan cheese.

Crust: On a large cookie sheet, press the crescent rolls into a 15 x 13 inch rectangle. Spoon half the meat mixture onto the dough, leaving a border on the sides and enough dough at the top and the bottom to enclose ingredients like a letter inside an envelope. Follow meat mixture with cheese mixture, then the other half of the meat mixture, placing the sliced mozzarella cheese on last. Enclose ingredients pressing dough together with fingers. Brush with milk and sprinkle with sesame seeds. Bake in a 375 degree oven for about 25 minutes or until crust is golden brown. Serves 6. Can be made ahead, but not more than 2 hours.

TRIPE STEW

1 Pkg. Tripe
1 Large Can Hominy
5 Med. Potatoes
2 Small Cans Hot Sauce
3 Large Green Peppers (Chili Peppers)
1 Tsp. Salt
1 Tbs. Black Pepper

Dice tripe into small squares; add hominy and potatoes. Cover with water. Cook 1 hour on medium heat. Add hot sauce, chili peppers, salt and black pepper. Cook on low heat 2 hrs. Stir from bottom often to keep from sticking to pan. This recipe can be prepared in MW.

OATMEAL COTTAGE CHEESE PATTIES

1 Cup Cottage Cheese (may use low fat)
1½ Cups Rolled Oats (old-fashioned)
2 Eggs, slightly beaten
1 Medium Onion, chopped (or onion powder)
½ Tsp. Salt
½ to 1 Cup Walnuts, coarsely chopped

Sauce:
2 - 10¾ Oz. Cans Cream of Mushroom Soup
1 - 10¾ Oz. Can Evaporated Milk (may use it diluted for less calories)

Mix ingredients well. Heat prepared frying pan on medium or low heat and spread large spoonfuls of mixture into shape of patties about ½ to ¾" thick in frying pan. Cover and cook until lower side is brown, about 5 minutes; turn patties and brown other side.

Place in casserole pan or shallow dish. Pour hot sauce over patties. Bake at 350 degrees for 30-45 min. [MW: 10 min. on full power]. Serves six.

To prepare sauce, place the contents of two cans mushroom soup in saucepan. Add one can of evaporated milk; stir well to mix, then stir occasionally while heating.

Optional: May use tomato soup instead of mushroom soup for sauce.

SOPA SECA

1 Dozen Corn Tortillas
1/3 Cup Shortening
1 Cup Minced Onion
2 Tbs. Shortening
1 - 4 Oz. Can Ortega Green Chilies,
    diced
1 Cup Whipping Cream
1 - 16 Oz. Can Tomato Puree, or
    Stewed Tomatoes
Salt
½ Lb. Shredded Jack Cheese
2 Tbs. Butter

Cut tortillas in thin strips; saute' them in 1/3 cup shortening until crisp. Make sauce. Saute' onion in 2 tbs. butter until transparent; add chilies, cream, tomato puree and simmer 10 minutes. Add salt to taste. Grease a 2 qt. baking dish and cover bottom with half the tortilla strips. Pour over half of the sauce and add layer of half shredded cheese. Repeat layers, ending with cheese. Dot with butter. Bake at 350 degrees for 30 min. [MW: 10 min. on full power, covered with plastic wrap].

CHILI RELLENO SUPREME

6 Slices Jack Cheese, sliced ½ inch square
    by 3 inches long
5 Eggs, separated
1 Tsp. Flour
Pinch Salt
1 Pt. Cooking Oil
2 Small Cans Whole Ortega Brand Chilies

Take each chili and roll both sides in flour and wrap around cheese slice. After you have prepared all of the chilies, beat whites of eggs with mixer until very stiff, adding a pinch of salt and tsp. of flour while beating. Then fold in yolks of eggs slowly until batter is well mixed. Have oil in skillet very hot. Place dollop of batter in hot oil, lay cheese filled chili on top and then cover with more batter until the entire chili is covered. After one to two minutes when

batter has browned, flip chili over to cook the other side. Remove and serve. Warmed La Victoria Bottled Salsa Suprema may be poured over relleno if desired.

VENISON STROGANOFF

2 Lbs. Venison Steak
Butter or Margarine

1 Cup Onions
¼ Lb. Mushrooms
1 Garlic Clove
6 Tbs. Butter or Margarine
4 Tbs. Flour
1½ Cups Beef Broth or Bouillon
¼ Cup White Wine
1 Cup Sour Cream
1 Tsp. Dill
Buttered Noodles

Slice the venison into thin strips. Coat the strips in flour mixed with salt and pepper. Brown the strips in as much butter as needed. Take out and set aside.

In the same skillet, saute' the onions, sliced mushrooms and minced garlic in the butter. Add the flour to the mixture, then gradually pour in the beef broth, stirring till smooth. Bring this to a boil and then simmer for 5 min. Over low heat, add the wine, sour cream and dill. Put the venison strips in and heat thoroughly. Serve over hot buttered noodles.

Note: Beef can be used in place of venison if venison is unavailable or beef is preferred.

QUICHE LORRAINE

1 Pastry for a 10" Pie Shell
4 Thin Slices Ham
1 Cup Grated Swiss Cheese
3 Eggs
1¼ Cups Milk
1¼ Cups Light Cream
¼ Tsp. Salt
1/8 Tsp. Cayenne
½ Tsp. Season-All or Bon Appetit
Dash Nutmeg
Dash MSG

Line a 10" pie plate with pastry. Cut ham into small pieces, should have about ¾ cup. Heat in frying pan for a few minutes. Sprinkle over pastry. (12 slices bacon may be substituted for ham). Cook bacon until crisp, them crumble into small pieces. Sprinkle cheese over ham. Beat eggs, add remaining ingredients and mix well. Pour over cheese and ham. Bake in 375° F. oven for about 40 minutes.

You can cut Quiche Lorraine into wedges and serve as a first course or for a light luncheon. Or cut into small squares for appetizers. Serves 8 to 10.

CHEESE CASSEROLE

2 - 4 Oz. Cans Green Chilies, drained
1 Lb. Monterey Jack Cheese, coarsely grated
1 Lb. Cheddar Cheese, coarsely grated
4 Egg Whites
4 Egg Yolks
2/3 Cup Can Milk, undiluted
1 Tbs. Flour
½ Tsp. Salt
1/8 Tsp. Pepper
2 Medium Tomatoes, sliced or Canned Tomatoes, drained & sliced

Preheat oven to 325 degrees. Remove seeds from chilies and dice. In a large bowl, combine the grated cheese and green chilies. Turn into a well buttered shallow 12 x 8 x 2 inch 2 quart casserole. In a large bowl with electric mixer at high speed, beat egg whites just until stiff peaks form when beater is slowly raised. In small bowl, combine egg yolks, milk, flour, salt and pepper and mix until well blended. Using rubber scraper, gently fold beaten whites into egg yolk mixture in casserole and using fork, "ooze" it through the cheese. Bake for 30 min. [MW: 10 min. on full power]. Remove from oven and arrange sliced tomatoes overlapping around the edge of casserole. Bake for 30 min. longer [MW: 10 min. on full power] or until a silver knife inserted comes out clean. If desired, garnish with a sprinkling of chopped green chilies. Makes 8 to 10 servings.

SOUPE AU PISTOU

1 Cup Diced Onions
1 Leek, sliced, white part only
2 Tbs. Butter
1 to 2 Cups Green Beans, cut in ½ inch slices
1 Cup Diced Potatoes
1 Cup Canned Tomatoes
6 Cups Beef Broth
½ Cup Spaghetti, broken up
2 Tsp. Salt
1 Tsp. Pepper
2 Cloves Garlic
2 Tsp. Basil
1 Tsp. Thyme
½ Tsp. Sage
2 Egg Yolks
¼ Cup Olive Oil
2 Tbs. Tomato Paste
¼ Cup Parmesan Cheese

Saute' onions and leek in butter, add beans, potatoes, tomatoes and broth, cook about 15 minutes. Add spaghetti, salt and pepper and cook until done, approximately 10 minutes. In a bowl, mash garlic and herbs together, add egg yolks, tomato paste and olive oil. Add a little soup to this mixture then stir back into soup. Sprinkle with parmesan and serve. Serves 6.

MEATLESS TAMALE PIE

1 Cup Yellow Corn Meal
2 Cups Milk
1 Large Onion, chopped fine
½ Green Pepper, chopped
½ Cup Salad Oil
1 - No. 2½ Can Tomatoes (3½ cups)
3 Eggs, slightly beaten
1 Can Whole Kernel Corn
2 Cups Ripe Olives, pitted
1 Tbs. Salt
½ Tsp. Pepper
1 Tbs. Spanish Pepper, mixed with 1
    tbs. water until smooth
½ Cup Grated Cheese

Cook cornmeal and milk as per instructions
for mush. Slightly brown onion and pepper
in oil. Add tomatoes and seasonings and
simmer for 20 minutes. Slightly beat 3 eggs
in a large bowl. Mix with mush, tomatoes,
corn and olives. Put in a greased casserole
dish. Top with ½ cup grated cheese. Bake
at 350 degrees for 1 hr. [MW: 15-20 min. on
full power], or until firm.

Note: Multiples of this recipe with a
green salad and a simple dessert is excellent for large groups and is a general favorite with all ages.

HEROINE SANDWICH

1 Long Loaf Sour French Bread, unsliced
3 Pkgs. Cream Cheese, 3 Oz. Size
3 Pkgs. Grated Cheddar Cheese
Mayonnaise
¾ Cup Chopped Parsley
Juice of ½ Lemon
1 Tbs. Worcestershire Sauce
3 to 4 Whole Lg. Dill Pickles
3 to 4 Thin Slices of Baked or Boiled
    Ham

Cut loaf in half lengthwise. Scoop out
center leaving crust shells (give it to the
birds). Spread insides of shells with the
mayonnaise (be generous). Sprinkle shells
liberally with the chopped parsley. Mix
cream cheese, cheddar cheese, Worcestershire sauce, lemon juice in a bowl until
creamy soft. Fill shell cavity of BOTH
loaf halves with the above mix. Wrap
slice of ham around each whole pickle
and press end to end into the bottom
half of the cheese filled loaf. Top with
the other half and press the 2 halves together back into the whole loaf shape.
Wrap tightly in foil or plastic and refrigerate for several hours. (Can be made a
day ahead of time.) To serve: Slice
the loaf as you normally would. Arrange
on a platter garnished with parsley sprigs
and apple quarters. Ideal luncheon dish
accompanied by Gaspatcho soup and / or
a mixed salad.

PIZZA LOAF

2 Loaves Frozen Bread Dough, unbaked
1 Lb. Ground Chuck
¾ Cup Minced Onion
1 - 8 Oz. Can Tomato Sauce
1 Tsp. Paprika
½ Tsp. Oregano
½ Tsp. Celery Salt
1/3 Tsp. Garlic Salt
1/8 Tsp. Pepper
¼ Cup Chopped Ripe Olives
¼ Cup Chopped Mushrooms
1 Tbs. Dried Sweet Pepper Flakes

Let dough rise according to package
directions.

Meat Filling: Combine in skillet, meat,
onion, tomato sauce, mushrooms and pepper flakes. Add paprika, oregano, celery
salt, garlic salt and pepper. Cover and
simmer for 30 to 40 minutes. Stir in
olives; cool to lukewarm. Press dough out
on greased cookie sheets to 14 x 12 inches.
Place half of meat mixture on each down
center third of dough to within 2 inches
of the ends. Sprinkle with cheese. Fold
ends over filling. Fold sides over filling.
Brush with milk, let rise in warm place
for 15 minutes. Bake at 375 degrees for
25 minutes.

PIZZA

¾ Cup Warm Water
1 Pkg. Active Dry Yeast
1 Tbs. Oil
½ Tsp. Salt
1½-2 Cups Flour
8 Oz. (½ can) Pizza Sauce (Contadina is good)
8 Oz. Mozzarella Cheese, grated
8 Oz. Pkg. Thinly Sliced Danish Ham or thinly sliced Beef Sausage or any other favorite pizza topping
1 Fresh Tomato, sliced thinly

Mix water and yeast until yeast is dissolved. Mix in oil and salt. Add flour. Knead 5-10 minutes or until smooth. Put in greased bowl and cover; let rise until double or about 1 hour. Spread dough out on greased 12 inch diameter pizza pan. Lightly grease top of dough. Bake in 425 degree oven about 10 minutes. Spread on pizza sauce, top with meat evenly. Bake another 5-10 minutes. Add grated Mozzarella cheese; bake another 5-10 minutes. Slice into 8 serving pieces and garnish with fresh tomato slices. Makes 1 large pizza.

GREEK—STYLE SANDWICHES

½ Cup Dry Red Wine
2 Tbs. Olive or Cooking Oil
1 Small Clove Garlic (optional)
½ Tsp. Dried Oregano, crushed
½ Tsp. Salt
Dash Freshly Ground Pepper
2 Lbs. Beef Sirloin Steak, cut ½" thick
1 Tbs. Butter or Margarine
4 Syrian or Pita Bread Envelopes
3 Cups Chopped Lettuce (½ Head)
1 Cup Diced, Seeded, Peeled Tomato (1 Large)
1 Cup Diced, Seeded, Peeled Cucumber (1 Medium)
2 Cups Sour Cream with Chives

Combine wine, oil, garlic, oregano, salt and pepper. Cut steak into bite-size pieces, ¼"

thick. Pour marinade over beef and let it set 1 hour at room temperature. Drain the meat. Cook meat, half at a time in hot butter or margarine, stirring to brown on all sides, 2 to 3 minutes. Serve meat in a chafing dish or a hot tray to keep warm. May also be kept in a 200 degree oven, covered. Open one end of Syrian bread to make a pocket, or cut bread in half and fill like a taco. Set out dishes of lettuce, tomato, cucumber and sour cream dip. Make your own sandwich. 4 individual servings.

Note: Steak is easier to cut if it is partially frozen.

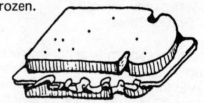

BARLEY PINE NUT CASSEROLE

1 Cup Pearl Barley
6 Tbs. Butter
¼ to ½ Cup Pine Nuts or Sliced Almonds
1 Medium Onion, chopped
½ Cup Minced Fresh Parsley
¼ Cup Minced Chives or Green Onions
¼ Tsp. Each Salt & Pepper
2 - 14 Oz. Cans Regular Strength Beef or Chicken Broth
Parsley (for garnish)

Rinse the barley in cold water and drain well. In a frying pan, heat 2 tbs. butter over medium heat. Add pine nuts and stir until lightly toasted. Remove the nuts with a slotted spoon and set aside. Add the remaining 4 tbs. butter to pan with the onions and drained barley. Cook, stirring, until lightly toasted. Remove from heat; stir in the pine nuts, parsley, chives, salt and pepper. Spoon into a 1½ quart casserole dish. This much may be done ahead. Cover and chill. Heat the broth to boiling; pour over barley mixture in casserole and stir to blend well. Bake, uncovered, at 375 degrees until the barley is tender and most of the liquid is absorbed, about 1 hour and 10 minutes [MW: 30 min. on full power].

CAKES - BREADS

ITALIAN CREAM CAKE

½ Cup Crisco
1 Stick Butter
2 Cups Sugar
1 Tsp. Vanilla
1 Tsp. Baking Soda
5 Eggs
1 Cup Buttermilk
2 Cups Flour
½ Tsp. Salt
2 Cups Coconut
1 Cup Pecans

Cream Crisco, butter and sugar together. Separate eggs and 5 yolks, one at a time. Add dry ingredients along with buttermilk. Stir in nuts. Fold in stiffly beaten egg whites. Bake in 3 greased and floured 9 inch pie pans. Bake for 30 minutes or until done.

Icing:
1 Stick Butter
1 - 8 Oz. Pkg. Cream Cheese
1 Box Powdered Sugar
1 Tsp. Vanilla
1 Cup Pecans

Warm butter and cream cheese to room temperature. Mix with remaining ingredients until smooth and spread.

TIN CAN BREAD

4 Cups Whole Wheat Flour
1 Pkg. Active Dry Yeast
½ Cup Water
½ Cup Milk
¼ Cup Honey
½ Cup Butter
1 Tsp. Salt
½ Cup Ground Sunflower Seeds
½ Cup Chopped Raisins
2 Eggs

Soak raisins for 2 to 3 hours in warm water. Mix 2 cups flour with yeast. Stir water, milk, honey, butter and salt over low heat until butter melts. Cool about 5 minutes. Add to flour and yeast mixture. Add eggs, remaining flour, sunflower seeds and raisins. Knead on a floured board until dough is smooth and elastic and raisins are well distributed. Divide dough in half and drop each roll into a tall tomato juice can that has been generously coated with butter. Cover each can with wax paper, held on by a rubber band. Let rise in a warm place, 85 degrees, until dough is within 1 inch of the top of the can. Remove covers and bake in a 375 degree oven for 35 minutes.

JEWISH CRUMB CAKE

½ Lb. Soft Butter or Margarine
2 Cups Sugar
2 Tsp. Vanilla
½ Tsp. Salt
4 Eggs
1 Pint Sour Cream
3 Cups Flour
2 Tsp. Baking Soda
1 Cup Sugar
3 Tsp. Cinnamon
3 Tbs. Chopped Nuts, optional
5 Tbs. Coconut, optional

Cream together first 4 ingredients. Add 4 eggs, one at a time, at high speed. Add 1 pint sour cream at low speed. Sift together next 2 ingredients and mix with first mixture. Mix sugar, cinnamon, nuts and coconut together in separate bowl.

Grease and flour 2 - 10" square pans [MW: omit grease & flour]. Put part of batter into each pan, then sprinkle with sugar mixture and cut through, using knife. Add balance of batter, then top with remaining sugar mixture, cut again. Bake in 350 degree oven 50-60 min. [MW: 15 min. on full power, covered with wax paper], or until toothpick inserted in center comes out clean. Cool on rack, in pan.

HEIRLOOM FRUITCAKE

2 Lbs. Candied Cherries
2 Lbs. Candied Pineapple
½ Lb. Candied Orange Peel
½ Lb. Candied Lemon Peel
½ Lb. Citron
11 Oz. Shelled Pecans
2 Lbs. Pitted Dates
2 Lbs. Golden Raisins
1 Lb. Dark Raisins
1 Lb. Currants
1 Lb. Butter
1 Lb. Brown Sugar
1 Dozen Large Eggs
3 Tsp. Vanilla
Juice of Large Lemon
Juice of Large Orange
4 Cups Sifted Flour
2 Tsp. Baking Powder
1 Tsp. Nutmeg
1 Tsp. Allspice
3 Tsp. Cinnamon
12 Oz. Jar Grape Jelly
1 Cup Brandy

Dice candied fruits and peels. Break nuts into coarse pieces and snip dates and raisins into small pieces with scissors dipped into hot water. Combine fruits and nuts into large bowl and toss with enough additional flour to coat well. Cream together butter and brown sugar until fluffy. Add eggs, one at a time, beating well after each addition. Stir in vanilla, lemon and orange juices. Sift together flour, baking powder, nutmeg, allspice and cinnamon. Beat together jelly and brandy until smooth. Alternately add flour mixture and jelly to creamed mixture, blending well. Stir in fruit and nut mixture. Dough will be very stiff, so a wooden paddle or scraper will mix most efficiently.

Grease pans; line with brown paper and grease the paper. Turn batter into pans. Fill three-fourths full and smooth tops. Bake at 300 degrees until a wooden pick inserted near center of cake comes out clean. Loaf cakes bake about 2½ hours, or a 10" tube pan bakes for about 6½ hours. Cool cakes in pans. Remove cakes from pans and pour a little brandy over tops. Wrap in cloth soaked in brandy. Wrap in foil. Store in cool place, but do not refrigerate. Store at least 4 months before you serve it. Makes about 10 lbs.

Fruit-cake Glaze:
1 Cup Sugar
1/3 Cup Light Corn Syrup
½ Cup Water

Combine sugar, corn syrup and water in saucepan. Cook, stirring constantly, until syrup spins a fine thread (300 degrees on candy thermometer). Brush hot syrup over cooked fruitcakes. Let dry until tacky, then arrange candied cherries, citron and pineapple in design on top of cake and brush with more glaze. Let glaze thoroughly dry before covering cake for storage.

NEW ENGLAND TOMATO SOUP CAKE

2 Cups Flour
2 Tsp. Baking Powder
1 Tsp. Soda
½ Tsp. Salt
½ Tsp. Cloves
2 Tsp. Cinnamon
½ Tsp. Nutmeg
½ Cup Shortening
1 Cup Sugar
1 Can Tomato Soup + ½ Can Water
½ Cup Nutmeats
1 Cup Raisins
Candied Fruits, optional
Dates, optional
Mincemeat, optional

Measure all ingredients into large bowl excluding nuts and raisins. Beat for 2 minutes at medium speed. Add nutmeats and raisins that have been powdered with flour (Keeps them from settling to the bottom.) Bake in 8-½ X 11 inch glass cake pan in 350 degree oven for 40 to 45 minutes. This cake can be served warm as a coffee cake with butter or cooled and frosted with cream cheese frosting and decorated with nuts. It can also be baked in 2 loaf pans to slice. It has been a family favorite for 4 generations of New Englanders.

TANGERINE BREAD

1 Cube Butter or Margarine
1 Cup Water
2 Cups Sugar
2/3 Cup Orange Juice
4 Tbs. Tangerine Rind
2 Eggs
4 Cups Flour
1 Cup Nuts
1 Tsp. Salt
2 Tsp. Baking Powder
2 Tsp. Baking Soda

Boil butter and water. Put all other ingredients in mixing bowl; add boiled mixture; beat with electric mixer for 30 seconds to mix; then beat for 3 minutes. Pour into 2 greased and floured loaf pans. Bake at 350 degrees for 1 hour. Test with toothpick after 1 hour. Set pans on rack to cool 15 minutes. Turn out of pans; cool 1 hour. Enjoy! Freezes well.

POTATO DOUGHNUTS

1¾ Cups Milk
½ Cup Shortening
½ Cup Sugar
½ Cup Mashed Potatoes
1 Pkg. Active Dry Yeast
½ Cup Warm Water
2 Eggs, beaten
1 Tsp. Vanilla
7 Cups Flour
1 Tsp. Baking Powder
2 Tsp. Salt

Scald milk; stir in the shortening, sugar and mashed potatoes. Cool to lukewarm. Blend well. Sprinkle yeast over the ½ cup warm water and stir until yeast is dissolved. Add to lukewarm mixture. Stir in vanilla and beaten eggs.

Sift the flour with baking powder and salt; add gradually to the liquid mixture. Mix well after each addition. This is a very soft

dough. Turn out on a floured board; knead just enough to shape up the dough. Turn into a greased bowl; cover with a piece of plastic wrap and let rise until double in bulk, about 1½ hours.

On a well-floured board, roll out dough to ½" thickness. Cut with floured doughnut cutter. Place cut doughnuts on waxed paper; cover with a cloth and let rise until double in bulk, about ½ hour. Fry a few at a time in oil or melted shortening, heated to 375 degrees. Drain on absorbent paper. Shake a few at a time in a bag containing sugar - or cinnamon and sugar. Makes about 4 dozen. They freeze well.

SLAVIC ZWIEBACK

1 Cup Shortening
2 Cups Sugar
6 Eggs
6 Cups Flour
5 Tsp. Baking Powder
1 Tsp. Salt
2 Cups Chopped Walnuts
2 Tsp. Anise Oil

Combine shortening and sugar. Mix until smooth. Add eggs, one at a time. Beat until smooth. Add anise oil. Sift flour. Add baking powder, salt and nuts to flour. Gradually add this to basic. Mix thoroughly. Grease 3 metal ice-tray pans. Divide dough into 3 parts, with floured hands. Press each part evenly into ice-tray pan. Bake in 350 degree oven for 25 to 30 minutes. Cool for 10 to 15 minutes at room temperature. Turn out onto a cutting board. Slice whole loaf. Place slices flat, onto a cooky-sheet. Bake in 350 degree oven for 6 minutes. Turn each piece to other side and bake 6 minutes more. Delicious plain or buttered. Loaves may be stored whole in refrigerator or freezer until ready to slice and bake again.

AUSTRALIAN CHRISTMAS CAKE

½ Lb. Butter
½ Lb. Brown Sugar
5 Eggs
4 Tbs. Rum
¾ Lb. Flour
½ Tsp. Baking Powder
1½ Lbs. Mixed Fruit
¼ Lb. Cherries
¼ Lb. Lemon Peel
1 Tsp. Mixed Spice
Almonds

Line a 3 lb. Christmas tin with 3 thicknesses of wax paper. Cream butter and sugar until fluffy. Beat eggs well and gradually add to mixture. Gradually add the rum. Fold in the sifted flour, baking powder and spice alternately with the fruit. Place in Christmas tin and decorate with split almonds. Bake in a 350 degree oven for 2½ to 3 hours. Leave in tin until cold.

GHIRARDELLI CHOCOLATE CAKE

Cake:

6 Oz. Ghirardelli Milk Chocolate
½ Cup Boiling Water
1 Cup Soft Butter
1-½ Cups Sugar
4 Egg Yolks
4 Egg Whites
1 Tsp. Vanilla
½ Tsp. Salt
1 Tsp. Baking Soda
2-½ Cups Sifted Cake Flour
1 Cup Buttermilk

Frosting:

3 Tbs. Butter
2 Oz. Unsweetened Chocolate
2 Cups Powdered Sugar
1/8 Tsp. Salt
½ Tsp. Vanilla
4 Tbs. Hot Milk
½ Small Carton Whipping Cream

Melt chocolate in boiling water. Cool. Cream butter and sugar until light add egg yolks, one at a time, beating until very smooth. Add chocolate and vanilla. Sift flour, salt and soda. Add alternately with buttermilk to chocolate mixture, beating well after each addition. Beat egg whites stiff, fold into batter. Pour batter into 3 greased 8 or 9 inch cake pans. Bake in 350 degree oven 30 to 40 minutes, or until toothpick inserted in center comes out clean. Cool on wire racks. After cool, frost. Frosting: Melt chocolate over top of a double boiler. Cream butter and sugar together. Add chocolate, vanilla and salt. Add enough of the milk to make good spreading consistency. Spread frosting between bottom 2 layers and sides of cake. Whip cream until stiff and spread on top layer. Garnish with shaved chocolate.

CINNAMON TORTE

¾ Cup Sugar
¾ Cup Crisco
9 Tbs. Milk
1½ Cups Flour
1½ Tsp. Baking Powder
6 Egg Yolks

Filling:
1 Cup Sugar
1 Cup Water
Butter (size of a walnut)
1 Heaping Tbs. Cornstarch
Grated Rind & Juice of 1 Lemon
1 Egg

Topping:
6 Egg Whites, beaten stiff
1 Cup Sugar
1 Tsp. Cinnamon
½ Cup Nuts

Cook filling ingredients and cool while baking cake. Cream sugar and Crisco; add milk, flour, baking powder and egg yolks. Bake. Spread lemon filling over cake; then topping, and brown in oven.

CALICO APPLE CAKE

½ Cup Shortening
¾ Cup Granulated Sugar
2 Eggs
2 Cups Flour
1 Tsp. Cinnamon
1 Tsp. Baking Soda
½ Tsp. Salt
½ Tsp. Nutmeg
1 Cup Canned Applesauce
1 Pkg. Semi-Sweet Chocolate Bits
½ Cup Raisins
½ Cup Chopped Nuts

Cream shortening and sugar. Add eggs and beat. Add dry ingredients alternately with applesauce and beat. Add remaining ingredients and mix. Bake in a greased 13 x 9 x 3 inch pan in a 350 degree oven for 40 minutes. Cool in pan and sift confectioner's sugar lightly over the top.

CHIPS OF CHOCOLATE PEANUT BUTTER CAKE

2¼ Cups Flour
2 Cups Brown Sugar
1 Cup Peanut Butter
½ Cup Butter or Margarine
1 Tsp. Baking Soda
½ Tsp. Baking Powder
1 Cup Milk
3 Eggs
1 Tsp. Vanilla
1 - 12 Oz. Pkg. Chocolate Chips

In a large mixer bowl, combine flour, brown sugar, peanut butter and butter or margarine. Blend at low speed until crumbly; reserve 1 cup of this mixture. Add to remaining crumb mixture the baking soda, baking powder, milk, eggs and vanilla; mix until blended. Batter will be slightly lumpy. Pour this batter into a greased 13 x 9 inch cake pan. Sprinkle with the 1 cup reserved crumbs. Over the crumbs, sprinkle the chocolate chips. Bake at 350 degrees for 35 to 40 minutes or until a toothpick inserted in the center comes out clean. If you prefer, you may also adapt this recipe for cupcakes. Fill paper baking cups ½ full, sprinkle each with a bit of the reserved crumb mixture and some chocolate chips. Bake for 15 to 20 minutes, or until a toothpick inserted in the center comes out clean.

YUGOSLAV DOUGHNUTS

1½ Cups Milk
1 Cube Butter
2 Tbs. Brandy
2 Tsp. Vanilla
1 Tsp. Orange Rind
1 Tsp. Lemon Rind
2 Cups Flour
1½ Tsp. Salt
½ Cup Sugar
1 Pkg. Dry Yeast
3 Eggs
1 Pint Cooking Oil

Heat 1½ cups milk in a saucepan; add 1 cube butter, 2 tbs. brandy, 2 tsp. vanilla, 1 tsp. orange rind and 1 tsp. lemon rind. Put into a mixing bowl 1 cup flour, 1½ tsp. salt, ½ cup sugar and 1 package dry yeast. Add milk mixture to flour mixture and beat for 3 minutes. Add 1 cup additional flour and beat. Add 3 eggs, one at a time, beating after each addition. If necessary, add a little flour to make a thick batter that drops off the spoon in sheets.

Turn into a warm bowl; cover with warm damp cloth and let rise for 1 hour. Beat again; cover and let rise for 30 minutes.

Fill a 2-quart saucepan with 1 pint oil and heat to frying temperature. Drop dough into oil by teaspoon; when brown on underside, turn over and brown on second side. Drain on paper towels. Sprinkle with sugar. If desired, you may add ½ cup chopped prunes or raisins to the dough.

UKRANIAN KOLACH

12 Cups Flour
1 Cup Sugar
2 Tsp. Salt
2/3 Lb. Butter
1 Quart Scalded Milk
1 Large Compressed Yeast
3 Eggs and 2 Egg Yolks, slightly beaten

Dissolve yeast in ¼ cup warm water; add
½ tsp. sugar; let it foam. Put 12 cups of
flour, salt and sugar (sifted) in a large bowl
and cut the butter in like pie dough. Add
lukewarm milk, beaten eggs and yeast to
flour - butter mixture. Knead until dough
is smooth and elastic and shows bubbles.
Dust top of dough with 3 tbs. flour. Cover
bowl with cloth; set in warm place to rise
until double in bulk, or a little more, about
2 hours. Put dough on bread board and
divide into 8 to 10 pieces. Knead each
piece a little. Cover with cloth; roll one
piece at a time into rectangular shape,
about ¼" thick (a little thicker than pie
crust). Spread filling on, leaving about 1"
of dough clear all around. Roll as for jelly
roll; pinch ends of roll to hold filling in.
Place on oiled pan, with smooth part on
top. Let rise in warm place ½ hour. Brush
top with 1 egg yolk mixed with 2 tbs.
melted butter. Bake at 350 degrees for
30 to 35 minutes.

Fillings for Kolach:
Walnut:
½ Cup Water
1/3 Cup Sugar
1 Lb. Ground Walnuts
Rind of 1 Lemon
1 Tsp. Melted Butter

Make a syrup of water and sugar; let boil
1 minute. Cool, then add walnuts, rind of
1 lemon and melted butter.

Poppy Seed:
1½ Cups Water
1 Cup Sugar
1 Lb. Ground Poppy Seeds
1 Lemon (juice and rind)
1 Tbs. Melted Butter

Make syrup of water and sugar; boil 1
minute. Cool. Add poppy seeds, juice
and rind of lemon and the melted butter.

Dry Cottage Cheese:
1½ Lbs. Dry Cottage Cheese
Rind and Juice of 1 Lemon
2 Egg Yolks
2 Tbs. Sugar
1/8 Tsp. Salt
½ Cup Yellow Raisins (optional)
2 Cups Hot Water

Cream dry cottage cheese until light; add
rind and juice of lemon, 2 egg yolks, 2
tbs. sugar and salt. Add raisins that have
been soaking in hot water for 2 hours,
drained and patted dry.

Prunes:
1½ Lbs. Prunes
1 Cup Water
1/3 Cup Sugar
Juice of 1 Lemon
1 Tsp. Butter, melted

Cook prunes in water with sugar and juice
of lemon slowly for ½ hour after it comes
to boiling point. Stir occasionally; cool.
Remove pits and add melted butter.

Note: Each of these fillings will fill 4 to 5
rolls.

DOUGHNUTS

3 Eggs, well beaten
1 Cup Sugar
1 Tsp. Vanilla
1/3 Cup Cream
2/3 Cup Buttermilk
3 Cups Flour
1 Tsp. Baking Soda
1 Tsp. Salt
1 Tsp. Baking Powder
Dash Nutmeg

Beat eggs well. Add sugar, vanilla,
cream and buttermilk. Sift and add
flour, baking soda, salt, baking powder and nutmeg. Chill dough before
rolling out. Fry at 375 degrees.

HOT MILK SPONGE CAKE

2 Eggs
1 Cup Sugar
½ Cup Hot Milk
1 Tbs. Butter
1 Tsp. Vanilla
1 Tsp. Baking Powder
¼ Tsp. Salt
1¼ Cups Flour

Beat eggs until thick. Gradually add sugar and beat some more. Sift flour, baking powder, and salt together. Heat milk to boiling. Add butter, vanilla, egg mixture. Add dry ingredients and mix well. This will be a thin batter. Bake in 350 degree oven for 30 minutes.

MIAMI BEACH BIRTHDAY CAKE

1 Cup Semi-sweet Chocolate Morsels
½ Cup Graham Cracker Crumbs
1/3 Cup Butter, melted
½ Cup Chopped Walnuts
2 Cups Flour
1 Tsp. Baking Soda
1 Tsp. Salt
½ Cup Butter
1½ Cups + 2 Tbs. Sugar
2 Eggs
1 Tsp. Vanilla
1¼ Cups Buttermilk or Sour Milk
1 Cup Heavy Cream

Melt 1/3 cup chocolate morsels. Grease and flour bottoms of two 9" layer pans [MW: omit grease and flour and use 2 - 9" plastic round cake pans]. Combine graham cracker crumbs and melted butter. Stir in walnuts and 2/3 cup morsels. Set aside. Combine flour with soda and salt. Cream butter. Gradually add 1½ cups sugar. Cream well. Add eggs, one at a time. Beat well. Blend in melted morsels and vanilla. At low speed add dry ingredients alternately with buttermilk, beginning and ending with dry ingredients. Turn into pans. Sprinkle with crumb mixture. Bake at 375 degrees for 30 to 40 min. [MW: 8-10 min. on full power, covered with wax paper]. Cool. Beat cream with 2 tbs. sugar until stiff. Fill and frost sides, keeping layers top-side up. Refrigerate.

SODA CRACKER CAKE

4 Egg Yolks
1 Cup Sugar
1 Cup Chopped Walnuts
1 Tsp. Vanilla
2 Tbs. Melted Butter
1 Cup Crushed Soda Crackers, salted
4 Egg Whites, beaten
1 Cup Raspberry Jam
1 Pkg. Macaroons
1 Cup Cream, whipped
Powdered Sugar
Flavoring

Add sugar to beaten yolks. Add chopped nuts, vanilla, butter and crackers. Fold in beaten egg whites. Pour into two 9 inch pans, lined with wax paper that has been greased. Bake 15 to 20 minutes at 325 degrees. Cool. Then spread bottom layer with ½ cup of the jam, cover with macaroons that have been dipped in water. Repeat with top layer. Cover with whipped cream flavored with rum if desired.

AVOCADO CAKE

2-2/3 Cups Sugar
1 Cup Shortening
2 Cups Mashed Avocado
4 Eggs
1 Tsp. Cinnamon
1 Tsp. Nutmeg
1 Tsp. Allspice
1 Tsp. Salt
2 Tsp. Soda
1 Cup Sour Milk
1 Cup Dates
3-½ Cups Flour

Cream sugar, shortening, avocado. Beat in eggs. Mix together dry ingredients. Add dry mix and sour milk alternately. Add dates, stir well. Bake for 30 min. in preheated oven at 300 degrees. [MW: 7-8 min. on full power covered with wax paper].

BUTTERSCOTCH NUT ROLL

¾ Cup Firmly-packed Brown Sugar
½ Cup Light Corn Syrup
¼ Cup Butter or Margarine
½ Cup Walnut or Pecan Halves
½ Recipe Sweet Yeast Dough
2 Tbs. Softened Butter
1/3 Cup Sugar
½ Tsp. Cinnamon
½ Cup Raisins

Combine brown sugar, corn syrup, ¼ cup butter in a small pan; simmer 2 minutes. Pour into a 9" x 9" x 2" baking pan and sprinkle with nuts. Roll out sweet yeast dough (already made) into a 15" x 8" rectangle on a lightly-floured surface. Set aside. Combine sugar, cinnamon and raisins. Spread butter on dough; sprinkle the cinnamon, raisin mixture. Roll up in jelly-roll fashion. Cut into 12 equal pieces. Place cut-side down in prepared pan; cover. Let rise 1 hour, or until double in size. Bake in moderate oven, 375 degrees, for 25 minutes or until golden brown. Turn upside down on plate. Leave pan in place for 5 minutes to allow topping to run over the rolls. Lift off pan.

Sweet Yeast Dough:
½ Cup Milk
½ Cup Sugar
½ Tsp. Salt
2/3 Cup Vegetable Shortening
½ Cup Very Warm Water
1 Envelope Active Dry Yeast
4 Eggs
4½ Cups Sifted Flour

Combine milk, sugar, salt and shortening in saucepan. Heat just until shortening is melted; cool until lukewarm. Sprinkle the yeast into very warm water. Put into large bowl. Add lukewarm milk mixture, eggs & 2 cups flour. Beat until smooth. Add just enough of remaining flour to make soft dough. Turn onto slightly-floured surface and knead into smooth dough - about 5 minutes. Place dough in large greased bowl. Turn; cover and let rise in warm place for about 1½ hours. Punch down; knead again and let rise 5 minutes; shape into rolls.

SCONES

6 Cups Sifted Flour
3 Tbs. Baking Powder
3 Eggs
2 Cups Milk
¾ Cup Vegetable Oil

Whisk together eggs, milk and oil. Add to flour and baking powder; mix well. Pat out on floured board and cut. Place closely together on cookie sheet. Bake 5 to 10 minutes at 450 to 500 degrees.

Variations: Add one of the following; 4 tbs. sugar (and use as shortcake with fresh fruit); 1 cup grated cheese; 1 cup raisins, dates or other dried fruit. Or serve plain with lots of butter, honey and jam.

FILLED COFFEE CAKE

½ Cup Butter or Margarine
1 Cup Sugar
2 Eggs
½ Tsp. Salt
2 Tsp. Vanilla
2 Cups Flour
1 Tsp. Baking Powder
1 Tsp. Baking Soda
1 Cup Buttermilk

Cream together butter, sugar and eggs. Sift dry ingredients together and add alternately with buttermilk to first mixture; add vanilla. Pour half the batter into greased [MW: ungreased] 9" x 9" pan. Top with nut mixture; repeat. Bake at 350 degrees for 35-40 min [MW: 8-10 min. on full power covered with wax paper].

½ Cup Brown Sugar
¼ Cup White Sugar
2 Tbs. Flour
2½ to 3 Tbs. Margarine
½ Cup Finely-chopped Nuts
1½ Tsp. Cinnamon

Work all ingredients together until crumbly.

SPINACH BREAD

1 Cube Butter
1 Cup Flour
1 Tsp. Salt
1 Tsp. Baking Powder
1 Cup Milk
3 Eggs
1 Lb. Grated Cheddar Cheese
4 Cups Spinach, chopped

Melt butter in a 9 x 13 inch pan in oven.
Beat eggs, add flour, milk, salt and baking powder. Mix together, then add the
cheese and spinach. Pour into pan.
Bake 35 minutes at 375 degrees. Cool.
Cut into small squares. Use as appetizer
with a beverage.

SQUASH BREAD

1 Cup Granulated Sugar
½ Cup Packed Brown Sugar
1 Cup Mashed, Cooked Squash
½ Cup Cooking Oil
2 Eggs
¼ Cup Water
2 Cups Flour
1 Tsp. Baking Soda
½ Tsp. Salt
½ Tsp. Nutmeg
½ Tsp. Cinnamon
¼ Tsp. Ginger
½ Cup Crushed Pineapple
½ Cup Walnuts

In mixing bowl, combine granulated sugar,
brown sugar, cooked squash, cooking oil &
eggs; beat until well blended. Stir in water.
Sift flour, baking soda, salt, nutmeg, cinnamon and ginger; add to squash mixture and
mix well. Stir in pineapple and nuts.

Turn batter into a well greased 9'' x 5'' x 3''
loaf pan [MW: ungreased tube or bundt pan].
Bake in 350 degree oven for 65-70 min. [MW:
17-20 min. on full power covered with wax
paper], or until bread is done. Remove from
pan; cool on rack. Wrap and store overnight
if desired. Makes 1 loaf.

EGG NOG CAKE MAGNIFIQUE

Egg Nog Cake:
1 Pkg. Yellow Cake Mix (one that
   calls for 2 eggs & 1-1/3 cups water)
2 Eggs
1½ Cups Egg Nog
¼ Cup Melted Butter
½ Tsp. Nutmeg
½ Tsp. Rum Extract

Egg Nog Filling:
3 Tbs. Cornstarch
2 Cups Egg Nog
½ Tsp. Rum Extract

Whipped Cream Frosting:
2 Cartons of Whipping Cream
¼ Cup Granulated Sugar
Dash of Salt
1 Tsp. Vanilla Extract
1 Tsp. Unflavored Gelatin, dissolved
   in 2 tbs. of water (optional)
1 Tsp. Rum Extract

Egg Nog Cake:
1. In large bowl, combine first 6 ingredients. Beat for 4 minutes.
2. Pour batter into wax paper lined,
greased and floured pans.
3. Bake for 30 minutes at 375 degrees.
When cooled, spread cooked egg nog
filling between the two cakes.

Egg Nog Filling:
1. In stainless steel saucepan, combine
cornstarch with a little bit of egg nog until smooth.
2. Blend remaining egg nog in over boiling water. Stir frequently until thick and
bubbly.
3. Add extract and cool.

Whipped Cream Frosting:
1. Combine cream, sugar, salt, vanilla and
rum extract in mixing bowl. Refrigerate,
with beaters.
2. When chilled, begin whipping.
3. If cake is to stand for more than two
hours after frosting, beat in dissolved gelatin.
Dissolve in cup set in boiling water. Dribble
into cream, beating constantly until stiff
and spreadable.

GUMDROP CAKE

1 Lb. Golden Raisins
1 to 2 Lbs. Gumdrops (do not
  use black gumdrops)
1 Cup Pecans
4 Cups Flour
1 Tsp. Cinnamon
¼ Tsp. Cloves
¼ Tsp. Nutmeg
¼ Tsp. Salt

1 Cup Butter
2 Cups Sugar
2 Eggs
1½ Cups Applesauce

1 Tsp. Soda, dissolved in 1 tbs. hot
  water
1 Tsp. Vanilla

Fry pecans in a little butter. Sift dry
ingredients (flour, salt and spices). Use
some of flour mixture to dredge raisins
and gumdrops (use scissors to cut gum
drops and raisins before dredging in flour
mixture).

Cream butter and sugar; add well-beaten
eggs. Add flour mixture alternately with
applesauce to creamed mixture. Stir in
soda, dissolved in water; add vanilla.
Add raisins, gumdrops and pecans. Pour
batter into two or three small loaf pans
lined with greased brown or parchment
paper. Bake 2 hours in 300 to 325 degree oven.

If oven glass pans are used, do not line
with paper, just grease them and bake
at lower temperature, 275 to 300 degrees.

Cakes may be decorated by placing
candied fruits (cherries, pineapple, etc.)
in bottom of pan before pouring batter
(Pam sprayed in pans to avoid sticking
of fruit).

Cool on racks after removing from pans.
Wrap in brandy-soaked cloths, wax paper
and foil.

CRANBERRY—ORANGE TEA BREAD

1 Cup Sugar
2 Cups Flour
1½ Tsp. Double-Acting Baking Powder
½ Tsp. Baking Soda
1 Tsp. Salt
¼ Cup Soft Butter or Margarine
¾ Cup Orange Juice
1 Egg, beaten
1 Tbs. Grated Orange Rind
½ Cup Chopped Nuts
1 Cup Fresh Cranberries, chopped

Toss sugar, flour, baking powder, baking
soda and salt to mix. Cut in butter with
a pastry blender or two knives to make
very fine crumbs. Combine orange juice
and egg; add all at once and stir to
moisten. Fold in orange rind, nuts and
cranberries. Avoid overmixing. Spread
in a greased 9" x 5" loaf pan; flatten the
center slightly. Bake in a moderate oven,
350 degrees F, about 1 hour - until loaf
is browned and a skewer inserted at the
center comes out dry. Cool thoroughly
on a rack before slicing.

CHEOREG

1 Cup Lukewarm Milk
1½ Cups Melted Butter
3 Eggs
1 Pkg. Yeast, dissolved in ½ cup warm
  water
1 Tsp. Salt
3 Tbs. Sugar
6 Cups Flour
1 Egg, for brushing top

Mix warm milk, melted butter, 2 eggs
(beaten), yeast, salt and sugar. Add flour
to make a soft dough. Let stand in warm
place until it rises double in size.

Roll small pieces of dough into strips about
8" long and as thick as your finger; shape
into circles or twist. Lay flat on cookie
sheet and brush with egg. Brush top with
sesame seeds if desired. Let stand again for
2 hours. Bake in 375 degree oven until
brown.

MOCHA OATMEAL CAKE

2 Tbs. Instant Powdered Coffee
1-1/3 Cups Boiling Water
1 Cup Quick Cooking Oats
   (uncooked)
¾ Cup Butter
1 Cup Granulated Sugar
1 Cup Brown Sugar, firmly packed
2 Eggs
1½ Tsp. Vanilla
2 Cups Flour
1¼ Tsp. Soda
¾ Tsp. Salt
3 Tbs. Powdered Cocoa

Combine coffee and boiling water; pour over oatmeal. Let stand 20 minutes. Beat butter till creamy; gradually add sugars and beat till fluffy. Beat in eggs, one at a time. Add vanilla and oat mixture. Sift together flour, soda, cocoa & salt. Add to creamed mixture. Blend well. Pour into greased and floured bundt pan [MW: omit grease and flour]. Bake in 350 degree oven for about 50 min. [MW: 12½-14 min. on full power, covered with wax paper]. Test with toothpick. Cool 10 min. on rack; remove from pan and frost with mocha frosting.

Mocha Frosting:
2½ Tbs. Butter
1½ Cups Sugar
Dash of Salt
½ Tsp. Vanilla
1½ Tbs. Instant Powdered Coffee
1 Cup Coconut
¾ Cup Canned Milk
½ Cup Chopped Nuts

Put all ingredients into a saucepan and boil slowly for about 4 minutes. If you want a harder icing, boil a minute or two longer.

CHOCOLATE INTRIGUE

3 Cups All Purpose Flour
2 Tsp. Baking Powder
½ Tsp. Salt
1 Cup Butter or Margarine
2 Cups Sugar
3 Eggs
1 Cup Milk
1½ Tsp. Vanilla
¾ Cup Chocolate Syrup
¼ Tsp. Baking Soda
¼ Tsp. Peppermint Extract

Cream butter and sugar til light and fluffy. Add eggs one at a time beating well after each. Combine the milk and vanilla, add alternately with the dry ingredients to creamed mixture. Turn 2/3 of batter into 10" tube pan greased on the bottom [MW: omit grease]. Add to the remaining batter the chocolate syrup, baking soda and mint extract. Pour over white batter. DO NOT MIX! Bake at 350 degrees for 65-70 min. [MW: 17-18 minutes, covered with wax paper]. Cool in pan.

CARROT CAKE

3 Cups Sifted All-Purpose Flour
2 Cups Sugar
2 Tsp. Cinnamon
1½ Tsp. Soda
1¼ Tsp. Salt
1 Tsp. Baking Powder
1 (8¾oz.) Can Crushed Pineapple, drained
3 Eggs, beaten
1½ Cups Salad Oil
2 Tsp. Vanilla
2 Cups Grated Raw Carrots, loosely packed
1½ Cups Broken Pecans

Combine flour, sugar, cinnamon, soda, salt and baking powder, mixing well. Drain pineapple, saving syrup, set aside. Make a well in center of dry ingredients, add pineapple syrup, eggs, oil and vanilla, blend thoroughly. Stir in pineapple, carrots and nuts. Turn into greased 10" tube pan [MW: omit grease]. Bake in 325 degree oven for 1½ hours [MW: 18-20 min. on full power, covered with wax paper] or until done. Cool 10 min., turn out onto rack to cool completely. Wrap and freeze.

BUTTERHORNS

2 Cups Flour, sifted
½ Tsp. Cinnamon
½ Lb. Butter
¾ Cup Sugar
¾ Cup Chopped Pecans
¾ Cup Sour Cream
1 Egg Yolk

Cut butter into flour with fingertips. Add 1 egg yolk, ¾ sour cream; mix well and when blended, shape into ball. Sprinkle with flour. Wrap well in waxed paper and chill in refrigerator for several hours.

COMBINE:
¾ Cup Sugar
¾ Cup Chopped Pecans
1 Tsp. Cinnamon

Sprinkle board lightly with flour. Remove dough from refrigerator. Divide into three parts. Roll out, one portion at a time on board making a large circle about 1/8 inch thick. Sprinkle with sugar and nut mixture. Cut into 12 wedge shaped sections. Roll up each wedge starting with the widest portion. Place rolls on a lightly greased cookie sheet, and bake in moderate oven 375° for 25 to 30 min.

This recipe is over 100 years old, and its origin is Czechoslovakia.

CHERRY—NUT POUND CAKE

Cake:
1½ Cups Shortening
3 Cups Sugar
6 Eggs
½ Tsp. Almond Flavoring
½ Tsp. Vanilla Flavoring
3¾ Cups Plain Flour
¾ Cup Milk
5 Oz. Maraschino Cherries, chopped
  and drained

Frosting:
1 - 3 Oz. Pkg. Cream Cheese
2 Cups Confectioner's Sugar
5 Oz. Maraschino Cherries, chopped
  and drained
1 Tsp. Almond Flavoring
½ Stick Margarine
½ Cup Walnuts, chopped
½ Cup Coconut (optional)

Cake: Cream together shortening and sugar until very creamy. Add eggs, one at a time, beating after each addition. Add flavorings and blend well. Alternately add flour and milk, beating well after each addition until all is added. Fold in the cherries last. Pour into a large tube pan. Place in cold oven set at 275 degrees and bake for 2 hours. Cool thoroughly.

Frosting: Blend margarine and cream cheese together at room temperature. Gradually add in confectioner's sugar and beat until smooth. Add flavoring; blend well. Fold in nuts, cherries and coconut. Spread over entire cooled cake.

OATMEAL CAKE

1 Cup Quick Oats
1½ Cups Boiling Water
1 Cup Brown Sugar
1 Stick Margarine
1 Cup White Sugar
2 Eggs
1½ Cups Flour
1 Tsp. Soda
2 Tsp. Cinnamon
½ Tsp. Salt
1 Tsp. Vanilla
½ Cup Nuts

Topping:
1 Cup Brown Sugar
½ Stick Margarine
Coconut
Nuts
Milk (enough to make topping spreadable)

Mix oats and boiling water. Let stand while mixing rest of ingredients together. Cream both sugars with margarine; add eggs. Add the rest of the ingredients, including the oats. Mix well and bake at 325 degrees (glass pan) or 350 degrees (metal pan). Use a 13x9" pan. While cake is still warm, spread with topping.

ORANGE RUM CAKE

1 Cup Butter or Margarine, salted, not
  whipped
2 Cups Granulated Sugar
Grated Rind of 2 Large Oranges
Grated Rind of 1 Lemon
2 Eggs
2½ Cups Sifted All-Purpose Flour
2 Tsp. Baking Powder (double-acting)
1 Tsp. Soda
½ Tsp. Salt

1 Cup Buttermilk
1 Cup Finely Chopped Walnuts or
  Pecans
2 Tbs. Rum
Juice of 2 Large Oranges
Juice of 1 Lemon
½ Cup Confectioner's Sugar
Walnut or Pecan Halves, about 16 to 20

To make cake:
1. With a little butter grease a 9" or
10" tube pan. If using a fluted or other
fancy pan be sure it holds at least 2 qts.
when measured to the brim with water).
2. Turn on oven, set at 350 degrees F.
If oven has no control, use a portable
oven thermometer and keep correct temperature by controlling heat.
3. With an electric mixer or a large
spoon beat 1 cup butter (or margarine)
in a large bowl until fluffy.
4. Gradually add 1 cup granulated
sugar, beating after each addition until
fluffy.

5. Add grated rind and juice of oranges
and lemon.
6. Add eggs, one at a time, beating
after each addition until very light.
7. Sift, then lightly spoon flour into
measuring cup. Level top with spatula;
put 2½ cups flour into sifter. If instant
type is used, do not sift, but mix with
other ingredients. Do NOT use cake flour
or self—rising flour.
8. Add 2 tsp. double-acting baking powder, 1 tsp. soda, ½ tsp. salt ; sift into
bowl.
9. To butter mixture add flour mixture
alternately with 1 c. buttermilk in small
amounts, beating after each addition until
smooth. Fold in 1 c. finely chopped nuts.

10. Pour batter into pan, bake about one
hour. Cake is done when it shrinks from
sides of pan and surface springs back when
pressed lightly with finger.
11. Meanwhile strain juice of 2 large
oranges and 1 lemon, add 1 c. granulated
sugar and 2 tbs. rum.
12. When cake is done, remove from
oven, bring mixture in saucepan to boil.
Pour slowly over cake in pan. If cake
does not absorb all mixture, reserve and
spoon on later. Remove from pan, sprinkle cake lightly with granulated sugar. Mix
½ C. confectioner's sugar with enough
water or milk to make of spreading consistency. Spread on nut halves on wax
paper, let stand until hard. Then press
on sides of cake.

SWEDISH RYE BREAD

2 Pkgs. Yeast
3 Cups Milk, scalded and cooled
8 to 10 Cups Flour (white)
2 Cups Rye Flour
½ Cup Brown Sugar
½ Cup Molasses
1 Tbs. Sugar
1 Tbs. Salt
2 Tbs. (heaping) Shortening
¾ Cup Warm Water
Grated Rind of 1 Orange

Scald milk; cool to lukewarm. Grate the
orange peel. Stir lukewarm milk, yeast,
water, sugar, molasses, brown sugar,
orange peel, salt, melted and cooled shortening and rye flour together. Add 8 to 10
cups all-purpose flour. Knead 5 minutes.

Place in greased bowl; turn over once.
Cover and let rise in warm place until
doubled, about 1 hour. Grease & flour
4 - 7" x 4" bread pans; divide dough into
4 pieces, kneading each piece 1 minute.
Place in pans and let rise 1 hour. Bake
in 350 degree oven 1 hour. Especially
good toasted with butter, sliced cheese
and fresh, hot coffee.

QUICK BUTTER CROISSANTS

1 Pkg. Yeast, dry or compressed
1 Cup Warm Water, for yeast
¾ Cup Evaporated Milk
1½ Tsp. Salt
1/3 Cup Sugar
1 Egg
5 Cups Flour
¼ Cup Butter or Margarine, soft
1 Cup Firm Butter
1 Egg

In a bowl, let yeast soften in water. Add milk, salt, sugar, egg and 1 cup of the flour. Beat to make a smooth batter; blend in melted butter; set aside. In a large bowl, cut the 1 cup firm butter into remaining 4 cups flour until butter particles are the size of dried kidney beans. Pour yeast batter over this and carefully turn the mixture over with a spatula to blend, just until all flour is moistened.

Cover with clear plastic film and refrigerate until well chilled, at least 4 hours or up to 4 days.

Remove dough to a floured board; press into compact balls and knead about 6 turns to release air bubbles. Divide dough into four equal parts. Shape one at a time. Refrigerate the remaining dough.

Roll one part of the dough on a floured board into a circle 17" in diameter. With a sharp knife, cut the circle into 8 equal pie-shaped wedges. Add softened butter, sugar, cinnamon and nuts (pecans or walnuts). Roll the wedges loosely toward the point. Shape each roll into a crescent and place on an ungreased baking sheet. Allow 1½" space between them. Cover and let rise at room temperature until almost double in bulk - about 2 hours. Bake at 325 degrees for about 35 minutes. They may be reheated.

HONEYSUCKLE CAKE
(From New Zealand)

½ Can Sweetened Condensed Milk
¼ Lb. Butter or Margarine, melted
¾ Cup Rolled Oats (quick-cooking)
2¼ Cups Crushed Vanilla Wafers
½ Cup Chopped Walnuts
1 Tsp. Grated Orange Peel

Mix all ingredients and press into a 9" square, flat pan. Bake at 350 degrees, till toothpick comes out clean when tested. Cool and cover with icing.

Icing:
1 Oz. Butter, melted
2 Tbs. Eagle Brand Milk
1 Cup Powdered Sugar
Pinch of Salt

Mix together till smooth.

WHITE LEMON FRUIT CAKE

1 Lb. Margarine
3 Cups Sugar
2 Oz. Lemon Extract
3 Tbs. Wine or Grape Juice
6 Eggs
5 Cups Flour
1 Tsp. Soda
1 Tbs. Warm Water
1 Lb. Golden Raisins
2 Pkgs. Candied Pineapple
2 Pkgs. Candied Cherries
1 Pint Pecans or Walnuts

Cream together margarine and sugar; add lemon extract and grape juice. Separate eggs; add egg yolks to mixture. Save whites to fold in at the end. Add 3 cups flour gradually; save other 2 cups for dredging fruit. Mix soda in warm water; add to above mixture. Stir well. Add the fruit and nuts to the 2 cups of flour, then add all to dough mixture. Fold in beaten egg whites. Makes 10 small loaves or 1 angel cake pan plus 1 large loaf. Bake at 250 degrees for 2 hours.

WHOLE WHEAT DATE CAKE

1 - 8 Oz. Pkg. Dates, chopped (2 cups)
1 Cup Water
1 Cup Butter
1½ Cups Enriched Flour
1½ Cups Whole Wheat Flour
2 Tbs. Baking Powder
1 Tsp. Salt
½ Tsp. Ground Nutmeg
1 Tsp. Ground Cinnamon
1 Cup Light Brown Sugar, packed
4 Eggs, beaten
1 Tbs. Vanilla Extract

Cook dates with water and butter over low heat until caramel colored and thickened. Refrigerate to cool completely. Stir together dry ingredients and add date mixture. Add eggs and vanilla; stirring until well-blended. Pour batter into greased and sugared bundt pan or a 10" tube pan (or use a large HI-C juice can). Bake at 350 degrees for 50 to 55 minutes. Cool for 10 minutes; remove from pan and cool completely on wire rack. Serve plain or add your choice of topping on top of cake.

STRAWBERRY—BANANA BREAD

1 Tsp. Grated Lemon Peel*
1¾ Cups Sifted All-purpose Flour
2½ Tsp. Baking Powder
½ Tsp. Salt
1/3 Cup Crisco Shortening
2/3 Cup Sugar
1 or 2 Eggs, beaten
1 Cup Ripe, Mashed Bananas
½ Cup Pureed Strawberries
½ Cup Chopped Nuts or Rolled Oats

Have all ingredients at room temperature. *When using real lemon rind, combine the lemon rind with the Crisco and sugar mixture rather than the dry ingredients.

Preheat oven to 350 degrees. Sift flour with salt, baking powder and lemon peel; set aside.

Cream shortening with sugar. Add the beaten eggs and blend until smooth. Add strawberry pureé and mashed bananas.

CARROT—PINEAPPLE BUNDT CAKE

3 Cups Sifted Cake Flour
2 Cups Sugar
2 Tsp. Cinnamon
1½ Tsp. Baking Soda
1½ Tsp. Salt
1 Tsp. Baking Powder
1 - 8¾ Oz. Can Crushed Pineapple
2 Cups Raw Carrots, grated and
  loosely packed
3 Eggs, beaten
1½ Cups Salad Oil
2 Tsp. Vanilla
1½ Cups Finely-chopped Nuts

Grease & lightly flour a bundt pan [MW: do not grease or flour]. Mix together cake flour, sugar, cinnamon, baking soda, baking powder and salt. Drain pineapple, saving syrup. Add pineapple syrup to dry mixture; add eggs, oil and vanilla. Beat for 3 min. Stir in pineapple, carrots and nuts. Bake at 325 degrees for about 1½ hours [MW: 18-20 min. on full power, covered with wax paper]. Cool 10 min. in pan before unmolding. Frost with currant-nut icing.

Currant-Nut Icing:
4½ Cups Confectioner's Sugar
1 - 8 Oz. Pkg. Cream Cheese, soft
¼ Cup Butter
2 Tbs. Milk
2 Tbs. Vanilla
¼ Cup Chopped Walnuts
¼ Cup Currants

Beat sugar, cream cheese, butter, milk and vanilla together until smooth. Fold in walnuts and currants. Spread over cooled bundt cake.

Note: To plump currants, soak in ¼ cup of hot water for 5 minutes; drain well.

BROWN BREAD

1 Egg
1/3 Cup Molasses
1½ Cups White Flour
½ Tsp. Baking Powder
1 Tsp. Baking Soda
½ Tsp. Salt
¾ Cup Oatmeal
½ Cup Sugar
¼ Cup Raisins
½ Cup Chopped Dates
1 Cup Sweet Milk
1 Tsp. Vinegar, add to milk

Beat egg, add molasses and beat again. Add dry ingredients along with milk, then add raisins and dates. Bake 1 hour at 350 degrees in greased and floured loaf pan (9¼x 5¼x2¾") or slightly smaller. Makes nice lunch box sandwiches with cheddar cheese, slightly sweet and filling. Check for doneness at 45 to 50 minutes.

BLACK WALNUT CAKE

2½ Cups Flour
1-2/3 Cups Sugar
1¼ Tsp. Baking Powder
1¼ Tsp. Baking Soda
1 Tsp. Salt
2/3 Cup Soft Shortening
2/3 Cup Buttermilk
3 Eggs (½ to 2/3 cup)
2/3 Cup English Walnuts, finely
   chopped
2/3 Cup Black Walnuts
1 Tsp. Black Walnut Flavoring

Heat oven to 350 degrees. Grease and flour two layer cake pans, 9" x 1-1/3" or two oblong pans, 13" x 9½". Measure flour by spoon, level, pour method. Mix flour and sugar, baking powder, soda and salt. Add shortening, half of buttermilk and beat two minutes at medium speed on mixer, or three hundred strokes by hand (vigorous strokes). Scrape sides & bottom of bowl constantly and add eggs, black walnut flavor and the rest of the

buttermilk. Beat two minutes more, scraping bowl. Fold in nuts. Pour into prepared pans. Bake layers about 35 minutes. Bake oblong pans about 45 to 50 minutes, or until cake tests done. Cool and finish with butter icing or whipped cream.

ROSE VELVET CAKE

1 Cup Crisco
1½ Cups Sugar
2 Eggs
1 Tsp. Lemon Extract
1 Tsp. Orange Extract
1 Oz. Red Food Coloring
1 Cup Buttermilk
2 Cups Flour
1 Tsp. Cinnamon
¼ Tsp. Salt
1 Tsp. Vinegar
1 Tsp. Soda

Cream together the first 6 ingredients. Sift flour, cinnamon and salt together; add alternately with buttermilk to creamed mixture. Add vinegar and soda to the last part of buttermilk; add to batter & mix well. Pour into 3 layers. Bake at 350 degrees about 30 min. [MW: 10-12 min. on full power, covered with wax paper], or until done.

Frosting:
1 Cup Sugar
1 Cup Milk
4 Tbs. Flour
½ Cup Crisco
1 Stick Oleo, at room temperature
1 Tsp. Vanilla
Coconut

Mix sugar, milk and flour; cook until thick as pie filling, stirring constantly. Set in refrigerator to chill while making the cake. After cake has cooled, finish icing by creaming Crisco, oleo and vanilla; add chilled mixture and whip until thick as whipped cream. Spread on cake and sprinkle with coconut.

This makes a nice cake for Christmas by putting red and green coconut on top.

COCONUT CREAM CAKE

Cake:
½ Cup Shortening
½ Cup Margarine
2 Cups Sugar
5 Eggs, at room temperature
1 Cup Buttermilk
1 Tsp. Baking Soda
2 Cups Flour
1 Tsp. Vanilla
1-2/3 Cups Coconut

Frosting:
½ Cup Margarine
8 Oz. Cream Cheese
1 Lb. Powdered Sugar
1 Tsp. Vanilla
1 Cup Coconut
1 Cup Chopped Nuts

Cake: Blend shortening, margarine and sugar until creamy. Blend egg yolks into mixture. Add baking soda to buttermilk. Stir buttermilk and flour, alternately, into egg mixture. Beat egg whites until stiff; add vanilla. Fold into cake mixture. Fold in coconut. Bake in 3 - 8" or 9" layer pans, greased and floured [MW: omit grease and flour]. Bake at 350 degrees for 30 min. [MW: 8-10 min. on full power, covered with wax paper].

Frosting: Blend margarine and cream cheese. Add sugar and vanilla. Fold in coconut and nuts. Sprinkle some coconut on top of cake after it is frosted.

RHUBARB CAKE

1½ Cups Sugar
½ Cup Margarine
1 Egg
1 Cup Buttermilk
1 Tsp. Vanilla
2 Cups Flour
1 Tsp. Soda
½ Tsp. Salt
2 Cups Rhubarb, cut in ½" to
   ¾" pieces

Topping:
½ Cup Sugar
¼ Cup Margarine
1 Tsp. Cinnamon

Topping: Mix sugar, margarine and cinnamon with fork until crumbly. Place in refrigerator until ready to use.

Cake: Cream sugar and margarine together. Add egg and beat till smooth. Add buttermilk and vanilla. Combine flour, soda and salt. Add to creamed mixture and beat well. Fold in cut-up rhubarb. Pour into a lightly-greased well-floured 13" x 9" x 2" pan. Sprinkle topping over cake batter. Bake 35 to 45 minutes in 350 degree oven.

FRUIT COCKTAIL CAKE

Cake:
1¼ Cup Sugar
2 Cup Flour
1 Tsp. Baking Powder
1 Tsp. Soda
2 Eggs - Well Beaten
2 Cups Fruit Cocktail - Undrained
   No. 303 or 1 Lb. size can

Topping:
¼ Cup Brown Sugar
½ Cup Chopped Nuts

Frosting:
¾ Cup Sugar
½ Cup Canned Milk
¼ Lb. Oleo
1 Tsp. Vanilla
1 Can Angel Flake Coconut

Preheat oven 350°
Grease and flour 9 x 12 x 3 cake pan. Combine cake ingredients in large mixing bowl. Pour into pan. Sprinkle top with brown sugar and nuts. Bake at 350° for 45 minutes or until nice and brown.

Frosting:
Combine the following frosting ingredients: Sugar, canned milk, oleo and vanilla. Boil 1 minute stirring constantly. Cool slightly before adding coconut. Spread evenly over warm cake.

RUSSIAN CHRISTMAS WALNUT HORNS

2½ Cups Flour
½ Tsp. Salt
1 Pkg. Compressed Yeast
2 Cubes of Butter
2 Eggs
½ Cup Sour Cream

Walnut Filling:
2 Cups Finely Ground Nuts
1 Cup Sugar
1 Tsp. Cinnamon
2 Tbs. Melted Butter

Mix all ingredients together with a few drops
of milk.

Cheese Filling:
1 Pkg. Cream Cheese
2-3 Tbs. Sugar
1 Egg Yolk
1 Tsp. Lemon Juice

Mix all ingredients together.

Sift flour; measure 2½ cups and sift again
with ½ tsp. salt into a large mixing bowl.
Crumble 1 pkg. yeast into flour. With a
pastry blender or 2 knives, cut 2 cubes of
butter into flour until particles look like
corn meal. Separate 2 eggs; beat whites until stiff but not dry; set aside. Beat yolks
until thick and lemon colored; blend in
half of sour cream. Stir into flour mixture.
Fold the rest of sour cream into beaten egg
whites and add to dough. Mix; cover and
chill until it can be handled (about 30 min.).
Turn out onto a floured board and knead
quickly until smooth and soft. Form dough
into balls about the size of a baseball. Wrap
tightly in waxed paper or foil; refrigerate
overnight. Roll out dough less than ¼"
thick on board sprinkled with flour & sugar
(mixed in equal parts). With pastry wheel
or a sharp knife, cut into 2" squares. Put
a spoonful of walnut or cheese filling in the
center of each square. Roll diagonally.
Press overlapping corner into cooky roll to
secure. Place on ungreased baking sheet.
Bake at 350 degrees for 15 minutes or until light brown. Remove cookies to wire
racks and cool. Sprinkle lightly with sifted
powdered sugar. Makes about 8 dozen.

RUM FRUITCAKE

2 Cups Sugar
1 Tsp. Cinnamon
1 Tsp. Salt
1 Cup Dates, pitted
1 Cup Walnuts
1 - 1 Lb. 12 Oz. Can Borden's
   None-Such Mincemeat
2 Cups Water
1 Tsp. Cloves (ground)
1 Cup Raisins
½ Cup Candied Cherries
½ Cup Pecans
½ Cup Salad Oil

Bring ingredients to a good rolling boil.
Remove from stove and let cool to lukewarm; then add:

½ Cup Dark Rum
3 Cups All-purpose Flour
2 Tsp. Baking Soda

Mix well. Turn into a well-greased and
floured pan or pans. Bake at 375 degrees
for 45 minutes to 1 hour, or until a cake
tester comes out clean.

EGGLESS, MILKLESS, BUTTERLESS
CAKE

2 Cups Water
1 Cup Sugar
1 Cup Shortening
1 Tsp. Cloves
1 Tsp. Cinnamon
1 Tsp. Salt
1 Pkg. Raisins
3 Cups Flour
1 Tsp. Soda
1 or 2 Cups Chopped Walnuts

Boil raisins, water, sugar and shortening
5 minutes; cool. Add spices, soda, flour
and mix well. Add chopped walnuts.
Bake at 350 degrees in two loaf pans
for about 1 hour. Needs no icing.

The longer the cake is kept, it seems the
more moist it is. Should be wrapped in
wax paper if keeping for quite a while.

CURRANT SPICE CAKE

1 Cup White Sugar
1 Cup Brown Sugar
¾ Cup Oil
1 Cup Sour Milk
2 Tbs. Sour Cream
2 Eggs
¾ Cup Currants, soaked in hot
   water and drained
2½ Cups Flour
1 Tsp. Cinnamon
1 Tsp. Cloves
½ Tsp. Salt
1 Tsp. Soda
1 Tsp. Baking Powder
½ Cup Chopped Nuts

Sift all dry ingredients in bowl; add 2 eggs, ¾ cup oil, 1 cup sour milk plus sour cream. Mix until all dry ingredients are moist. Add currants and nuts. Bake in layer pans 35 minutes at 350 degrees [MW: 10-12 min. on full power, covered with wax paper]. Frost with favorite frosting. Can be baked in a bundt pan.

ZUCCHINI CARROT CAKE

2 Eggs
1 Cup Sugar
2/3 Cup Oil
1¼ Cups All-Purpose Flour
1 Tsp. Baking Powder
1 Tsp. Baking Soda
1 Tsp. Cinnamon
½ Tsp. Salt
1 Cup Carrot, grated
1 Cup Zucchini, grated and drained
½ Cup Nuts, walnut
Frosting:
3 Oz. Pkg. Cream Cheese
3 Tbs. Margarine
1 Tsp. Vanilla
2 Cups Powdered Sugar

Beat eggs with sugar until frothy. Gradually beat in oil. Add dry ingredients. Beat at high speed, 4 minutes. Stir in carrot, zucchini and nuts. Pour into a greased [MW: ungreased] 9" square pan. Bake in 350 degree oven about 35 min. [MW: 8-10 min. on full power, covered with wax paper]. Top springs back when touched.

Frosting: Mix cream cheese and margarine; add sugar & vanilla. Beat well until smooth.

CREAM CHEESE ROLLS

1 Cup Milk
½ Cup Water
¼ Cup Margarine
5-6 Cups Flour
½ Cup Sugar
2 Pkgs. Dry Yeast
1 Tsp. Salt
2 Eggs
1 Large Pkg. Cream Cheese
¾ Cup Raisins
¼ Cup Powdered Sugar

Heat milk, water and margarine until warm. Combine 2 cups flour, ½ cup granulated sugar, yeast and salt in large bowl of mixer; add the milk mixture. Beat on low speed until blended; add eggs and 1 cup flour. Beat 2 minutes on medium speed.

With a large mixing spoon, stir in 2 cups flour to make a firm dough. Turn out on floured board and knead in 1 cup flour gradually until dough is smooth & elastic.

Grease large bowl, turn dough into bowl & turn over to bring greased side up. Cover with towel and let rise in warm place for 1 hour. Punch dough down, turn out onto floured board and let rise 15 minutes.

While dough rests, combine cream cheese, raisins and powdered sugar in small bowl; set aside. Grease 3 round or square pans. Divide dough into 18 pieces; roll 1 piece at a time on floured board to a 4½" circle. Spoon 1 tbs. cheese mixture in center. Gather circle along edge to form pouch; pinch firmly to seal. Place bun, sealed side down, in pan. Repeat with other pieces. Cover pans with towels; let rise 45 minutes. Bake in 350 degree oven for 30 minutes. Remove from pans and serve while warm or hot.

Note: If you like a soft crust, brush with butter after finished baking. Do not use butter if you want a crispy crust.

HEATH BRUNCH COFFEE CAKE

¼ Lb. Butter
2 Cups Flour
1 Cup Brown Sugar, packed
½ Cup White Sugar

1 Cup Buttermilk
1 Tsp. Baking Soda
1 Egg, beaten
1 Tsp. Vanilla

6 Heath Candy Bars
¼ Cup Pecan Pieces

Blend first 4 ingredients; reserve ½ of above mixture for later. To ½ of mixture add the next 4 ingredients and pour into a greased & floured 9x13 inch cake pan. Crush with rolling pin 6 Heath Candy Bars, mix together crushed candy bars, pecans and remainder of mixture and sprinkle over batter already in pan. Bake in 350° oven for 30 minutes.

COCOA COLA CAKE

1 Cup Oleo or Butter
2 Cups Sifted Flour
1¾ Cups Sugar
3 Tbs. Cocoa
1 Tsp. Baking Soda
1 Tsp. Vanilla
2 Eggs
½ Cup Buttermilk
1 Cup Coke
1½ Cups Miniature Marshmallows

Icing:
½ Cup Butter or Oleo, soft
3 Tbs. Cocoa
½ Cup Coke
4 Cups Powdered Sugar
1 Cup Toasted Pecans, chopped

Combine all cake ingredients, except Coke & marshmallows, in large mixing bowl. Beat 1 minute at high speed; add Coke and blend well. Stir in marshmallows by hand; bake at 350 degrees for 40-45 minutes. Use a 13x9" pan.

Icing: Combine all ingredients and beat until smooth. Add pecans last. Spread on cake when cooled.

BLACK BOTTOM CUPCAKES

1 Cup Cream Cheese - 8 Oz.
1/3 Cup Sugar
1 Unbeaten Egg
1/8 Tsp. Salt
6 Oz. Chocolate Chips
2-1/4 Cup Flour
1-1/2 Cup Sugar
¼ Cup + 2 Tbs. Cocoa
1-1/2 Tsp. Soda
¾ Tsp. Salt
1-1/2 Cup Water
1/3 Cup + 3 Tbs. Oil
1-1/2 Tsp. Vanilla

Beat cream cheese, sugar, egg, salt until smooth. Add chocolate chips. Set aside. Sift flour, sugar, cocoa, soda and salt in a large bowl. Add water, oil and vanilla and mix until smooth. Fill paper muffin cups 1/3 full of chocolate batter. Top each with a heaping tsp. of cheese mixture. Bake at 350 degrees for 30 min. [MW: 3-4 min. on full power, using plastic muffin pans].

Makes 24 cupcakes.

JOHNNY CAKE

1 Cup Flour
1 Cup Yellow Corn Meal
3 Tsp. Baking Powder
1 Tsp. Salt
1 Egg
½ Cup Sugar
3 Tbs. Honey
3 Tbs. Cooking Oil
1 Cup Milk

Preheat the oven to 400 degrees. Grease an 8 x 8 x 2 inch baking pan [MW: ungreased]. Sift flour, corn meal, baking powder and salt together. Beat the egg and add the sugar. Warm the milk slightly with honey, stirring thoroughly. Add the sugar, milk and cooking oil. Mix thoroughly. Combine with the dry ingredients gradually to avoid lumps. Bake at 400 degrees for 30 min. [MW: 7-9 min. on full power, covered with wax paper], or until a toothpick inserted in the center comes out clean. Serve while hot.

BEER & SAUERKRAUT FUDGE CAKE

2/3 Cup Butter
1½ Cups Sugar
3 Eggs
1 Tsp. Vanilla
½ Cup Cocoa
2¼ Cups Sifted Flour
1 Tsp. Baking Powder
1 Tsp. Soda
1 Cup Beer
2/3 Cup Sauerkraut
1 Cup Raisins
1 Cup Chopped Nuts

Cream butter and sugar until light. Add eggs, one at a time, beating well after each addition. Blend in vanilla. Sift cocoa, flour, baking powder, soda and salt together. Add to creamed mixture alternately with beer, beginning and ending with dry ingredients. Stir in sauerkraut. Raisins and/or nuts are optional. Turn into two 8" or 9" greased and floured layer cake pans. Bake at 350° for 35 minutes; cool and frost as desired.

RAISIN DELIGHT

1½ Cups Raisins
2½ Cups Water
1½ Cups Sugar
½ Cup Crisco
2 Eggs
2¾ Cups Flour
¼ Tsp. Salt
1 Tsp. Soda
1 Tsp. Baking Powder
1 Tsp. Cinnamon
1 Tsp. Vanilla
1 Cup Chopped Nuts

Glaze:
½ Cup Butter
¼ Cup Milk
¾ Box Powdered Sugar
1 Tsp. Vanilla
1 Tsp. Lemon Extract

Boil raisins and water together until there is only 1 cup of juice. Cool. Combine in mixing bowl the sugar, Crisco and eggs & mix well. Sift together flour, salt, soda, baking powder and cinnamon. Add dry ingredients to Crisco mix and add raisin water. Add vanilla. Fold in raisins and nuts. Grease and flour a 14" x 12" baking pan. Bake at 350 degrees for 25 to 35 minutes.

Glaze: Heat butter and milk; add powdered sugar. Mix and beat well in electric mixer. Add vanilla and lemon extract; pour over cake while hot.

FILLED ANGEL FOOD CAKE

1 Baked Angel Food Cake
1 - 3 Oz. Pkg. Strawberry Jello
1 Pint Whipping Cream
1 Pkg. Frozen Strawberries

Filling: Use 1 cup boiling water to dissolve jello. Cut unthawed berries into pieces and stir into hot jello until berries are melted. Chill jello until it begins to set. Fold in broken pieces of angel food cake and spoon into the cavity of the cake.

How to cut cake for filling:

1. Place a 10" cake upside down on plate or wax paper. Slice entire top from cake 1" down. Lift top and lay aside.

2. Cut down into the cake 1" from outer edge and 1" from center hole, leaving a substantial "wall" of cake about 1" thick.

3. Remove center with fork - be careful - leave base of cake at bottom thick. Place cake on serving plate. Save cake pieces for filling above.

4. Completely fill cake with filling. Avoid "holes."

5. Replace top of cake; frost with chilled whipped cream. Chill until well set (about 4 hours).

RHUBARB UPSIDE-DOWN CAKE

3 or 3½ Cups Rhubarb
10 Large Marshmallows
¾ Cup Sugar
Few Red Hots

Dice rhubarb into 10" skillet. Top with marshmallows, sugar and red hots.

¼ Lb. Butter
1 Cup Sugar
2 Eggs, beaten
1¾ Cups Cake Flour
3 Tsp. Baking Powder
¼ Tsp. Salt
½ Cup Milk

Cream butter and sugar, add egg yolks. Mix dry ingredients and add to sugar mixture alternately with milk and vanilla. Add stiffly beaten egg whites. Bake in 365 degree oven for 30 min. [MW: 7-10 min. on full power, covered with wax paper] in 2 - 9" layer pans.

IRISH SODA BREAD

¾ Cup Seedless Raisins
2 Cups All-purpose Flour
1 Tbs. Sugar
2 Tsp. Baking Powder
½ Tsp. Soda
1 Tsp. Salt
1/3 Cup Butter or Margarine
1 Tsp. Caraway Seed
1 Egg
1 Cup Sour Milk or Buttermilk

Rinse and drain raisins. Sift flour, baking powder, soda and salt; cut in butter with pastry blender until mix resembles coarse corn meal. Stir in raisins and caraway seeds. Beat egg slightly and add to sour milk. Make a "well" in center of flour mix and add the liquids all at once. Stir with fork until all are moistened. Do not overmix. Turn into greased 8" round baking pan. Preheat oven to 400 degrees. Bake about 20 minutes. Makes 8 large wedges. Also makes good toast if left over.

GRAHAM SPICE CAKE

½ Cup Shortening
1¼ Cups Sugar
3 Eggs, separated
1 Cup Milk
1 Tsp. Vanilla
3 Cups Finely Rolled Graham Crackers
1 Tsp. Cinnamon
½ Tsp. Nutmeg
¼ Tsp. Cloves
3 Tsp. Baking Powder
½ Tsp. Salt

Cream butter and sugar, add egg yolks. Mix dry ingredients and add to sugar mixture alternately with milk and vanilla. Add stiffly beaten egg whites. Bake in 365 degree oven for 30 minutes in 2 9 inch layers.

Frosting:
6 Oz. Cream Cheese
2½ Cups Powdered Sugar
¾ Tsp. Vanilla
¼ Tsp. Salt
1½ Tsp. Milk

Beat cream cheese and milk till light. Add rest of ingredients.

PLUM CAKE

2 Cups Self-rising Flour
2 Cups Sugar
3 Eggs
1 Cup Vegetable Oil
2 - 4¾ Oz. Jars Plum Baby Food
1 Tsp. Cloves
1 Tsp. Cinnamon
½ Tsp. Nutmeg
1 Cup Chopped Nuts
1 Tsp. Vanilla

Mix all ingredients together; DO NOT USE electric mixer. Stir as little as possible, just until well blended. Bake in greased and floured tube or bundt pan [MW: ungreased]. Bake at 350 degrees for 1 hr. [MW: 10-15 min. on full power, covered with wax paper]. Test at 50 min. [MW: 10 min.]. Remove from pan after 5 minutes. No frosting is needed. Great for lunch boxes, picnics and teas.

HARVEY WALLBANGER'S CAKE

1 Pkg. Yellow Cake Mix
1 Pkg. Vanilla Instant Pudding (3¾ oz.)
½ Cup Liquid Shortening
4 Eggs
¼ Cup Vodka
¼ Cup Galliano
¾ Cup Orange Juice

Mix all ingredients together and beat for 4 min. Pour batter into well greased and lightly floured Bundt pan [MW: omit grease and flour]. Bake at 350 degrees for 45-50 min. [MW: 10-13 min. on full power, covered with wax paper]. Dust with confectioners' sugar.

INDIAN FRY BREAD

2 Cups All-purpose Flour
¼ Cup Nonfat Milk Powder
2 Tsp. Baking Powder
1 Tsp. Salt
1 Tbs. Crisco
¾ Cup Warm Milk
Cooking Oil for Deep Fat Frying

Stir together flour, nonfat dry milk powder, baking powder and salt; cut in Crisco until mixture resembles coarse crumbs. Stir in water. Turn out onto floured surface and knead to smooth. Divide dough into eight balls; cover and rest ten minutes. On a floured surface, roll each ball to a 6" circle. With finger, make hole in center of each circle. Fry one at a time in deep, hot fat until golden brown!

APPLE—NUT CAKE

Cake:
2 Cups Whole Wheat Flour
½ Cup Sugar
1 Tbs. Baking Powder
Dash of Salt
½ Cup Soft Butter
1 Egg

Filling:
5 Pippin Apples
½ Cup Sugar
1 Cup Diced Walnuts
Juice of 1 Lemon
½ Tsp. Cinnamon

1. Sift flour, sugar, baking powder and salt into a mixing bowl. Add butter & egg. Knead until dough is firm and shapes easily into a ball. Wrap in wax paper; refrigerate 1 hour.

2. Peel apples; cut into small pieces. Add sugar, nuts, lemon juice and cinnamon. Let mixture steep until dough is ready.

3. Preheat oven to 350 degrees.

4. Butter a 9" springform pan. Divide dough into thirds. Roll out 1/3 to line bottom of pan. Roll another 1/3 and line inside halfway to top of pan, pressing bottom rim to seal sides and bottom.

5. Drain fruit and pour into pastry-lined pan. Roll out last 1/3 of dough and make strips. Place strips crisscross on top of filling. Bake until golden brown, 45 to 55 minutes. Cool and serve.

CHILI CHEDDAR CORN BREAD

2 Cups Yellow Corn Meal
½ Cup All-purpose Flour
1 Tsp. Baking Powder
1 Tsp. Sugar
1¼ Tsp. Salt
2½ Cups Milk
2 Eggs
2 Tsp. Shortening, melted (or oil)
1 Tsp. Minced, Dried Onion
1 Cup Shredded Cheddar Cheese (4 Oz.)
1 - 8¾ Oz. Can Whole Corn, drained
1 - 4 Oz. Can Green Chili Pepper,
  seeded, rinsed and chopped
¼ Cup Chopped Red Pepper

Mix corn meal, flour, baking powder, sugar
and salt together. Add milk, eggs and
shortening; mix together. Add onion & let
stand 5 minutes. Fold in cheese, corn,
green chili peppers and red peppers. Spoon
about 1/3 cup batter into greased & floured
2½" muffin cups. Bake at 375 degrees for
25 to 30 minutes. Makes 15 muffins. This
is a bread which is real good with barbecues.

SPICE CAKE

2 Cups Sugar (white)
2 Cups Brown Sugar
2 Cups Raisins
2 Cups Salad Oil
4 Cups Water
2 Tsp. Cloves
2 Tsp. Nutmeg
2 Tsp. Salt
4 Tsp. Cinnamon

6 Cups Sifted Flour
4 Tsp. Soda
1 Tsp. Vanilla
1 Tsp. Lemon
2 Cups Walnuts

Combine first group of ingredients in a large
kettle and boil one or two minutes; cool.

Combine second group of ingredients and
add to first mixture. Bake in greased and
floured pan, 15" x 11", at 325 degrees for
1½ hours. Can be frozen for as long as 6
months.

100% WHOLE WHEAT VEGETABLE BREAD

½ Cup Warm Water
2 Tbs. Dry Yeast
½ Cup Cooking Oil
2 Eggs
1 Can Evaporated Milk
1 Stalk Celery
2 Large Carrots
2" Wedge Cabbage
3 Tbs. Honey
1 Tbs. Salt
6 Cups Whole Wheat

Grind 6 cups of whole wheat on fine.
While it is grinding, pour warm water &
yeast into mixing bowl. Put cooking oil,
eggs, canned milk, celery, carrots, cabbage
and honey into blender & liquidize thoroughly. Pour this liquid into mixing bowl
with yeast. Add flour and salt and knead
for 10 minutes. Form into loaves & place
in 3 oiled pans. Let rise until not quite
double in bulk. Don't let it get too light.
Bake 45 minutes at 350 degrees. Very
tender and fine-textured!

SESAME TEA LOAVES

1 Can (2¼ Oz.) Sesame Seed, divided
2½ Cups Flour
2½ Tsp. Baking Powder
1 Tsp. Salt
1/3 Cup Butter or Margarine, softened
2/3 Cup Sugar
2 Eggs
1 Cup Milk

Toast sesame seed till lightly golden, about
10 minutes, while preheating oven to 350 degrees. Stir together flour, baking powder,
salt and 2 tbs. sesame seed. Beat together
butter, sugar and eggs until well blended.
Stir in flour mixture alternately with milk.
Mix until blended. Turn into 2 well-greased
8x4x2" loaf pans; sprinkle with remaining
sesame seed. Bake about 45 minutes, or
until pick comes out clean.

PANNATONE (Italian Sweet Bread)

2 Cups Warm Milk
1½ Cups Sugar
1 Tsp. Salt
2 Fresh Yeast Cakes
4 Eggs
1 Cup Melted Crisco
4 Tbs. Vanilla
4 Tbs. Lemon Juice
1 Small Bottle Anise Extract
1 Small Bottle Rum or Brandy Extract
9 to 10 Cups Sifted Flour
2 Cups Nuts, chopped
2 Cups Raisins
1 Cup Candied Fruits

Mix the milk, sugar, salt and yeast together; add well-beaten eggs, melted crisco, vanilla, lemon juice, anise extract and rum or brandy extract and mix well; add the flour. Don't make dough too hard, make it as you would make regular bread. Put into a greased bowl and let rise in a warm place till double in size. Then spread it out on floured board, add nuts, candied fruits and raisins; knead well until all fruit is well blended. Divide dough into 3 or 4 loaves and put on greased pan and let rise till double in size.

Topping: Beat 1 egg well; add 1 tbs. sugar and brush mixture on bread before baking. Bake at 350 degrees for 40 to 45 minutes.

CHERRY CHOCOLATE CAKE

1½ Cups Sugar
½ Cup Butter
2 Eggs, well beaten
2¼ Cups Sifted Flour
1½ Tsp. Salt
1½ Cups Liquid: Cherry Juice with Sour
   Milk to make 1½ cups or Buttermilk
2 Squares Chocolate, melted
20 Cherries, cut rather fine

Cream sugar and butter; melt chocolate and add to ingredients. Add well-beaten eggs. Mix flour and salt and add with liquid to batter. Add cherries, cut up. Pour into greased and floured cake pan [MW: omit grease and flour, use bundt pan]. Bake at 350 degrees for 25 min., finish at 325 degrees [MW: 8-9 min. on full power, covered with wax paper].

Frosting:
2 Cups Sugar
1 Stick Butter
2 Squares Chocolate
1 Cup Hot Water

Boil to 236 degrees, add ½ cup butter; cool and beat.

6 WHOLE GRAIN BREAD

6 Cups Warm Water
2 Tbs. Sugar
2 Tbs. Molasses
3 Packets Dry Yeast
6 Tsp. Salt
3 Tbs. Corn Oil
2 Tbs. Lecithin Granules
1 Cup Rolled Oats
1 Cup Soya Flour
1 Cup Barley Flour
1 Cup Rye Flour
1 Cup Corn Meal
4 Cups Whole Wheat Flour
3-5 Cups Unbleached White Flour

Dissolve sugar, molasses and yeast in warm water. Add salt, oil and lecithin. Beat in the whole grain flours, using electric mixer or large, wooden spoon (100 strokes at least) until glutenous sponge is formed. Cover large bread board with 3 cups white flour. Place sponge in center of board and knead white flour into sponge (200 strokes) until proper elasticity of dough is achieved. Additional flour may be needed. Divide the dough into 4 equal parts and form into loaves on a slightly oiled board. Place the loaves in greased 5x9" pans. Set in a warm place to raise. Cover with a damp tea towel. When loaves fill pan, or about double their size, put in 350 degree preheated oven. Bake for 45 minutes. Remove pans from oven and loaves from pans and place loaves on their sides on wire rack to cool.

PUMPKIN BREAD

2-2/3 Cup Sugar
2/3 Cup Butter or Shortening
4 Eggs
1 - 1 Lb. Can Pumpkin
2/3 Cup Orange Juice, Prune Juice or Water
3-1/3 Cup Flour
½ Tsp. Baking Powder
½ Tsp. Soda
1-1/2 Tsp. Salt
1 Tsp. All Spice
1 Tsp. Cinnamon
1 Cup Dates or Raisins
1 Cup Nuts - Walnuts - Orange Peel -
  grated if you like

Cream together sugar, butter or shortening and eggs add pumpkin and juice. In another bowl sift flour, baking powder, soda, salt, all spice and cinnamon together.

Add to first mixture. Mix until blended. Add nuts and dates. Place in two greased loaf pans. Bake in 350° oven about 1 to 1-1/2 hours or until bread springs back at touch.

Makes 2 loaves.

PINTO BEAN CAKE

1 Cup Sugar
¼ Cup Shortening
1 Egg
1½ Cups Flour
2 Cups Cooked and Mashed Pinto
  Beans
2 Cups Diced Raw Apples
1 Cup Walnuts
½ Tsp. Soda
½ Tsp. Salt
½ Tsp. Cloves
½ Tsp. Allspice
1 Tsp. Cinnamon
1 Cup Raisins
1 Tsp. Vanilla

Cream sugar, shortening; add egg. Sift together dry ingredients. Add creamed mixture. Stir in beans, apples, raisins, nuts & vanilla. Pour into greased and floured loaf pan. Bake at 350 degrees for 1 hr. 15 min. or until toothpick comes out clean.

Topping:
6 Oz. Cream Cheese
2 Lbs. Powdered Sugar
½ Lb. Margarine
1 Cup Walnuts

Blend cream cheese, powdered sugar, margarine and nuts.

SUGAR PLUM RING

1 Pkg. Dry Yeast (1 tbs.)
¼ Cup Water
½ Cup Milk
1/3 Cup Sugar
1/3 Cup Shortening
1 Tsp. Salt
3¾ to 4 Cups Flour
2 Eggs
¼ Cup Butter or Margarine, melted
¾ Cup Sugar
1 Tsp. Cinnamon
½ Cup Whole, Blanched Almonds
½ Cup Candied Whole Cherries
½ Cup Dark Corn Syrup

Combine sugar and yeast; add warm water (110 degrees). Let stand until bubbly; add scalded milk (or use dry milk & warm water), shortening (softened), eggs; beat well. Stir in 1 cup of flour; beat well. Add remaining flour and salt. Make a soft dough. Mix thoroughly; place in greased bowl, turning once to grease surface. Cover; let rise till double (about 2 hours). Punch down; let rest 10 minutes. Divide dough into 4 parts. Cut each part into 10 pieces; shape into balls. Dip balls in melted butter, then in the ¾ cup sugar blended with some of the almonds and cherries. Repeat with 2 more layers. Mix corn syrup with butter left from dipping balls; drizzle over top. Cover, let rise in warm place till double, about 1 hour. Bake at 350 degrees for 35 minutes. Cool 5 minutes. Invert pan; remove ring. Makes 1 ring.

MARDI GRAS PARTY CAKE

2/3 Cup Nestles Butterscotch
  Morsels
¼ Cup Water
1¼ Cups Sugar
½ Cup Shortening (part butter)
1 Cup Buttermilk or Sour Cream
2¼ Cups Sifted Flour
1 Tsp. Salt
1 Tsp. Soda
½ Tsp. Baking Powder
3 Eggs, unbeaten

Melt morsels in water in pan & cool. Sift flour with salt, soda and baking powder; set aside. Cream shortening; add sugar and cream well. Add eggs, one at a time; beat well after each one. Add melted morsels. Mix well. Add dry ingredients alternately with buttermilk. Turn into 9" pans. Bake at 375 degrees 25 to 30 min. [MW: 8-9 min. on full power, covered with wax paper, cooking one layer at a time]. Cool. Spread filling on top of each layer.

Butterscotch Filling:
½ Cup Sugar
1 Tbs. Cornstarch
½ Cup Evaporated Milk
1/3 Cup Water
1/3 Cup Morsels
1 Beaten Egg Yolk
2 Tbs. Butter
1 Cup Coconut
1 Cup Pecans or Walnuts, chopped

Combine the sugar and cornstarch in a 2-quart pan. Stir in evaporated milk and water and morsels. Add beaten egg yolk and cook, stirring constantly, till thick. Remove from heat; add 2 tbs. butter, the coconut, pecans or walnuts (chopped) and dash of salt. Cool.

Sea Foam Icing:
1/3 Cup Brown Sugar
1/3 Cup White Sugar
1/3 Cup Water
1 Tbs. Corn Syrup
1 Egg White
¼ Tsp. Cream of Tartar

Combine in saucepan the brown sugar, white sugar, water and corn syrup. Cook until syrup forms a soft ball in cool wa-

ter. Beat 1 egg white with the cream of tartar until stiff peaks form. Add syrup to egg white in a slow, steady stream, beating constantly. Spread around sides of cake. This is good, if not better, made the day before it is served.

BEER BREAD

3 Cups Self-Rising Flour
1 Can 12 Oz. Beer
3 Tbs. Sugar

Stir together all ingredients until well mixed. Pour into buttered 9 x 5 x 3 loaf pan. Bake at 350° about 1 hour or until loaf tests done.

ORANGE GLAZED CAKE

1½ Cups Flour
1½ Tsp. Double-Acting Baking Powder
¼ Tsp. Salt
1 Stick Butter
1 Cup Sugar
1 Tsp. Vanilla
2 Eggs
1 Tbs. Grated Orange Rind (1 orange)
½ Cup Milk

For the Glaze:
1-2 Tbs. Rum
3 Tbs. Orange Juice
1 Tbs. Butter or Margarine
5 Tbs. Sugar

Mix flour, baking powder and salt together. Add butter and sugar and beat in the 2 eggs. Add vanilla and orange rind. Pour milk slowly and beat vigorously until all ingredients are well mixed. Bake at 350 degrees for about 35 min. [MW: 7-10 min. on full power, covered with wax paper]. Let it cool. In a frying pan [MW: browning dish], pour 3 tbs. orange juice, the rum, butter and sugar. Fry over medium heat for about 2 minutes. Spread this glaze over the cake and serve. Buon Appetito! (This is an Italian recipe).

WHITE BREAD

1 to 2 Pkgs. Yeast
½ Cup Water
1½ Cups Other Liquid (potato water
    or scalded milk)
3 Tbs. Sugar
1 Tbs. Salt
2 Tbs. Melted Shortening
5 to 7 Cups Flour

Put yeast into large bowl. Add ½ cup water and stir. Add 3 tbs. sugar, 1 tbs. salt and 2 tbs. shortening; then add remaining liquid which has been cooled. Blend 2 to 3 cups of flour and remaining flour at intervals as dough becomes workable. Add more flour if needed until dough is not sticky. Put dough on board and knead for 10 to 15 minutes. Let dough rest 20 minutes. Then shape in a ball. Place in bowl with oil to grease dough thoroughly. Let rise 1 hour and then punch down. Let rise ½ hour longer and shape into loaves or buns. Let stand 20 minutes and bake in a 350 degree oven for 25 to 30 minutes.

CRANBERRY NUT BREAD

1 Cup Sugar
1 Cup Cranberries, chopped
2 Cups Flour
1½ Tsp. Baking Powder
½ Tsp. Baking Soda
½ Tsp. Salt
1 Tsp. Cinnamon
1 Egg
¼ Cup Salad Oil
1 Tsp. Grated Orange Rind
¾ Cup Orange Juice
½ Cup Chopped Walnuts

Stir 1 tbs. sugar into chopped cranberries; set aside. In large bowl, combine remaining sugar with dry ingredients; blend thoroughly With hand beater, beat egg, oil, rind and juice together. Stir into dry ingredients, mixing just enough to moisten. Fold in the nuts and cranberries. Bake in greased loaf pans, at 350 degrees, for about 1 hour or until done. Best after frozen and thawed.

SPECIAL CHOCOLATE CHIP BUNDT CAKE

1 Pkg. Betty Crocker Milk Chocolate Cake Mix
1 Small Pkg. Royal Dark & Sweet Chocolate Pudding
4 Eggs
½ Cup Oil
½ Cup Water
1 Small Container Sour Cream
1 Large Pkg. Chocolate Chips

Mix cake mix with the dry pudding, eggs, oil, water and sour cream until well blended. Fold in 1 large pkg. chocolate chips. Spray Bundt pan with Pam. [MW: omit spray]. Fill pan ¾ full. Bake at 350 degrees for 50-55 minutes. [MW: 13-15 min. on full power, covered with wax paper]. Cool upright 15 min. Turn up side down on plate until it releases itself. Dust with powdered sugar. Serves 8-10.

RAISIN CAKE

2 Cups Water
2 Cups Sugar
2 Cups Raisins
1 Cube Butter
2 Tsp. Cinnamon
1 Tsp. Nutmeg
1 Tsp. Cloves
½ Tsp. Allspice
4 Cups Flour
2 Tsp. Baking Powder
2 Tsp. Baking Soda
½ Tsp. Salt
½ Cup Chopped Walnuts

In a saucepan, put the 2 cups water, raisins, sugar, butter and spices; bring to a boil. Simmer 5 min.; cool to room temperature. Sift flour, baking powder, baking soda and salt into a mixing bowl. Stir in nuts; add cooled raisin mixture and mix well. Don't beat - just mix until all flour is absorbed. Pour into a well greased tube pan [MW: ungreased]. Bake in a preheated 325 degree oven for 45 min. [MW: 15 min. on full power, covered with wax paper]. This is an inexpensive cake (no eggs or milk) and very easy to prepare - no mess. It's a heavy, moist cake.

THE PERFECT CHOCOLATE CAKE

Cake:
1 Cup Unsifted Unsweetened Cocoa
2 Cups Boiling Water
2¾ Cups Sifted All-purpose Flour
2 Tsp. Baking Soda
½ Tsp. Salt
½ Tsp. Baking Powder
1 Cup Butter or Regular Margarine,
   softened
2½ Cups Granulated Sugar
4 Eggs
1½ Tsp. Vanilla Extract

Frosting:
1 - 6 Oz. Pkg. Semisweet Chocolate
   Pieces
½ Cup Light Cream
1 Cup Butter or Regular Margarine
2½ Cups Unsifted Confectioner's Sugar

Filling:
1 Cup Heavy Cream, chilled
¼ Cup Unsifted Confectioner's Sugar
1 Tsp. Vanilla Extract

In medium bowl, combine cocoa with boiling water, mixing with wire whisk until smooth. Cool completely. Sift flour with soda, salt & baking powder. Preheat oven to 350 degrees. Grease well and lightly flour three 9" x 1½" layer-cake pans [MW: omit grease and flour]. In large bowl of electric mixer, at high speed, beat butter, sugar, eggs and vanilla, scraping bowl occasionally, until light, about 5 min. At low speed, beat in flour mixture (in fourths), alternately with cocoa mixture (in thirds), beginning and ending with flour mixture. Do not overbeat. Divide evenly into pans; smooth top. Bake 25 to 30 min. [MW: 7-8 min. on full power for each layer pan, covered with wax paper], or until surface springs back when gently pressed with fingertip. Cool in pans 10 min. Carefully loosen sides with a spatula; remove from pans; cool on racks.

Frosting: In medium saucepan, combine the chocolate pieces, cream, butter; stir over medium heat until smooth. Remove from heat. With whisk, blend in 2½ cups confectioner's sugar. In bowl set over ice, beat until it holds shape.

Filling: Whip cream with sugar and vanilla; refrigerate.

To assemble cake: On plate, place a layer, top-side down; spread with half of cream. Place second layer, top-side down; spread with rest of cream. Place third layer, top-side up. To frost, with spatula frost sides first, covering whipped cream; use rest of frosting on top, swirling decoratively. Refrigerate at least 1 hour before serving. To cut, use a thin-edged sharp knife; slice with a sawing motion. Serves 10 to 12.

Follow the recipe exactly - accurate measurements, no substitutions, the right pan size, and you'll have a perfect dessert that you can really be proud of.

HONEY ZUCCHINI BREAD

3 Cups Unsifted, Unbleached, All-
   purpose Flour
1 Tsp. Salt
1 Tsp. Soda
½ Tsp. Baking Powder
1 Tbs. Cinnamon
2 Cups Finely-grated, Raw, Unpeeled Zucchini
3 Eggs, slightly beaten
2/3 Cup Salad Oil
1-2/3 Cups Honey
1 Tbs. Vanilla
1 Cup Finely-chopped Nuts

In large bowl, measure and mix together dry ingredients. Set aside. Grate zucchini; measure and set aside. In medium bowl, mix together slightly beaten eggs, salad oil, honey, vanilla and zucchini. Add to dry ingredients, stirring only enough to moisten. Do not beat! Add nuts. Pour into 2 well-greased, lined 8½" x 4½" x 2½" loaf pans. Push batter into corners.

Heat oven to 325 degrees. Bake 1 hour, or until bread tests done in center. Cool on rack 10 minutes. Remove from pans. Complete cooling on rack. Makes 2 loaves. Note: Sliced bread freezes well.

NEW BACARDI CHOCOLATE RUM CAKE

1 - 18½ Oz. Pkg. Chocolate Cake
  Mix
1 Pkg. (4-serving size) Jello
  Chocolate Instant Pudding and
  Pie Filling
4 Eggs
½ Cup Bacardi Dark Rum (80 proof)
½ Cup Cold Water
½ Cup Wesson Oil

Filling:
1½ Cups Cold Milk
½ Cup Bacardi Dark Rum
1 Pkg. (4-serving size) Jello
  Chocolate Instant Pudding and
  Pie Filling
1 Envelope Dream Whip Topping
  Mix

Use two round 9" layer cake pans, greased and floured [MW: omit grease and flour]. Combine all cake ingredients together in large bowl. Blend well, then beat at medium speed for 2 minutes. Turn into prepared pans. Bake at 350 degrees for 30 to 35 min. and let cool. [MW: cook each layer separately 5 min. on full power, covered with wax paper in plastic layer cake pans].

Split layers in half horizontally. Spread 1 cup filling between each layer. Stack and spread mixture over top of cake also. Keep cake chilled. Serve cold.

CHOCOLATE PINEAPPLE UPSIDE DOWN CAKE

½ Cup Shortening
1 Cup Sugar
¼ Cup Hershey's Chocolate
2 Eggs
2 Cups Sifted Flour
3 Tsp. Baking Powder
½ Tsp. Salt
1 Tbs. Vanilla
¾ to 1 Cup Cold Water
1 Cup Brown Sugar
¼ Cup Margarine
5 Slices Pineapple
5 Maraschino Cherries

Cream shortening; add sugar and beat. Add eggs, one at a time; beat well. Sift flour, baking powder, salt and chocolate together. Add vanilla to water. Alternately add dry and liquid ingredients; blend until smooth. Sprinkle pan with brown sugar; dot with margarine. Arrange pineapple slices in pan, place cherry in center of each slice. Spread cake batter evenly over pineapple; may be baked with or without a cover. Bake at 375 degrees for 5 min. Reduce heat to 350 degrees and bake for 40-50 min. [MW: 13-15 min. on full power, covered with wax paper]. Allow to stand 5 min. before turning cake upside down on platter.

ORANGE CANDY SLICE CAKE

1 Cup Butter or Shortening
1 Cup Sugar
4 Eggs
3 Cups Flour
½ Cup Buttermilk
1 Tsp. Soda
2 Cups Orange Candy Slices, chopped
1 - 10 Oz. Pkg. Dates, chopped
2 Cups Nuts, chopped
½ Cup Flour

Cream butter & sugar; add eggs, one at a time, beating well after each addition. Combine buttermilk & soda & add alternately with flour; beat well. Dredge orange candy, dates and nuts in the ½ cup of flour. Stir into cake mixture. Bake in a well-greased and floured tube pan at 300 degrees for 1½ hours, or until done. Ice when you take it from the oven.

Topping:
2 Cups Powdered Sugar
1 Cup Orange Juice

Combine and heat (do not boil) and pour over hot cake while still in pan. Punch holes in cake to allow to penetrate cake. Loosen from sides and remove from pan when cool. Let cool overnight if planning to freeze it.

SCOTCH SHORT BREAD

1 Lb. Butter (or ½ lb. butter and
  ½ lb. margarine)
½ Cup Brown Sugar, packed
½ Cup White Sugar
4½ Cups Flour, approximate

Note: No leavening or salt are used.

Sift the flour twice. Cream the butter
by hand; add the sugars and cream well,
still by hand. Gradually add the flour,
adding until the creamed mixture doesn't
stick to the hands. Chill the dough for
½ hour.

Sprinkle the bread board liberally with
flour and pat out the dough to about
1¼" thickness. Cut into oblongs and
place on an ungreased cookie sheet.
Prick with a fork.

Bake at 300 degrees for 20 to 25 min.
These cookies do not brown.

APRICOT NIBBLE BREAD

2 3-Oz. Pkg. Cream Cheese, Softened
1/3 Cup Sugar
1 Tbs Flour
1 Egg
1 Tsp. Grated Orange Peel
1 Slightly Beaten Egg
½ Cup Orange Juice
½ Cup Water
¾ Cup Chopped Dried Apricots
1 17-Oz. Apricot-Nut Quick Bread Mix

Combine cream cheese, sugar and flour, beat
in the first egg, the orange peel. Set mixture
aside. Combine the slightly beaten egg, orange
juice and water. Add Quick Bread and apricots,
stirring till moistened. Turn two-thirds of the
apricot batter into greased and floured 9x5x3
inch loaf pan. Pour cream cheese mixture
over top; spoon on remaining apricot batter.
Bake in 350º oven for 1 hour. Cool 10 min.;
remove from pan. Cool, wrap in foil; refrigerate.

GERMAN APPLE PUDDING CAKE

2 Cups Peeled Diced Apples
1 Cup Sugar
1 Egg
1 Cup Flour
1-1/2 Tsp. Cinnamon
1 Tsp. Baking Soda
1 Cup Nuts (chopped)
3/4 Cup Raisins
1 Tsp. Vanilla

Topping
1/2 Cup Brown Sugar
1 Cup Water
1/2 Cup White Sugar
2 Tbs. Flour
1/4 Lb. Butter or Margarine
1 Tsp. Vanilla
1/2 Cup Chopped Nuts
1/2 Cup Raisins

Mix apples and sugar together. Let stand
until sugar is thoroughly dissolved. Add
eggs and mix well.

Sift dry ingredients together. Stir into apple
mixture. Add nuts, raisins and vanilla. Pour
into 8 x 8 pan which is slightly oiled [MW:
omit oil].
Bake at 375 degrees for 40-45 min. [MW: 10-
12 min. on full power].

If preferred use unsweetened can sliced
apples instead of fresh apples.

Topping
Mix sugar, water and flour. Cook until
slightly thick and clear.

Add the rest of the ingredients and
stir until butter has melted.

Pour over hot baked cake while still in
pan.

BUDAPEST COFFEE CAKE

Nut Filling:
¾ Cup Dark Brown Sugar
1 Tbs. Cinnamon
1 Tbs. Powdered Unsweet Cocoa
2-3 Tbs. Currants or Raisins, coarsely chopped
3½ Oz. Walnuts, finely cut

In a small bowl, stir brown sugar, cinnamon, and cocoa to mix thoroughly. Stir in currants or raisins and then the walnuts. Set aside.

Cake Batter:
3 Cups Sifted All-Purpose Flour
1½ Tsp. Double–Acting Baking Powder
1½ Tsp. Baking Soda
½ Tsp. Salt
6 Oz. Butter
2 Tsp. Vanilla Extract
1½ Cups Sugar
3 Eggs
2 Cups Sour Cream

Adjust rack 1/3 up from bottom of oven. Preheat to 375 degrees. Butter a 10" Bundt pan [MW: omit butter]. (This is best baked in a Bundt pan, but a tube pan of similar size may be substituted.) Even if the pan is Teflon, it should be buttered for this recipe.

Sift together flour, baking powder, baking soda and salt. Set aside. In large bowl of electric mixer cream the butter. Add vanilla and sugar, beat for a minute or two. Add eggs individually, beating until thoroughly incorporated after each. Scrape bowl with rubber spatula as necessary to keep mixture smooth and beat at high speed for a minute or so until mixture is light and creamy. On lowest speed alternately add dry ingredients in 3 additions and sour cream in 2 additions, continuing to scrape bowl as necessary with the rubber spatula and beating only until smooth after each addition.

Spread a thin layer of the batter in the bottom of the pan. Sprinkle very generously with about 1/3 of nut filling. Continue making layers, 4 of the batter and 3 of the filling. The top layer should be batter. It will take a bit of patience to spread the batter thin. It will be easier if the batter is placed on by many small spoonfuls and then spread with the back of the spoon, instead of just being dropped on in 2 or 3 large amounts.

Bake 50-60 min. [MW: 12-15 min. on full power, covered with wax paper] or until cake tester comes out dry and the top feels firm and springy. Remove from oven. Leave cake in pan 5 min., no longer. The cake should be hot when glaze is applied. Meanwhile prepare glaze.
Glaze:
2 Cups Confectioner's Sugar
1 Tsp. Vanilla Extract
2-3 Tbs. Hot Milk

In a small bowl, with a rubber spatula, mix sugar with vanilla and about 2 tbs. hot milk. Very gradually add more milk, just a bit at a time, using only enough to make a semi-fluid mixture about as thick as thick cream sauce.

Cover cake with a rack and invert over a large piece of wax paper or aluminum foil. Remove pan, leaving cake upside down. Immediately pour on the glaze, just pour it on quickly, don't spread it or work over it, and let it run down the sides unevenly. When the glaze has set, use a small cookie sheet as a spatula to transfer cake to cake plate. Serve the cake while still slightly warm or after it has cooled completely.

TROPICAL POUND CAKE

2¼ Cups Unsifted Flour
½ Tsp. Soda
½ Tsp. Salt
1 Cup Butter or Margarine
1 8-Oz. Carton Yogurt (Peach, Orange, Pineapple or Apricot) or
1 Cup Dairy Sour Cream
2 Cups Sugar
3 Eggs
1 Tsp. Vanilla

Combine all ingredients. Blend on low speed, then beat 3 min. at med. speed. Pour batter in greased & floured 10" bundt pan [MW: omit grease & flour]. Bake 60 min. at 325⁰, cool 15 min. in pan [MW: 15-17 min. on full power, covered with wax paper]. Remove and drizzle with glaze.

WHITE GERMAN CHOCOLATE CAKE

2½ Cups Sifted Cake Flour
1 Tsp. Baking Powder
½ Tsp. Salt
1 Cup Butter or Margarine
2 Cups Sugar
4 Eggs, separated
1 Tsp. Vanilla
1 Cup Buttermilk
¼ Lb. White Chocolate
1 Cup Chopped Pecans
1 Cup Angel Flaked Coconut

Melt white chocolate in double boiler. Sift and measure sugar. Add the baking powder and salt and sift again. Soften butter or margarine and cream with the sugar, beating until light and fluffy. Add the 4 yolks and beat again very well. Then add the melted chocolate and vanilla. After beating well, add the flour and buttermilk alternately and beat after each addition. Fold in the beaten egg whites. Stir in the nuts and coconut. Bake in two 9" pans at 350 degrees for 45 minutes or in a loaf pan for about 75 min. [MW: 12 min. on full power, covered with wax paper]. If you prefer, leave the coconut and nuts out and use them in the filling instead. This is the recipe for filling with nuts and coconut:

Filling:
1 Cup Nuts
1 Cup Coconut
1 Cup White Sugar
½ Cup Half & Half
½ Cube Butter
1 Tsp. White Karo Syrup
1 Tsp. Vanilla

Put in pan. Stir well to dissolve. Then boil for 8 to 10 minutes. Let cool and put between layers. Or you may use a cream cheese frosting:

½ Cup Butter
3 Oz. Cream Cheese

Melt in double boiler, then add 3 cups powdered sugar and beat until smooth. Add 1 tsp. vanilla. Use more sugar if needed, and luck to you!

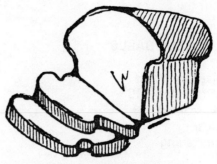

SHREDDED WHEAT BREAD

3-4 Shredded Wheat Biscuits
½ Cup Shortening (vegetable)
½ Cup Molasses
2¾ Cups Boiling Water
1 Tsp. Salt
1 Pkg. Yeast
¼ Cup Lukewarm Water
7-8½ Cups Sifted Flour

Crush shredded wheat biscuits into a large mixing bowl. Measure shortening and place on top of crushed shredded wheat. Measure ½ cup molasses in a one cup measuring cup; pour over shredded wheat. Use the same cup to measure the boiling water and pour over shredded wheat, shortening and molasses. Add salt and set aside to cool.

Meanwhile, soften yeast in lukewarm water and add to cooled mixture. When shortening begins to congeal again, the mixture is usually cool enough. Gradually add flour until it makes a very thick dough that is difficult to stir. Turn out on a floured surface (you may use some of allowed flour); knead lightly for 1 to 2 minutes. Return to greased or oiled bowl and place in a warm place to let rise until double in bulk; at least an hour. Return to floured surface and divide into three equal parts. Form into loaves or round loaves and put in WELL GREASED pans. I like to use 46 oz. fruit juice cans. These make nice cylindrical loaves. Set in a warm place to rise again, at least an hour, or until double

Bake 45 minutes to 1 hour at 375 degrees. Remove from cans or pans immediately & put on a rack. This is excellent to freeze. Slice and wrap securely in heavy aluminum foil. To serve, thaw in oven and serve warm. Delicious!

APRICOT BUBBLE BALLS

1 Pkg. Active Dry Yeast
¼ Cup Warm Water, 110°
½ Cup Milk, scalded
1/3 Cup Sugar
1/3 Cup Shortening
1 Tsp. Salt
3¾ - 4 Cups Sifted All-Purpose Flour
2 Beaten Eggs
¼ Cup Melted Butter
¾ Cup Sugar
1 Tsp. Cinnamon
2/3 Cup Apricot Preserves
¾ Cup Finely Chopped Walnuts

Soften active dry yeast in warm water. Combine scalded milk, 1/3 cup sugar, shortening and salt. Cool to lukewarm. Stir in 1 cup of the flour; beat well. Add softened yeast & eggs. Add remaining flour, or enough to make a soft dough. Mix thoroughly & place in a greased bowl, turning once to grease the surface. Cover and let rise until double, about 2 hours. Punch down and let rest 10 min. Divide dough into 20 pieces and form into balls. Roll each ball in melted butter. Combine sugar and cinnamon; roll ball in mixture. Place a layer of 10 balls in well-greased 10" tube pan. Place a spoonful of the preserves between each ball and sprinkle with half the nuts; repeat with second layer. Cover and let rise in warm place until double, about 45 minutes. Bake in moderate oven, 350 degrees, for about 30 to 35 minutes. Cool about 8 minutes, invert pan and remove ring. Makes 1 coffee cake. Pull balls apart to eat.

YULECAKE
(Norwegian Christmas Bread)

12 Cups Flour
2 Tbs. Salt
2 Cubes Butter
1½ Cups Sugar
4½ Cups Milk
1 Lb. Dark Raisins
1½ Lbs. Chopped Citron
3 Squares Yeast
4 Tsp. Cardamom Seed

Melt butter in milk in large cooking utensil. When lukewarm, add cardamom, sugar, yeast (dissolved in small amount of water), salt and flour (2 cups at a time); mix well after each addition. When all flour is used, knead the dough well. Put back in pan. Cover with clean cloth; set in warm place to rise until double in size. Sprinkle a large area with flour; roll dough all out flat. Cover half with raisins and citron; cover with other half and roll out again. Keep doing this until all raisins & citron are used.

Cut into four parts and shape into loaves. Put in greased loaf pans; cover and let rise till up above pan. Bake at 350 degrees for 1 hour; when removed from oven, butter tops of loaves. May be frozen.

WACKY CAKE

1 Cup Sugar
3 Tbs. Cocoa
1½ Cups Flour
1 Tsp. Baking Soda
1 Pinch Salt
1 Cup Cold Water
6 Tbs. Salad Oil
1 Tbs. Vinegar
1 Tsp. Vanilla

Frosting:
1 Cup Powdered Sugar
2 Tbs. Cocoa
2 Tbs. Melted Butter
2 Tbs. Cream, or evaporated milk
1 Pinch Salt

Sift dry ingredients together into an ungreased 8" x 8" baking pan. Make 3 holes in dry ingredients. Put vinegar in one hole; oil in one hole, and vanilla in the last hole. Pour cold water over all and stir with a fork until moistened. Do not beat. Bake 25-30 min. at 350 degrees [MW: 6-8 min. on full power, covered with wax paper]. Leave in pan and frost.

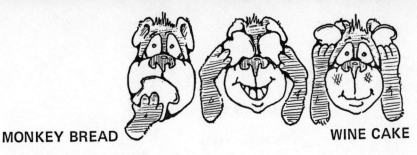

MONKEY BREAD

2 Cups Milk
2 Pkgs. Dry Yeast
2 Eggs
2 Tbs. Sugar
1/3 Cup Crisco (or pure lard)
1/8 Tsp. Salt
4-1/3 Cups Flour
1 Lb. Real Butter
3 Tbs. Water

Very Important: Kitchen must be heated (or hot) to make bread. Butter is to be set on top of stove and melted by rising heat, not cooked.

Put milk on fire and let it come to a boil (or let it get hot; do not scorch milk or let it get cold).

While milk is yet on fire, take a large bowl and put 1/3 cup Crisco (or 2 heaping tbs. Crisco or lard), 2 tbs. sugar, and 1/8 tsp. salt into it.

Put enough faucet water into a coffee cup to dissolve the yeast. Take eggs, beat and pour over yeast mixture and mix very thoroughly - let sit until needed.

Pour hot milk over into the bowl of Crisco, sugar and salt; stir real good until dissolved. After dissolved thoroughly, pour eggs and yeast into the milk mixture. Finally, sift flour in portions over into the mixture, stirring until thickened.

1. Grease hands with Crisco and knead the dough for 15 minutes.
2. Let dough sit and rise for 45 minutes to 1 hour.
3. Put a damp rag over rising dough (do not let rag dry out).
4. After bread has risen, knead 15 minutes to ½ hour. Break dough in small pieces, dip into butter and drop in baking pan. Let bread sit on stove top and rise half way. Place in oven and bake for 1 hour, or until brown.
5. Take leftover melted butter and cut slits in baked bread and pour the butter over the top of bread. Let sit for 5 minutes, then serve hot.

WINE CAKE

1 - 1 Lb. 3 Oz. Pkg. Yellow Cake Mix
1 - 3½ Oz. Pkg. Instant Vanilla
   Pudding Mix
4 Eggs
¾ Cup Oil
¾ Cup Cream Sherry
1 Tsp. Nutmeg
Confectioner's Sugar

Combine cake mix, pudding mix, eggs, oil, sherry and nutmeg in mixer bowl. Beat about 5 min. Pour batter into a greased 10" tube pan [MW: ungreased] and bake at 350 degrees for 45 min. [MW: 11-12 min. on full power], or until cake springs back when touched. Cool in pan for 5 min., then turn out on rack. When cool, sprinkle with confectioner's sugar.

Note: can also be baked in two loaf pans, 9-5/8" x 5½" x 2¾". [MW: omit this note].

EGGPLANT PUDDING CAKE

1 Pkg. Yellow Cake Mix, 2-layer size
1 Pkg. Vanilla Flavor Instant Pudding
   and Pie Filling, 4-serving size
4 Eggs
1 Cup (½ Pint) Sour Cream
¼ Cup Oil
2 Cups Grated, Peeled Eggplant
½ Tsp. Nutmeg
¼ Tsp. Cinnamon
1/8 Tsp. Cloves
1/8 Tsp. Salt

Combine all ingredients in a large mixing bowl. Blend, then beat at medium speed of electric mixer for 4 minutes. Pour into a greased and floured fluted tube pan. Bake at 350 degrees for 1 hour 10 minutes, or until cake tests done. Do not underbake. Cool in pan 15 min. Remove from pan & finish cooling on rack. Sprinkle with sifted powdered sugar, if desired.

Note: For mellowing of flavors, cover & store overnight. Do not use cake mix which has pudding added.

DILLY BREAD

1 Pkg. Dry Yeast
¼ Cup Warm Water
1 Cup Cream Cottage Cheese
2 Tbs. Sugar
1 Tsp. Instant Minced Onion (rounded)
1 Unbeaten Egg
1 Tsp. Salt
¼ Tsp. Baking Soda
1 Tbs. Butter
2 Tbs. Dill Seed
2¼ Cups Flour, or more

Fix yeast first by combining it in a bowl with the ¼ cup warm water. Soak for 5 minutes. Combine in a bowl, all ingredients, adding the yeast and flour to make a stiff dough. Cover and let rise until double in size. For about 30 to 60 minutes. Work down, put in a greased 8 inch casserole or a 2 quart dish. Let rise until light. Bake at 350 degrees for 30 to 40 minutes. Butter the top with soft butter and sprinkle with salt.

FRENCH APPLESAUCE CAKE

2 Cups Flour
1-1½ Cups Sugar
1 Tsp. Baking Soda
1 Tsp. Cinnamon
½ Tsp. Nutmeg
½ Tsp. Salt
½ Tsp. Cloves
3 Tbs. Cocoa
1 Tbs. Cornstarch
½ Cup Oil
2 Cups Applesauce

Optional:
1 Cup Nuts
1 Cup Raisins

Combine first 9 ingredients in large bowl. Heat applesauce in oil and add to dry ingredients; if desired, add nuts and raisins. Mix thoroughly. Pour into tube pan which has been greased and floured [MW: omit grease and flour]. Bake 1 hr. at 325 degrees. [MW: 15 min. on full power, covered with wax paper].

RAISIN SPICE BAGELS

2 Pkgs. Yeast
2 Cups Warm Potato Water
4 Eggs
1 Tbs. Salt
¼ Cup Sugar
¼ Cup Salad Oil
8 Cups Unsifted Flour (approx.)
2 Tsp. Cinnamon
1 Tsp. Nutmeg
½ Tsp. Cardamom
1 Cup Raisins
2 Tbs. Sugar
2 Qts. Boiling Water
2 Egg Yolks
2 Tbs. Water

Soften yeast in ½ cup potato water (water in which peeled potatoes have been boiled). Beat eggs in a large bowl, blend in yeast, extra water, sugar, salt, oil, 2 cups flour, cinnamon, nutmeg, cardamom and raisins. Stir in extra flour to make a soft dough. Knead for 10 minutes on a light, floured board. Place in a greased bowl. Cover and let rise until doubled. Punch down, knead until smooth. Roll out to rectangle and divide into 32 parts. Roll each to form 6 inch strands. Wet ends and make into doughnut shapes. Let rise on board for 15 minutes. Dissolve sugar in water. Drop bagels in, one at a time. Don't crowd. Turn them over, as they rise to the surface. Boil 3 minutes. Remove, place on a greased baking sheet. Brush with mixture of the 2 egg yolks that have been beaten with the water. Bake at 425 degrees for 15 to 20 minutes, or until golden brown. Makes 32 bagels.

Note: This bread recipe will take all day. Start early in the morning and you will finish around 5 or 6 o'clock in the evening. Use them as muffins for dinner or toast them for breakfast. Spread them with cream cheese and smoked salmon for sandwiches.

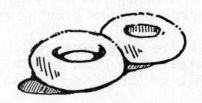

SHERRY HOLIDAY LOAF

3 Cups Pecans, halved
4 Oz. Glace Cherries, left whole
4 Oz. Glace Pineapple
½ Lb. Dates, pitted and chopped lg.
¾ Cup Flour
¾ Cup Sugar
½ Tsp. Baking Powder
½ Tsp. Salt
3 Eggs, beaten
1 Tsp. Vanilla
Sherry Wine

Mix fruit and nuts. Sift together flour, sugar, baking powder and salt. Mix eggs and vanilla into flour mixture. Stir in fruits and nuts until well blended. Pour into 2 foil loaf pans. Bake one hour and 30 minutes at 300 degrees. When cool, pierce top with fork or tester and pour Sherry wine over. If made in advance, cover with cheesecloth and keep moist with Sherry. Freezes well.

MINI LUNCHEON LOAVES

2½ to 3 Cups Unbleached Flour
1 Pkg. Dry Yeast
2 Tbs. Very Warm Water
½ Cup Warm Milk
1/3 Cup Butter
3 Eggs
1½ Tsp. Salt
1½ Tsp. Dill Weed
1 Tbs. Dry Minced Onion
1 Tbs. Poppy Seed

Measure and set aside the flour. More flour can be used if needed. Dissolve the yeast in water and put in a warm place. In a bowl or saucepan, add the milk and butter. Heat just until the butter melts. In a large mixing bowl, beat the eggs. Add the dill weed, onion, poppy seed and the milk and yeast mixtures. Beat slightly. Gradually add the flour while beating by hand or mixer until thick enough to turn out on a well-floured board. Knead dough, adding as much flour as dough needs to keep it from sticking. Knead for 10 to 15 minutes. Place in a well greased bowl, turning several times to grease the top and sides of the dough. Let rise for 1½ hours in an oven over a pan of hot water or in another warm place. Punch down and shape into 4 round loaves. Place in Corning Ware bowls or other similar 5 inch shallow bowls that have been well greased. Brush the tops with melted butter and let rise for 1 hour. Bake at 350 degrees for 12 to 15 minutes. Remove from pans and place on racks to cool. This freezes well.

REVANI

Syrup:
4 Cups Sugar
5 Cups Water

Combine sugar and water in a saucepan and bring mixture to a boil. Lower the flame, and let the syrup boil for 20 min. Set aside to cool.

Batter:
1 Cup Farina
1 Cup Flour
1 Cup Sugar
2 Tsp. Baking Powder
5 Eggs, beaten
½ Lb. Butter, melted
1 Cup Chopped Walnuts

Preheat oven to 375⁰. Combine the Farina, flour, sugar and baking powder in a mixing bowl. Add the beaten eggs and the melted butter and beat with an electric mixer. Add the chopped nuts, and mix. Pour into a buttered 9x9 inch baking pan. Place the pan in the oven and lower the temp. to 350⁰. Bake for 45 min. When you remove the pan from the oven, while the revani is still hot, cut into diamond-shaped serving pieces and pour half of the cooled syrup evenly over the entire surface. Pour the balance of the syrup over the cake 1 hour before serving. Bon Appetit!

SHEPHERD'S BREAD

This recipe makes an excellent snowy white round loaf. Best if baked on an earthenware bread plate, but a regular baking sheet will do.

Sponge:
1 Cake or Pkg. Yeast
2 Cups Lukewarm Water
4 Cups Flour (use a blend of flours if preferred)
2 Tbs. Malt or Honey

Dissolve yeast in water slowly, thoroughly blend in the flour and malt or honey. Cover with a clean towel and let rise in a warm place for approximately 4 hours.

Dough:
1 Cake or Pkg. Yeast
1 Cup Lukewarm Water
1 Tbs. Salt
2 Tbs. Malt or Honey
3 to 4 Cups Flour

Dissolve the yeast in the water. Blend in the salt, malt or honey and flour. Blend well. Thoroughly incorporate with the sponge until pliable and smooth. Dough will pull away from bowl. Turn out on a lightly floured board and knead for 3 to 5 minutes, then let rest for 10 minutes. Shape into one long or one round loaf, cut a cross in center, and place on a corn meal-sprinkled baking tin. Cover and let rise until almost doubled. Then place a pan of boiling water on the floor of the oven, place bread in oven, set temperature for 400 degrees, and bake the bread for 45 minutes or until golden brown and done. Brush with egg white glaze before and after baking. Do not preheat the oven.

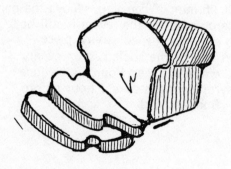

GRAPE NUT BREAD

1 Cup Grape Nuts
2 Cups Buttermilk
2 Cups Sugar
2 Eggs
3½ Cups Flour
½ Tsp. Salt
1 Tsp. Soda
2 Tsp. Baking Powder

Soak grape nuts in buttermilk for 10 minutes. Cream sugar and eggs. Add milk and grape nuts mixture. Sift dry ingredients and add to above mixture. Pour into 2 loaf pans, greased and floured [MW: omit grease and flour]. Bake at 350 degrees for about 45 min. [MW: 11-12 min. on full power, covered with wax paper], or until toothpick comes out clean when stuck into center of loaf.

"AMOR POLENTA" - FLORENTINE CORN MEAL CAKE

2/3 Cup Soft Butter
2-2/3 Cups Sifted Powdered Sugar
1 Tsp. Vanilla
2 Whole Eggs + 1 Egg Yolk
1¼ Cups Cake Flour
1/3 Cup Yellow Corn Meal
2 Tbs. Powdered Sugar

In a large bowl of electric mixer, beat butter until creamy. Gradually add the powdered sugar, beating until fluffy. Beat in vanilla. Add eggs and egg yolk, one at a time, beating well after each addition. Add flour and corn meal, beat until well mixed. Generously grease and lightly flour either a 10" deerback loaf pan, an 8½ x 4½" loaf pan or a 3½ to 4 cup mold or tube pan [MW: omit grease and flour and use tube pan]. Bake in a 325 degree oven for about 1 hr. and 15 minutes [MW: 18-20 min. on full power, covered with wax paper] or until a wooded pick stuck in the center comes out clean, and when the center of the cake springs back when lightly touched. Cool cake in pan for 3 minutes and then turn it out on a rack. Sift the 2 tbs. powdered sugar over the warm cake. Cool for serving. Makes about 15 servings.

FINNISH VIIPURI TWIST

5-½ to 5-¾ Cups All-Purpose Flour
2 Pkgs. Active Dry Yeast
½ Tsp. Ground Cardamom
½ Tsp. Ground Nutmeg
2 Cups Milk
¾ Cup Sugar
¼ Cup Butter Or Margarine
1 Tsp. Salt
1 Slightly Beaten Egg

In large mixer bowl combine 2-½ cups flour, yeast, cardamom and nutmeg. In saucepan heat milk, sugar, butter and salt until warm, 115 degrees to 120 degrees, stirring constantly to melt butter. Add to dry mixture. Beat at low speed with mixer for ½ minute, scraping bowl. Beat at high speed for 3 minutes. By hand, stir in remaining flour to make a moderately stiff dough. Knead until smooth. 5 to 8 minutes. Place in greased bowl, turning once, cover & let rise until doubled, 1 to 1-½ hours. Punch down. Divide in thirds. Cover, let rest 10 minutes. On floured surface shape one part into a roll 36 inches long. Cross ends to form a circle, extending each end about 6 inches. Holding ends toward center or circle, twist together twice. Press ends together, tuck under center or top of circle, forming a pretzel-shaped roll. Place on greased baking sheet. Repeat with remaining dough. Let rise until almost double, about 45 minutes. Bake in 375 degree oven about 20 minutes. Combine egg and 1 tbs. water and brush on hot breads. Makes 3 loaves.

SOFT GINGER BREAD

½ Cup Sugar
1 Cup Molasses
½ Cup Shortening
½ Tsp. Cinnamon
½ Tsp. Cloves
½ Tsp. Ginger
1 Tsp. Baking Soda (dissolved in 1 cup boiling water)
2½ Cups Flour
2 Well Beaten Eggs

Beat sugar and shortening. Add molasses, baking soda and hot water. Sift flour and spices and add to mixture. Add the two well beaten eggs last. Bake in a 350 degree oven for about 40 min. [MW: 10-12 min. on full power, covered with wax paper] or until a toothpick inserted in the middle comes out dry. Serve hot with whipped cream.

CHALLAH BREAD

1 Pkg. Active - Dry Yeast
¼ Cup Warm Water (105 to 115 deg.)
½ Cup Lukewarm Milk (scalded & cooled)
1 Tbs. Sugar
1 Tsp. Salt
1 Egg
1 Tbs. Shortening or Butter
2½ to 2¾ Cups Flour

Dissolve yeast in warm water. Stir in lukewarm milk, sugar, salt, shortening and 1¼ cups flour. Beat until smooth. Mix in enough remaining flour to make the dough easy to handle. Turn dough out on a lightly floured board. Knead until smooth and elastic, about 5 minutes. Round up dough in greased bowl, turn greased side up. Cover & let rise in warm place until it doubles. About 1½ to 2 hours. Punch down dough and divide into 3 equal parts. Roll each part into a strand 14 inches long. Place strands close together on lightly greased cookie sheet. Braid loosely and gently. Fasten ends and tuck under securely. For round Challah, roll braid and tuck outside end under. Brush with melted butter or shortening. Let rise until it doubles. About 40 to 50 minutes. Heat oven to 375 degrees and bake 25 to 30 minutes. Brush again with butter.

Variations: Beat egg yolk and 2 tbs. cold water, brush over braid and bake. Can add cinnamon or can use honey instead of sugar.

KENTUCKY BUTTER CAKE

1 Cup Butter, softened
2 Cups Sugar
4 Eggs
3 Cups Flour
1 Tsp. Salt
1 Tsp. Baking Powder
½ Tsp. Baking Soda
2 Tsp. Vanilla
1 Cup Buttermilk or Sour Milk

Grease bottom only of a 10 inch tube pan. Cream butter, gradually add sugar until fluffy. Add eggs, one by one, beating well after each addition. Add remaining ingredients. Blend at low speed until moistened. Beat 2 minutes at medium speed, scraping bowl occasionally. Bake in a 325 degree oven for 60 to 65 minutes, until top springs back when touched lightly in the center. Prepare butter sauce. Prick top of cake with fork. Pour warm butter sauce over warm cake. Cool cake completely before removing from pan.

Butter Sauce:
1 Cup Sugar
¼ Cup Hot Water
½ Cup Butter
1 or 2 Tbs. Rum Flavoring

In a small saucepan, combine sugar, water and butter. Heat until butter is melted. Do not boil. Remove from heat, add rum and pour over cake. Bundt pan may be used if desired.

MISSISSIPPI MUD CAKE

Cake:
2 Cups Sugar
1 Cup Shortening
4 Eggs
1½ Cups Flour
1/3 Cup Cocoa
¼ Tsp. Salt
2 Tsp. Vanilla
1 Cup Chopped Pecans or Walnuts
1 Large Pkg. Marshmallows

Frosting:
1 Box Powdered Sugar
1 Cube Margarine, melted
¼ Cup Evaporated Milk
1/3 Cup Cocoa
1 Tsp. Vanilla

Cake: Cream sugar and shortening. Beat in eggs by hand. Sift flour, cocoa and salt together. Add to creamed mixture. Add vanilla and nuts. Pour into a greased and floured oblong cake pan. Bake for 25 minutes in a 300 degree oven. Sprinkle cake with rows of marshmallows. Increase oven to 350 degrees and bake for 10 minutes longer, cool cake completely.

Frosting: Sift powdered sugar and cocoa. Add melted margarine, milk and vanilla. Stir in nuts and spread on cake.

TEXAS SHEET CAKE

Cake:
2 Cups Flour
2 Cups Sugar
½ Tsp. Salt
1 Cup Water
2 Cubes Margarine
4 Tbs. Cocoa
2 Eggs
½ Cup Sour Cream
1 Tsp. Baking Soda

Frosting:
1 Cube Margarine
4 Tbs. Cocoa
6 Tbs. Milk
1 Box Powdered Sugar
1 Cup Chopped Nuts

Cake: Sift together flour, sugar and salt; bring to a light boil the water, margarine and cocoa. Add eggs, sour cream and baking soda. Combine with the flour mixture and mix well. Pour into a 10½ x 18 x 1 inch cookie sheet and bake in a 400 degree oven for 20 minutes.

Frosting: Bring to a light boil the margarine, cocoa and milk. Remove from stove and add the powdered sugar and nuts. Beat well and pour over cake as soon as it is removed from the oven.

COFFEE CHIFFON CAKE

1¾ Cups Flour
1 Cup Sugar
1 Tbs. Baking Powder
1 Tsp. Salt
½ Cup Salad Oil
5 Egg Yolks
¾ Cup Water
½ Tsp. Cream of Tartar
1 Cup Egg Whites
3 Tbs. Instant Coffee
1½ Tsp. Vanilla

Spoon or pour flour into dry measuring cup. Level off & pour into mixing bowl. Add sugar, baking powder, coffee & salt; stir well to blend. Add oil, egg yolks, water and vanilla to dry ingredients in bowl. Blend them with electric mixer at medium speed until smooth. Beat egg whites in large bowl until foamy. Add cream of tartar and beat until very stiff peaks are formed. Fold egg yolk mixture into beaten egg whites very carefully, using rubber scraper. Turn batter into ungreased 10" tube pan. Bake on lower rack at 325 degrees for 55 min. [MW: 14-15 minutes on full power, covered with wax paper]. Invert pan on funnel and allow cake to hang suspended until cold. When cooled, run knife around edge to loosen cake; shake out gently. Frost the cooled cake if desired. Yield: 1 - 10" tube cake.

SWISS CHEESE BREAD

1 Cup Milk
2 Tbs. Sugar
3 Tsp. Salt
1 Tbs. Butter
1 Envelope Dry Active Yeast
1 Cup Warm Water
5 Cups Sifted Flour
2 Cups (8 oz.) Grated Swiss Cheese

Scald milk with sugar, salt and butter in a small saucepan. Cool just until warm. In a large bowl sprinkle yeast into warm water & stir until yeast dissolves. Stir in cooled milk mixture. Beat in 2 cups of the flour mixture to form a smooth soft dough. Beat in the cheese. Gradually beat in the 3 remaining cups of flour to make a stiff dough. Turn out onto a lightly floured pastry cloth or a cutting board. Knead until smooth and elastic, adding only enough extra flour to keep the dough from sticking. Place in a greased bowl, turn to coat all over with shortening. Cover with a towel. Let rise in a warm place, away from drafts, for about 1 hour or until it doubles in bulk. Punch dough down and divide in half. Knead each half a few times. Shape each into a ball. Place in a greased 8 inch round layer cake pan. Cover and let rise again in a warm place for about 1 hour or until it doubles in bulk. Bake in a moderate oven of 350 degrees for 50 minutes or until the bread gives a hollow sound when tapped. Remove from pans and cool on a wire rack. Slice in wedges.

7—UP CAKE

1 Pkg. Yellow Cake Mix
1 Pkg. French Vanilla Instant Pudding
¾ Cup Oil
3 Eggs
1 - 12 Oz. Bottle 7-Up
½ Cup Walnuts, chopped
½ Cup Shredded Coconut

Topping:
2 Envelopes Dream Whip
1½ Cups Cold Milk
1 Pkg. French Vanilla Instant Pudding

Prepare cake from first five ingredients. Bake in an oiled and floured 12" x 9" pan for 45 minutes. When cool, frost.

Beat Dream Whip and cold milk until very stiff, then add the French vanilla instant pudding and beat well. Spread on cake. Sprinkle with the chopped walnuts and coconut.

EGYPTIAN CAKE WITH NOUGAT FILLING

Cake:
5 Tbs. Chocolate (baking)
5 Tbs. Water, boiling
½ Cup Butter
1½ Cups Sugar
½ Cup Milk
4 Egg Yolks
1¾ Cups Cake Flour
2 Tsp. Baking Powder
Pinch of Salt
4 Egg Whites
1 Tsp. Vanilla

Nougat Filling:
2 Eggs
2 Cups Heavy Whipping Cream
Pinch of Salt
1 Cup Walnuts, chopped
5 Tbs. Powdered Sugar
1 Tsp. Vanilla

Cake: Dissolve 5 tbs. of baking chocolate in 5 tbs. of boiling water. Cream ½ cup of butter; blend with it 1½ cups sugar. Add 4 well-beaten egg yolks. Add ½ cup milk, then the melted chocolate. Mix and sift 1¾ cups flour with 2 level tsp. baking powder & a pinch of salt. Add to the above mixture. Fold in the stiffly-whipped egg whites and flavor with 1 tsp. of vanilla. Bake in layers. Bake at 350 degrees for 25-30 minutes, or until done.

Nougat Filling: Beat 2 egg whites until they are stiff and dry. Have 2 cups of double cream whipped until it will hold its shape. Beat 2 egg yolks until they are thick and creamy. Add a few grains of salt. Add 1 cup of finely chopped nut meats and 5 tbs. of powdered sugar to whipped cream; add the beaten egg yolks and the stiffly-beaten egg whites; flavor with vanilla.

This recipe is a very old family recipe; it is over 100 years old.

SHREWSBURY CAKE

½ Lb. Butter
3 Eggs
1 Tsp. Baking Powder
1 Cup Milk
3 Cups Sugar
3 Cups Sifted Flour

Cream butter and sugar well. Add eggs, one at a time, beating for 5 min. after each addition. Add flour and baking powder alternately with the milk. Add vanilla. Bake in a tube pan for 1 hour in a 350 degree oven. [MW: 15 min. on full power, covered with wax paper]. Test for doneness with a toothpick. This sugar-crusted cake needs no frosting.

BLACKBERRY JAM CAKE

6 Eggs, beaten separately
1 Cup Butter
2 Cups Sugar
1 Cup Buttermilk
1 Tsp. Soda
4 Cups Flour
1 Cup Seedless Jam (blackberry)
1 Cup Chopped Nuts
½ Tsp. Cinnamon
½ Tsp. Cloves
1 Tsp. Vanilla

Beat the eggs separately; add the butter, sugar and buttermilk. Sift flour, soda, cinnamon and cloves together. Add to creamed mixture. Stir in the jam and nuts. Bake at about 350 degrees. Makes a 4-layer cake.

Icing:
3 Cups Sugar
1 Cup Milk
1 Cup Seedless Raisins or Dates
1 Cup Nuts
½ Cup Butter
1 Tsp. Vanilla

Cream together butter, milk and sugar well. Add raisins, nuts and vanilla.

YOGURT WHEAT BREAD

8 to 9 Cups Unbleached White Flour
¾ Cup Nonfat Dry Milk
5 Tsp. Salt
1 Pkg. Active Dry Yeast
2¾ Cups Water
1 Cup Plain Yogurt
¼ Cup Honey
2 Tbs. Oil
1 Cup Wheat Germ

Mix 3½ cups flour, dry milk, salt & yeast. In a saucepan, heat water, yogurt, honey and oil till warm. Gradually add dry ingredients and beat 2 minutes on medium speed; add 1 cup flour and beat 2 minutes on high speed. Stir in wheat germ and enough flour to make dough stiff. Knead 10 minutes. Place in greased bowl, greased-side up. Cover and let rise until double, approximately 1 hour. Punch dough down and divide into 2 pieces. Divide each piece into 3 pieces and roll each piece into a rope approximately 16" long. Braid. Place each loaf on greased cookie sheet. Cover and let rise until double, approximately 1 hour.

Top Spread:
1 Egg Yolk
Sesame Seeds (optional)

Brush tops with egg yolk & sprinkle with sesame seeds. Bake at 350 degrees for 35 minutes. Yield: 2 loaves. Delicious served warm! No need to cut it as it's fun to break off pieces!

SCRIPTURE CAKE

½ Cup Judges 5:25 (last clause)
1½ Tbs. 1 Samuel 14:25 (2nd clause)
2 Cups 1 Kings 4:22 (1st clause)
½ Tsp. Leviticus 2:13
1 Tsp. Amos 4:5 (use modern powder)
1 Tsp. 2 Chronicles 9:9 (or to taste)
½ Cup Judges 4:19 (2nd part)
1 Cup 1 Samuel 30:12 (2nd item)
1 Cup Nahum 3:12 (dried, chopped)
1 Cup Numbers 17:8 (chopped)
4 of Isaiah 10:14 (separated & beaten)

Cream first 2 ingredients together well. Sift next 4 ingredients together and add alternately with next ingredient. Follow Solomon's advice for making a good boy Proverbs 23:14. Add next 3 ingredients. Fold in beaten yolks and stiffly beaten whites carefully. Bake in lined 9x13 in. pan. Temperature 350 degrees F. Time 35 to 40 minutes. Yield: 1 cake. You may frost the cake with white or chocolate frosting. A fun cake to make.

CHEESE BREAD KNOTS

5 to 5½ Cups Flour
2 Pkgs. Active Dry Yeast
2 Cups Milk
1½ Cups Grated Swiss Cheese (6 Oz.)
½ Cup Sugar
4 Tbs. Butter or Margarine
1 Tbs. Salt
1 Egg

In large mixer bowl, combine 2 cups flour and the yeast. In saucepan, heat milk, cheese, sugar, butter, and salt just until warm (115 to 120 degrees), stirring constantly until butter almost melts. Add to dry mixture in mixer bowl; add egg. Beat at low speed of electric mixer for ½ min., scraping sides of bowl constantly. Beat 3 minutes at high speed. By hand, stir in enough remaining flour to make a soft dough. Turn out onto lightly-floured surface; knead until smooth and elastic, 5 to 8 minutes. Shape into a ball. Place in lightly-greased bowl, turning once to grease surface. Cover and let rise in a warm place until double, about 1½ hrs.

Punch dough down; turn out on lightly-floured surface. Divide dough into four equal pieces; shape each into a ball. Cover and let rest 10 minutes. Roll each ball into a 12" x 6" rectangle. Cut crosswise into 6" x 1" strips. Tie each strip into a loose knot. Place 2 to 3 inches apart on a greased baking sheet; cover and let rise until double, 40 minutes. Bake in 375 degree oven for 10 to 12 minutes. Makes approximately 48 rolls. Hint: If dough strips shrink, pull gently before tying knots. Preparation time, including rising, is approximately 3 to 3½ hours.

SPUMONI CAKE

¾ Cup Boiling Water
½ Cup Cocoa
1¾ Cups Sifted Cake Flour
1¾ Cups Sugar
1½ Tsp. Baking Soda
1 Tsp. Salt
½ Cup Salad Oil
7 Unbeaten Egg Yolks, medium
2 Tsp. Vanilla
1 Cup Egg Whites, 7 or 8
½ Tsp. Cream of Tartar

Custard Filling:
1 Cup Sugar
4½ Tbs. Flour
4½ Tbs. Cornstarch
½ Tsp. Salt
2¾ Cups Milk
2 Beaten Eggs
1½ Tbs. Butter
2½ Tsp. Rum Flavoring
½ Pint Sweetened Whipped Cream or 2
  Cups Cool Whip
2 or 3 Tbs. Finely Chopped Candied
  Fruitcake Mixture
Few Drops Yellow Food Coloring
Shaved Chocolate

Heat oven to 325 degrees. Combine the boiling water and cocoa. Cool. Sift into smaller bowl the flour, sugar, soda and salt. Make a well in center and add egg yolks, oil, cocoa mixture and vanilla. Beat until smooth. In a large bowl, beat egg whites and cream of tartar until very stiff. Pour egg yolk mixture gradually over beaten egg whites, gently folding in with rubber scraper, just until blended. Bake in 2 ungreased 9" layer pans 25-30 min. [MW: 6-7 min. per layer, one at a time, on full power, covered with wax paper]. Invert pans to cool. When cold, split layers in half and spread with custard filling.

Custard Filling:
Combine sugar, flour, cornstarch and salt in a saucepan. Gradually stir in milk and cook over low heat, stirring constantly, until mixture thickens and comes to a boil. Stir a little hot mixture into beaten eggs, then add to hot mixture. Continue cooking, stirring and bring to a boil. Remove from heat, add food coloring, butter and flavoring. Cool before spreading between layers. Reserve enough custard to spread on top of cake, also. Frost sides of cake with whipped cream or Cool Whip and sprinkle sides of cake with shaved chocolate. Sprinkle top of cake with finely chopped fruit. This topping is what makes it a Spumoni Cake.

STICKY CINNAMON BUNS

1 Pkg. Yeast
1/3 Cup Very Warm Water
½ Cup Shortening
¾ Cup Milk, scalded
3½ Cups Flour
1 Tsp. Salt
10 Tbs. Granulated Sugar
2 Eggs
1 Cup Light Corn Syrup
¼ Cup Soft Butter
¾ Cup Brown Sugar
2 Tsp. Cinnamon
½ Cup Nuts

Add yeast to water; let stand. Stir till dissolved. Add shortening to milk; cool to lukewarm; add yeast. Add 1½ cups of the flour, the salt and 2 tbs. granulated sugar. Beat till smooth. Cover; let stand till spongy and bubbly. Add eggs, one at a time, beating well after each. Add remaining sugar. Beat in about 2 cups flour to make a soft dough. Turn out on floured board. Knead for 10 minutes. Put in a greased bowl; cover and let rise till double.

Punch dough down; turn out on floured board and let stand for 5 minutes. Grease 2 - 9" square cake pans and pour ½ cup syrup into each pan. Divide dough. Roll each to a rectangle. Spread with half of butter and sprinkle with half of brown sugar, cinnamon and nuts. Roll as a jelly roll; cut into 1" slices. Arrange, cut-side down, in pan of syrup. Repeat with the second portion of dough. Cover pans of buns; let rise till doubled in bulk. Bake at 350 degrees F for 35 minutes. Turn out of pans immediately.

DATE CAKE

16 Oz. Can Applesauce
1 Pkg. Pitted Dates, cut up
1 & ¾ Tsp. Baking Soda
1½ Cups Unsifted Flour
¼ Tsp. Salt
½ Cup Shortening
1 Cup Plus 2 Tbs. Sugar
2 Eggs
6 Oz. Pkg. Semi-Sweet Chocolate Chips
½ Cup Chopped Walnut Meats

Grease and flour a baking pan 13x9x2". In a medium saucepan, bring applesauce to a boil, remove from heat, stir in dates and 1 tsp. soda. Cool. On waxed paper, thoroughly stir together the flour, remaining ¾ tsp. soda and the salt. In a large mixing bowl cream shortening and 1 c. sugar; stir in applesauce mixture. Turn into prepared pan. Stir together the remaining 2 tbs. sugar, chocolate chips and nuts. Sprinkle over cake batter. Bake in preheated 350 degree oven until a cake tester inserted in center comes out free of batter. Cool cake in pan on wire rack; cut in pan.

RAW APPLE CAKE

½ Cup Butter
1 Cup Sugar
2 Tbs. Dry, Unsweetened Cocoa
2 Eggs, beaten
1½ Cups Flour
¼ Tsp. Baking Powder
1 Tsp. Baking Soda
½ Tsp. Salt
1 Tsp. Cinnamon
½ Tsp. Cloves
½ Cup Water
1 Cup Peeled, Shredded Raw Apple

Cream together butter, sugar and cocoa. Add eggs. Mix dry ingredients in small bowl. Add mixture to butter mixture alternately with water, beating after each addition. Fold in shredded apple. Grease and flour an 8" x 8" cake pan [MW: ungreased]. Pour in batter. Bake at 350 degrees for about 45 min. [MW: 11-12 min. on full power, covered with wax paper]; until cake bounces back from touch.

MAPLE-NUT COFFEE TWIST

1 Pkg. Pillsbury Hot Roll Mix
¾ Cup Warm Water
1 Egg
3 Tbs. Sugar
1 Tsp. Maple Flavoring
6 Tbs. Melted Butter or Margarine

Filling:
½ Cup Sugar
1 Tsp. Cinnamon
1 Tsp. Maple Flavoring
1/3 Cup Chopped Nuts

Glaze:
1½ Cups Powdered Sugar
¼ Tsp. Maple Flavoring
2 to 3 Tbs. Milk

Preheat the oven to 375 degrees. In a large mixing bowl, dissolve the yeast (from mix) in warm water. Stir in egg, sugar and maple flavoring. Add the flour mixture and blend well. Knead on a floured surface for 2 to 3 minutes until smooth and satiny. Place in a greased bowl. Cover and let rise in a warm place until light and doubled in size, for about 30 to 45 minutes. Prepare the filling. Divide the dough equally into 3 balls. On a lightly floured surface, roll out one ball of dough to a 12 inch circle. Fit onto bottom of a greased 12 inch pizza pan. Brush dough with 2 tbs. melted butter and sprinkle with about 1/3 cup of the filling. Use a glass to mark a 2 inch circle in center of dough (do not cut through the dough). Cut from outside edge just to circle forming 16 pie shaped wedges. Twist each of the 3 layered wedges 5 times. Let rise in a warm place until light and doubled in size, for about 30 to 40 minutes. Bake at 375 degrees for 20 to 25 minutes until golden brown. Drizzle with glaze while still warm. Serve warm or cold.
Filling: Combine all ingredients & mix well.
Glaze: In a small mixing bowl, combine the powdered sugar, maple flavoring and enough milk until thin enough to spread.

Tip: Pillsbury Vanilla Ready to Spread Frosting may be used for the glaze. Heat ¾ cup over low heat until thin enough to drizzle. Stir in Maple Flavoring.

CARAMEL APPLE CAKE

1¾ Cups Flour
1½ Cups Firmly Packed Brown Sugar
1½ Tsp. Cinnamon
½ Tsp. Salt
½ Tsp. Baking Soda
½ Tsp. Baking Powder
1 Tsp. Vanilla Extract
¾ Cup Butter or Margarine, softened
3 Eggs
1½ Cups Peeled & Diced Apples
1 Cup Chopped Nuts
½ Cup Raisins, if desired

Frosting:
1½ Cups Powdered Sugar
¼ Tsp. Cinnamon
¼ Cup Butter or Margarine, softened
½ Tsp. Vanilla Extract
3 or 4 Tsp. Milk

Preheat oven to 350 degrees. 325 degrees for glass dish. Grease a 13 x 9 inch pan. Lightly spoon flour into measuring cup and level off. In a large bowl combine first 9 ingredients & beat for 3 minutes at medium speed. Stir in apples, nuts and raisins. Pour into a greased pan. Bake 30 to 40 minutes until toothpick comes out clean. Let cool. In a small bowl put the frosting ingredients together & blend until smooth. Spread over cake. If using Pillsbury's Best Self-Rising Flour, omit the salt, baking powder and baking soda.

SOPAIPILLAS
(Deep-fat Fried Bread)

4 Cups Flour
1½ Tsp. Salt
1 Tsp. Baking Powder
1 Tbs. Granulated Sugar
1 Tbs. Shortening
1 Cake Yeast, or 1 Pkg. Dry Yeast
¼ Cup Warm Water
1¼ Cups Scalded Milk

Combine the dry ingredients and cut in shortening. Dissolve yeast in warm water. Add to scalded milk that is cooled to room temperature. Make a well in center of dry ingredients. Pour liquid into well and work into dry ingredients to make dough. Knead dough 15 to 20 times and set aside for approximately 10 minutes.

Roll dough to ¼" thickness or slightly thinner, then cut into squares or triangles and fry in melted shortening at 420 degrees F. Fry only a few at a time so fat stays hot. Drain sopaipillas on absorbent towels and serve as a bread.

WALDORF ASTORIA CAKE

½ Cup Crisco
2 Eggs
1½ Cups Sugar
2 Cups Cake Flour
1 Tbs. Cocoa
½ Tsp. Salt
1 Cup Buttermilk
1 Tsp. Vanilla
2 Oz. Red Food Coloring
1 Tbs. Vinegar
1 Tsp. Soda

Frosting Ingredients:
1 Cup Milk
¼ Cup Flour
1 Cube Nucoa
1 Cup Sugar
½ Cup Crisco
1 Tsp. Vanilla
Coconut

Cake: Beat together eggs, Crisco and sugar. Sift together cake flour, cocoa and salt. Mix all above ingredients with buttermilk. Add vanilla and red food coloring and mix well. In separate dish, mix vinegar with baking soda; mix well and add to batter (it will fizz). Bake at 350 degrees for 30-35 min. [MW: 6-7 min. on full power per layer, covered with wax paper].

Waldorf Astoria Frosting: Make pudding, using 1 cup milk and ¼ cup flour. Mix well and cook over medium fire till thick. Let cool. Beat with a mixer the Nucoa, sugar, Crisco and vanilla. When pudding is cooled, add to the well-beaten mixture which will be real fluffy. Keep beating until real creamy. Frost cake, then cover it completely with angel flake coconut.

SPICY PINEAPPLE—ZUCCHINI BREAD

3 Eggs
1 Cup Salad Oil
2 Cups Sugar
2 Tsp. Vanilla
2 Cups Zucchini, coarsely shredded
1 - 8¼ Oz. Can Crushed Pineapple, well drained
3 Cups Flour
2 Tsp. Soda
1 Tsp. Salt
½ Tsp. Baking Powder
1½ Tsp. Ground Cinnamon
¾ Tsp. Ground Nutmeg
1 Cup Walnuts, finely chopped
1 Cup Currants

With a rotary mixer, beat eggs to blend. Add salad oil, sugar and vanilla. Continue beating mixture until thick and foamy. With a spoon, stir in zucchini and pineapple. Combine all-purpose flour (unsifted), soda, salt, baking powder, cinnamon, nutmeg, walnuts and currants; stir dry ingredients gently into zucchini mixture just until blended.

Divide the batter equally between 2 greased and flour dusted 5" x 9" loaf pans. Bake in a 350 degree oven for 1 hr. [MW: 15 min. on full power], or until a wooden pick inserted in center comes out clean. Cool in pans 10 min.; turn out on wire racks to cool thoroughly. Makes 2 loaves.

BOREGO SPRINGS BUTTERMILK BREAD

1½ Cups Lucerne Buttermilk
1 Egg
3 Cups Biscuit Mix
2 Tbs. Sugar
1 Cup (about ¼ Lb.) Grated Swiss Cheese
1 Cup Sliced Pimiento Stuffed Olives, drained
¾ Cup Chopped Walnuts (optional)

Combine buttermilk, egg, biscuit mix and sugar. Beat one minute to blend thoroughly. Gently stir in Swiss cheese, olives and walnuts; spoon into well-buttered loaf pan (9" x 5" x 3" or comparable size).

Bake in moderate oven, 350 degrees, for 50 to 55 minutes (a crack along the top of the loaf usually occurs); cool 5 minutes before removing from pan.

Continue cooling. Unused portions will keep well when wrapped and stored in refrigerator or freezer.

"MEA'ONO HULIHIA MIKANA" (Papaya Upside Down Cake)

Topping:
2 Tbs. Lemon Juice
2 Cups Sliced Ripe Papaya
3 Tbs. Butter
½ Cup C&H Dark Brown Sugar, packed

Cake:
¼ Cup Butter
¾ Cup C&H Granulated Sugar
1 Egg
1¼ Cups All Purpose Flour
2 Tsp. Baking Powder
¼ Tsp. Salt
½ Cup Milk

Pour lemon juice over papaya; let stand 15 min. Melt butter and brown sugar in an 8" square baking pan. Place a layer of papaya slices on top of the sugar mixture. Decorate with almonds, if desired. Set aside. Cream together butter and sugar. Beat in egg. Combine flour, baking powder and salt. Add to creamed mixture alternately with milk, beginning and ending with the flour mixture. Pour batter over papaya. Bake in 350 degree oven for 40-45 min. [MW: 10-12 min. on full power, covered with wax paper]. Turn cake upside down on a large plate. Makes 1 cake. 6-8 servings.

FRUIT FANTASIA
(A Three-layer Cake)

1¼ Cups Sifted Softasilk Flour
5/6 Cup Sugar
5/8 Tsp. Baking Powder
5/8 Tsp. Soda
½ Tsp. Salt
1/3 Cup Imperial Margarine
1/6 Cup Buttermilk
5/8 Cup Mashed Ripe Bananas
1 or 2 Eggs
1/6 Cup (another) Buttermilk
1/3 Cup Chopped Nuts

Be ready to spend time on this one! Individual layers may be made in any succession. Egg whisks work better than spoon.

BANANA NUT LAYER:
Grease and flour a 9" layer pan. Sift all dry ingredients together. Add margarine, mashed bananas and first 1/6 cup of buttermilk. Beat 2 min. or stir by hand, if preferred. Fold in nuts. Pour batter into pan.

CHERRY CAKE LAYER:
1 Cup Plus 1 Tbs. Sifted Flour
2/3 Cup Sugar
1½ Tsp. Baking Powder
½ Tsp. Salt
¼ Cup Imperial Margarine
1/8 Cup Maraschino Cherry Juice
10 Maraschino Cherries, cut in eighths
¼ Cup Milk
2 Egg Whites, unbeaten
¼ Cup Chopped Nuts

Sift dry ingredients together. Add margarine, cherry juice, cherries and milk. Beat 2 min., or until well blended with spoon or egg whisk. Add egg whites and nuts and beat, mix, for 2 more min. Pour batter into a greased and floured 9" pan.

APPLE CAKE LAYER:
1½ Cups Sifted Flour
1 Cup Sugar
1½ Tsp. Cinnamon
½ Tsp. Salt
½ Tsp. Baking Soda
1½ Cups Diced Apples
½ Cup Chopped Nuts
½ Cup Oil
2 Eggs, beaten

Mix dry ingredients together, then mix in eggs and oil and add to dry ingredients. Blend well Add apples and nuts. Pour into a 9" cake pan. Note: If you feel that this layer will appear too high in comparison, then pour most of the batter into the cake pan and use the excess to make approximately 2 to 3 cupcakes

Pudding Filling:
2 Pkgs. Instant Vanilla Pudding

Prepare pudding according to package directions.

All cakes are baked at 350 degrees, until a toothpick comes out clean, about 20 to 30 minutes. Next decide order of layers. Place 1 layer on bottom; spread over it freshly-chilled instant French vanilla pudding. Add second layer and do the same. You may wish to balance the cake by inserting a couple of toothpicks through the layers. Place last layer on top, then frost sides & top with your favorite butter frosting, or, if you choose, use a lighter fluffy egg-white-base frosting.

CRANBERRY COFFEE CAKE

¼ Cup Melted Butter
1 Cup Sugar
2 Cups Raw Cranberries
1½ Cups Flour
2 Tsp. Baking Powder
½ Cup Sugar
½ Tsp. Salt
1 Egg, beaten
2/3 Cup Milk
3 Tbs. Wesson Oil

In a square or oblong pan [MW: square] melt butter. Stir in sugar till dissolved, then pour cranberries on top. Set aside. Sift together dry ingredients. Mix liquid ingredients together and add to dry, stirring only until mixed. Pour batter over cranberries. Bake 45 min. at 350 degrees [MW: 11-13 minutes on full power, covered with wax paper]. Serve warm with whipped cream.

RUSSIAN EASTER BREAD
(Koolitch)

3 Cakes Yeast
¾ Cup Lukewarm Water
4 Cups Scalded Milk
1 Cup Sugar
4 Cups Flour
1 Tbs. Ground Cardamom
1½ Cups Butter
3 Cups Sugar
2 Tbs. Salt
1 Tbs. Vanilla
1 Tbs. Grated Orange Peel
9 Eggs
3 Quarts Flour
½ Cup Candied Orange & Lemon Peel*
½ Cup Citron*
½ Cup Candied Cherries*
3 Cups Raisins
1 Cup Chopped Nuts
6 - 48 Oz. Juice Cans, cleaned
1 Box Powdered Sugar
1 Bottle Candy Decor

Allow 8 hrs. preparation time, from the time you start until you take bread out of oven.

1. Dissolve 3 cakes of yeast in ¾ cup lukewarm water. Scald 4 cups milk, cool to 90° F. Add yeast, 1 cup sugar, 4 cups flour, 1 tbs. ground cardamom and mix to a smooth sponge; set in warm place for about 2 hours, until light.

2. Melt & warm carefully 1½ cups butter, 3 cups sugar, 2 tbs. salt, 1 tbs. vanilla, 1 tbs. grated orange peel, and 9 beaten eggs. Add to sponge; work in about 3 quarts flour and knead for 5 min. Add fruit, raisins and nuts and knead for another 5 min. Set in a warm place to rise till double in bulk. Mold into loaves of any shape. Put into juice cans or loaf pans that have been greased. Let rise; bake in 350 degree oven for 1½ hours. Makes 6 large loaves. When cold, frost with a runny powdered sugar white frosting and decorate with candied decorations in the form of a cross or whatever. Baking in a round tin and the white frosting and cross are traditional. Then invite friends over to break bread with and wish them a good crop, or good things for the coming year.

*In place of candied fruits listed, you may substitute 2 cups of fruit cake mix. For a sweeter taste, use 2 cups of fruit medley (apricots, apples, peaches, pears and dried raisins). The 1 cup of chopped nuts may be walnuts, pecans, or a combination of both.

Note: When dividing recipe in half, use 2 cakes yeast, ½ cup water, and 4 eggs.

BANANA CAKE

2 Cups Flour
1/2 Tsp. Baking Powder
3/4 Tsp. Baking Soda
1/2 Tsp Salt
1/2 Cup Soft Shortening
1 1/2 Cup Sugar
2 Beaten Eggs
1 Tsp. Vanilla
2 or 3 Mashed, ripe, bananas
1/4 Cup Buttermilk

Fluffy Butter Frosting

1/3 Cup Soft Butter
1/4 Tsp. Salt
1 Tsp. Vanilla
1 Lb. Powdered Sugar
2 Egg Whites, unbeaten
1 Tbs. Milk

Prepare 2-9" cake pans [MW: plastic, ungreased] by oiling and dusting with flour. Sift together flour, baking powder, soda and salt. In another bowl mix shortening, sugar, beaten eggs, and vanilla. Beat 1½ min. Add buttermilk to flour mixture alternately with bananas while beating for about 2 min. Pour into 2 pans and bake 30-35 min. at 350 degrees [MW: 6-8 minutes on full power, covered with wax paper]. Remove from pans while cake is still warm. Cream butter, salt, and vanilla until light and fluffy. Add sugar alternately with eggs, beating well. Add milk and beat until smooth and of spreading consistency.

BOURBON—PECAN CAKE

2 Cups Whole Red Candied Cherries
2 Cups White Seedless Raisins
2 Cups Bourbon
1 Lb. Butter or Margarine
2 Cups Dark Brown Sugar, firmly packed
2 Cups Sugar
8 Eggs, separated
5 Cups Sifted Flour
5 Cups Pecan Halves
1½ Tsp. Baking Powder
1 Tsp. Salt
2 Tsp. Ground Nutmeg

Combine cherries, raisins and bourbon in a large mixing bowl. Cover tightly and let stand overnight in the refrigerator. Drain fruits and reserve bourbon. Place butter in a large bowl of an electric mixer and beat on medium speed until light and fluffy. Add sugars gradually, beating on medium speed until well blended. Add egg yolks, beating until well blended.

Combine ½ cup of the flour with pecans. Sift the remaining flour with the baking powder, salt and nutmeg mixture and mix thoroughly. Add the reserved bourbon and the remainder of the flour mixture, alternately, ending with the flour. Then add the flour and pecans, beating well after each addition.

Beat egg whites until stiff but not dry; fold gently into the cake batter; blend thoroughly. Grease a 10" tube cake pan; line with wax paper. Grease and lightly flour the paper. Pour batter into pan within 1" of the top. Bake remaining batter in a small loaf pan. Bake at 275 degrees for 4 hours for tube pan, 2 hrs. for loaf pans. Cool cakes in pans on rack for two to three hours. Remove cakes from pans and remove wax paper. Wrap cakes in cheesecloth saturated with bourbon, then wrap in aluminum foil or plastic wrap and store in tightly-covered container for several weeks. Cut into thin slices to serve.

PINEAPPLE NUT CAKE

1 Cube Butter or Margarine
1-1/2 Cups Sugar
2 Eggs - slightly beaten
2 Cups Flour
½ Tsp. Salt
2 Tsp. Soda
1 - 1 Lb. 4 Oz. Can Crushed Pineapple
¾ Cup Chopped Walnuts
1 Cup Brown Sugar

Cream butter and sugar. Add eggs and beat until smooth. Sift flour, salt and soda and blend with creamed mixture. Mix in pineapple including liquid. Sprinkled walnuts and brown sugar over top.

Bake in 350 degree oven for 45 min. [MW: 11-12 min. on full power, covered with wax paper].

APRICOT BRANDY CAKE

2 Sticks Butter
3 Cups Sugar
6 Eggs
3 Cups Flour
¼ Tsp. Baking Powder
½ Tsp. Salt
1 Cup Sour Cream
½ Tsp. Rum Extract
½ Tsp. Lemon Extract
¼ Tsp. Almond Extract
1 Tsp. Orange Extract
½ Cup Apricot Brandy
1 Tsp. Vanilla

Cream butter and sugar; add eggs one at a time. Sift dry ingredients; add to butter and sugar. Mix alternately with sour cream; beat well. Mix extracts and brandy together. Add to batter. Make at 350 degrees for 60-75 min. in a bundt pan or 10" tube pan [MW: 15-19 min. on full power, covered with wax paper]. Dust with confectioner's sugar after it has been cooled. Can drizzle more apricot brandy over top also.

PUMPKINUT TEA LOAF

½ Cup Shortening
1 Cup Brown Sugar
½ Cup White Sugar
2 Large Eggs
2/3 Cup Canned Pumpkin
3 Tbs. Molasses (light)
½ Cup Buttermilk
2 Cups + 2 Tbs. All-purpose Flour
1 Tsp. Baking Powder
1 Tsp. Baking Soda
1 Tsp. Salt
1 Tsp. Cinnamon
½ Tsp. Ginger
½ Tsp. Nutmeg
1 Tsp. Vanilla
1 Cup Chopped Walnuts

Icing:
1 Cup Powdered Sugar
2 Tbs. Melted Butter
Orange Juice (frozen concentrate)

Cream shortening and sugar. Add eggs, one at a time, and continue mixing. Add molasses and pumpkin. Add dry ingredients alternately with buttermilk. Add vanilla and chopped nuts. When cool, ice top of loaves only and sprinkle with chopped nuts if desired. Bake in 1 large loaf 5½" x 9½", or 2 small loaves, 3½" x 7½" (preferable). Large loaf should bake approximately 1 hr. and 20 min. or until done in center. Small loaves bake for 1 hour, or until done in center. Bake in 350 degree oven. When cool, loaves may be wrapped in foil and kept in refrigerator. For icing, add sugar and butter and just enough orange juice to make soft icing.

FRUIT COCKTAIL CAKE

1½ Cups Sugar
2 Cups Flour
2 Tsp. Baking Soda
2 Tsp. Vanilla
2 Eggs
1 Medium Can Fruit Cocktail
1 Cube Margarine
¾ Cup Sugar
½ Cup Milk
1 Tsp. Vanilla

Mix together sugar, flour, baking soda, vanilla, eggs and fruit cocktail. Sprinkle ½ cup brown sugar and nuts on top. Bake for 40 minutes in a 400 degree oven. [MW: 10 minutes on full power]. While baking, mix 1 cube margarine, sugar, milk and vanilla in saucepan and melt. Pour over top of cake while still hot.

ANGEL FLAKE BISCUITS

5 Cups Flour
¾ Cup Shortening
1 Tsp. Soda
1 Tsp. Baking Powder
1 Tsp. Salt
3 Tbs. Sugar
1 Pkg. Powdered Yeast (or 1 Cake)
½ Cup Warm Water
2 Cups Buttermilk

Sift dry ingredients together; cut in the shortening. Add buttermilk and the yeast, dissolved in water. Mix with a spoon until all flour is moist. Cover the bowl and put in refrigerator until ready to use. Can also be used right away. The dough will keep several weeks in refrigerator.

Roll out as much dough as you need on floured board, dough should be ½" to ¾" thick. Cut out. Bake at 400 degrees for 12 minutes.

DESSERTS

CHEDDAR CHEESECAKE with STRAWBERRIES

Courtesy of California Strawberry Advisory Board

Note: This recipe is shown on the cover of this book.

1¼ Cups Vanilla Wafer Crumbs
2 Tbs. Butter or Margarine, melted
2 - 8 Oz. Pkgs. Cream Cheese, softened
½ Cup Shredded Sharp Cheddar Cheese
¾ Cup Sugar
3 Eggs
½ Tsp. Grated Orange Peel
¼ Tsp. Grated Lemon Peel
2 Tbs. Flour
1 Cup Heavy Cream
1 Pint Fresh California Strawberries
Light Corn Syrup

Mix crumbs with butter; press over bottom of 9" springform pan. Bake in 350 degree (moderate) oven 5 minutes. Combine the cheeses and sugar in bowl; beat until fluffy. Beat in eggs, 1 at a time. Blend in peels, flour and ½ cup of the cream. Pour over crumb crust in pan. Bake at 350 degrees for 40 minutes, until the cake is set in center. Cool on rack.

Arrange the whole strawberries on top of the cake. Brush with corn syrup. Whip remaining cream until stiff; then, using a pastry tube, pipe in a border around the strawberries.

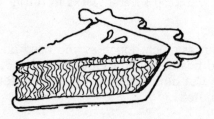

CANTALOUPE CHIFFON PIE

1 Med. Cantaloupe, peeled
3 Eggs, separated
½ Tsp. Salt
1 Cup Cream, whipped
1 Pkg. Gelatin
¾ Cup Sugar
¼ Cup Lemon Juice
1 - 9" Baked Pie Crust

Peel and seed melon; cut into small pieces. Put in blender and make 1 cup pulp; put in top of double boiler, over boiling water. Soften gelatin in pulp; add slightly beaten egg yolks and ¼ cup sugar and salt. Cook over boiling water, stirring, until thickened. Add lemon juice and cool. Cut remaining melon into small cubes and add to cooled mixture. Beat egg whites; add rest of sugar and beat until stiff. Fold with half of cream into cooled mixture. Pour into crust; chill and serve with rest of cream.

CHOCOLATE BREAD PUDDING

1 Cup Very Fine, Dry Bread Crumbs
1 Cup Sugar
6 Tbs. Cocoa OR 2 Oz. Unsweetened Chocolate
2 Cups Milk
2 Eggs, beaten

Combine first 4 ingredients in saucepan. Boil for 1 minute. Add eggs. Bake in a greased casserole 20 to 25 minutes at 350 degrees. Serve with brown sugar sauce.

Sauce:
1 Cup Brown Sugar, packed
1 Tbs. Butter
4 Tbs. Heavy Cream

Combine in a small pan the brown sugar, butter and cream, or evaporated milk. Heat slowly, stirring constantly, until smooth.

RAISIN CRUNCH PUDDING

5 Oz. Raisins
1 - 20 Oz. Can Crushed Pineapple
2 Oz. Sugar
1 Tbs. Lemon Juice
1 Tsp. Corn Flour

Crumbly Mixture:
3 Oz. Flour, sifted
1 Tsp. Salt
½ Tsp. Baking Soda
6 Oz. Butter or Margarine
7 Oz. Brown Sugar
1-2/3 Cups Quick Oats

For the filling: Combine raisins, drained, crushed pineapple, 1 tbs. syrup from pineapple and remaining filling ingredients. Cook and stir until thickened.

For Crumbly Mixture: Resift flour with salt and baking soda. Cream butter until soft; blend in brown sugar. Stir in flour mixture and oats. Press half of this mixture in layer on bottom of greased square pan. Pat down evenly. Spread with filling. Cover with remaining crumbly mixture. Press down to make crust. Bake at 375 degrees F until lightly browned, about 20 to 25 minutes. Serve with ice cream or cream.

PUMPKIN PIE

1 Large Can Pumpkin
2 Tsp. Cinnamon
½ Tsp. Ginger
½ Tsp. Salt
4 Eggs, well beaten
3 Cups Milk
2½ Cups Sugar

Pie Crust:
4 Cups Flour
1 Cup Liquid Shortening
1 Tsp. Salt
1 Tsp. Baking Powder
1 Tbs. Sugar
1 Beaten Egg
½ Cup Ice Water
1 Tbs. Vinegar

Pie: Beat eggs well; add spices and salt. Add pumpkin and beat. Continue beating as you add milk and sugar. Mix well. Pour into 2 pie pans lined with unbaked pastry and bake. Bake in hot oven, 450 degrees, for 15 minutes (no longer), then reduce heat to slow oven, 325 degrees, and continue baking until set or until a silver knife inserted in the center will come out clean. Serve with or without whipped cream.

Note: Broken nut meats may be added if desired. Serves 12.

BROKEN GLASS CAKE

3 - 3 Oz. Pkgs. Fruit Flavored Gelatin, assorted
2 Cups Vanilla Wafer OR Graham Cracker Crumbs
½ Cup Sugar
1 Stick Margarine, melted
1 Envelope Unflavored Gelatin
2 Tbs. Cold Water
½ Cup Hot Fruit Juice
2 Pkgs. Whipped Topping
1 Tsp. Vanilla Extract
¼ Cup Sugar
1 Cup Milk
Chopped Nuts, if desired

Prepare 3 fruit gelatins according to package directions (select assorted colors and flavors). Pour into 3 shallow pans and keep in refrigerator overnight. Mix 1¾ cups of the crumbs with ½ cup of sugar and melted margarine. Use to line bottom and sides of a 13" x 9" pan. Dissolve unflavored gelatin in cold water; let stand 5 minutes. Add hot juice & heat until gelatin is dissolved; cool. Whip packaged topping with vanilla, ¼ cup sugar and 1 cup milk. Fold unflavored gelatin mixture into this mixture. Cut fruit gelatin into small cubes and fold into topping mixture. This dessert gives the appearance of colored glass cubes. Pour into crumb-lined pan and sprinkle with remainder of crumbs and nuts. Chill and serve. Yield: 12 to 16 servings.

SUPER NUT ROLL

1 Cake of Yeast or 2 Pkgs. Yeast
½ Pt. or 1 Cup Sour Cream
3½ Cups Flour
¼ Tsp. Salt
2 Tbs. Sugar
2 Cubes Margarine
4 Egg Yolks

Nut Mixture:
3 Cups Ground Nuts
1 Cup Brown or White Sugar (whatever you
   prefer)

Mix margarine and egg yolks together. Add
the salt and sugar. Add flour and mix until
crumbly like corn meal. Make a hole in the
center of the mixture. Mix yeast and sour
cream together and add to the flour mixture.
Knead until dough pulls away from the bowl.
Divide into four parts. Let stand for 8 hours
in the refrigerator. Roll thin like pie crust
into a rectangle. Spread nut mixture over it
and roll like a jelly roll. Place on a cookie
sheet and let stand for 1 or 2 hours. Bake at
350 degrees until lightly brown.

CONCORD GRAPE PIE

1½ Quarts Washed Concord Grapes
1 Cup Sugar
2 Tbs. Cornstarch
3 Cups Sifted Flour
1 Tsp. Salt
1¼ Cups Solid Shortening
1 Egg, well beaten
1 Tbs. Vinegar
4 Tbs. Cold Water

Squeeze pulp out of grapes and set skins
aside. Sieve seeds out of pulp and combine skins and pulp in saucepan. Add the
sugar and cornstarch and mix well. Cook
over low heat until thick; set aside to cool.

Sift flour & salt into a bowl; add shortening & mix with pastry blender. In another
bowl, combine the egg, vinegar & water.
Drizzle over flour mixture and mix until
it holds together in a ball. Divide dough
in half. Roll into two rounds 1/8" thick.

Place one round into a 9" pie pan. Pour
in grape mixture. Top with remaining
crust, seal and cut several slits in top.
Bake at 400 degrees for 30 minutes or until crust is done and pie is bubbly.

THREE—WAY BUTTERSCOTCH PIE

¾ Cup Firmly-packed Light Brown
   Sugar
1/3 Cup Flour
½ Tsp. Salt
1 Tall Can (1-2/3 Cups) Evaporated
   Milk
½ Cup Water
3 Egg Yolks, beaten
3 Tbs. Butter or Margarine
1 Tsp. Vanilla
3 Egg Whites
6 Tbs. White Sugar
1 Baked Pie Shell

Combine brown sugar, flour and salt in a
saucepan. Mix well. Blend in evaporated
milk and water. Cook over medium heat,
stirring constantly, until thick and smooth.
Add a small amount of hot mixture to the
beaten egg yolks; return to mixture in
saucepan. Cook, stirring constantly, for 3
minutes longer. Remove from heat; add
butter and vanilla. Cool slightly. Pour
into baked pie shell.

To make meringue, beat egg whites until
they begin to stiffen; add sugar, 1 tbs. at
a time, and continue to beat until stiff
peaks form. Spread over filling. Bake at
350 degrees for 15 minutes, or until the
meringue is lightly browned. Cool, then
chill before serving, if desired.

For variety, add ¼ cup chopped nuts to
pie crust dough before rolling out; or
sprinkle 3 tbs. grated orange rind over
filling and carefully spread meringue over
orange rind. Or grate 2 oz. semisweet
chocolate and sprinkle over filling; spread
meringue carefully over chocolate.

STRAWBERRY CREAM ROLL

7/8 Cup Eggs (about 4)
¼ Tsp. Salt
1 Tsp. Baking Powder
¾ Cup Sugar
¾ Cup Sifted Cake Flour
1 Tsp. Vanilla

2 Cups Heavy Cream
½ Cup Sugar
½ Tsp. Vanilla

2 Cups Sliced Strawberries, sweetened
  with about ¼ cup sugar

Preheat oven to 375 degrees. Grease a 10"
x 15" x 1" pan; line with waxed paper and
then grease paper.

Place eggs in a 2-quart mixing bowl; set over
slightly smaller bowl of hot water. Add salt
and baking powder. Beat until foamy, by
hand or with electric mixer.

While beating rapidly, slowly add the sugar
by the tablespoonful. Continue beating till
thick and tripled in volume. Remove bowl
from hot water and quickly fold in flour &
vanilla.

Pour into pan, spreading evenly. Bake in
375 degree oven for 10 to 12 minutes.
Cake should be LIGHT brown. Turn out on
dish cloth which has been laid on cake rack
and sprinkled with powdered sugar. Quickly
peel off waxed paper and cover with a towel
till cool.

When cake is cool, whip cream with sugar &
vanilla. Spread on cake and sprinkle with
strawberries. With both hands, carefully roll
up cake from narrow side, pushing away as
little filling as possible. Finish with open
end underneath.

Chill in refrigerator at least 2 hours before
serving. Sprinkle with powdered sugar. Will
serve 10.

TEXAS PECAN PIE

1 9" Unbaked Pie Shell
1 Cup Sugar
½ Cup Light Corn Syrup
¼ Cup Melted Butter
3 Well-Beaten Eggs
1½ Cups Pecan Halves

Mix sugar, corn syrup and melted butter.
Add well-beaten eggs and pecans. Fill pie
shell. Bake 10 minutes at 400°. Reduce
heat to 350° for 30 to 35 minutes. Cool
thoroughly before slicing.

ANGEL CHARLOTTE RUSSE

1 Level Tbs. Knox Gelatin
½ Dozen Rolled, Stale Macaroons
1 Dozen Marshmallows, cut in small
  pieces
2 Tbs. Chopped, Candied Cherries
¼ Lb. Blanched and Chopped Almonds
¾ Cup Sugar
2 Cups Cream or Evaporated Milk
¼ Cup Boiling Water
¼ Cup Cold Water
Salt
Vanilla

Soak gelatin in cold water about 5 minutes.
Dissolve in boiling water and add sugar.
When mixture is cold, add cream or evaporated milk, beaten until stiff. Add almonds,
macaroons, marshmallows and candied cherries. Flavor with vanilla. Turn into a wet
mold and chill. Remove from mold and
serve with angel food cake.

This dessert may be made more elaborate by
cutting the top from an angel food cake and
removing some of the inside, leaving a case
with ¾" walls. Fill case with mixture, replace top of cake and cover with frosting.
Garnish with candied cherries and blanched
almonds.

DESSERT VEGETABLE PUDDING

1½ Cups Flour
1 Cup Sugar
1 Cup Grated Raw Carrot
1 Cup Grated Raw Potato
1 Cup Raisins
1 Cup Suet
1 Tsp. Soda, dissolved in 1 tbs. hot
  water
1 Tsp. Salt
¾ Tsp. Cinnamon
½ Tsp. Nutmeg
¼ Tsp. Cloves
½ Cup Nuts, if desired

Combine sugar, carrots and potatoes. Add soda. Sift flour, salt and spices and add gradually. Add raisins, suet and nuts. Turn into a buttered bowl or mold; cover with aluminum foil and steam for 3 hours.

Note: You may also steam in your pressure cooker as per manufacturer's instructions. Serve with your favorite lemon or brandy sauce. Serves 6.

MAI TAI PIE

1 - 9'' Pie Crust

Filling:
1 Cup Pineapple-Grapefruit Juice
1½ Tbs. Frozen Orange Juice Concentrate
3 Tbs. Cornstarch
6 Tbs. Sugar
¼ Tsp. Salt
2 Egg Yolks, beaten
2 Egg Whites, beaten
3 Tbs. Rum
½ Cup Heavy Whipping Cream, whipped

Topping:
½ Cup Heavy Whipping Cream, whipped
  with 1 Tsp. Orange Juice Concentrate
6 Cherries for Garnish

1. Combine juices, cornstarch, sugar and salt in a saucepan. Cook until thickened, stirring constantly.

2. Stir a little of this hot mixture into egg yolks, then add this to remaining hot mixture, stirring constantly. Cook 4 minutes over very low heat.

3. Cool mixture; add rum; beat until smooth.

4. Fold in whipped cream.

5. Fold in egg whites.

6. Pour into pie crust.

7. Top with the additional whipped cream.

8. Garnish with cherries.

9. Refrigerate.

CRANBERRY RING

1 Large Pkg. Strawberry Jello
1 - 10½ Oz. Can Cranberry Relish
  (Whole Berries)
1 - 13½ Oz. Can Crushed Pineapple
1¼ Cups Boiling Water
1 - 3 Oz. Pkg. Cream Cheese
½ Cup Miracle Whip Salad Dressing
1 Cup Boiling Water
1 Large Pkg. Lemon Jello
2 Cups Miniature Marshmallows
½ to 1 Cup Whipping Cream

First Layer: Dissolve strawberry jello in hot water (1¼ cups); add cranberry sauce and pour into a 6½ cup jello mold. Chill until firm.

Second Layer: Drain pineapple (reserve syrup). Dissolve lemon jello in boiling water (1 cup). Add marshmallows & stir until melted. Add pineapple syrup. Chill until partially set. Blend cream cheese & Miracle Whip. Stir in pineapple (if mixture is too thin, chill until it mounds slightly when spooned). Fold in whipping cream; pour over first layer and chill until firm. Serves 12 or more.

PINEAPPLE ICE CREAM

2 Quarts Half & Half
½ Quart Extra Rich Milk
2½ Cups Sugar
1 Tbs. Vanilla
6 Eggs
1 Large Can Crushed Pineapple (Dole),
  in heavy syrup

Pour milk in a large bowl; add sugar and vanilla. Add eggs, one at a time, to separate bowl; beat well with mixer. Pour eggs into milk mixture. Add can of sweetened, crushed pineapple (do not drain). Stir well; beat 1 minute with mixer. Let foam die down, then pour mixture into freezer container and follow ice-cream freezer directions.

Note: If you have a 4 quart freezer, omit the ½ quart of extra rich milk and it should be about the right amount. The recipe, as given, is for a 5 quart freezer. If you have a 6 quart freezer, use the whole quart of extra rich milk.

This recipe is the result of trial and error & has been tried on a lot of people. Some, who don't like homemade ice cream, usually say they love it. The best pineapple ice cream you'll ever taste.

If you like vanilla ice cream, just add 2¾ cups sugar and 1½ tbs. vanilla and omit the pineapple. Use this recipe as a base and make up your own recipe by adding crushed strawberries, peaches, etc. Have fun!

YULETIDE CHOCOLATE DISH

2 Cups Fine Vanilla Wafer Crumbs
1/3 Cup Melted Butter
½ Cup Butter
1½ Cups Sifted Powdered Sugar
2 Eggs
¼ Cup Sugar
2 Tbs. Cocoa
1 Fully Ripe Banana, mashed
1 Cup Heavy Cream
1 Cup Chopped Walnuts
¼ Cup Sliced Maraschino Cherries

Mix together crumbs and melted butter. Reserve 2 tbs. for top. Press remainder in bottom of oblong pan 13" x 9". Cream together ½ cup butter and powdered sugar. Add eggs one at a time, beating well after each. Spread over crumbs. Combine ¼ cup sugar, cocoa and cream, whip. Fold in nuts and fruit, pile atop mixture in pan. Sprinkle reserved crumbs over top. Chill overnight or freeze. Defrost couple hours ahead of time. Best if made night before!

PUDDING DESSERT

Layer 1:
1 Stick Butter or Oleo
1 Cup Flour
1 Cup Walnuts, chopped
1 Tbs. Sugar

Layer 2:
1 Cup Powdered Sugar, sifted
1 - 8 Oz. Pkg. Philadelphia Cream Cheese
1 Cup Cool Whip

Layer 3:
1 - 3¾ Oz. Pkg. Chocolate Instant Pudding
1 - 3¾ Oz. Pkg. Vanilla Instant Pudding

Layer 4:
1 Small Carton Cool Whip
1 Hershey's Chocolate Bar, shavings
½ Cup Chopped Nuts

Mix melted butter, flour, walnuts and sugar together and press into an 8x8" pan. Bake at 325 degrees for 20 minutes. Let cool. Mix layer 2 ingredients together; pour this onto layer 1. For layer 3, prepare instant puddings as directed and pour over layer 2. For layer 4, pour cool whip on top of layer 3, add grated or shaved chocolate and add chopped nuts, sprinkled on top.

IMPOSSIBLE PIE

2 Cups Milk
¾ Cup Sugar
½ Cup Bisquick Mix
4 Eggs
¼ Cup Soft Butter or Margarine
1 Cup Shredded Coconut OR
  Crushed Banana Flakes
1½ Tsp. Vanilla

Heat oven to 350 degrees. Mix all ingredients together in a blender except coconut or banana flakes. Pour into a 9" empty pie pan. Let set 5 minutes then sprinkle coconut or banana flakes on top. Bake 40 minutes or until knife comes out clean.

PERSIMMON PUDDING

1 Cup Persimmon Pulp
1 Cup Sugar
1 Egg
2 Tbs. Melted Butter
1 Cup Milk
1 Cup Flour
2 Tsp. Soda
½ Tsp. Cinnamon
½ Cup Raisins
½ Tsp. Salt
¼ Cup Dates
½ Cup Nuts

Sauce:
1 Cup Brown Sugar
1 Cup Water
2 Tbs. Flour
Pinch of Salt

Pudding: Mix sugar, pulp, egg, melted butter and milk. In separate bowl, combine all dry ingredients. Gradually add pulp mixture, mixing well. Dust raisins, dates and nuts with flour to keep them from sinking to bottom; add them to mixture. Pour into a 9" x 13" pan and bake at 325 degrees for 45 to 60 minutes.

Sauce: Cook ingredients on low heat until thick. Pour over squares of pudding when serving.

CREAM PUFFS

1 Cup Water
½ Cup Butter
1 Cup Flour
4 Eggs

Filling:
¾ Cup Sugar
3 Tbs. Cornstarch
¼ Tsp. Salt
2 Eggs
2 Cups Milk
1 Tbs. Butter
1 Tsp. Vanilla

Cream Puffs: Heat water and butter to rolling boil. Stir in flour all at once. Stir vigorously over low heat until mixture leaves the pan and forms into a ball, about 1 minute. Remove from heat. Beat in eggs thoroughly one at a time. Beat until mixture is smooth and velvety. Drop from spoon onto ungreased baking sheet. Bake until dry in 400 degree oven approximately 45 to 50 minutes. Cool slowly. Cut top from puff and dip in powdered sugar. Fill with cream filling.

Filling: Combine sugar, salt, cornstarch. Add 1½ cups of milk. Cook until thickened. Beat egg yolks; add to the other half cup of milk. Add egg mixture to custard and cook 2 minutes more. Add butter & vanilla. Cool. Fill puffs.

PUMPKIN PIE SQUARES

1 - 13 Oz. Can Canned Milk
3 Eggs, beaten
2 Tsp. Pumpkin Pie Spice
½ Tsp. Salt
1 Cup Sugar
1 - 13 Oz. Can Pumpkin
1 Pkg. Yellow Cake Mix
½ Cup Margarine

Combine the first 6 ingredients. Pour into an 11 x 13 pan. Sprinkle dry cake mix over top. Slice butter over top of cake mix. Bake at 350 degrees for 30 to 40 minutes. Serve with whipped cream.

CHERRIES JUBILEE

2 - 1 Lb. Cans Sweet Dark Cherries
2 Tbs. Cornstarch
¾ Cup Brandy
Vanilla Ice Cream

Drain cherry syrup into automatic fry pan. Heat to boiling with heat at 350 degrees. Pit cherries. Mix cornstarch to a smooth paste with small amount of water; stir into cherry juice. Cook and stir until transparent and slightly thickened. Add the drained, pitted cherries to syrup. Heat brandy and add. Ignite and ladle, flaming, over vanilla ice cream.

PERSIMMON PUDDING

1 Cup Mashed Persimmon Pulp
1 Egg
¼ Cup Milk
1 Tsp. Vanilla
1 Tbs. Melted Butter
½ Cup Chopped Nuts
½ Cup Chopped Raisins
1 Cup Sugar
1 Cup Flour
½ Tsp. Salt
2 Tsp. Baking Powder
1 Tsp. Soda
1 Tsp. Cinnamon

Topping:
1 Egg
2 Tbs. Melted Butter
2 Cups Powdered Sugar
½ Pint Whipping Cream

Beat together persimmon pulp with all ingredients through raisins. Sift together remaining ingredients and add to persimmon mixture. Blend until all flour is absorbed; bake in covered baking dish, approximately 8" x 8", at 350 degrees for 45 to 50 minutes.

Topping: Whip whipping cream until stiff; add egg, powdered sugar and melted butter. Beat until smooth.

Better for Christmas dinner than plum pudding.

VINA TERTA

Filling (Prepare in advance):
2 - 12 Oz. Pkgs. Ready-to-eat Pitted Prunes
2 Cups Cold Water
1 Cup Sugar
1 Tsp. Cinnamon
1 Tsp. Vanilla Extract

Cookie Layers (Makes 8 layers):
1 Cup Melted Butter
1 Cup Sugar
2 Eggs
¼ Cup Sweet Milk
4½ Cups Sifted Flour
1½ Tsp. Baking Powder
½ Tsp. Salt
1 Tsp. Freshly-ground Cardamom Seed

Icing:
1 Cup Powdered Sugar
1 Tbs. Melted Butter
½ Tsp. Vanilla
Milk (about 2 Tsp.), enough to make spreading consistency

Filling: Bring prunes and water to a boil over low heat. Add sugar & cinnamon. Simmer and stir until thick; remove from heat. Add vanilla; cool.

Cookie Layers: Sift flour, baking powder, salt. Mix melted butter with sugar, eggs and ground cardamom until light & fluffy. Mix in flour mixture alternately with milk. Divide dough into 8 equal parts. Roll each part into a round cookie, 8½" in diameter. Place on ungreased cookie sheet; prick lightly with a fork and bake at 375 degrees for 10 to 12 minutes (until done). Cool on cookie racks.

Apportion filling into 7 portions and layer cookie and filling alternately, ending with cookie. Frost top cookie with icing. Cover torte and let rest 2 days before slicing. To serve, slice into 3/8" thick slices and cut each slice diagonally into 2" sections. Freezes well.

GERMAN CHOCOLATE CHEESECAKE

1 Pkg. German Chocolate Cake Mix
½ Cup Shredded Coconut
1/3 Cup Butter or Margarine, softened
1 Egg
2 - 8 Oz. Pkgs. Cream Cheese, softened

2 Eggs
¾ Cup Sugar
2 Tsp. Vanilla
2 Cups Dairy Sour Cream
¼ Cup Sugar
1 Tbs. Vanilla

Heat oven to 350 degrees. In large mixer
bowl, blend cake mix, coconut, butter and
1 egg on low speed until mixture is crumbly.
Press very lightly into an ungreased baking
pan, 13x8x2".

Beat cream cheese, 2 eggs, sugar and vanilla
until smooth and fluffy. Spread over cake
mixture. Bake 20 to 25 minutes.

Mix sour cream, ¼ cup sugar and 1 tbs. of
vanilla until smooth. Spread over cheesecake. Cool. Refrigerate at least 8 hours.
Let sit at room temperature about ½ hour
before cutting. Serves 20.

CUSTARD PIE

4 Eggs
½ Cup Sugar
½ Tsp. Salt
2½ Cups Scalded Milk
1 Tsp. Vanilla
¼ Tsp. Nutmeg
Pastry for 9" Crust

Prepare pastry and make an unbaked 9"
pastry shell; chill thoroughly. Beat eggs
slightly; add sugar and salt. Slowly stir
in hot scalded milk; add vanilla and mix
well. Pour mixture into pastry shell.
Sprinkle with nutmeg. Bake on lower
shelf of a hot oven, 425 degrees, for 25
to 30 minutes, or until custard is firm.

RHUBARB CRUNCH

2 Cups Brown Sugar
2 Cups Flour
1½ Cups Quick Oats
1 Cup Melted Oleo
2 Tsp. Cinnamon
5 Cups Rhubarb, raw, diced
1½ Cups Sugar
2 Tbs. Cornstarch
1 Cup Water
1 Tsp. Vanilla Flavoring

Mix first 5 ingredients until crumbly. Press
½ of this mixture into greased 9x13" pan.
Cover with 5 cups raw, diced rhubarb. Cook
sugar, cornstarch and water until thick and
clear; remove from heat. Add vanilla and
pour syrup over rhubarb. Sprinkle rest of
crumbly mixture over all and pat lightly.
Bake in 350 degree oven for 45-55 minutes.

ORANGE BAKED ALASKA

1 Pint Vanilla Ice Cream, or Orange,
  Lemon or Lime Sherbert
3 Large Oranges
3 Egg Whites
¼ Tsp. Cream of Tartar
¼ Cup Plus 2 Tbs. Sugar

Scoop ice cream into 6 balls, freeze until
very firm, at least 5 hours. Cut oranges
crosswise in half, cut thin slice from bottom
of each half. Cut around edges and membranes. Remove fruit and membranes from
orange shells. Line bottom of each shell
with fruit. Refrigerate. Heat oven to 500
degrees. Beat egg whites and cream of tartar until frothy. Beat in sugar, 1 tbs. at a
time. Continue beating until stiff and glossy. Do not overbeat. Place orange cups on
an ungreased baking sheet; fill each up with
an ice cream ball. Completely cover ice
cream with meringue, sealing it to edge of
shells. Bake for 2 to 3 minutes, or until
meringue is light brown. Serve immediately.
Makes 6 servings.

SCOTCH BETTY

2 Cups Coarsely-chopped Peaches
¼ Tsp. Cinnamon
¼ Cup Shortening or Oil
1/3 Cup Brown Sugar, firmly packed
¼ Tsp. Baking Soda
1 Tbs. Butter
2/3 Cup Flour
1/8 Tsp. Salt
½ Tsp. Vanilla
2/3 Cup Rolled Oats

Arrange peaches in buttered baking dish; sprinkle with cinnamon and dot with butter. Combine melted shortening or oil & sugar. Sift flour, salt and soda together; stir in oats. Blend with sugar mixture, crumbling well with hands. Add vanilla and spread over peaches. Bake at 350 degrees for 50 minutes.

STRAWBERRY CRUNCH

1 Cup Flour
¼ Cup Brown Sugar
½ Cup Chopped Walnuts
½ Cup Melted Butter
2 Egg Whites
1 Cup Sugar
10 Oz. Frozen Strawberries
1 Tbs. Lemon Juice
1 Tsp. Vanilla
1 Cup Whipping Cream, whipped

Crunch: In a 9" x 13" x 2" pan, mix flour, brown sugar, nuts and melted butter. Bake at 350 degrees for approximately 15 minutes; stir often. Set aside.

Filling: Beat 2 egg whites till firm; add 1 cup sugar, thawed strawberries, lemon juice and vanilla. Beat 20 minutes at high speed. Add whipping cream, whipped, and fold into filling mixture with spoon. Pour on top of crunch. Freeze for 6 hours. Serves 15 or more.

BANANA MALLOW PIE

2 Cups Vanilla Wafer Crumbs
1/3 Cup Margarine
3-1/8 Oz. Pkg. Vanilla Pie Filling
1¾ Cups Milk
2 Bananas
1½ Cups Miniature Marshmallows
1 Cup Whipped Cream

1. Combine 2 cups vanilla wafer crumbs & 1/3 cup margarine, melted. Press into a 9" pie plate. Bake at 375 degrees for 8 min.

2. Prepare one 3-1/8 oz. package vanilla pie filling, using 1¾ cups milk. Cover surface with transparent wrap and chill. Fold in 1½ cups miniature marshmallows and 1 cup whipped cream.

3. Slice 2 bananas into crust. Pour filling over bananas. Chill several hours.

LEMON LUSH

1 Cup Sugar
3 Tbs. Flour
¼ Tsp. Salt
2 Eggs, separated
1 Cup Milk
1 Lemon (juice & rind of)

Mix the sugar, flour and salt. Beat the egg whites until stiff, but not dry, put aside. Beat egg yolks, add about 1/3 of the milk, beat in gradually the mixed dry ingredients. Add the remaining milk, the juice and rind of the lemon and beat well. Fold in the stiffly beaten egg whites. Do not fold in the egg whites until all lumps have disappeared! Pour into buttered casserole dish or individual molds, about ¾ full. Set in pan of hot water and bake in a slow 325 degree oven for 1 hour, cool. Remove from casserole and serve upside down with or without whipped cream. Makes 4 servings.

MOCHA LADYFINGER DESSERT

1 Lb. Pkg. Marshmallows
2 Pkgs. Bakery Ladyfingers
1 Tsp. Instant Coffee
½ Cup Boiling Water
1 Pint Heavy Whipping Cream

Line sides and bottom and middle of a buttered 8" springform pan with split ladyfingers. Put ¾ of bag of marshmallows in top of double boiler. Dissolve coffee in water and add to marshmallows. Let mixture melt, then mix and cool thoroughly.

Whip cream, but don't add sugar, and mix with cooled marshmallows and coffee. Pour into prepared springform pan and refrigerate at least 3 hours. Can be made a day ahead. Serves 8 deliciously!

SWEDISH FRUIT SOUP

1 Cup Pear Juice, from canned fruit
1 Cup Peach Juice, from canned fruit
1 Cup Plum Juice, from canned fruit
1 Cup Orange, Grapefruit OR Cranberry juice
1/8 Tsp. Ground Cinnamon
Dash of Ground Clove
6 Purple Plums, canned
1 Canned Peach
1 Canned Pear
1 Tbs. Cornstarch
Water

Combine one cup each of pear, peach and plum juice from canned fruit. Put in a saucepan. Add one cup of orange, grapefruit or cranberry juice, ground cinnamon and dash of ground clove. Place over low heat and simmer for 1 hour. Coarsely chop and add the canned purple plums, one canned peach and one canned pear and bring to boil. Combine 1 tbs. cornstarch with a little water and add to mixture. Boil for approximately 10 minutes. Served hot or cold; delicious either way.

DEEP DISH RHUBARB PIE
with CREAM CHEESE PASTRY

2 Lbs. Rhubarb
½ Cup Flour
1 Cup Sugar
½ Cup Light Corn Syrup
1 Tbs. Butter

3 Oz. Cream Cheese
6 Tbs. Butter
¾ Cup Flour
½ Tsp. Salt

Wash 2 lbs. of rhubarb and trim and cut into 1" pieces (6 cups). Toss with ½ cup flour and turn into an 8" x 8" x 2" pan. Sprinkle remaining flour over rhubarb.

Mix 1 cup sugar and ½ cup light corn syrup and bring to boil, stirring constantly. Pour over rhubarb and dot with 1 tbs. butter.

Cover with cream cheese pastry rolled 1" bigger than pan. Turn under 1" and crimp against edge. Bake at 425 degrees for 25 minutes. Serve warm with whipped cream.

Pastry: Mix cream cheese with butter till fluffy. Add flour and salt with a fork. Chill and roll between waxed paper.

ZABAGLIONE ICE BOX CAKE

2 Dozen Lady Fingers
2 Cups Milk
3 Pkgs. Instant Vanilla Pudding
¾ Cup Marsala
1½ Pints Whipping Cream

Line lightly buttered spring-form pan and the bottom with split Lady Fingers (you will need about 2 dozen). Beat 2 cups milk into 3 pkgs. instant vanilla pudding. Slowly add ¾ cup Marsala. Beat 1 pint whipping cream until stiff and fold into pudding mixture. Spoon gently into pan and chill overnight. Before serving, top with ½ pt. cream, whipped.

KOLACHE

Pastry:
4 Cups Flour
½ Tsp. Salt
1 Tsp. Vanilla
1 Cake Yeast
2 Sticks Butter
3 Egg Yolks
1 Cup Sour Cream

Filling:
3 Egg Whites
1 Cup Sugar
1 Cup Chopped Pecans
1 Tsp. Vanilla

Let butter soften overnight. Preheat oven to 400 degrees.

Pastry: Sift flour in bowl; add salt, yeast in flour; add butter and cut in. Add egg yolks, sour cream, vanilla and mix. Form ball. Divide into 9 or 10 balls. Roll out each ball 1/8" thick on sugar. Cut each piece into 8 wedges.

Filling: Whip egg whites stiff. Gradually fold in 1 cup sugar, 1 cup chopped pecans and 1 tsp. vanilla and spread on wedges. Roll wedge, starting with wide edge of wedge. Bake 15 minutes in greased or teflon cookie sheet. Yield: 72 to 80 pastries.

IDAHO APPLE PUDDING

½ Cup Sugar
¼ Cup Shortening
1 Egg
½ Tsp. Salt
2 Cups Chopped Apples
1 Cup Sifted Flour
1 Tsp. Cinnamon
½ Tsp. Nutmeg
1 Tsp. Baking Soda

Whipped Topping
3 Oz. Heavy Whipping Cream
1½ Tsp. Sugar
1 Tsp. Vanilla

Cream sugar and shortening until fluffy. Beat in egg. Sift dry ingredients in a separate bowl, add to shortening mixture and stir well. Add chopped apples. Batter will be stiff. Put in a greased loaf pan. Bake at 350 degrees for ½ hour, or until golden brown.

Whipped Topping: While pudding is in oven, whip the cream until not quite stiff. Add sugar and vanilla. Beat until stiff. Chill. Serve pudding warm, topped with chilled whipped cream topping. Dee-licious!

FLORIDA KEY LIME PIE

1 Cup Vanilla Wafer Crumbs
¼ Cup Butter or Margarine
½ Cup Chopped Pecans

Filling:
3 Eggs, separated
¼ Cup Lime Juice
1 Tsp. Grated Lime Rind
1 Can Sweetened Condensed Milk
3 Drops Green Food Coloring
¼ Tsp. Cream of Tartar
6 Tsp. Sugar

Crust:
Mix the vanilla wafer crumbs, butter or margarine and the chopped pecans thoroughly. Reserve a small amount for topping meringue. With back of spoon, press this mixture into pie pan.

Filling:
Beat egg yolks. Add lime juice, rind, condensed milk and food coloring. Mix well at medium speed. Pour into pie shell. Beat egg whites until frothy. Add cream of tartar and beat until stiff. Beat in sugar gradually, until stiff and glossy. Pile meringue on pie lightly, sealing outside edges, brushing toward center. Bake at 425 degrees for 4 minutes, or until lightly browned.

GRAHAM CRACKER PIE

Crust:
20 Graham Crackers, reserve some
½ Cup Melted Butter
½ Cup Sugar

Filling:
2 Cups Milk
3 Tbs. Sugar
3 Egg Yolks
3 Tbs. Cornstarch
1 Tsp. Vanilla
½ Tsp. Salt

Topping:
3 Egg Whites
6 Tbs. Sugar

Crust: Roll graham crackers until fine.
Mix with sugar and melted butter. Line
a pie plate with mixture.

Filling: Cook in double boiler the above
filling ingredients. Dissolve cornstarch in
small amount of milk. Add rest of milk,
sugar and salt and cook about 20 minutes,
stirring constantly. Add slightly beaten
egg yolks and cook until thickened. Add
vanilla, then pour into shell.

Topping: Beat the 3 egg whites and the 6
tbs. sugar together, put on top of pie.
Sprinkle any remaining cracker crumbs on
top of meringue. Bake in a slow 325 deg.
oven for 30 minutes. Delicious.

KENTUCKY PIE

1 Qt. Fresh Strawberries
1 Cup Sugar
3 Tbs. Cornstarch
1 Baked Pie Shell

Put ½ quart berries in baked pie
shell. Mash the other ½ quart and
bring to a boil. Add sugar and the
cornstarch. Let cool and then pour
over berries that are in pie shell. Refrigerate until set. Serve with whipped
cream if desired.

WATERMELON DESSERT

2 Cups Flour
1 Cup Brown Sugar
1 Tsp. Soda
1 Tsp. Salt
2 Tsp. Cinnamon
½ Tsp. Nutmeg
1 Cup Sour Cream
½ Cup Shortening
2 Eggs
1 Cup Chopped Pickled Watermelon

Mix all ingredients together except the
pickled watermelon. Stir in watermelon.
Spread batter in greased and floured pan.
Bake at 350 degrees for 30 to 35 minutes,
or until done. When slightly cooled, sprinkle with powdered sugar.

PEACH—BERRY COBBLER

¼ Cup Sugar
¼ Cup Brown Sugar
1 Tbs. Cornstarch
½ Cup Water
1 Tbs. Lemon Juice
2 Cups Sliced Peaches (4 medium)
1 Cup Blueberries
1 Cup Sifted Flour
½ Cup Sugar
1½ Tsp. Baking Powder
½ Tsp. Salt
½ Cup Milk
¼ Cup Butter, soft
2 Tbs. Sugar
¼ Tsp. Nutmeg

Bake at 375 degrees for 40 to 45 minutes.
Serves 6 to 8.

Combine in saucepan sugars, cornstarch. Add
water; blend well. Cook over medium heat,
stirring constantly, until thick. Add lemon
juice, peaches and blueberries. Turn into a
2-quart baking dish.

Sift together into mixing bowl flour, sugar,
baking powder and salt. Add milk and
softened butter; beat until smooth. Spoon
over fruit. Sprinkle with mixture of sugar
and nutmeg. Bake at 375 degrees for 40 to
45 minutes.

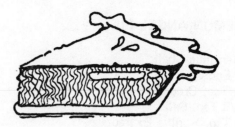

OLALLIE BERRY PIE

1¾ Cups Water
1 Cup Sugar
2 Tbs. Cornstarch
1 Large Pkg. Raspberry Jello
8 Cups Olallie Berries or Boysenberries
2 Graham Cracker Pie Crusts

Put water, sugar and cornstarch into a saucepan. Bring to a boil, then cook for 3 minutes. Remove from heat and add 1 pkg. of raspberry jello and stir well. Let cool. Wash 8 cups fresh or frozen berries and drain. Then put into jello mixture. If berries are frozen, just thaw them enough to separate them. Pour mixture into graham cracker pie shells. Cool in refrigerator until firm. Serve, when firm, with whipped cream. Makes 2 - 9" pies.

ZWIEBACK PUDDING

1 Pkg. Zwieback, rolled fine
   (save 1/3 cup)
½ Cup Melted Butter (1 cube)
½ Cup Sugar
1 Cup Coconut
4 Egg Yolks (large eggs)
1 Quart Milk
¾ Cup Sugar
3 Heaping Tbs. Cornstarch

Mix together the zwieback (reserve 1/3 cup), melted butter, coconut and sugar. Mix all this together very well. Pat into a pan and put in slow oven for 10 min.

Beat egg yolks; add milk and sugar and cornstarch; cook until thick. Add 1 tsp. vanilla. Pour this over the first mixture. On top of this put the egg whites, stiffly beaten with 4 tbs. sugar. Sprinkle remaining crumbs on top and bake in 350 degree oven until brown. Set in ice box for 24 hours. Good while warm, too.

MACAROON PIE

Pastry:
1-2/3 Cups Flour
1/3 Cup Sugar
1 Tsp. Baking Powder
¼ Tsp. Salt
2 Oranges (grated peel)
1 Egg, lightly beaten
1 Cube Butter (¼ Lb.)

Filling:
2 Eggs, lightly beaten
1 Cup Sugar
¼ Cup Flour
¼ Tsp. Salt
2 Cups Angel Flake Coconut
½ Cup Orange Juice
¼ Cup Melted Butter
¼ Cup Coconut Syrup or Apricot
   Jam

Pastry: Mix first 5 ingredients together; cut in butter with pastry blender until fine. Add egg and stir with fork until blended. Work by hand into ball. Save 1/3 of dough. With the 2/3, roll on waxed paper to fit 10" pie pan, but not over edge. Bake for 8 minutes at 325 degrees. Meantime, roll other 1/3 into ropes for lattice strip.

Filling: Beat eggs lightly; stir in sugar, flour and salt. Add coconut, orange juice and butter. Mix and pour into pastry. Make lattice; trim and press into edges of pie. Bake 40 minutes at 325 degrees, until set and brown.

Heat jam or coconut syrup and brush on while pie is warm. Let cool. Is best a day or more old. Also can be made as small tarts.

LEMON ANGEL PIE

Meringue Shell:
4 Egg Whites
½ Tsp. Cream of Tartar
1/8 Tsp. Salt
1 Tsp. Vanilla Extract
1 Cup Granulated Sugar

Lemon Filling:
2 Tbs. Flour
1 Cup Granulated Sugar
1/8 Tsp. Salt
¼ Cup Water
¼ Cup Lemon Juice
4 Egg Yolks, beaten
¼ Tsp. Almond Extract
2 Cups Heavy Whipping Cream

Meringue Shell:
Place egg whites in large mixing bowl. Beat until foamy. Add cream of tartar, salt and vanilla. Beat until stiff and dry. Add sugar gradually and continue beating until sugar has dissolved. On a greased 10x14" cookie sheet, spoon mixture into a 9" round, having sides at least 1" high. Bake for 1 hour in a preheated 275 degree oven. When done, turn off heat and allow to dry in oven for 10 to 15 minutes. Cool slightly before removing from pan onto a serving dish or platter.

Lemon Filling:
Mix flour, sugar and salt. Add water and lemon juice. Stir until smooth; add beaten egg yolks and mix well. Cook over low heat until mixture is thick, stirring constantly. Remove from range; add almond extract & chill. Whip the heavy cream until stiff; fold half or all of the whipped cream into the chilled filling. Pour into meringue shell. Top with the second half of whipped cream, if desired. Let stand 24 hours in the refrigerator before serving. Be sure it is covered to prevent it from absorbing other flavors in the refrigerator. Serves 8 to 10.

CARROT PIE

4 Large Carrots
¼ Cup Butter
½ Cup Milk
1½ Tsp. Vanilla
2 Eggs
½ to ¾ Cup Sugar
½ Cup Flour or Cornstarch
1¼ Tsp. Nutmeg
¼ Tsp. Salt
¼ Tsp. Baking Powder

Heat oven to 375 degrees. Cook carrots in boiling water until well done. Skin carrots and mash, add melted butter, milk, egg and vanilla. Sift flour, sugar, nutmeg, salt and baking powder. Beat all ingredients together with a rotary beater. Pour into pastry-lined pie pan and bake 50 to 60 minutes.

BLACKBERRY ROLY-POLY

2 Cups Flour
½ Tsp. Salt
3 Tsp. Baking Powder
2 Tbs. Sugar
1 Beaten Egg
½ Cup Milk
3 Tbs. Crisco
3 Cups Berries
½ Tsp. Ginger
¾ Cup Sugar
2 Tbs. Sugar

Sift dry ingredients. Cut in Crisco. Blend with beaten egg and milk. Toss on floured board. Roll to ¼ inch thickness. Mix berries, ginger and sugar. Spread dough with melted Crisco. Spread on berries and roll. Bake in a greased pan for 25 minutes in a 375 degree oven. For glass dish size 8 x 12 in. bake at 350 degrees. Serve warm.

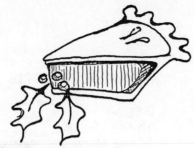

WHITE CHRISTMAS PIE

1 Tbs. Knox Unflavored Gelatine
¼ Cup Cold Water
¼ Cup Sugar
4 Tbs. Flour
½ Tsp. Salt
1½ Cups Milk
¾ Tsp. Vanilla
¼ Tsp. Almond Extract
½ Cup Fresh Whipping Cream
3 Egg Whites
¼ Tsp. Cream of Tartar
½ Cup Sugar
1 Cup Angel Flake Coconut
2 Baked Pie Shells

Soften gelatine in cold water in a bowl; set aside. Mix ¼ cup sugar, flour, salt and milk together in a saucepan. Cook it over low heat, stirring until it comes to a boil. Boil it for 1 minute. Remove from heat; stir in softened gelatine. Let it all cool. When partially set, beat with rotary beater until smooth; blend in vanilla and almond extract. Gently fold in whipping cream that has been whipped stiff. Make a meringue of 3 egg whites, the cream of tartar and the ½ cup of sugar. Carefully fold it into the mix. Put in 1 cup of coconut; put it all into 2 baked pie shells; sprinkle coconut on top. Chill until set, about 2 hours. Serve cold.

CHOCOLATE ROLL

5 Egg Yolks
½ Cup Sugar
2 Tbs. Melted Chocolate
2 Tbs. Flour
1 Pint Whipping Cream
5 Egg Whites
1/3 Cup Powdered Sugar

Chocolate Sauce:
¾ Cup Sugar
½ Cup Melted Chocolate
½ Cup Cream (light)
1 Tbs. Butter
½ Tsp. Vanilla

Heat oven to 375 degrees. Line jelly-roll pan, 15½" x 10½" x 1", with waxed or foil paper. Grease. In mixer bowl, beat eggs till thick and lemon colored. Gradually beat in granulated sugar, then chocolate and flour. Add the egg whites that have been beaten stiff. Put batter in pan and bake 10 to 15 minutes; test with wooden pick inserted in center - should come out clean. Loosen cake from edges of pan. Invert on towel sprinkled with confectioner's sugar. Remove wax or foil paper. Trim off stiff edges if necessary. While hot, roll cake and towel. Cool on wire rack. Unroll cake; remove towel. Fill with whipped cream that has been sweetened. Roll up and serve with hot chocolate sauce.

PERSIMMON HOLIDAY PIE

1½ Cups Graham Cracker Crumbs
3 Tbs. Sugar
½ Cup Melted Butter or Margarine
2 Cups Persimmon Pulp (heaping)
3 Eggs
1¼ Cups Sugar
1½ Cups Flour
1 Tsp. Baking Powder
1 Tsp. Baking Soda
1 Tsp. Vanilla (optional)
½ Tsp. Salt
½ Cup Melted Margarine
2½ Cups Milk
2 Tsp. Cinnamon
1 Tsp. Nutmeg
1 Cup Walnut Meats (optional)

Mix first three ingredients and pat firmly on the bottom and sides of pie pan. Bake at 375 degrees for 15 minutes, or if desired, chill. It can be baked with the filling. Place persimmon pulp in large mixing bowl and beat in all other ingredients in order given. Pour into a graham cracker crust and bake in a moderate 325 degree oven for about one hour, until firm. Serve with whipped cream topped with chopped walnut meats, if desired. A light, delicious dessert for holiday meals.

KID'S JELLO TREAT

2 Pkgs. Raspberry Jello
1 Pkg. Mixed Fruit Jello
1-½ Cups Party Whip, heaping
1 Box Strawberries
1 Large Banana
1 Cup Colored Miniature Marshmallows

Make jello as directed on packages. Chill in a large bowl until set. When jello is set, add 1 heaping cup of Party Whip and use electric mixer to blend very well. Cut up banana into small pieces and fold into jello mixture. Save 6 uniform strawberries and cut the rest up into small pieces and fold into mixture. Smooth over top of jello mixture and make it flat as possible. Drop rest or Party Whip with a teaspoon in little mounds over top of jello. Put miniature colored marshmallows on each mound of Party Whip. Slice the 6 uniform strawberries in half and garnish between mounds of Party Whip.

PEACH CUSTARD "PIE"

1½ Cups Flour
½ Tsp. Salt
½ Cup Margarine or Butter
1 Can (1 Lb. 14 Oz.) Sliced Peaches
  (drain and reserve ½ cup syrup)
½ Cup Sugar
½ Tsp. Cinnamon
1 Egg, slightly beaten
1 Cup Evaporated Milk

Mix the flour, salt and margarine or butter with pastry blender or two knives until mixture looks like coarse meal. With back of spoon, press mixture firmly on bottom and half way up sides of a 10" pie pan (glass). Arrange well the drained peach slices on crust. Sprinkle with mixture of sugar and cinnamon and bake in 375 degree oven for 20 minutes. Mix ½ cup of peach syrup, 1 slightly beaten egg and 1 cup evaporated milk. Pour over peaches. Bake 30 minutes longer or until custard is firm, except in center.

JAPANESE FRUIT PIE

3 Eggs
1½ Cups Sugar
1 Stick Margarine, melted
¾ Cup Coconut, shredded
½ Cup Chopped Nuts
½ Cup Raisins
1 Tsp. Vanilla

Beat eggs; add other ingredients. Pour into an unbaked pie shell. Bake on bottom shelf of oven at 300 degrees for 50 minutes. This makes nice bars also, by placing dough into oblong pans, filling and baking as above.

SCHAUM TORTE

TORTE:
4 Egg Whites
¼ Tsp. Salt
¼ Tsp. Cream Tartar
1 Cup Sugar
½ Tsp. Vanilla

FILLING:
1 Pint Fresh Strawberries (2 Cups) OR 2 Pkgs.
  Frozen, thawed and drained
1 Cup Heavy Cream

To make torte: Grease and flour a large cookie sheet. Make 3 circles in the flour coating, using a 6" plate as a guide. Place egg whites in a large bowl, sprinkle with salt and cream of tartar. Beat egg whites until they fold soft peaks. Add sugar gradually, beating hard and constantly until the mixture holds firm, shiny peaks. Fold in vanilla. Spoon onto circles on cookie sheet. Bake in 250 degree oven for 60 min., or until meringues are firm to touch. Loosen carefully with a spatula. Slide onto cake rack and cool. To make filling: Wash and hull berries. Save a few for garnish, crush remaining and sweeten with sugar to taste. Whip cream, drain berries and fold into cream. Spoon 1/3 of the filling between each of the meringues and the remainder on top. Decorate top with reserved berries. Makes 6 to 8 servings.

PINEAPPLE TURNOVERS

6 Cups Sifted Flour
2 Cups Lard (no substitute)
1 Tbs. Sugar
3 Eggs, well beaten
1 Cake Yeast (dissolved in ½ cup warm
  water)

Filling:
1 Cup Sugar
3 Tbs. Cornstarch
1 Can Crushed Pineapple

Mix the first 4 ingredients as for a pie crust. Add yeast mixture and chill overnight. Roll chilled dough on sugared board. Cut into squares and fill in center of squares. Lap over opposite ends in middle over the filling. Bake at 400 degrees for 10 to 14 minutes or until lightly browned.

Filling: Cook all ingredients until clear then let chill.

APRICOT CHEESE DELIGHT

1 - 29 Oz. Can Apricots, drained & finely
  cut
1 - 29 Oz. Can Crushed Pineapple, drained
2 Pkgs. Orange Flavored Gelatin
2 Cups Hot Water
1 Cup Combined Apricot & Pineapple
  Juice
¾ Cup Miniature Marshmallows (optional)

Drain and chill the fruits, reserving the juice. Dissolve gelatin in boiling water. Add 1 cup fruit juice, reserve remaining juice for topping. Chill until slightly congealed. Fold in fruit and marshmallows. Pour into a cold-water rinsed 13 x 8 inch baking dish. Chill until firm. Spread with Fruit Cheese:

Fruit Cheese Topping:
½ Cup Sugar
3 Tbs. All-Purpose Flour
1 Egg, slightly beaten
1 Cup Combined Pineapple & Apricot
  Juice
2 Tbs. Butter
1/3 Cup Whipping Cream, whipped
¾ Cup Grated Cheddar Cheese

Combine sugar and flour and blend in the beaten egg. Gradually stir in juices. Cook over low heat until thickened, stirring constantly. Remove from heat. Stir in butter. Cool. Fold in whipped cream and spread over chilled gelatin layer. Sprinkle top with grated cheese. Chill. To serve, arrange squares of salad on lettuce. Makes approximately 18 servings. May be used as a dessert, without lettuce, serve a small cookie on the side.

PAPER BAG APPLE PIE

4 - 5 Large Apples (2½ Lbs.)
1 Cup Sugar
2 Tbs. Flour
1 Tsp. Nutmeg
2 Tbs. Lemon Juice
½ Cup Flour
½ Cup Butter
1 Unbaked Pie Shell

Place sliced and peeled apples in large bowl. Combine ½ cup sugar, 2 tbs. flour, nutmeg and sprinkle over apples. Toss to coat well and put into pastry shell. Drizzle apple mixture with 2 tbs. lemon juice. Combine ½ cup sugar and ½ cup flour (for topping) in bowl. Cut in butter and sprinkle over apples evenly. Slide pie into heavy brown bag (regular large shopping market bag). Fold bag end and fasten with paper clips or staple. Place on cookie sheet. Bake at 400 degrees for 1 hour. Split bag open; remove pie and cool. Very good and all mess is inside paper bag.

ORANGE BAVARIAN CREAM

2 Large Bright Skinned Oranges
2 Large Sugar Lumps
1½ Tbs. Gelatin
7 Egg Yolks
1 Cup Granulated Sugar
2 Tsp. Cornstarch
1½ Cups Boiling Milk
5 Egg Whites
Pinch Salt
1 Tbs. Granulated Sugar
½ Cup Chilled Whipping Cream
2 Tbs. Orange Liqueur

Wash and dry oranges. One at a time, rub sugar lumps over them until all sides of each lump are impregnated with orange oil. Mash sugar lumps into a 4 qt. mixing bowl. Grate orange peel into bowl; squeeze juice of oranges into measuring cup to make ½ to ¾ cup of strained juice. Sprinkle gelatin over the orange juice and set aside to soften. Add the egg yolks to the orange sugar in the mixing bowl. Gradually beat in the granulated sugar and continue beating for 2 to 3 min. until mixture is pale yellow and forms ribbons. Beat in cornstarch. Beat boiling milk in a thin stream of droplets into the egg yolk mixture. Pour into a 2 qt. enameled saucepan and set over moderate heat. Stir with wooden spoon until mixture thickens enough to coat spoon lightly. Do not over-heat or egg yolks will scramble. Remove from heat and immediately add orange juice and gelatin mixture, beating a moment or two until gelatin has dissolved completely. Rinse out mixing bowl and pour in the custard. Beat egg whites and pinch of salt until soft peaks form. Using a rubber spatula, fold egg whites into hot custard. Set in refrigerator. Fold delicately with spatula several times while mixture is cooling, to keep from separating. When cold, but not quite set, beat the cream lightly, until doubled in volume and beater leaves faint traces on the surface. Fold the whipped cream and orange liqueur into the custard. Rinse an 8 cup ring mold in cold water and shake out excess water. Turn Bavarian Cream into mold and cover with wax paper. Chill for 3 to 4 hours or overnight. Remove wax paper & dip mold in very hot water for 1 second, run a knife around edge of cream and remove onto a chilled serving platter. Serve surrounded with the orange segments. As delightful to the eye as it is to the taste!

RASPBERRY WALNUT TORTE

1 Cup Flour
1/3 Cup Conefectioner's Sugar
½ Cup Butter, softened
1 - 10 Oz. Pkg. Frozen Raspberries, thawed
¾ Cup Chopped Walnuts
2 Eggs
1 Cup Sugar
¼ Cup Flour
½ Tsp. Baking Powder
½ Tsp. Salt
1 Tsp. Vanilla

Torte:
In small bowl, combine 1 c. flour, confectioner's sugar & butter; blend well. Press into bottom of ungreased 9 in. square pan. Bake at 350 degrees for 15 minutes. Cool. Drain raspberries; reserve liquid for sauce. Spread berries over crust; sprinkle with walnuts. In small bowl, combine eggs, sugar, ¼ cup flour, salt, baking powder and vanilla at low speed. Blend well. Pour over walnuts. Bake at 350 degrees for 35 to 40 minutes until golden brown. Cool. Cut into squares. Serve with whipped cream and raspberry sauce.

Raspberry Sauce:
½ Cup Sugar
2 Tbs. Cornstarch
½ Cup Water
Reserved Raspberry Juice
1 Tbs. Lemon Juice

In small saucepan, combine all ingredients except lemon juice. Cook, stirring constantly until thick and clear. Stir in lemon juice. Cool.

KIWI FRUIT CREAM CHEESE PIE

1 Baked Pie Shell
3 to 4 Medium Kiwis, soft
½ Cup Water
1¼ Cups Sugar
3 Tbs. Cornstarch
1 - 3 Oz. Pkg. Cream Cheese,
  softened
1 Squirt (½ Tsp. approximately) Lemon
  Juice

Liquefy peeled kiwi fruit. Simmer kiwi fruit and water about 3 minutes. Blend in sugar and cornstarch. Boil 1 minute, stirring constantly. Cool. Spread cream cheese over bottom of cooled pie shell; cover with cooked mixture. Refrigerate until firm (about 2 hours). Serve with whipped cream or ice cream.

"VERY SPECIAL" BOSTON CREAM PIE

2 Egg Whites
½ Cup Sugar
2¼ Cups Flour
1 Cup Sugar
3 Tsp. Baking Powder
1 Tsp. Salt
1/3 Cup Salad Oil
1½ Tsp. Vanilla
2 Egg Yolks
1 Cup Milk

French Custard Filling:
1/3 Cup Sugar
1 Tbs. Flour
1 Tbs. Cornstarch
¼ Tsp. Salt
1½ Cups Milk
1 Egg, slightly beaten
1 Tsp. Vanilla

Chocolate Gloss:
½ Cup Sugar
1½ Tbs. Cornstarch
1 Oz. Chocolate
Dash of Salt
½ Cup Boiling Water

Beat egg whites until foamy. Gradually beat in ½ cup sugar. Beat until very stiff and glossy. Sift remaining dry ingredients into another bowl. Add salad oil, half of the milk and half of the vanilla. Beat 1 minute at medium speed. Add remaining milk and egg yolks. Beat 1 minute. Gently fold in egg white mixture with down-up-over motion. Bake in paper-lined 9" pans at 350 degrees for 25 minutes; cool.

French Custard Filling: Mix sugar, flour, cornstarch and salt. Gradually stir in milk. Cook and stir until mixture thickens and boils. Cook and stir 2 to 3 minutes longer. Stir a little of hot mixture into egg yolk. Return to hot mixture, stirring constantly, bring just to boiling. Add vanilla; cool. Beat with wire whisk until smooth. Fill between layers and refrigerate.

Chocolate Gloss: Add all ingredients to small saucepan. Cook and stir until blended and thickened. Remove from heat and add 1½ tbs. butter and ½ tsp. vanilla. Pour over top layer while still hot and let drip down the sides.

CREEPING CRUST COBBLER

½ Cup Butter or Margarine
1 Cup Flour
1 Cup Sugar
1 Tsp. Baking Powder
½ Cup Milk
2 Cups Fruit: Blackberries, Raspberries,
  Apricots, Peaches, etc.
1 Cup or less Sugar

Melt butter in 10 inch baking dish. Mix flour, sugar, baking powder; add milk and mix. Spoon over melted butter. Heat fresh or canned fruit with sugar, adjusting less sugar if fruit is canned. Pour over dough. Bake in a 350 degree oven about 30 minutes until crust is golden brown. Crust will rise to the top. Serve warm or cold, if any lasts that long.

BAKED APPLE PUDDING WITH RUM

PUDDING:
1 Cup Sifted Flour
1 Tsp. Baking Soda
1 Tsp. Cinnamon
¾ Tsp. Nutmeg
¼ Tsp. Salt
¼ Cup Butter
1 Cup Sugar
1 Egg, unbeaten
2 or 3 Medium Apples, washed, unpared

SAUCE:
½ Cup Butter
1 Cup Sugar
½ Cup Light Cream
Dash Nutmeg
1 Tsp. Vanilla
1 Tsp. Rum Extract OR 2 to 3 Tbs. Rum

Heat oven to 400 degrees. Grease an 8x8"
pan. Sift first 5 ingredients. With mixer at
cream, mix butter with sugar and egg until
light and fluffy. Grate apples, medium fine.
Measure 2 Cups. Add to egg mixture. At low
speed, beat in flour mixture, just until mixed.
Pour into pan. Bake 20 to 30 min. Cool;
store in pan. Cut into 8 squares. Rum
Butter Sauce: In double boiler, mix butter
with sugar and cream. Cook, stirring 10 to 15
min., or until slightly thickened. Add nutmeg,
vanilla and rum extract. Serve over baked
apple pudding.

BUTTERSCOTCH PIE

6 Tbs. Butter
2½ Cups Scalded Milk
3 Tbs. Cornstarch
1½ Cups Brown Sugar
2 Eggs, separate whites & yolks
4 Tbs. Sugar
¼ Tsp. Cream of Tartar
½ Tsp. Vanilla
1 - 8" Baked Pastry Shell

Melt butter and brown sugar. Mix cornstarch with ½ cup of milk. Scald 2 cups
milk and add cornstarch mixture. When
thick, add brown sugar mixture. Cook until thick. Add egg yolks. Pour into baked
pastry shell. Spread meringue over filling;
seal to edge. Bake at 350 degrees for 12 -
15 minutes. Cool before cutting.

CREAM PUFFS

½ Cup Butter or Margarine
1 Cup Boiling Water
1 Cup Sifted All-Purpose Flour
½ Tsp. Salt
4 Eggs, unbeaten

Cream Puff Filling:
1 Cup Granulated Sugar
½ Cup All-Purpose Flour
1/8 Tsp. Salt
3 Eggs, beaten
3 Cups Bottled Milk or ½ Cup Evapor-
    ated Milk and 1½ Cups Water
1 Cup Heavy Cream, whipped
1½ Tsp. Vanilla

Add butter to boiling water and heat until butter melts. Add flour and salt all
at once, stirring vigorously. Cook, stirring until mixture leaves sides of pan.
Add eggs (unbeaten), one at a time,
beating with a spoon after each addition
until smooth. Drop by heaping tbs. (it
helps to have the spoon wet) 2 inches
apart on greased baking sheets, shaping
with a wet spoon into rounds, with point
up in center. Bake in a hot 450 degree
oven for 20 minutes, then at 400 degrees
for 25 minutes. The cream puffs should
be puffed high and golden brown. Cool,
cut a slit in 1 side of each puff and fill
with cream puff filling, or serve dusted
with confectioner's sugar.

Cream Puff Filling: Combine the dry ingredients and eggs in a double boiler.
Stir in the milk gradually. Cook over boiling water for 15 minutes, while stirring.
Let cool. Add vanilla and cream. Fill 20
cream puffs generously.

NO—BAKE CHEESE CAKE

2 Envelopes Knox Unflavored Gelatine
1 Cup Sugar
¼ Tsp. Salt
2 Eggs
1 Cup Milk
1 Tsp. Lemon Rind
3 Cups Cottage Cheese
1 Tsp. Lemon Juice
1 Tsp. Vanilla
2 Tbs. Butter
½ Cup Graham Cracker Crumbs
¼ Tsp. Cinnamon
¼ Tsp. Nutmeg
1 Cup Heavy Cream

1. Mix together 2 envelopes unflavored gelatine, 1 cup sugar and ¼ tsp. salt in a double boiler.

2. Beat together 2 egg yolks and 1 cup milk. Add to gelatin mixture; cook over boiling water, stirring constantly until gelatin is dissolved and mixture thickens, about 10 minutes.

3. Remove from heat; add 1 tsp. grated lemon rind; cool.

4. Stir in 3 cups creamed cottage cheese (24 oz. sieved), 1 tbs. lemon juice and 1 tsp. vanilla. Chill, stirring occasionally, until mixture mounds slightly when dropped from a spoon.

5. While mixture is chilling, make crumb topping as follows: Mix 2 tbs. melted butter with 1 tbs. sugar, ½ cup graham cracker crumbs, ¼ tsp. cinnamon and ¼ tsp. nutmeg. Set aside.

6. Fold in 2 egg whites, stiffly beaten, and 1 cup heavy cream, whipped, into the gelatine mixture.

7. Turn into an 8" springform pan and sprinkle with crumb mixture. Chill until firm.

Note: If desired an 8" or 9" square pan, or a 9" x 5" loaf pan may be used. Line with waxed paper and press crumb mixture into bottom of pan. Turn in gelatine mixture; chill until firm then unmold. For family-size, use ½ gelatine recipe, but full amount of crumb mixture in an 8" layer pan or 9" pie plate.

This is a party-size recipe; makes 10 to 12 servings.

KEY LIME PIE

1 Tbs. Unflavored Gelatin
½ Cup Sugar
¼ Tsp. Salt
4 Egg Yolks
½ Cup Lime Juice
¼ Cup Water
1 Tsp. Grated Lime Peel
Few Drops Green Food Coloring
4 Egg Whites
½ Cup Sugar
1 Cup Cream or Dream Whip
1 - 9 Inch Baked Pastry Shell or Graham
    Cracker Crust

Thoroughly mix gelatin, ½ cup sugar, and salt in a saucepan. Beat together egg yolks, lime juice and water; stir into gelatin mixture. Cook and stir over med. heat just till mixture comes to boiling. Remove from heat; stir in grated peel. Add food coloring sparingly to tint pale green. Chill, stirring occasionally until mixture mounds slightly when dropped from a spoon. Beat egg whites till soft peaks form; gradually add ½ cup sugar, beating to stiff peaks. Fold gelatin mixture into egg whites. Fold in whipped cream. Pile into cooled pastry shell, chill till firm. Spread with more whipped cream; edge with grated pistachio nuts.

BANANA SPLIT DESSERT

½ Cup Oleo or Butter, melted
2 Cups Graham Cracker Crumbs
2 Eggs
2 Cups Powdered Sugar
¾ Cup Oleo, soft
1 Tsp. Vanilla
1 - 20 Oz. Can Crushed Pineapple, well
   drained
4 Medium Bananas, sliced
9 Oz. Dessert Topping
½ Cup Chopped Pecans
4 Oz. Maraschino Cherries

Combine oleo and crumbs and pat into
bottom of a 13 x 9 inch pan. Beat eggs
4 minutes. Add powdered sugar, butter
and vanilla and beat 5 minutes more.
Spread over crumbs and chill. Spread
pineapple and sliced bananas over former.
Then topping, nuts and cherries. Refrigerate 6 hours.

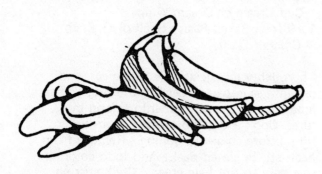

BICENTENNIAL SURPRISE

Red Layer:
1 - 3 Oz. Pkg. Strawberry Jello
1-1/3 Cups Boiling Water
1 - 10 Oz. Pkg. Birds-Eye Quick Thaw
   Strawberries

White Layer:
1 - 3 Oz. Pkg. Lemon Jello
1 Cup Boiling Water
1 Pt. Vanilla Ice Cream

Blue Layer:
1 - 3 Oz. Pkgs. Black Cherry jello
¼ Cup Sugar
½ Cup Cold Water
1½ Cups Fresh or Frozen Blueberries,
   mashed

Red Layer: Dissolve strawberry jello in
1-1/3 cups water; add fruit, stir gently until fruit thaws. Chill until thickened.
Pour into an 8 cup mold or a 9 cup bundt
pan. Chill until set, but not firm.

White Layer: Dissolve 1 pkg. lemon jello
in 1 cup of boiling water. Blend ice cream,
beating until smooth. Chill until thickened.
Spoon over strawberry mixture in mold.
Chill until set, but not firm.

Blue Layer: Dissolve the last pkg. of jello
and the sugar in 1 cup boiling water. Add
½ cup water, chill until thick. Stir in fruit
and spoon over second mixture. Chill overnight. Unmold. Makes 8 cups, about 12
to 14 servings.

TOASTED SNOW SQUARES

1 Envelope Knox Gelatine
4 Tbs. Cold Water
1 Cup Boiling Water
2/3 Cup Sugar
3 Egg Whites, unbeaten
½ Tsp. Vanilla
16 Graham Crackers

Soak gelatine in cold water for 5 minutes.
Add boiling water and stir till dissolved.
Add sugar and egg whites and cool. Cooling is very important. Beat at high speed
until mixture resembles thick cream; turn
into a 9x9x2" pan. Refrigerate until very
firm. Cut in small squares (marshmallow
size) and roll each one in graham cracker
crumbs. Serve 4 or 5 to a sauce dish and
cover with sauce (drizzle sauce).

Butter Sauce:
2 Egg Yolks
1/3 Cup Sugar
½ Cup Melted Butter
1 Tbs. Lemon Rind
2 Tbs. Lemon Juice
1/3 Cup Whipped Cream

Beat egg yolks till thick and lemon colored
Gradually add sugar and continue to beat.
Add butter, lemon rind and juice. Blend
and fold in the cream.

BLUEBERRY YUM YUM

1 Large Pkg. Cream Cheese
¾ Cup Sugar
2 Envelopes Dream Whip (follow
  package instructions)
3 Cups Graham Cracker Crumbs
2 Cans Comstock Pie Filling, any
  desired flavor
½ Cup Butter

Cream together cream cheese and sugar.
Add to already prepared Dream Whip.
Mix melted butter and graham cracker
crumbs. Use half of graham cracker
crumb mixture and pat down on bottom
of a large glass pyrex pan. Use half of
Dream Whip mixture, half of pie filling
(blueberry or whatever desired). Then
layer the other half of Dream Whip, pie
filling and the rest of the graham cracker
crumbs on top.

FRENCH PEAR PUDDING

1 Egg
1 Cup Dairy Sour Cream
1 Tsp. Vanilla
2 Tbs. Sugar
1 Tbs. Flour
1 - 1 Lb. Can Pears, drained
¼ Cup Brown Sugar, firmly packed
1/3 Cup Flour
½ Tsp. Nutmeg
2 Tbs. Butter

Heat oven to 350 degrees. Beat eggs
slightly in small bowl; stir in sour cream
and vanilla. Mix sugar and 1 tbs. flour;
add these ingredients to sour cream mixture; mix well. Quarter pears; arrange
in a shallow baking dish. Top with sour
cream mixture. Bake 15 minutes.

While pudding bakes, combine brown
sugar, 1/3 cup flour and nutmeg in a
second small bowl. Cut in butter with
pastry blender until mixture resembles
corn meal. Sprinkle over pudding and
bake 15 minutes more. Makes 6
servings.

PINEAPPLE CREAM PIE

1 Cup Crushed Pineapple
¾ Cup Sugar
3 Tbs. Cornstarch
¼ Tsp. Salt
3 Egg Yolks, slightly beaten
1 Cup Whole Milk
1 Cup Canned Milk
2 Tbs. Butter or Margarine
1 Baked 9" Pastry Shell

Snow Mountain Meringue:
3 Egg Whites
1 Tsp. Vanilla
3 Tbs. Sugar
3 Tbs. Powdered Sugar

Pie Crust for 9" Pie:
1½ Cups All-purpose Flour
½ Tsp. Salt
½ Cup Crisco Shortening
4 to 5 Tbs. Water
½ Tsp. Baking Powder
1 Tsp. Vanilla Flavoring

Crust: Mix flour, salt, baking powder
together. Add shortening, vanilla and
water. Mix well and roll out on floured
board. Bake until brown in 450 degree
oven.

Filling: In saucepan (double boiler), mix
sugar, cornstarch, salt; gradually stir in
milk. Add pineapple, stirring slowly.
Cook and stir until mixture thickens.
Add butter, stirring until smooth. Pour
into 9" pastry shell that is baked and
cool. Top with Snow Mountain Meringue.

Snow Mountain Meringue: Beat egg
whites until soft peaks form. Add vanilla slowly. Add sugar, beating slowly;
add powdered sugar. Continue to beat
at high speed until high peaks form.

RICE CUSTARD PUDDING

1 Cup Steamed Rice
1½ Cups Scalded Milk
2 Eggs, slightly beaten
3½ Tbs. Sugar, or sweeten to taste
¼ Tsp. Salt
¼ Cup Seeded Raisins
½ Tsp. Vanilla
½ Tbs. Butter

Mix the sugar and the salt with the eggs; mix well. Add vanilla. Add milk slowly to the egg mixture. Add rice and raisins, mixing well. Use ½ tbs. butter to grease a baking dish. Pour mixture into baking dish. Bake as for custard, in 325 degree oven, in a pan of hot water. Do not let the water in the pan boil or the custard mixture will be coarse. Serves 4 people.

CRANBERRY REFRIGERATOR DESSERT

2 Cups Fresh Cranberries, ground
1 Large Banana, diced
½ Cup Sugar
2 Cups Graham Cracker Crumbs
6 Tbs. Butter
½ Cup Butter
1 Cup Sugar
2 Eggs
½ Cup Nuts
1 Cup Whipping Cream

Grind 2 cups (½ lb.) fresh cranberries. Combine with 1 large banana, diced (1 cup), and ½ cup sugar; set aside. Combine 2 cups graham cracker crumbs and 6 tbs. butter, melted. Press half the crumb mixture into bottom of a 9" x 9" x 2" pan. Cream ½ cup butter and 1 cup sugar until light. Add 2 eggs and beat until fluffy. Fold in ½ cup chopped nuts (pecans are best). Spread over the crumb mixture layer. Top with cranberry mixture. Whip 1 cup whipping cream just until soft peaks form; spread over all. Sprinkle with remaining crumbs; press down slightly. Chill 6 hours or overnight. Makes 12 servings. It is fantastic!

BLUEBERRY STRATA PIE

1 Lb. Can Blueberries
1 - 8¾ Oz. Can Crushed Pineapple
1 - 8 Oz. Pkg. Cream Cheese, softened
3 Tbs. Sugar
1 Tbs. Milk
½ Tsp. Vanilla
1 - 9" Baked Pastry Shell, cooled
¼ Cup Sugar
2 Tbs. Cornstarch
¼ Tsp. Salt
1 Tsp. Lemon Juice
½ Cup Whipping Cream, whipped

Drain fruits, reserving syrups. Blend cream cheese and next 3 ingredients. Reserve 2 tbs. pineapple; stir remainder into cheese mixture. Spread over bottom of pastry shell. Chill. Blend ¼ cup sugar, cornstarch and salt. Combine reserved syrups, measure 1½ cups, blend into cornstarch mixture. Cook and stir until thickened. Stir in blueberries and lemon juice; cool. Pour over cheese layer; chill. Top with whipped cream and reserved pineapple.

SHOO FLY PIE

¾ Cup Dark Molasses
¾ Cup Boiling Water
½ Tsp. Baking Soda
1 Tsp. Vanilla

Top Layer:
1½ Cups Flour
¼ Cup Crisco
½ Cup Brown Sugar
1 Unbaked 9" Pie Crust

Dissolve baking soda in boiling water, add molasses and vanilla. Combine brown sugar, flour and crisco to make crumbs. Pour 1/3 of liquid into unbaked pie crust, add 1/3 of crumbs. Repeat until all of the mixture is used; bake at 375 degrees for 35 min. Serve warm with whipped cream.

FROZEN SOUFFLE' WITH STRAWBERRY SAUCE

Souffle:
1 Pt. Vanilla Ice Cream
4 Macaroons, crumbled
4 Tsp. Orange Juice or Grand Marnier
½ Cup Heavy Cream
1 to 2 Tbs. Chopped Toasted Almonds
1 to 2 Tsp. Confectioner's Sugar

Strawberry Sauce:
1 Pt. Fresh Strawberries, washed, hulled and cut in half or
1 - 10 Oz. Pkg. Frozen Sliced Strawberries, thawed
Sugar to taste
4 Tsp. Orange Juice or Grand Marnier

Souffle: Soften ice cream slightly. Stir in the crumbled macaroons and orange juice or grand marnier. Whip the cream until thick and shiny. Fold into ice cream mixture. Spoon into a 4 cup serving dish or mold. Sprinkle surface lightly with almonds and confectioner's sugar. Cover with saran. Freeze until firm, about 4 to 5 hours or overnight. Bring the frozen souffle to the table on a serving dish. To unmold, wrap the serving dish for 4 or 5 seconds in a towel wrung out of very hot water. Loosen the edge with a spatula and turn out onto a cold platter. Makes 4 servings.

Strawberry Sauce: Mix this sauce just before serving. Put berries in a saucepan with sugar added to taste (about ¼ cup sugar for fresh berries, less for frozen berries) & simmer until soft but not mushy. Remove from heat and stir in juice or grand marnier.

PEANUT BUTTER BANANA CRUNCH

4 Cups Sliced Bananas (6 medium)
1 Tbs. Lemon Juice
½ Tsp. Ground Cinnamon
½ Cup Flour
½ Cup Brown Sugar, packed
1/3 Cup Chunk-style Peanut Butter
1 Tbs. Butter or Margarine

Place bananas in 8" round baking dish. Add lemon juice and cinnamon, stirring lightly to coat fruit. In small bowl, combine flour and brown sugar. Cut in peanut butter and margarine until mixture is crumbly. Sprinkle over bananas. Bake in 375 degree oven for 25 minutes. Serves 6.

TEMPTATION TURTLE SUNDAE

Hot Chocolate Sauce:
2 to 4 Squares Unsweetened Chocolate or 6 to 8 Tbs. Cocoa
½ Cup Butter
½ Tsp. Salt
3 Cups Sugar
1 Large Can Evaporated Milk (13 Oz.)

Butterscotch Sauce:
1-1/3 Cups Light Corn Syrup
3 Cups Light Brown Sugar
1/8 Tsp. Salt
½ Cup Butter
1-1/3 Cups Evaporated Milk

Hot Chocolate Sauce: Melt chocolate, butter and salt together in a double boiler. Add sugar, ½ cup at a time while stirring often after each addition. Add the evaporated milk a little at a time & continue stirring until well mixed.

Butterscotch Sauce: Combine all ingredients except the milk. Boil to consistency of heavy syrup. Cool. Add milk. Keep refrigerated. Heat in jar in a pan of hot water.

Serve sauces heated with scattered pecan halves over 2 or 3 scoops of vanilla ice-cream. Top with whipped cream and a red cherry.

SEAFOAM PIE

½ Lb. Marshmallows
½ Cup Milk
½ Cup Walnuts, chopped
½ Cup Fruit, Pineapple, Banana, Nuts
1 Cup Whipping Cream
1/8 Tsp. Salt
8 Graham Crackers
8 Large Ginger Snaps
1 Tsp. Vanilla
¼ Cup Melted Butter

Quarter marshmallows and cook with milk until melted. Stir until smooth. Heat should be low so marshmallow will not stick. Cool. Fold in nuts, fruit, whipped cream, vanilla and salt. Roll crackers and snaps to crumbs. Place a layer in pie pan 8 or 9 inch. Pour ¼ cup melted butter over crumbs and press firmly to pan. Bake 5 minutes at 375 degrees. Pour marshmallow mixture over crush and refrigerate overnight. Variations: Use favorite crumb recipe for shell, or place half crumb mixture in pan 8 or 9 inches. Sprinkle remaining crumbs over top. Serve with whipped cream or plain.

OZARK PUDDING

1 Egg
¾ Cup Sugar
1 Cup Chopped Apple
¾ Cup Walnuts
3 Tbs. Flour
1½ Tsp. Baking Powder
Dash of Salt

Beat egg lightly and add sugar; add the apple and nuts; mix well. Add the flour, baking powder and salt; mix well. Pour into a greased baking dish and bake at 350 degrees for 25 minutes. Serve warm or cold with cream, whipped cream or ice cream.

AVOCADO PIE

2 Egg Yolks
1 Large Avocado
1 - 15½ Oz. Can Borden's Condensed Milk
¼ Cup Lemon Juice
½ Tsp. Salt
1 Tsp. Vanilla

Crust: (See Note below)
26 Graham Crackers, crushed fine
1 Cube Butter
¼ Cup Sugar

Topping:
1 Pint Sour Cream
½ Cup Sugar
1 Tsp. Vanilla

Beat egg yolks until thick; add avocado and vanilla. Continue beating; add milk and other ingredients in given order. Continue beating until smooth. Pour into graham cracker crust. Bake at 325 degrees for 20 minutes.

Let cool; prepare topping. Pour on topping and refrigerate till thoroughly chilled before serving.

This recipe is great for the person who likes cheese cake! It takes practically no time at all to prepare!

Note: You may use recipe from back of Nabisco graham cracker box.

PEPPERMINT DESSERT

½ Lb. Peppermint Candy, crushed
1 Cup Nuts, chopped
20 Marshmallows, cut up
1 Pint Cream, whipped
¾ Lb. Vanilla Wafers, ground

Whip cream; add candy, nuts, marshmallows and mix all together. Put layer of wafer crumbs in bottom of pan; spread a thin layer of cream mixture. Add another layer of crumbs and remainder of cream mixture. Top with crumbs. Set in refrigerator 24 hrs. Top with whipped cream.

PETITS FOURS

Quick Petits Fours Icing:
4½ Oz. Water (½ Cup + 1 Tbs.)
6 Cups Powdered Sugar (measure, then sift)
2 Tbs. Light Corn Syrup
Few Drops of Vanilla
Color, if desired

You will also need a pound cake or heavy sponge cake 1" thick.

In double boiler, blend together & heat over hot water the icing ingredients to lukewarm temperature to pour. Do not overheat or white sugared spots will appear on the finished petits fours. If icing is too thin, add powdered sugar; if too thick, add water. Real fondant may be used the same as this.

If desired, split & fill cake. Trim edges. Ice sheet of cake with buttercream or hot sieved apricot preserves. Let set. Chill the sheet cake. Cut with hot, wet knife into 1" x 1" or ¾" x 1½" pieces as squares, rectangles, diamonds, triangles - these save waste - or use special round, oval, crescent, etc., cutters dipped into hot water to cut petits fours.

Set a cake rack over a pan or over waxed paper to catch dripping icing, which may be rewarmed and reused. Petits fours may be entirely immersed (dipped) and then set on the rack to dry; or set the little cakes on the rack and then pour the fondant over them. Pour icing over a second time if needed.

Set the little cakes, one at a time, on a slotted spoon over the fondant, which is kept warm in the double boiler. Dip the fondant over the cake with a spoon, tilting the slotted spoon to pour the sides. Transfer with small spatula to rack and continue to next one. When the fondant is set, decorate with candied fruits, or use icing bag or parchment cone to pipe lines, flowers, etc., with royal icing, buttercream, chocolate, etc. Trim excess icing off bottom edges. You may dip the base in melted semi-sweet chocolate and let set again. Place each petite four in a paper case.

197 DESSERTS

LEMON TORTE

Crust:
1 Stick Oleo
1 Cup Graham Crackers
1 Cup Soda Crackers

Combine Crust ingredients and press into a 9x13" pan. Bake at 375 degrees for 10 minutes. Cool.

Torte:
1 Small Box Lemon Jello
1 Cup Boiling Water
13 Oz. Can Evaporated Milk, chilled
8 Oz. Pkg. Cream Cheese
1 Cup Sugar
1 Tbs. Vanilla

Mix jello with boiling water and let cool. Cream the cheese and add sugar and vanilla. Add cooled jello and blend thoroughly. Whip the evaporated milk until thick. Combine the whipped milk and the cheese mixture; blend well. Pour onto the prepared crust.

Topping:
Whipped Cream or Dream Whip

Spread the whipped cream on top of the cheese-milk layer. Decorate with small amount of slivers of unsweetened baking chocolate over the cream.

SKY—HIGH LEMON PIE

2¼ Cups Sugar
4 Tbs. Cornstarch
4 Tbs. Flour
¼ Tsp. Salt
2 Cups Water
4 Eggs, separated
1 Tbs. Grated Lemon Rind
6 Tbs. Lemon Juice
2 Tbs. Butter or Margarine
¼ Tsp. Lemon Extract
4 Oz. Can Toasted Coconut Chips
1 Recipe Plain Pastry

Plain Pastry:
Combine 1¼ cups sifted regular flour and 1 tsp. salt in medium size bowl; cut in ½ cup shortening with pastry blender until mixture is crumbly. Sprinkle 3 to 4 tbs. water at a time; mix lightly with a fork just until the pastry holds together and leaves side of bowl clean. Makes enough for 1 - 9" single-crust pie.

Pie:
1. Prepare pastry recipe or use ½ package pie crust mix, following label directions. Roll out to a 12" round on a lightly floured pastry cloth or board; fit into a 9" pie plate. Trim overhang to ½"; turn under flush with rim & flute to make a stand-up edge; prick well all over with a fork.
2. Bake in hot oven, 425 degrees, for 15 minutes or until golden; cool completely on a wire rack.
3. Mix 1¾ cups of the sugar, cornstarch, flour, and salt in a medium-size bowl; set the remaining ½ cup sugar aside for step 7.
4. Heat water to boiling in a medium-size saucepan. Lower heat to medium; slowly add sugar mixture, stirring gently but constantly. Cook, stirring constantly, 5 to 7 minutes or until mixture holds a line when cut with a spoon; remove from heat at once. Do not let mixture boil.
5. Beat egg yolks slightly in bowl; stir in ½ cup hot mixture; quickly stir back into mixture in saucepan. Cook, stirring constantly over medium heat, for 3 minutes or until mixture thickens. Remove from heat.
6. Stir in lemon rind, juice, butter or margarine until blended. Pour into cool pastry shell.
7. Beat egg whites with lemon extract until foamy, white and double in volume in bowl. Sprinkle in ½ cup sugar, 1 tbs. at a time, beating all the time until sugar dissolves and meringue stands in firm peaks.
8. Pile onto hot filling, spreading to edge of crust. This keeps meringue from shrinking. Sprinkle with coconut chips, or place them in a pretty pattern on top.
9. Bake in moderate oven, 350 degrees, 12 minutes, or until peaks of meringue are a golden brown. Cool completely on a wire rack before cutting.

ALMOND CHEESECAKE

Crust:
4 Oz. Butter or Oleo
8 Tbs. Sugar
2 Eggs
2 Cups Flour
1 Tsp. Baking Powder
Pinch of Salt

Cheesecake:
2 Eggs
1 - 12 Oz. Pkg. Cream Cheese
¾ Cup Sugar
1 Tsp. Lemon Juice
1 Tsp. Almond Extract

Sour Cream Topping:
3 Tbs. Sugar
1 Tsp. Lemon Juice
1 Tsp. Almond Extract
1 Cup Sour Cream

Crust: Add ingredients in order, blend it together until it looks like soft dough, press into spring-form 9 inch pan.
Cheesecake: Mix 2 beaten eggs with cream cheese at room temp. Cream together sugar, lemon juice and almond extract. Add to cheese mixture and beat until creamy. Pour into prepared crust. Bake 30 minutes, at 350 degrees. Cool 5 minutes.
Sour Cream Topping: Mix together, spread on baked cheesecake. Bake 10 min. at 350 degrees. When cool, sprinkle with almonds.

TRIFLE (Traditional English)

4 Plain Sponge Cupcakes
Raspberry or Strawberry Jam
6 Macaroons
12 Miniature Macaroons
¼ Pt. Sherry
Grated Rind of ½ Lemon
1 Oz. Almonds, blanched & shredded
½ Pt. Custard, using ½ Pt. Milk, 1 Egg & 1 Egg Yolk
½ Pt. Double Cream (Whipping)
1 Egg White
1 to 2 Oz. Sugar
Glace Cherries and Angelica (for decoration)

Split the sponge cakes into two and spread the lower halves with jam. Replace tops. Arrange in a glass dish and cover with macaroon miniatures. Soak with sherry and sprinkle with lemon rind and almonds. Cover with the custard and leave to cool. Whisk cream, egg white and sugar together until stiff and pile on top of the trifle. Decorate with glace cherries and angelica. Fruit trifles, such as apricot or gooseberry, are made by substituting layers of purees or chopped fruit for jam.

BAKLAVA (Syrian-Armenian Pastry)

2 Lbs. Filo Dough, 1 Lb. for top and 1 Lb. for bottom
1 Lb. Chopped Walnuts or Pistachio Nuts.
3-½ Cups Granulated Sugar
1 Lb. Unsweetened or Unsalted Butter, fresh
1 Cup Water

Mix ½ cup sugar and chopped nuts in bowl. Set aside. Melt butter and skim off top foam until clear. Brush pan bottom with butter 2 or 3 times. Spread first sheet of dough on bottom of pan, fold over excess, brush with butter. Do this for remaining 1 lb. of dough. Spread nut mixture over this. Repeat layering process, (dough, butter) with second pound of dough. Cut into diamond shapes in pan. Bake in 325 degree oven for 1 hour and check. Bake 10 to 15 minutes more or until top is light brown, check often to prevent bottom layer from burning. Use 14 X 28 inch pan.

Syrup or Glaze:

3 Cups Sugar
1 Cup Water

Combine sugar and water over slow heat until it boils and spins a fine thread. Let syrup cool slightly and pour over hot Baklava. Let stand overnight, covered with moist dish towel or cloth.

BREAD PUDDING SOUFFLE

2 Cups Milk
1 Cup Dry Bread Crumbs
4 Egg Whites (beat whites separately)
½ Tsp. Salt
½ Cup Packed Brown Sugar
½ Cup Honey, or enough to taste
2 Tbs. White Sugar
1 Tsp. Vanilla
Grated Rind of 1 Orange
Nuts & Raisins, if desired

In a large mixing bowl add all of the ingredients except the egg whites. Beat the egg whites separately until very stiff but not dry. Add the white sugar 1 tbs. at a time, beating well after each addition. Fold in the egg whites. Pour into a lightly greased oven-wear baking dish. Place in a pan of cold water. Bake 1 hour at 325 degrees or until done. Use a straw or silver knife, when it comes out clean and the pudding is a golden brown is when it is done. Serve warm.

CRUNCH—TOP PEAR PIE

1 Unbaked 9" Pie Shell
6 Sliced, Cored, Large Pears
½ Cup Sugar
1 Orange
½ Cup Brown Sugar, packed
½ Cup Flour
½ Tsp. Cinnamon
¼ Tsp. Ginger
¼ Tsp. Mace
1/3 Cup Butter or Margarine

Preheat oven to 400 degrees. Gently mix pears with sugar, 2 tsp. grated orange rind and 3 tbs. orange juice. Arrange in pie shell. Combine brown sugar, flour and spices; cut in butter until mixture is crumbly. Sprinkle over pears. Bake 45 minutes. Partially cool and serve with whipped cream.

POACHED PEARS IN RED WINE

2 Cups Port or Dry Red Wine
2 Cups Sugar
6 to 8 Med. Pears, ripe and peeled
Few Drops Red Food Coloring
4 Thin Strips Lemon Peel

Put wine & sugar in saucepan. Cover and cook on high until sugar is dissolved. Peel pears, keeping whole and leaving stems on. Peel into saucepan (turn to coat well). Add food coloring and lemon peel. Cover and cook on low heat for 4 to 6 hours, turning occasionally. Serve with wine poured over pears.

RHUBARB CHIFFON PIE

4 Cups Sliced Rhubarb
2 Cups Sugar
2 Tbs. Unflavored Gelatin
4 Tbs. Cold Water
1 Egg, separated
Dash of Salt
1 Cup Whipping Cream
½ Tsp. Almond Extract
9" or 10" Baked Pie Shell

Wash rhubarb; cut off the leaves and root ends. Slice into 1" lengths. Put in glass bowl; sprinkle sugar over, cover and refrigerate, for at least 12 hours. Turn the rhubarb-sugar mixture into a pan; cover and cook over low heat without adding water until rhubarb is tender, about 20 minutes. Soften the gelatin in the water; add the gelatin to the hot rhubarb and stir until well-blended. Beat the egg yolk and stir some of the hot rhubarb mixture into the yolk. Gradually add the yolk to the remaining hot mixture; stir in the salt and cook 2 minutes. Remove the mixture from the heat and cool until it begins to set. Stir in the almond extract. Beat egg white until stiff but not dry. Carefully fold into the rhubarb mixture. Whip the cream and fold in mixture gently. Pour the filling into the baked pie shell and chill it until it is set, about 3 hours.

CHOCOLATE - GLAZED CREAM PUFF RING

A. Cream Puffs:
 1 Cup Boiling Water
 ½ Cup Shortening
 1 Cup Flour
 4 Eggs
B. Chocolate Whipped Cream:
 1 Cup Whipping Cream
 1/3 Cup Powdered Sugar
 ¼ Cup Cocoa, unsweetened
C. Chocolate Glaze:
 1 Sq. Unsweetened Chocolate
 1 Tbs. Butter
 2 Tbs. Water
 ½ Cup Powdered Sugar

Optional: Chopped Walnuts & 6 Maraschino Cherries

A. 1. Prepare cream puff recipe.
 2. Draw a seven inch circle on greased cookie sheet.
 3. Spoon cream puff paste into six puffs, almost touching, within the seven inch circle.

Cream Puffs:
 1. Preheat oven to 400 degrees.
 2. Add the boiling water to the shortening in a small pot. Bring to a boil, slowly.
 3. Stir in flour and mix well.
 4. Remove from heat, let cool slightly.
 5. Add eggs, one at a time, beating each one for sometime before the next.
 6. Spoon onto seven inch circle as described above.
 7. Bake at 400 degrees for 10 minutes, then reduce heat to 350 degrees and continue to bake for another 20 minutes.
 8. After baking, cool for 30 minutes.

B. 1. After cream puff ring has cooled, split the whole ring in half very carefully.
 2. Fill with chocolate whipped cream as follows, (saving 6 tbs.)

Chocolate Whipped Cream:
 1. Combine all ingredients.
 2. Beat with mixer until very fluffy.

C. 1. Put top half of ring back on filled cream puffs.
 2. Top with chocolate glaze as follows:

Chocolate Glaze:
 1. Combine first 3 ingredients in double boiler. Heat until melted.
 2. Remove from heat. Mix in powdered sugar. Spoon over puffs.
 3. Top with chocolate whipped cream that you set aside from before.
 4. Optional: Sprinkle with nuts and one cherry for each puff. Serves 6.

PINEAPPLE TORTE

1 Large Can Crushed Pineapple
½ Lb. Vanilla Wafers
½ Cup Butter
1½ Cups Powdered Sugar
2 Eggs
1 Pint Whipping Cream

Drain pineapple. Butter a pyrex pan. Roll vanilla wafers to make crumbs. Put wafers into pan and sides, saving a few for the top.

Cream together butter and powdered sugar. Add well beaten eggs. Pour this mixture over crumbs. Spread crushed pineapple on top of creamed mixture. Whip cream and spread on top of pineapple. Sprinkle well with vanilla wafer crumbs. Let stand overnight in refrigerator.

BREAD PUDDING

3 Cups Milk
2 Cups Soft Bread Cubes
1½ Tbs. Butter
¾ Cup Sugar
1/3 Tsp. Salt
1 Cup Raisins (if desired)
3 Beaten Eggs

In a pot, heat milk, blend in bread cubes and butter. In a bowl, combine sugar, salt, raisins and eggs. Blend milk mixture into egg mixture. Pour into a greased baking dish. Place in a pan of hot water. Bake in a 350 degree oven for 1 hour or until set. Serves 6.

CHOCOLATE ÉCLAIRS

Eclair Cream Puff Paste:
¾ Cup Water
1/3 Cup Butter or Margarine
1/8 Tsp. Salt
¾ Cup All-purpose Flour, sifted
3 Large Eggs

Custard Filling:
2½ Cups Milk
5 Egg Yolks
½ Cup Sugar
2/3 Cup Sifted Flour
2 Tbs. Butter or Margarine
1 Tbs. Vanilla

Chocolate Glaze:
1 Cup (6 Oz.) Chocolate Chips
2 Tbs. Butter or Margarine
2 Tbs. Corn Syrup
3 Tbs. Milk

Éclair Cream Puff Paste:
1. Preheat oven to 400 degrees. In medium saucepan, bring water, butter and salt to boiling. Remove from heat. Quickly add flour all at once. With wooden spoon, beat constantly over low heat until mixture forms ball and leaves side of pan. Remove from heat.
2. Using mixer or wooden spoon, beat in the eggs, one at a time, beating well after each addition. Continue beating till dough is shiny and breaks away in strands. It will be stiff and hold its shape.
3. Drop dough by rounded tablespoonsful 3" apart on ungreased cookie sheet. Shape into 4" x 1½" strips, rounding ends. Bake 35 to 40 minutes, or till puffed and golden. Cool on rack.

Filling:
1. Heat milk in large saucepan till bubbles appear around edge.
2. Beat egg yolks and sugar in large bowl with mixer until pale yellow and thick. Beat in flour and mix well. Gradually beat in hot milk; pour all back into saucepan and cook, stirring constantly, over medium-high heat till boiling and thick. Lower heat; continue cooking 2 to 3 minutes over low heat, stirring constantly. Remove from heat.

3. Stir in butter and vanilla. Place a piece of wax paper over it to prevent skin from forming. Chill 2 hours.

To Fill: Cut off tops of Éclairs crosswise. Remove some soft dough inside. Fill each éclair and replace top.

Glaze: Melt chocolate with butter. Blend in corn syrup and milk. Cool 5 minutes. Spoon over eclairs. Serve at once or refrigerate. Makes about 10 to 12.

SWEET POTATO PIE

2 Medium Sweet Potatoes (about 1 cup when mashed)
½ Cup Brown Sugar
¼ Tsp. Salt
¼ Tsp. Cinnamon
¼ Tsp. Allspice
½ Tsp. Vanilla
2 Eggs
1 Small Can Evaporated Milk

To prepare sweet potatoes, set oven at 350 degrees and bake potatoes for 1½ to 2 hours until very soft. Cut off about 1 inch of the pointed end of the potato to eliminate some of the stringy fiber. Then peel and slice in about ½ inch slices, crosswise of the grain. Mash with a potato masher before adding the other ingredients. When mixing the custard with an electric mixer, the rest of the little pieces of stringy fiber will cling to the beaters, therefore, getting rid of almost all of them. This is important for a smooth, creamy texture. To mashed sweet potatoes, add all ingredients except evaporated milk. Beat well with an electric mixer. Reduce speed of mixer and gradually add the milk. Pour into an unbaked pie crust and bake in a 350 degree oven for about 35 to 40 minutes, or until the custard appears set.

MOCK MINCE MEAT

1 Cup Bread Crumbs
1 Cup Grated Carrots
1 Cup Grated Yams or Sweet Potatoes
1 Cup Raisins
1 Egg
1 Lump Margarine, size of egg yolk
1 Cup Grated Apples
1 Cup Applesauce
½ Tsp. Soda
1 Tsp. Salt
1 Tsp. Cinnamon
¼ Tsp. Ginger
1 Tsp. Ground Cloves
½ Cup Brown Sugar

Mix all grated items together in a sauce-pan and cover with water. Cook until soft, 20 min. or so. Drain off water and mix all other ingredients. Use in tarts or pie as you would real mincemeat.

CRANBERRY CHEESECAKE

4 - 8 Oz. Pkgs. Cream Cheese
3 Cups Ocean Spray Cranberry Juice
    Cocktail
2 Cups Sugar
1 Cup Whole Fresh Cranberries
3 Envelopes Knox Gelatine
2 Cups Whipping Cream
1 Graham Cracker Crust, (line bottom of 1
    large or 2 small spring-form pans)

Graham Cracker Crust:
1 Wax Paper Pkg. of Graham Crackers
1 Cube Butter or Margarine
¼ Cup Sugar

Melt butter, roll graham crackers into fine crumbs, add sugar to crumbs, stir in melted butter. Press into spring-form pan and bake 3 or 4 minutes at 450 degrees till crisp.

Stir 2 cups cranberry juice and 2 envelopes gelatine over low heat till dissolved. Whip cream, set aside. Soften cream cheese in lg. bowl, add 1 cup sugar and mix well. Squeeze 3 tsp. lemon juice, add to gelatine. Fold in whipped cream. Pour into spring-form pan and refrigerate for 4 hours.

Topping:
Cook Together:
1 Cup Cranberries
1 Cup Sugar
¾ Cup Cranberry Juice, till berries burst
Add:
1 Envelope Gelatine
¼ Cup Cranberry Juice, and dissolve
Refrigerate about 30 minutes before topping cake. Spoon on.

SOUR CREAM APPLE SQUARES

2 Cups Flour
2 Cups Firmly-packed Brown Sugar
½ Cup Butter or Margarine, softened
1 Cup Chopped Nuts
1 to 2 Tsp. Cinnamon
1 Tsp. Soda
½ Tsp. Salt
1 Cup Dairy Sour Cream
1 Tsp. Vanilla
1 Egg
2 Cups (2 medium) Peeled, Finely-
    chopped Apples

Preheat oven to 350 degrees. Lightly spoon flour into measuring cup; level off. In large bowl, combine first three ingredients; blend at low speed until crumbly. Stir in nuts. Press 2¾ cups crumb mixture into ungreased 13" x 9" pan.

To remaining mixture, add cinnamon, soda, salt, sour cream, vanilla and egg; blend well. Stir in apples; spoon evenly over base. Bake 25 to 35 minutes, until toothpick inserted in center comes out clean. Cut into squares; serve with whipped cream, if desired. Makes 12 to 15 squares.

SPICY PUMPKIN PIE

1½ Cups Canned Pumpkin
¾ Cup Sugar
½ Tsp. Salt
1¼ Tsp. Cinnamon
1 Tsp. Ginger
½ Tsp. Nutmeg
½ Tsp. Cloves
2 Slightly Beaten Eggs
1 13-Oz. Can Evaporated Milk
1 9-Inch Unbaked Pastry Shell

Thoroughly combine pumpkin, sugar, salt and spices. Blend in eggs & evaporated milk. Pour into unbaked pastry shell (have edges crimped high as filling is generous). Bake in hot oven 400° for 50 minutes or until knife inserted halfway between center and outside comes out clean. Cool.

COCONUT CREAM PIE

¼ Cup Flour
½ Cup Sugar
¼ Tsp. Salt
1½ Cups Scalded Milk
3 Eggs, separated
2 Tbs. Butter
½ Tsp. Vanilla
6 Tbs. Sugar
1 Baked 8" Pie Shell
½ Cup Moist, Shredded Coconut

Mix flour, ½ cup sugar and salt in top of double boiler; add scalded milk and stir well. Cook over direct heat until thick & smooth, stirring constantly. Beat egg yolks well, stir in a little hot mixture and pour back into double boiler; cook over boiling water 2 minutes, stirring constantly. Remove from heat and add butter and vanilla. Beat egg whites until light; gradually beat in 6 tbs. sugar. Fold ½ cup moist, shredded coconut into cooled filling; fold 1/3 meringue into cooled pie filling also.

Pour filling into cooled pie shell and spread remaining meringue over filling, so as to touch the edges of the crust all around. Place in a moderate oven, 350 degrees, and bake 12 to 15 minutes or until golden brown. Remove to a cake rack to cool before cutting. Makes 5 to 6 servings.

GERMAN CHOCOLATE PIE

2 Oz. German Chocolate
2 Tbs. Butter
1/3 Cup Flour
¾ Cup Sugar
¼ Tsp. Salt
2½ Cups Milk, scalded
3 Eggs, separated
¾ Tsp. Vanilla
1 Baked 8" Pie Shell
1/3 Cup Sugar
Chopped Nuts or Coconut

Melt chocolate and butter over low heat or hot water in top of double boiler. Mix flour, sugar and salt and stir into chocolate mixture. Slowly add milk, stirring constantly. Cook until mixture is fully thickened, about 15 minutes. Beat egg yolks well; stir in a little of the chocolate mixture, then pour into rest of hot mixture and cook about 2 minutes longer, stirring constantly.

Remove from heat; cool partially and stir in vanilla. Pour into pie shell. Beat egg whites until stiff, then slowly beat in the 1/3 cup sugar. Swirl meringue over pie filling. Sprinkle with nuts or coconut and brown in moderate oven, 350 degrees, about 15 minutes. This can be used as a pudding by following pie directions, then folding the meringue into finished pie filling. Put into custard cups and chill.

GLORIFIED RICE

1 Cup Raw Rice
2 Cups Cold Water
1 Tsp. Salt
1 Tbs. Butter
1/3 Cup Granulated Sugar
1 - 8¾ Oz. Can Pineapple Tidbits
1 Red Apple, coarsely chopped
1½ Cups Miniature Marshmallows
1 Cup Heavy Whipping Cream
½ Tsp. Vanilla Extract

In a saucepan, combine 1 cup raw regular rice, cold water, salt and butter. Turn heat to high. When water just begins to boil, stir once with fork, reset heat to medium-low, cover and simmer for 18 to 20 minutes, or until all liquid is absorbed. Measure 2 cups warm rice and combine with sugar. Add pineapple, apple and marshmallows. Let stand 1 hour. Whip cream with vanilla and fold into rice mixture. Serves 6.

STRAWBERRY PIZZA

Crust:
1 Cup Flour
¼ Cup Powdered Sugar
½ Cup Margarine

Topping:
1 - 8 Oz. Pkg. Philadelphia Cream
   Cheese
½ Cup Granulated Sugar

1 Can Pie Filling (Comstock), strawberry,
   cherry, or whatever flavor you desire

Crust: Blend ingredients together; spread onto 12" pizza pan. Bake at 325 degrees until light brown, approximately 12 min. Cool.

Topping: Blend together cream cheese & sugar. Spread over cooled pie crust.

Top with pie filling. Chill for 1 hour and serve.

RHUBARB DESSERT

6 Cups Rhubarb
2 Cups Sugar
1 Pkg. Strawberry Jello
2 Cups Small Marshmallows
½ Cup Sugar
¼ Cup Crisco
1 Egg
½ Cup Milk
¾ Cup Flour
1/8 Tsp. Salt
1½ Tsp. Baking Powder

Cut rhubarb in small pieces, put in bottom of a 9 x 13 inch pan. Put sugar over rhubarb. Sprinkle the jello over the sugar and add the marshmallows. Cream the sugar and Crisco; add egg and beat well. Add the milk, flour and baking powder; drizzle this over top. Bake 50 minutes at 300 degrees.

CHOCOLATE MOUSSE

4 Cups Milk
1 Cup Sugar
3 Egg Yolks
1½ Oz. Cornstarch
1½ Lbs. Hershey's Semi sweet Baking
   Chocolate
1½ Pints Heavy Cream, whipped

Melt chocolate in double boiler over hot water. Mix sugar in saucepan with most of milk; place over low flame and bring to boil. Separately beat egg yolks with the balance of the milk, gradually adding the cornstarch. Combine this mixture with the boiling milk and sugar. Continue to cook over low flame, stirring constantly, until mixture reaches the consistency of custard. Add melted chocolate. Remove from heat and let cool.

When mixture is thoroughly cool, fold in whipped cream. Spoon into cups or parfait glasses and chill. Makes twelve servings. It is delicious.

COOKIES

ITALIAN NEOPOLITAN COOKIES

Dark Mixture:
3 Cups Flour
½ Tsp. Cinnamon
½ Tsp. Cloves
¼ Tsp. Salt
1 Tsp. Soda
1 Cup Chopped Nuts
1 Cup Shortening
1½ Cups Brown Sugar
2 Eggs

Light Mixture:
2 Cups Flour
¼ Tsp. Soda
½ Tsp. Salt
¾ Cup Seedless Raisins
12 Candied Cherries
½ Cup Shortening
¾ Cup Sugar
1 Egg
1 Tsp. Vanilla
½ Tsp. Almond Extract
2 Tbs. Water

Dark Mixture: Sift flour, measure; sift again with spices, soda and salt. Cream shortening; add sugar, beat until fluffy. Beat in eggs, slowly add flour and nuts.

Light Mixture: Sift and measure flour, add soda and salt. Chop raisins fine, cherries in fourths. Cream shortening and sugar until fluffy. Beat in egg, vanilla, almond extract and water. Mix in flour, add raisins and cherries. Pack half of the dark mixture into a 9 x 5 x 3 inch pan. Pack light on top of the dark mixture. Cover with dark. Chill overnight. Bake for 10 to 12 minutes at 400 deg. Slice ¼" thick. Makes 6 to 8 dozen. Very good for the holidays.

NORWEGIAN COCONUT PUFFS

1 Cups Butter
1 Cup Crisco
2½ Cups Sugar
2-2/3 Cups Flour (reg. or cake)
1 Cup Coconut
2 Tsp. Ammonium Carbonate (powdered)

Sift flour with ammonium carbonate, add to creamed sugar and shortening mixture. Add coconut. Roll into balls, size of a walnut. Bake at 350 degrees about 10 minutes until very light tan. Makes a large batter. Note: Ammonium carbonate can be purchased at the drug store. If in lumps, crush to powder.

WAFFLE BROWNIES

1 Cup Sugar
½ Cup Shortening
2 Eggs
½ Cup Milk
1½ Cups Flour
1 Tsp. Baking Powder
2 Squares Chocolate, melted
½ Tsp. Salt
1 Tsp. Vanilla
1 Cup Finely-cut Walnuts, optional

Cream shortening and sugar. Add eggs and beat well. Add chocolate and mix well. Mix and sift dry ingredients. Add to creamed mixture alternately with the milk.

Note: The waffle iron should not be as hot as for plain waffles. Drop about 1 tbs. batter into each section of the iron and bake 2 to 3 minutes. Remove and roll in powdered sugar while warm. Serve with whipped cream or ice cream, in layers or single.

Note: Use three sections, cream in between each section and on top. Place a cherry on the top cream.

CRESCENT NUT ROLL COOKIES

Cookie Mixture:
6 Cups Flour
2½ Cups Shortening
6 Egg Yolks
1 Cup Milk
1 - 6 Oz. Yeast Cake
1 Tsp. Salt

Nut Mixture:
1 Cup Chopped Nuts
½ Cup Sugar
½ Tsp. Cinnamon
1 Tsp. Soft Margarine or Butter

Cookie Mixture: Cut shortening into flour and salt. Dissolve yeast in milk. Add egg yolks and yeast mixture to flour; knead until smooth. Let rise in refrigerator overnight.

Cut dough in four equal parts. Sprinkle sugar on rolling board. Roll dough very thin. One section at a time, cut into 3" squares. Put 1 tsp. nut mixture on each square. Roll squares from corner to corner. Roll in sugar and place on cookie sheet; bend to form crescent. Bake at 350 degrees about 15 minutes, or until golden brown.

BROWNIES FOR A CROWD

½ Cup Butter or Margarine
1 Cup Sugar
4 Eggs
1 Tsp. Vanilla
1 Lb. Can Chocolate Syrup (1½ Cups)
1 Cup Sifted Flour
½ Tsp. Baking Powder
¼ Tsp. Salt
½ Cup Chopped Nuts
6 Tbs. Butter or Margarine
6 Tbs. Milk
1 Cup Sugar
½ Cup Semisweet Chocolate Pieces
1 Tsp. Vanilla

Cream together ½ cup butter and 1 cup sugar until light and fluffy. Beat in eggs and 1 tsp. vanilla; blend well. Stir in chocolate syrup. Sift together flour, bak-ing powder and salt; pour into well-greased 15½" x 10½" x 1" jelly roll pan. Bake in 350 degree oven 22 minutes, or until done. Cool in pan on rack.

Combine 6 tbs. butter, milk and 1 cup of sugar in saucepan. Bring to a boil; boil 30 seconds. Remove from heat. Add choco-late pieces and 1 tsp. vanilla; stir until mix-ture thickens slightly. Spread over brownies; cut into 2½" x 1½" bars. Makes 60. Very rich and very good!

FINNISH STAR COOKIES

Pastry:
1½ Cups Flour
1 Cup Butter (no margarine)
½ Cup Water

Apricot Filling:
1 Cup Sugar
½ Lb. Dried Apricots
1 Cup Water

or

Date Filling:
1 Cup Sugar
½ Lb. Dates
1 Cup Water

Dough: Mix ½ of butter with flour as for pie crust. Add water slowly until well mixed. Chill and then roll to a ½ inch thickness. Spread half of the dough with some of the remaining butter. Fold over and roll again. Repeat until all the butter is used, then roll out thin. Cut 2½ inch squares. Cut each cor-ner of the squares. Put a spoonfull of filling in the center and fold opposite corners togeth-er to the center of the filling. Brush with cream and sprinkle with sugar. Bake in a 375 degree oven for a few minutes until pastry is golden brown.

Fillings: Cut fruit up fine. Put all of the in-gredients in a saucepan. Boil slowly until it is very thick. Let cool. Dough and filling is best when chilled overnight. Fillings may be frozen. The dough may be kept in the re-frigerator for several weeks if it is sealed.

APPLE—OATMEAL SQUARES

Crumb Mixture:
1 Cup Sifted Flour
½ Cup Brown Sugar
½ Tsp. Salt
½ Tsp. Cinnamon
1 Cup Quick Oatmeal
½ Tsp. Soda
1/3 Cup Vegetable Oil

Filling:
2½ Cups Thinly Sliced Apples
½ Cup Brown Sugar
2 Tbs. Butter
Few Shakes Cinnamon

Sift together salt, flour, cinnamon and soda.
In separate bowl, mix sugar and oatmeal; add
to flour mixture. Stir, then add oil and mix
thoroughly. If the flour mixture is not completely moistened, add a little more oil.

Spread ½ mixture in a 9" or 10" square pan;
pan down evenly. Cover with apples;
with cinnamon, dot with butter, and spread
sugar evenly over all. Cover with remaining
crumb mixture. Bake at 350 degrees for 40
to 45 minutes, or until apples are soft when
speared with a fork. Cut in squares when
cooled, or can be served spooned while warm.
Delicious either way. Whipped cream sprinkled with a tiny bit of cinnamon adds a
gourmet touch.

This recipe is great since one can change its
flavor so easily by adding one or more of
the following:

½ Cup Nuts, chopped
½ Cup Crushed Pineapple
½ Cup Chopped Dates
½ Cup Stewed Rhubarb
½ Cup Raisins (plumped in water or juice)

Mix with apples before spreading on crumb
mixture.

GUM DROP COOKIES

2/3 Cup Shortening
¾ Cup Brown Sugar
¾ Cup White Sugar
2 Eggs
1 Cup Oatmeal
2/3 Cup Nuts
1 Cup Coconut
1 Cup Gum Drops (no black ones)
1 Tsp. Salt
1 Tsp. Soda
1 Tsp. Baking Powder
1 Tsp. Vanilla
2 Cups Flour

Cream shortening, sugars, eggs and vanilla.
Add all dry ingredients one at a time. Drop
dough by teaspoonfuls on greased cookie
sheet. Bake 12 minutes at 375 degrees.
Makes 3 dozen.

POLISH DELIGHTS

2 Cups Unsifted Flour
1 Tbs. Melted Butter
2 Tbs. Sugar
1 Egg, lightly beaten
1 Tbs. Vinegar
½ Cup Sour Cream

Sift flour, combine following ingredients:
butter, sugar and egg; stir. Add vinegar
and sour cream to form a biscuit dough
consistency, solid enough to roll. Divide
into 4 parts; roll one piece very thin on
a floured board. Keep the rest of dough
covered. Cut into strips about ¾ inch
or 1 inch wide and 3 inches long. Cut
a short lengthwise slit in the center of
each strip. Pass one end of the strip
through the slit and repeat. Fry in deep
fat until golden brown, drain on paper
towel and sprinkle with confectioner's
sugar. Serve at Tea Time or as a dessert
with coffee.

POLYNESIAN BARS (Sugar-free)

1½ Cups Flour, whole wheat &
  unbleached
1½ Cups Rolled Oats
½ Tsp. Salt
¾ Cup Soft Margarine
½ Cup Unsweetened Coconut (optional)
½ Cup Chopped Nuts (optional)

Filling:
4 Cups Chopped Dates
1 No. 2 Can Unsweetened, Crushed
  Pineapple
¾ Cup Water
1 Tsp. Vanilla

Combine filling ingredients and cook until
thick and smooth.

Combine remaining ingredients to form a
crumb mixture; pat half of crumb mixture
into greased pyrex pan, 9" x 12", firmly.
Add date mixture and then remaining topping. Pat down well. Bake at 350 degrees
for 30 minutes, or until light brown. Let
cool and cut into squares. For those trying
to avoid fats, substitute ¾ cup margarine
with 1 cup orange juice.

For a more tangy-sweet flavor, use two cups
chopped, dried apricots and 2 cups of
chopped dates instead of 4 cups chopped
dates in the filling.

SNICKERDOODLES (Cookies)

1 Cup Shortening
1¼ Cups Sugar
2 Eggs
2¾ Cups Flour
2 Tsp. Cream of Tartar
1 Tsp. Soda
½ Tsp. Salt
1 Tsp. Vanilla
3 Tbs. Sugar
1½ Tbs. Cinnamon

Cream shortening, 1¼ cups sugar and
eggs together. Add flour, cream of tartar,
soda, and salt; add vanilla. Form dough
into small balls, walnut size. Roll in cinnamon and sugar mixture. Bake at 450
degrees for 8 minutes.

TOASTED OATMEAL COOKIES

¾ Cup Butter or Margarine
2½ Cups Raw Oats
½ Cup Flour
1 Tsp. Cinnamon
½ Tsp. Salt
½ Tsp. Baking Soda
1 Cup Brown Sugar
1 Egg
1 Tsp. Vanilla

Makes about 4 dozen.

1. Preheat oven to 375 degrees F.

2. In medium skillet, over medium heat,
heat butter until lightly browned. Add
oats; stir constantly until golden, about
5 minutes. Remove from heat and cool.

3. Meanwhile, sift flour with cinnamon,
salt and soda; set aside.

4. In large bowl, combine sugar, egg and
vanilla. Beat until light with wooden
spoon or mixer at medium speed.

5. Stir in oats and flour mixtures and
mix well.

6. Drop by teaspoon onto ungreased
cookie sheet.

7. Bake 10 to 12 minutes; cool and enjoy.
A truly delicious oatmeal cookie.

Note: You may add ½ cup of coconut,
nuts, raisins or whatever sounds good.
May combine 2 or three of the foregoing
together.

PEANUT BUTTER BARS

1¼ Cups Graham Cracker Crumbs
¼ Cup Sugar
½ Tsp. Cinnamon
½ Tsp. Nutmeg
½ Cup Peanut Butter
1/3 Cup Light Corn Syrup
1 - 6 Oz. Pkg. Chocolate Chips

Combine graham cracker crumbs, sugar, cinnamon and nutmeg. Add peanut butter and light corn syrup. Mix thoroughly. Press into an 8" square cake pan. Melt chocolate chips over low heat, then spread over mixture in pan. Chill at least 1 hour. Cut into 2" pieces.

CHINESE CHEWS

First Layer:
½ Cup Butter of Margarine
1 Cup Flour
2 Tbs. White Sugar
1 Tsp. Salt

Mix ingredients and press into bottom of greased 8" square baking pan. Bake in a 375 degree oven for 12 to 15 minutes; remove from oven.

Second Layer:
1½ Cups Brown Sugar
2 Beaten Eggs
½ of 3½ Oz. Can Coconut
½ Cup Chopped Pecans
1 Tsp. Vanilla
2 Tbs. Flour

Mix ingredients and spread evenly over baked layer. It is not necessary to wait until first layer has cooled. Return to a 375 degree oven & bake 25 to 30 min. longer. Cool and cut into squares.

POLISH FINGER COOKIES

1½ Lbs. Ground Nuts
1/3 Cup Sugar
2 Lbs. All-purpose Flour
1 Lb. Butter
5 Egg Yolks
¾ Cup + 1 Tbs. Milk
1 Tbs. Sugar
1 Pkg. Dry Yeast
1 Box Powdered Sugar (to roll dough in)

Mix sugar and nuts together for filling. Mix flour and butter together; add egg yolks and mix in well. Boil milk and sugar. Add yeast. Let this rest and bubble, then mix into flour mixture until dough feels like pie dough. Dough does not raise.

Measure half teaspoon of dough; roll out on powdered sugared board. Put ½ tsp. nut mixture on and roll up lengthwise. Place on greased cookie sheets, ¼" apart. Bake at 350 degrees for 12 to 15 minutes. Sprinkle with powdered sugar. May be frozen.

SOFT MOLASSES COOKIES

2¼ Cups Flour
2 Tsp. Baking Powder
1 Tsp. Soda
¼ Tsp. Salt
1 Tsp. Cinnamon
1 Tsp. Ginger
½ Cup Nucoa
½ Cup Sugar
1 Large Egg
½ Cup Molasses
½ Cup Water

Cream nucoa, sugar, egg, molasses; beat well and add flour, dry ingredients and spices alternately with water just until smooth. Drop by tbs. 2" apart. Bake at 375 degrees for 10 minutes.

SUNFLOWER CHEWS

¼ Cup Cooking Oil
1 Cup Brown Sugar, well packed
1 Egg
1 Tsp. Vanilla
½ Cup Shelled Sunflower Seeds
1 Cup Flour
¼ Tsp. Salt
1 Tsp. Baking Powder

Beat oil, sugar, egg and vanilla thoroughly. Add sunflower seeds; mix well. Add dry ingredients. Dough will be thick to spread in an 8" x 8" pan that has been well oiled. Bake at 350 degrees for about 20 minutes, until mixture pulls away slightly from pan. Cool on rack for 5 minutes; cut into squares. Yield: 25 chews.

APPLESAUCE BARS

1 Cup Oil
1 Cup Sugar
1 Tsp. Soda
1 Cup Warm Applesauce
2 Cups Sifted Flour
½ Tsp. Salt
½ Tsp. Cinnamon
¾ Cup Raisins
1 Cup Chopped Nuts
1 Tsp. Vanilla

Mix oil with sugar. Add soda to applesauce and combine with sugar mixture. Add flour, salt, cinnamon, raisins, nuts and vanilla and blend thoroughly. Turn into greased and floured 8" x 12" x 2" pan. Bake at 350 degrees for 30 minutes. Cut into bars while slightly warm. Yield: 25 bars. Very good with any type of icing.

Icing:
2 Tbs. Butter
2 Tbs. Milk, heated
1½ Cups Powdered Sugar
½ Tsp. Vanilla
¼ Tsp. Lemon Flavoring

Mix all ingredients together well and spread on warm bars before cutting them.

WHOLE WHEAT and PEANUT BUTTER COOKIES

½ Cup Butter or Margarine
½ Cup Peanut Butter
1 Cup Brown Sugar
1 Egg
1 Tsp. Vanilla Extract
1¼ Cups Whole Wheat Flour
1½ Tsp. Baking Soda
¼ Tsp. Salt
½ Cup Toasted Wheat Germ

Thoroughly cream butter, peanut butter, sugar, egg and vanilla. Mix together the dry ingredients, except wheat germ. Blend into creamed mixture. Shape into 1" balls; roll in wheat germ. Place 2" apart on ungreased cookie sheet. Flatten in crisscross pattern with fork tines. Bake at 375 degrees for 10 to 12 minutes. Cool slightly. Remove from pan. Makes about 4 dozen.

CHOCOLATE DROP COOKIES

1 Cup Brown Sugar
½ Cup Shortening
2 Eggs
4 Tbs. Water
4 Tbs. Ground Chocolate
1 Tsp. Vanilla
2-1/3 Cups Flour
2½ Tsp. Baking Powder
¼ Tsp. Salt

Cream the shortening and sugar. Add eggs one at a time and stir. Add water & vanilla. Sift and measure flour. Sift again with chocolate, baking powder and salt. Add to the first mixture, stirring well.

Drop by teaspoon on greased baking sheet, 3" apart. Bake at 325 degrees for 10 min. Good iced and sprinkled with chopped nuts.

WALNUT SLICES

Crust:
¾ Square of Butter
1 Cup Flour

Filling:
2 Eggs, well beaten
½ Tsp. Salt
1½ Cups Brown Sugar
½ Cup Coconut
¼ Tsp. Baking Powder
2 Tbs. Flour
1 Cup Nuts
1 Tsp. Vanilla

Frosting:
2 Tbs. Butter
2 Tbs. Orange Juice
1½ Cups Powdered Sugar
Nuts

Crust: Mix ¾ square butter and 1 cup of flour together and press down in a 9" square pan. Bake slowly, 300 degrees, for 35 minutes, until delicate brown.

Filling: Combine ingredients and pour over crust; bake in slow oven again for 25 minutes. Let cool, then frost and sprinkle with nuts. Cut in squares.

SPRITZ COOKIES

1 Cup Shortening
¾ Cup Sugar
1 Egg
2¼ Cups Sifted All-purpose Flour
½ Tsp. Baking Powder
Dash of Salt
1 Tsp. Almond Extract

1. Cream shortening; add sugar gradually.
2. Add egg, unbeaten; beat well.
3. Add sifted dry ingredients and extract.
4. Fill cookie press. Form cookies on an ungreased Mirro aluminum cookie sheet & bake at 375 degrees for 10-12 minutes.

SWEDISH GINGER COOKIES

1 Cup Butter or Margarine
1½ Cups Sugar
1 Egg
1½ Tbs. Grated Orange Peel
2 Tbs. Dark Corn Syrup
1 Tbs. Water
3¼ Cups Sifted All-purpose Flour
2 Tsp. Soda
2 Tsp. Cinnamon
1 Tsp. Ginger
½ Tsp. Cloves

Cream butter and sugar; add egg and beat till light and fluffy. Add orange peel, corn syrup; add water and mix well. Sift dry ingredients together; stir into creamed mixture. Chill thoroughly. On lightly floured surface, roll to ¼" thickness. Cut with floured cookie cutters. Place on ungreased cookie sheet; bake at 375 degrees for 8 to 10 min. Cool on rack.

POTATO CHIP COOKIES

1 Cup Margarine
1 Cup Brown Sugar
1 Cup White Sugar
2 Eggs
1 Tsp. Vanilla
2½ Cups Flour
1 Tsp. Baking Soda
2 Cups Coarsely Crushed Potato Chips
1 - 6 Oz. Pkg. Butterscotch Morsels

Cream together margarine and sugars, add eggs and vanilla and beat well. Sift flour and soda together and add to creamed mixture, then add crushed potato chips and butterscotch morsels. Drop by tsp. on a greased cookie sheet about 2" apart. Bake at 375 degrees for 10 min. Makes approx. 3 doz. cookies.

APRICOT CHIP COOKIES

¼ Cup Butter or Margarine
¼ Cup Crisco
1/3 Cup Granulated Sugar
1/3 Cup Packed Brown Sugar
1 Egg
½ Tsp. Vanilla
1 Cup Flour
½ Tsp. Salt
½ Tsp. Baking Soda
2/3 Cup Finely Chopped Dried Apricots
½ Cup Chocolate Chips
¼ Cup Chopped Nuts

Cream together butter, shortening and sugars. Beat in egg and vanilla. Gradually stir flour, salt and soda into creamed mixture until smooth. Stir in apricots, chips and nuts.

Drop by teaspoonfuls onto greased baking sheets; bake at 375 degrees for 10 minutes, or until lightly browned. Cool on wire rack.

APPLE OATMEAL COOKIES

½ Cup Margarine, softened
½ Cup Honey
1 Egg
1 Tsp. Vanilla
¾ Cup Unsifted Stone Ground Flour
½ Tsp. Soda
¾ Tsp. Cinnamon
1 Medium-size Apple, chopped fine
1½ Cups Uncooked Oats

Beat margarine, honey, egg and vanilla together. Mix flour, soda and cinnamon together. Add to egg mixture. Add apple; mix well. Stir in oats. Drop by spoonfuls onto greased cookie sheet. Bake at 375 degrees for 10 minutes. Makes approximately 4 dozen cookies. You can add other fruits such as bananas, cherries, etc. These are low-sodium, no-sugar cookies.

OATMEAL CARMELITAS

50 Light Caramels (14 Oz. Pkg.)
½ Cup Evaporated Milk
2 Cups Flour
2 Cups Quick-cooking Rolled Oats
1½ Cups Packed Brown Sugar
1 Tsp. Soda
½ Tsp. Salt
1 Cup Butter, melted
2 Cups Chocolate Chips
1 Cup Chopped Walnuts

Melt caramels with milk in saucepan. Cool slightly. Combine remaining ingredients, except for chocolate chips and nuts.

Press half of oatmeal mixture into a greased 13" x 9" pyrex dish. Bake at 350 degrees for 10 minutes. Remove from oven; sprinkle crust with chocolate chips and nuts and drizzle caramel mixture over all. Cover with remaining oatmeal crumbs; press slightly. Bake for 15 to 20 minutes longer.

POLKA DATERS

1¼ Cups Sugar
1 Cup Soft Butter
2 Eggs
1 Tsp. Vanilla
1¾ Cups Sifted Flour
½ Tsp. Soda
¼ Tsp. Salt
1¼ Cups Chopped Dates
1 Cup Hot Water
1 Cup Nuts, chopped
6 Oz. Pkg. Chocolate Chips

Mix dates with hot water (chop dates first); set aside. Beat until creamy the soft butter, sugar, eggs and vanilla. Stir in date mixture. Sift in flour, salt and soda; add ½ cup nuts and ½ cup chocolate chips; mix well.

Spread dough in a greased 15" x 10" x 1" pan. Top with ½ cup chopped nuts and ½ cup chocolate chips. Bake 35 minutes at 350 degrees or until done. Cool and cut into bars.

ROCKY ROAD FUDGE BARS

BAR:
½ Cup Butter
1 Square Chocolate
1 Cup Sugar
1 Cup Flour
½ to 1 Cup Chopped Nuts
1 Tsp. Baking Powder
1 Tsp. Vanilla
2 Eggs

FILLING:
6 Oz. Cream Cheese
½ Cup Sugar
2 Tbs. Flour
¼ Cup Butter
1 Egg
½ Tsp. Vanilla
¼ Cup Chopped Nuts
6 Oz. Chocolate Chips

FROSTING:
2 Cups Miniature Marshmallows
¼ Cup Butter
1 Square Unsweetened Chocolate
2 Oz. Cream Cheese
¼ Cup Milk
1 Lb. Powdered Sugar
1 Tsp. Vanilla

Preheat oven to 350 degrees, grease and flour 9x13" pan. In large sauce pan over low heat, melt butter and chocolate. Add remaining bar ingredients. Mix well and spread in prepared pan. In small bowl combine cream cheese with next 5 ingredients. Blend until smooth and fluffy, stir in nuts. Spread over chocolate mixture. Sprinkle with chocolate pieces and bake 25 - 30 min. or until toothpick inserted in center comes out clean. Sprinkle with marshmallows and bake 2 min. longer. In large saucepan over low heat, melt butter, chocolate and cream cheese, milk. Stir in powdered sugar and vanilla until smooth, immediately pour over marshmallows and stir together.

CHERRY NUT NUGGETS

1 Cup Shortening
1 - 3 Oz. Pkg. Cream Cheese, softened
1 Cup Sugar
1 Egg
1 Tsp. Almond Extract
2½ Cups Sifted Flour
½ Tsp. Salt
¼ Tsp. Soda
1 Cup Finely-chopped Nuts
Maraschino Cherries, halved

Cream shortening, cream cheese, sugar, egg and almond extract. Sift dry ingredients together and stir into creamed mixture. Chill dough 1 hour. Form into 1" balls. Roll balls in chopped nuts and place on ungreased cookie sheet. Press a cherry half into the center of each ball. Bake at 350 degrees for 10 to 15 min. Makes 4½ dozen.

BLOND BROWNIES

1 Cup Oleo or Butter
2¼ Cups (1 Lb.) Brown Sugar
4 Eggs
2½ Cups Flour, sifted
2½ Tsp. Baking Powder
1 Tsp. Salt
1 Tsp. Vanilla
1 - 12 Oz. Pkg. Semi-sweet Chocolate
  Morsels
1 Cup Chopped Walnuts

Melt shortening in a large (6 quart) saucepan. Add brown sugar. Blend well. Remove from heat and cool 10 minutes. Add eggs, one at a time, beating well after each addition. Add dry ingredients. Mix well. Add vanilla; mix well. Add chocolate chips and walnuts; mix well.

Spread in greased pan (15" x 10" jelly roll pan) and bake at 350 degrees for 30 to 35 minutes. Cool and cut into squares. Makes fifty.

PASTRY SQUARES

¼ Lb. Margarine
½ Cup White Sugar
2 Egg Yolks
1 Tsp. Vanilla
1½ Cups Sifted Flour
1 Pinch of Salt
1 Pinch of Baking Soda
12 Oz. Jar Raspberry Preserves
1½ Cups Chopped Nuts
2 Egg Whites, beaten

Cream margarine and sugar; add egg yolks and beat until light and fluffy. Add vanilla and dry ingredients. Mix well. Pat into a greased 9" x 12" pan. Spread with preserves; sprinkle with half the nuts. Spread with the beaten egg whites; sprinkle with nuts again. Bake 25 to 30 minutes at 350 degrees; cut when cool.

APRICOT BUTTER BARS

1 Cup Sifted All-purpose Flour
¼ Cup Sugar
½ Cup Butter
1/3 Cup Sifted All-purpose Flour
½ Tsp. Baking Powder
½ Tsp. Salt
2 Eggs
1 Tsp. Vanilla Extract
1 Cup Firmly-packed Brown Sugar
1½ Cups Dried Apricots, snipped
1 Cup Walnuts, medium chopped

First Part: Mix 1 cup flour with the sugar in a bowl. Cut in the butter with pastry blender or two knives until the particles formed are the size of small peas. Turn into a 9" x 9" x 2" baking pan and press firmly into an even layer over bottom of pan. Bake at 350 degrees F for 25 min.

Second Part: Meanwhile, blend remaining 1/3 cup flour, the baking powder and salt; set aside. Beat eggs with extract; add the brown sugar gradually, beating until thick. Stir in the flour mixture, apricots & nuts.

Remove pan from oven; turn the apricot mixture onto the layer in pan and spread evenly. Return to the oven and continue baking 30 minutes. Cool completely on wire rack before cutting into bars. Makes about 2 dozen cookies.

CASHEW COOKIES

1½ Cups Margarine
2 Cups Brown Sugar
1 Cup White Sugar
3 Eggs
1½ Tsp. Vanilla
6 Cups Flour
2¼ Tsp. Baking Powder
2½ Tsp. Baking Soda
¾ Tsp. Salt
1½ Tsp. Cinnamon
¾ Tsp. Nutmeg
½ Pint Sour Cream
1½ Cups Cashews, in large chunks

Frosting:
1 Cube Butter
1¼ Pkgs. Powdered Sugar
2 Tsp. Vanilla
Milk

Cookies: Mix in order given and drop a rounded tbs. for each cookie as these are large cookies. Bake at 375 degrees to 400 degrees for 15 to 20 minutes. Frost while still warm.

For frosting, brown butter; beat in powdered sugar & vanilla and enough milk to make the right consistency for frosting cookies.

OLD-FASHIONED MOLASSES COOKIES

¾ Cup Oil
¼ Cup Brer Rabbit Molasses (green label)
1 Cup Sugar
1 Egg
2 Cups Flour
2 Tsp. Soda
½ Tsp. Ginger
½ Tsp. Cloves
1 Tsp. Cinnamon
½ Tsp. Salt

1. Mix oil, molasses, egg and sugar.

2. Sift all dry ingredients into above mixture. Blend thoroughly.

3. Chill dough at least 1 hour.

4. Roll into balls (about 1 tsp.) and then roll each ball in granulated sugar.

5. Bake on greased cookie sheets for about 10 minutes; do not overbake. Use a 375 degree oven.

LEMON BARS

1 Cup Margarine
2 Cups Flour
½ Tsp. Salt
½ Cup Powdered Sugar
4 Eggs
6 Tbs. Lemon Juice
6 Tbs. Flour
1½ Cups Sugar

Mix margarine, flour, salt and the powdered sugar and pat into cookie sheet with sides. Bake at 350 degrees for 20 minutes. Mix eggs, lemon juice, flour and sugar; beat. Pour on top at once. Bake 25 minutes more. Sprinkle with powdered sugar.

PINEAPPLE KRINGLE

1 Cup Milk, scalded
¼ Cup Sugar
1 Egg White
1 Yeast Cake
½ to 1 Cup Shortening
Flavoring (optional)
1 Tsp. Salt
3 Egg Yolks
4 Cups Flour

Filling:
8 Tbs. Cornstarch
2-No. 2 Cans Crushed Pineapple
1 Cup Sugar

Scald milk, dissolve the yeast in about ¼ cup of the milk that is just warm, use the milk for this before it gets too warm. In the scalded milk, dissolve shortening, butter is best. Add salt and sugar and stir to dissolve, cool to lukewarm and then add 3 egg yolks and 1 egg white plus ½ tsp. vanilla. Mix and blend well; add the yeast mixture. Add 2¾ cups of the flour and beat with a wooden spoon, or you can use a mixer, until dough is smooth. Add the rest of the flour gradually, as much of it as you need so the dough will not stick to the rolling pin. Cover dough and let rise until doubled in bulk. Divide dough in half and roll out each half, a little larger than a cookie sheet, place on cookie sheets and fill with the following filling, then turn edges of remaining extending dough over filling. Bake in a 375 degree oven for about 21½ minutes or until brown. Before baking, beat 2 remaining egg whites to foam consistency and spread over cakes.

Filling: Drain pineapple and set aside. In saucepan, put cornstarch and sugar, stir to blend. Gradually add the juice from the pineapple; cook and stir over medium heat until clear, cool. Add pineapple and spread on top of dough. Spread out as far as pan will allow, then turn edges of dough over the filling.

SUGAR PLUMS

1 Cup Butter or Margarine
½ Cup Sifted Confectioner's Sugar
1½ Tsp. Vanilla
2 Cups Sifted Enriched Flour
½ Tsp. Salt
1 Cup Oats (quick, uncooked)
30 Candied Cherries

Beat butter until creamy; add sugar gradually, beating until smooth. Add vanilla. Sift together flour & salt; add to butter mixture, mixing thoroughly. Stir in rolled oats, mixing until blended. Dough will be quite stiff. Shape into balls around candied cherries. Bake on ungreased cookie sheets in 325 degree oven for about 15 minutes. Start them on a rack in about the middle of the oven, then shift them to a higher rack until they are delicately browned. Ovens vary, therefore the baking depends much on the oven. While still warm, roll in sifted confectioner's sugar. Sometimes it seems necessary to roll the cookies twice in the sugar.

RAISIN BARS

Filling:
2½ Cups Raisins
1½ Cups Sugar
1½ Cups Water
3 Heaping Tbs. Flour

Crumb Mixture:
1½ Cups Brown Sugar
1 Cup Margarine
2 Cups Quick Oats
1 Tsp. Baking Soda
1½ Cups Flour

Boil the raisins, sugar, water & flour until thick. In a separate bowl, mix the brown sugar, margarine, quick oatmeal, baking soda and flour until crumbly. Pat ½ of the crumb mixture into a greased 9x13" pan. Spread raisin filling over this and sprinkle remaining crumb mixture on top. Pat down lightly so it will hold together. Bake 30 minutes at 325 degrees. Keeps well in refrigerator.

GOBS

Filling:
1 Cup Crisco Shortening
1 Cup Sugar
6 Tbs. Flour
2/3 Cup Warm Milk
1 Tsp. Vanilla
¼ Tsp. Salt

Cakes:
½ Cup Crisco Shortening
2 Cups Sugar
2 Eggs
1 Cup Milk
2 Tsp. Baking Soda
4 Cups Flour
½ Tsp. Baking Powder
¾ Cup Cocoa
1 Tsp. Vanilla
½ Cup Boiling Water

Prepare filling as directed and refrigerate. Beat Crisco and sugar until light & fluffy. Add flour to warm milk; shake to make a paste and add to Crisco-sugar mixture. Beat until creamy and thick; add vanilla & salt. Beat at high speed. Refrigerate.

Cakes: Sift all dry ingredients; set aside. Blend all other ingredients (except boiling water). Mix together with dry ingredients; add water. Drop by teaspoonful on cookie sheet; flatten and shape into circle with back of wet spoon. Bake 5 to 7 minutes at 350 degrees. Put filling between 2 cakes and wrap individually to store. Makes 3½ to 4 dozen.

Helpful hints: Do not try to double this recipe! It is impossible. Also, wet spoon before flattening each cake.

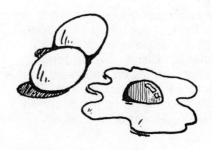

DANISH SPICE COOKIES

2 Cups Sifted All-purpose Flour
½ Tsp. Salt
¼ Tsp. Baking Soda
1 Tsp. Ground Cinnamon
¼ Tsp. Ground Cloves
½ Cup Butter or Margarine
1 Cup Firmly Packed Brown Sugar
½ Cup Dairy Sour Cream
1 Egg
1 Tsp. Vanilla
1 Cup Chopped Dates
½ Cup Finely Chopped Walnuts

1. Sift flour, salt, baking soda, cinnamon and cloves onto waxed paper.
2. Melt the butter in a medium-size sauce-pan over moderate heat. Remove from heat; add sugar and beat with a wooden spoon until combined. Beat sour cream, egg and vanilla until smooth.
3. Stir in flour mixture until thoroughly combined. Stir in dates and nuts. Spread evenly into greased 15x10x1" pan.
4. Bake in a moderate oven, 350 degrees, for 30 minutes or until top springs back when lightly touched with fingertip. Cool in pan on wire rack. Cut into diamond shapes. Makes about 4 dozen.

PINEAPPLE-RAISIN COOKIES

1/3 Cup Shortening
2/3 Cup Brown Sugar
1/3 Cup Granulated Sugar
1 Egg
1 Cup Drained Crushed Pineapple
2½ Cups Sifted All-Purpose Flour
1 Tsp. Salt
½ Tsp. Baking Powder
1 Cup Raisins

Cream shortening and sugars together until fluffy. Beat in egg. Add pineapple (drained as dry as possible) and sifted dry ingredients. Blend. Stir in raisins. Drop by teaspoonfuls on ungreased cookie sheets. Bake in preheated oven at 375° for 15 minutes or until lightly browned. Cool on racks. Makes 3 to 4 dozen cookies.

BANANA NUT BARS

2/3 Cup Shortening (or use 1/3 shortening and 1/3 oleo)
1½ Cups Sugar
2 Egg Yolks
¾ Cup Very-ripe Mashed Banana (2 medium)
1½ Cups Flour
1 Tsp. Baking Soda
¼ Tsp. Salt
4 Tbs. Sour Cream
½ Tsp. Vanilla
½ Cup Nuts (optional)
2 Egg Whites, stiffly beaten

Cream together shortening and sugar; add egg yolks and mashed banana. Sift together the flour, baking soda and salt and add alternately with sour cream and vanilla. Add nuts. Fold in stiffly-beaten egg whites last. Pour into greased 9" x 13" pan. Bake in slow oven, 325 degrees, for 45 minutes. Cut into squares while warm and roll in powdered sugar.

TEATIME TASSIES

1 - 3 Oz. Pkg. Cream Cheese
½ Cup Butter or Margarine
1 Cup Flour, sifted
¾ Cup Brown Sugar
1 Tbs. Butter or Margarine, softened
1 Tsp. Vanilla
2/3 Cup Coarsely Broken Pecans
1 Egg

Cheese Pastry: Let cream cheese and ½ cup butter soften at room temperature. Blend cream cheese, butter and flour; chill slightly (about 1 hour). Shape into 2 dozen 1" balls. Place in tiny ungreased 1¾" muffin cups. Press dough on bottom and sides of cups.

Pecan Filling: Beat together egg, sugar, 1 tbs. butter, vanilla and salt just till smooth. Divide half of the pecans among pastry-lined cups. Add egg mixture and top with remaining pecans. Bake in a slow oven, 325 degrees, for 25 minutes or till filling is set. Cool; remove from pans.

WALNUT CHEWIES

1 Egg
1 Cup Brown Sugar
½ Tsp. Vanilla
½ Cup Flour, sifted
½ Tsp. Salt
1/8 Tsp. Soda
1 Cup Cut-up Walnuts

Beat egg till foamy; beat in sugar and vanilla. Stir in flour, salt and soda. Add walnuts. Spread in well-greased 8" square pan; bake till crust has dull finish (25 to 30 minutes). Bake at 325 degrees. Cut into squares while still warm - about 16 2" squares. Ready to eat within minutes! These are quick cookies; best right out of oven. Super for last-minute company & overnight get-togethers!

APPLESAUCE—RAISIN COOKIES

½ Cup Butter or Shortening
1 Egg
1 Cup Sugar
1¾ Cups Sifted Flour
½ Tsp. Baking Powder
1 Tsp. Soda
½ Tsp. Salt
1 Tsp. Cinnamon
½ Tsp. Cloves
½ Tsp. Nutmeg
½ Cup Raisins
1 Cup Quick-cooking Oats
1 Cup Applesauce
½ Cup Finely-chopped Nuts, if desired

Preheat oven to 375 degrees. Cream butter & sugar; stir in egg. Sift together dry ingredients (except oats); add to creamed mixture alternately with applesauce and oats. Beat well. Stir in raisins and nuts. Drop by tsp. onto greased cookie sheet. Bake at 375 degrees about 15 minutes. Keeps well - not too sweet and kids love them.

PUMPKIN COOKIES

1 Cup Shortening
1 Cup White Sugar
1 Egg
1 Cup Pumpkin
2 Tsp. Vanilla
2 Cups Flour
1 Tsp. Baking Powder
1 Tsp. Soda
2 Tsp. Cinnamon
½ Tsp. Salt
½ Cup Nuts

Frosting:
1 Cup Brown Sugar
3 Tbs. Margarine
4 Tbs. Milk
1 Cup Powdered Sugar
1 Tsp. Vanilla

Cookies: Combine and mix first ten ingredients. Add nuts. Bake at 350 degrees for 10 to 12 minutes.

Frosting: Stir & boil first 3 ingredients for 2 minutes. Cool. Add last two ingredients. Frost cookies.

PUDDING COOKIES

¾ Cup Bisquick
1 Pkg. Instant Pudding Mix
¼ Cup Vegetable Oil
1 Egg

Heat oven to 350 degrees. Mix ingredients together until dough forms a ball. Shape into balls, using 1 tsp. dough for each. Flatten to about 2" size with hand. Bake 8 minutes. Makes 2½ to 3 dozen cookies.

EASY FILLED DROP COOKIES

2 Cups Dates, cut small
¾ Cup Sugar
¾ Cup Water
½ Cup Chopped Nuts
1 Cup Soft Shortening
2 Cups Brown Sugar
2 Eggs
½ Cup Water, Sour Milk or
  Buttermilk
1 Tsp. Vanilla
3½ Cups Sifted Flour
1 Tsp. Salt
1 Tsp. Soda
1 Tsp. Cinnamon

Filling: Cook until thick, stirring constantly, the dates, ¾ cup sugar and ¾ cup water. Add ½ cup chopped nuts; cool.

Heat oven to 400 degrees. Mix well 1 cup soft shortening, 2 cups brown sugar and 2 eggs. Stir in ½ cup water, or sour milk, or buttermilk. Add 1 tsp. vanilla. Sift together and stir in the sifted flour, salt, soda and cinnamon. Drop by teaspoon onto ungreased baking sheet. Place ½ tsp. of date filling on dough; cover with ½ tsp. dough. Bake 10 to 12 minutes.

JUMBO RAISIN COOKIES

1 Cup Water
2 Cups Raisins
1 Cup Shortening
2 Cups Sugar
3 Eggs
4 Cups Flour
1 Tsp. Soda
1 Tsp. Salt
1½ Tsp. Cinnamon
¼ Tsp. Nutmeg
½ Tsp. Allspice
1 Cup Walnuts
1 Tsp. Vanilla

Boil raisins and water for 5 minutes. Cream shortening, sugar and eggs; beat well. Add vanilla and raisins, with water liquid. Add chopped walnuts to mixture. Sift flour, soda, salt and spices and add to mixture. Drop by spoonfuls onto oiled cookie sheets. Bake at 375 degrees for 12 to 15 minutes.

CHOCO—MALLOW COOKIES

½ Cup Shortening
1 Cup Granulated Sugar
1 Egg
1 Tsp. Vanilla
¼ Cup Milk
1-2/3 Cups Flour
½ Cup Cocoa
½ Tsp. Salt
½ Tsp. Baking Soda
18 Marshmallows, cut in half

Cocoa Icing:
2 Cups Powdered Sugar
5 Tbs. Cocoa
1/8 Tsp. Salt
3 Tbs. Soft Butter or Margarine
4-5 Tbs. Canned Milk or Light
  Cream

Cream shortening and sugar; beat in egg, vanilla and milk. Sift dry ingredients together, then stir into creamed mixture. Drop on greased cookie sheet and bake at 375 degrees for 8 minutes. Remove from oven and press ½ marshmallow, cut side down, into each cookie. Return to oven for 2 minutes, then remove and cool. Frost with cocoa icing.

Cocoa Icing: Combine all ingredients with enough milk to make a spreading consistency. Beat until smooth.

CINNAMON SUGAR PLUMS

Combine and beat thoroughly:

1 Cup Shortening
1 Cup Firmly-packed Brown Sugar
1 Cup Granulated Sugar
½ Tsp. Salt
½ Tsp. Vanilla
2 Tsp. Cinnamon
¾ Tsp. Nutmeg
¼ Tsp. Allspice
2 Eggs, unbeaten
1 Tbs. Cold Coffee

Add:
¾ Cup Chopped Raisins
½ Cup Chopped Nuts

Sift together:
1¼ Cups Sifted All-purpose Flour
1 Tsp. Soda

Add dry ingredients to above mixture, then add:
3 Cups Rolled Oats

Mix well. Shape the dough into 1¼" balls and roll each ball in a mixture of ¼ cup sugar and ¼ tsp. cinnamon. Place balls on greased baking sheets. Bake in moderate oven, 350 degrees, for 12 to 15 minutes.

Cool about 2 minutes before removing from baking sheets. Makes 5½ dozen spicy crisp cookies.

WALNUT REFRIGERATOR COOKIES

1 Cup Butter or Margarine
2 Cups Light Brown Sugar
2 Eggs
3 Cups Flour
3½ Tsp. Baking Powder
½ Tsp. Salt
1 Cup Chopped Walnuts
1 Tsp. Vanilla

Cream the butter or margarine with sugar until light and fluffy. Add the well-beaten eggs and beat until light again. Sift the flour with baking powder and salt and work this thoroughly into creamed mixture. Stir in the walnuts and vanilla. Shape into long rolls 1¼" in diameter; wrap in waxed paper and chill at least overnight. The longer you chill the dough, the better the cookies.

Slice the dough as thin as possible and bake on greased baking sheet in moderately hot oven, 375 degrees, for about 8 minutes. Yield: 8 to 10 dozen cookies.

MOLASSES FRUIT BARS

¾ Cup Shortening
1 Cup Brown Sugar, firmly packed
¼ Cup Egg (1 Large)
¼ Cup Light or Dark Molasses

2 Cups Flour
2 Tsp. Baking Soda
½ Tsp. Salt
1 Tsp. Powdered Cinnamon
1 Tsp. Powdered Ginger
½ Tsp. Powdered Cloves

1 Cup Seedless Raisins

Cream together first 4 ingredients with electric mixer or by hand until ingredients are well blended.

Add dry ingredients and mix. It will be a moderately stiff dough. Add raisins. With floured fingers, press dough evenly into 2 - 9" x 9" x 1" greased and floured pans, or a 13" x 9" cookie sheet may be used.

Brush entire surface of dough with water and sprinkle with granulated sugar. Bake at 350 degrees for 15 to 20 minutes. Cool and cut into bars and store in airtight container. These cookies keep well and develop flavor and a chewy texture upon storage.

Makes approximately 3 dozen bars.

NO—BAKE COOKIES

2 Cups Sugar
½ Cup Milk
1 Stick Butter or Margarine
4 Tbs. Cocoa
½ Cup Crunchy Peanut Butter
3 Cups Quick-cooking Oats
1 Tsp. Vanilla

Boil sugar, milk, margarine and cocoa for 1½ minutes. Start timing after mixture reaches a full, rolling boil. Remove from heat; add peanut butter, oats, vanilla. Beat until blended, then drop on waxed paper by teaspoonfuls. Coconut or chopped dates may be added if desired. These may be placed in the refrigerator to hasten hardening.

NUTRITIONAL CAROB BALLS

1 Cup Carob
1 Cup Non-instant Powdered Milk
1 Cup Crunchy Peanut Butter (natural - no sugar)
1 Cup Raw Honey
¼ Cup Sunflower Seeds *
¼ Cup Coconut *
¼ Cup Raisins*

*Use all or any part of these ingredients.

Mix carob and powdered milk; add peanut butter and honey. Mix with a spoon. If too thick, add a little milk. Next add whatever you like of last three ingredients - all or part. When mixed, use a spoon and roll into balls. Keep in refrigerator. Ready to eat when you are.

SAND TARTS

½ Lb. Butter
½ Cup Confectioner's Sugar
2 Cups Sifted Cake Flour
1 Tsp. Vanilla
1 Cup Chopped Pecans or Walnuts

Cream butter. Add sugar, flour, vanilla and nuts. Mix well. Roll into crescents or balls and bake on ungreased cookie sheet in 350 degree oven for 20 minutes. Cool. Roll in powdered sugar.

EASY OATMEAL COOKIES

2 Cups Oatmeal
1 Cup Flour
1 Cup Sugar
1 Tbs. Syrup
6 Oz. Margarine
1 Tsp. Baking Soda

Melt margarine and syrup in pan over low heat. When melted, mix in baking soda. While margarine is melting, mix oatmeal, sugar and flour in bowl. When margarine mixture is cooled a bit, add to oatmeal mixture and mix well. Pour into jelly-roll type of pan and pat down with fingers, making sure all of mixture is patted down really well. Bake in 350 degree oven for 15 minutes.

Cut into squares as soon as taken out of oven. When cool, recut the squares and the cookies are ready to eat. This cookie is crumbly, but the crumbs are also good to eat as topping on fruit desserts.

OIL & CORN FLAKE COOKIES

2 Eggs, beaten
1 Cup White Sugar
1 Cup Brown Sugar
1 Cup Salad Oil
1 Cube Oleo
2 Cups Flour
1 Tsp. Soda
½ Tsp. Baking Powder
2 Cups Quick Cooking Oats
1 Cup Chopped Nuts
1 Cup Coconut
2 Cups Corn Flakes
1 Tsp. Vanilla
½ Tsp. Lemon Extract
1 Tsp. Salt

Add sugars to eggs and beat well; add oil and oleo, flour, soda and baking powder; continue stirring. Add vanilla, lemon and salt. Add oats, nuts and coconut and stir. Lastly add corn flakes. Drop by teaspoonfuls on greased cookie sheet and bake at 400 degrees for 10 minutes. If you prefer a harder and crisper cookie, add ½ cup more oats and ¾ cup more corn flakes. More nuts or coconut may be added if desired.

SOUR CREAM COOKIES

½ Cup Shortening
1 Cup Sugar
1 Beaten Egg
2 Cups Flour
½ Tsp. Baking Soda
½ Tsp. Nutmeg
½ Tsp. Cinnamon
¼ Tsp. Salt
½ Cup Sour Cream
½ Cup Raisins or Chopped Nuts,
  or a combination of both

Cream shortening and sugar. Add egg and continue creaming until light. Sift flour, baking soda, nutmeg, cinnamon and salt together. Add alternately with cream to creamed mixture. Stir in raisins or nuts. Drop by teaspoon onto greased baking sheets. Bake in moderately hot oven, 375 degrees, 10 to 12 minutes. Yield: 36 cookies.

CHOCOLATE COOKIES

½ Cup Softened Butter or Margarine
1 Cup Sugar
1 Egg
1½ Tsp. Vanilla
1½ Cups Flour
½ Cup Unsweetened Cocoa (carob
  powder can be substituted)
¼ Tsp. Salt
¼ Tsp. Baking Powder
¼ Tsp. Soda

Bake at 350 degrees. In large bowl, cream butter, sugar, egg and vanilla until light & fluffy. Add flour (no need to sift flour). Add remaining ingredients and mix well. The dough will be stiff. Shape dough into 1" balls and place 2" apart on an ungreased cookie sheet. Bake 10 to 12 minutes at 350 degrees. For a variation, add finely-chopped nuts or raisins, or chocolate chips, to the dough before baking.

COFFEE COOKIES

1 Cup Brown Sugar
1½ Cups Flour
1 Egg
½ Cup Shortening
½ Tsp. Cinnamon
½ Tsp. Allspice
½ Tsp. Baking Powder
½ Tsp. Soda
½ Tsp. Salt
½ Cup Raisins
½ Cup Nuts
½ Cup Hot Coffee

Icing:
1 Cup Powdered Sugar
1 Tbs. Hot Water
1 Tbs. Butter
1 Tsp. Vanilla

Mix sugar, egg, shortening; put in dry ingredients and hot coffee alternately. Add raisins and nuts. Bake in a 9" x 13" x 1" pan for 20 minutes in 350 degree oven. Ice while hot.

DELICIOUS COCONUT BARS

1 Stick Butter or Oleo
1 Cup Graham Crackers, crushed
1 Can Angel Flake Coconut
1 - 6 Oz. Pkg. Chocolate Chips
1 - 6 Oz. Pkg. Butterscotch Chips
1 Cup Nuts, pecans or walnuts
1 Can Eagle Brand Sweetened
   Condensed Milk

Melt butter in an 11½" x 8½" pan and
add each ingredient as a layer in order
given. Do not mix or stir. Bake at 350
degrees about 30 minutes. If pyrex dish
is used, bake at 325 degrees. Cool; cut
into bars.

BUTTER BALL CHIFFONS

1 Cup Butter or Margarine, softened
¼ Cup Confectioner's Sugar
1 - 3 Oz. Pkg. Lemon Instant Pudding
   Mix
2 Tsp. Water
1 Tsp. Vanilla
2 Cups All-purpose Flour
1 Cup Chopped Nuts
3 Bars (¾ Oz. each) Chocolate Coated
   English Toffee Bars, crushed
Confectioner's Sugar (optional)

Combine all ingredients except the nuts and
toffee in a large mixing bowl. Mix at low
speed until dough forms. Add nuts and
crushed candy and blend well. Shape into
1" balls. Place on ungreased cookie sheets.
Bake at 325 degrees for 12 to 15 minutes,
or until light golden brown. Cool cookies
completely before removing from the
cookie sheet. Dust with confectioner's
sugar, if desired.

BROWN SUGAR COOKIES

1 Cup Shortening (we use margarine)
2 Cups Light Brown Sugar
2 Eggs
2 Tbs. Water
2 Tsp. Vanilla
3½ Cups Flour
2 Tsp. Baking Powder
1 Tsp. Soda
1 Tsp. Salt
1 Tsp. Cinnamon

Cream shortening and sugar; add eggs,
water and vanilla. Sift dry ingredients
and mix well. We take little balls of
dough and mash down with fork; or
you can roll it out and cut with cookie
cutter. Bake 8 to 10 minutes at 350 degrees. A vanilla or caramel icing is good;
or sprinkle brown sugar or coconut on
top before baking. Easy to make and
a favorite with children.

GINGER SNAPS

1 Cup Butter
1 Cup Sugar
1 Cup Molasses
1 Tbs. Ginger
1 Tbs. Soda
Hot Water
Flour

Mix the butter, sugar and molasses thoroughly. Dissolve soda in a little hot water
Add to mixture. Add as much flour as
can be stirred in with spoon. Pinch off
pieces size of a walnut. Drop on greased
cookie pan and bake at 350 degrees;
leave room for cookies to spread.

SALADS

HEAVENLY FRUIT CUP

2 Cups Sliced White Grapes
2 Cups Miniature Marshmallows
1 Can or 2½ Cups Pineapple Tidbits, drained
2 Cups Sliced Bananas
1 Lemon, squeezed and poured over bananas
1 Cup Nuts

Prepare fruit dressing and chill before adding to salad. Mix 2 tbs. cornstarch and ½ cup sugar in double boiler. Stir in 2 cups pineapple juice and cook over hot water until smooth and thick, stirring constantly from 8 to 10 minutes. Add small amount to 2 beaten eggs, then add to mixture and cook 2 minutes more, stirring carefully. Cool. Whip 1 cup of whipping cream. Chill whipping cream and fruit dressing and pour over fruit mixture. Note: bananas and whipping cream may be added just before serving.

MORRO BAY SALAD

1 Large Cucumber
4 Hard Boiled Eggs, refrigerated
1 Lb. Small Cooked Shrimp*
1 Lb. Cooked Clean Crab Meat*
1 Lobster Tail*, cooked and chilled
1 Head Iceberg Lettuce
1 Pkg. Good Seasons "Italian" Dressing
1 Medium White Spanish Onion

*Note: Use fresh or fresh-frozen fish.

Prepare Italian dressing as directed on the package. Set aside or refrigerate. Rinse shrimp and crab in cold water. Combine together. Remove lobster meat from shell and flake. Add lobster to other fish. Shred ½ of lettuce head. Toss with fish. Slice cucumber. Dice onion. Toss with other ingredients. Add salad dressing and mix well. Arrange lettuce leaves on plates and serve salad over lettuce. Garnish with eggs, quartered. Makes 4 large salads.

POMEGRANATE SALAD

2 - 3 Oz. Pkgs. Raspberry Jello
1 Small Can Pineapple, crushed
1½ Cups Pomegranate Kernels
½ Cup Sour Cream
½ Cup Mayonnaise

Dissolve jello according to package. Refrigerate. When starting to jell, add pineapple and pomegranate kernels. Mix well. Pour into 8" x 11" pyrex dish and refrigerate until set. Top with mixture of sour cream and mayonnaise. Cut into squares and serve on lettuce leaf.

CRANBERRY—AVOCADO SALAD

Top Layer:
1 - 3 Oz. Pkg. Lime Gelatin
1 Cup Boiling Water
1 Avocado, mashed
1 Tsp. Lemon Juice

Middle Layer:
1 Cup Plain Low-fat Yogurt
2 Tsp. Unflavored Gelatin

Bottom Layer:
1 - 3 Oz. Pkg. Cherry Gelatin
1 Cup Boiling Water
1 - 8 Oz. Can Whole Cranberry Sauce

1. Dissolve lime gelatin in boiling water. Add mashed avocado and lemon juice. Pour into 6½-cup mold and refrigerate until firm.
2. Soften unflavored gelatin in 1 tbs. cold water; warm to dissolve. Cool until tepid. Stir into yogurt; blend well and put on top of firm first layer. Chill until firm.
3. Meanwhile, dissolve cherry gelatin in boiling water; add cranberry sauce, mixing thoroughly.
4. Allow mixture to thicken slightly, then pour on top of yogurt layer. Chill thoroughly before unmolding. Makes 10 servings.

KOREAN SALAD

2 Pkgs. Spinach
2 Cups Water Chestnuts
4 Hard Cooked Eggs
1 Can Bean Sprouts
2 Lbs. Bacon
Dressing:
½ Cup Salad Oil
½ Cup Wine or Taragon Vinegar
1 Med. Onion, sliced thin
¾ Cup White Sugar
1 Tsp. Salt
1/3 Cup Catsup

Break spinach into small pieces; drain water chestnuts and slice thin. To this, add eggs chopped, well drained bean sprouts and bacon fried crisp and crumbled. Serve with dressing listed.

SUNBURST SALAD

1 Small Pkg. Each Lemon and Orange Jello
1 No. 2 Can Crushed Pineapple
3 Bananas
1 Small Pkg. Miniature Marshmallows
3 Eggs, beaten
1 Cup Sugar
5 Tbs. Flour
2 Cups Pineapple Juice
2 Pkgs. Dream Whip
1 Cup Cold Milk
16 Oz. Philadelphia Cream Cheese
1 Cup Grated American Cheese

Drain pineapple well. Save juice for second layer. Dissolve jello in 1 cup boiling water. Add 2¼ cups cold water. Add drained pineapple, let partially set in large pyrex pan, 13" x 9" x 2". Add sliced bananas. Add marshmallows and push down into jello. Mix together sugar and flour, then add eggs. Stir in 2 cups pineapple juice. Put into a saucepan and cook slowly until thick. Cool, add to first layer, spreading evenly. Beat well the Dream Whip and milk. Add cream cheese; continue beating until smooth. Spread over second layer. Top with grated American cheese. Serve on lettuce and/or favorite crackers.

SAUERKRAUT SALAD

2 Lbs. Sauerkraut
1 Cup Sugar
½ Cup Vegetable Oil
¼ Cup Cider Vinegar
1 Cup Diced Celery
1 Med. Onion, chopped
1 Med. Green Pepper, chopped
3 Tbs. Pimiento, chopped

1. Drain and chop sauerkraut.
2. Combine sugar, oil and vinegar in a large mixing bowl; beat until thoroughly blended.
3. Add sauerkraut, celery, onion, green pepper and pimiento to mixture in bowl; stir well.
4. Refrigerate for 2 days.

Makes about 1 quart.

SIX—CUP SALAD

1 Cup Pineapple Tidbits, well drained
1 Cup Flaked Coconut
1 Cup Mandarin Orange Slices, well drained
1 Cup Miniature Marshmallows
1 Cup Commercial Sour Cream
1 Cup Pecans
Maraschino Cherries for garnish

Mix all ingredients together and chill several hours or overnight. Garnish with cherries.

TOMATO SOUP SALAD

1 Can Campbell's Tomato Soup
½ Can Water
1 Tbs. Gelatin
½ Cup Mayonnaise
½ Cup Celery, chopped fine
¼ Cup Green Pepper, chopped fine
¼ Cup Onion, chopped fine
1 - 8 Oz. Pkg. Philadelphia Cream Cheese

Soak gelatin in ½ cup cold water. Heat soup and water to boiling. Take from heat and add gelatin. Then add cheese and stir to dissolve. Cool to the consistency of egg whites. Add mayonnaise, pepper, onion and celery. Let chill until firm.

BAR-B-QUE BEAN SALAD

1 - 1 Lb. Can Cut Green Beans
1 - 1 Lb. Can Kidney Beans
1 - 1 Lb. Can Wax Beans
½ Cup Chopped Green Pepper
½ Cup Finely-chopped Parsley
1 Purple Onion

Marinade:
¾ Cup Sugar
2/3 Cup Cider or Wine Vinegar
1/3 Cup Corn or Safflower Oil
1 Tsp. Salt
1 Tsp. Coarse Pepper
½ Tsp. Garlic Salt

Open, drain and rinse beans. Drain well in colander. Place in 2"-deep flat container that can be covered in refrigerator. Add chopped green pepper, parsley and purple onion which has been thinly sliced and separated into rings.

Make marinade: In glass 2 or 4-cup measuring pitcher mix sugar well with vinegar to dissolve sugar. Add salad oil and the seasonings. Mix well with wire whisk or fork. Pour over container with vegetables in it. Cover and refrigerate for at least two days, mixing gently several times. Taste for seasoning. Add a bit more salt if desired (do not cut amount of sugar or it will not be as delicious).

Drain to serve, reserving marinade to keep over any remaining salad. This salad gets better and may be kept up to a week or more in the refrigerator. Serves 8 to 12, depending on the rest of the menu.

WINE JELLO

2 Tbs. Unflavored Gelatin
1 Cup Sugar
2 Cups Boiling Water
1/3 Cup Orange Juice
3 Tbs. Lemon Juice
1 Cup Wine, either Sherry, Claret or a Rose is
  delicious

Mix well in a bowl, the gelatin and sugar. Add boiling water, stir until dissolved. Add juices and wine. Mold and chill. Serves 6 to 8 as a dessert, 12 as an accompaniment for poultry.

SHRIMP & CRAB SALAD

1 Pkg. Star Shaped Macaroni
1 Medium Onion
1 Cup Finely Chopped Celery
1 Lb. Fresh Crab
1 Lb. Fresh Shrimp
Best Foods Mayonnaise
Salt & Pepper
Garlic Powder (optional)

Cook macaroni until tender but firm. Drain and put in bowl. Mix in mayonnaise till macaroni is covered. Salt and pepper and garlic powder to taste. Refrigerate. Chop onion and celery. Break up crab. Add onion, celery, crab and shrimp to macaroni. Refrigerate till served. Serves 20.

INDIAN SPINACH SALAD

¼ Cup White Wine Vinegar
¼ Cup Salad Oil
2 Tbs. Chutney, chopped
2 Tsp. Sugar
½ Tsp. Salt
1½ Tsp. Curry Powder
1 Tsp. Dry Mustard
8 Cups (10 Oz.) Fresh Spinach, torn
  into bite-size pieces
1½ Cups Chopped, Unpared Apple
½ Cup Light Raisins
½ Cup Peanuts
2 Tbs. Sliced Green Onion

In a jar combine vinegar, oil, chutney, sugar, salt, curry powder and mustard. Cover and chill. Place torn spinach in large salad bowl; top with apple, raisins, peanuts and green onion. Shake dressing well; pour over salad and toss. Makes 6-8 servings.

CHEDDAR—PINEAPPLE MOLDED SALAD

2 Pkgs. Gelatin
1 No. 2 or 2½ Can Crushed Pineapple in own juice
Juice of 1 Lemon
1 Cup Cheddar Cheese
½ Pint Whipping Cream, or 1 Pkg.
  Dream Whip
½ Cup Cold Water

Dressing:
1 Cup Mayonnaise
1 Tbs. Onion, chopped
1 Tbs. Green Bell Pepper, chopped
1 Tbs. Chopped Celery

Put gelatin in ½ cup cold water for 10 minutes. Heat pineapple and lemon juice; add gelatin to hot mixture; cool. When above is set, add cheddar cheese and cream (whipped). Turn into mold.

Dressing: Mix all ingredients together; chill.

Serves 10.

SPINACH MOUSSE (Salad)

1 - 3 Oz. Pkg. Lemon Jello
1 Cup Boiling Water
½ Cup Cold Water
1½ Tbs. Vinegar
½ Cup Mayonnaise
½ Cup Sour Cream
½ Cup Dream Whip
½ Tsp. Salt
Few Grains Pepper
2 Tbs. Finely-chopped Onions
1 Cup Chopped, Raw Spinach

Dissolve gelatin in boiling water. Add cold water and vinegar. Chill to egg-white consistency. Blend in bowl the mayonnaise, sour cream, whipped cream, seasoning, onion and spinach. Adjust seasoning to taste. When gelatin is partially jelled, add remaining ingredients. Stir well. Mold and chill. Eat with enjoyment. Serves 6.

CALICO SALAD

1 - 16 Oz. Pkg. Frozen Mixed Vegetables
1 Small Pkg. Frozen Lima Beans
¼ Cup Chopped Onion
½ Cup Chopped Celery
½ Cup Chopped Green Pepper
1 Small Can Black Pitted Olives, sliced
1 Pkg. Hidden Valley Mix (dry)
1 Cup Mayonnaise

Cook the frozen vegetables and drain thoroughly. Let cool. Add the remaining ingredients and marinate overnight.

RHODE ISLAND CRANBERRY SALAD

1 Can Pineapple Tidbits (about 1 lb.
  size), or Crushed Pineapple
1 - 3 Oz. Pkg. Lemon Jello (or red
  cherry + ¼ cup lemon juice)
1 - 1 Lb. Can Whole Cranberry Sauce
½ Cup Thinly-diced Celery
1 Pkg. Broken Walnuts or Slivered
  Almonds
1 - 8 Oz. Carton Cream-style Cottage
  Cheese, if desired
1 Carton Sour Cream
Mayonnaise

Drain pineapple juice into 1-cup measure. Add water, if necessary, to make 1 cup. Heat to boiling and stir into gelatin in a medium-size bowl; stir till dissolved. Beat in cranberry sauce (and lemon juice if cherry gelatin has been used). Chill for 45 minutes. Stir in pineapple, celery & nuts (also cottage cheese, if used). Chill until firm - overnight is best.

Serve with sour cream to which mayonnaise has been added.

BOILED SLAW

1 Large Head Cabbage
1 Green Bell Pepper
1 Large Onion
1 Cup Sugar
1 Tsp. Salt
1 Tbs. Celery Seed
¾ Cup Salad Oil
1 Cup Vinegar

Grate half of cabbage into a large airtight bowl. Add a layer of half bell pepper, grated, and half onion, grated. Sprinkle ½ cup sugar on. Repeat layers of grated cabbage, bell pepper and onion. Sprinkle with remaining half cup of sugar.

Bring to a boil the vinegar, oil, salt and celery seed. Pour boiling hot mixture over cabbage - DO NOT STIR! Refrigerate for at least 4 hours, then stir and serve.

The slaw tastes better on the second or third day, so make it ahead of time to really impress guests. You may wish to add black pepper to enhance taste. Just try it - it'll become your favorite.

HOT CURRIED FRUIT SALAD

1 - No. 2½ Can Salad Fruit, drained
½ Cup Brown Sugar
2 Tbs. Cornstarch
1 Tbs. Curry Powder
½ Cup Maraschino Cherries
2 Bananas, sliced
1 Can Pitted Black Cherries
¼ Cup Melted Butter

Drain salad fruit and place in the bottom of a greased 2 quart baking dish. Pour in the maraschino cherries and black cherries with the juice. Add the bananas. Mix the dry ingredients together and add the melted butter. Stir into the fruit. Bake at 350 deg. for 40 minutes. Serve hot. Yields 8 servings.

VEGETABLE DILL COMBO

¼ Cup Creamy French Salad Dressing
¼ Cup Mayonnaise
2 Tbs. Chili Sauce
2 Tsp. Lemon Juice
1 Tsp. Salt
1 Tsp. Dried Dill Weed
1/8 Tsp. Pepper
1½ Cups Diced Carrots, cooked & drained
½ Small Head Cauliflower, sliced, cooked & drained (1½ cups)
1 - 9 Oz. Pkg. Frozen Peas, cooked & drained
1 - 9 Oz. Pkg. Frozen Italian Green Beans (or regular green beans), cooked & drained
½ Cup Chopped Celery
¼ Cup Chopped Onion

Blend together French dressing, mayonnaise, chili sauce, lemon juice, salt, dill weed and pepper. Chill several hours or overnight. Arrange vegetables in large bowl; add dressing; toss to coat.

MEXICAN SALAD

1/3 Can Sliced Ripe Olives
1 Sliced Avocado
4 Green Onions, sliced
2/3 Cup Cheddar Cheese
3 Tomatoes
½ Pkg. Pumpkin Seeds (or can use sunflower seeds), toasted & salted
2 Kinds Greens

Dressing:
1 Avocado, mashed
½ Cup Sour Cream
1/3 Cup Salad Oil
1 Clove Garlic
2 Tsp. Chili Powder, Sugar and Salt
¼ Tsp. Tabasco Sauce
2 Tbs. Lemon Juice
½ Pkg. Fritos, added last

Mix salad greens with other salad ingredients. Mix dressing ingredients together. Pour on dressing and mix. At last minute add ½ pkg. crumbled Fritos.

CRAB SALAD SUPREME

1 - 8 Oz. Can Tomato Sauce
1 - 8 Oz. Can Water (use tomato
  sauce can to measure)
1 - 3 Oz. Pkg. Lemon Flavor Gelatin
2 Tbs. Vinegar
¼ Tsp. Salt
2 Tbs. Lemon Juice
½ Cup Pickle Relish
1 Cup Chopped Celery
4 Green Onions, chopped
1 Green Pepper, chopped
½ Cup Chopped Red Onions
1 Cup Crab Meat and/or Shrimp

Heat tomato sauce, water, salt and vinegar
to very hot, but not boiling. Stir in
package of gelatin; allow to cool slightly.
Add remaining ingredients, place in lightly-
oiled casserole or mold; refrigerate until
firm. Serve with a sprig of parsley and
½ tsp. mayonnaise. Serves 8.

FROSTED FRUIT SALAD

Salad:
1 Small Pkg. Lemon Jello
1 Small Pkg. Orange Jello
2 Cups Hot Water
1½ Cups Cold Water
1 Small Can Crushed Pineapple,
  drained (save juice)
2 Bananas, sliced
About 40 Little Marshmallows

Topping:
1 Egg, beaten
2 Tbs. Flour
2 Tbs. Margarine
½ Cup Sugar
1 Cup Pineapple Juice, left from can
  of pineapple
1 Small Pkg. Cream Cheese
1 Cup Whipped Cream
½ Cup Shredded Sharp Cheese

Salad: Dissolve jello in hot water; add cold
water. Let cool. Add fruits & marshmallows. Pour into large baking dish and chill
until firm. Then spread with topping.

Topping: In a little saucepan, combine egg,
flour, margarine, sugar and pineapple juice.
Stir over low heat until thickened. Cool &
fold in cream cheese and whipped cream.
Spread over top of chilled jello and sprinkle
with cheese. Cut into 13 to 15 squares and
serve on greens.

TOMATO ASPIC

2 Pkgs. Unflavored Gelatine
1-1/3 Cups Water, boiling
1 - 15½ Oz. Jar Spaghetti Sauce, with
  mushrooms
4 Tbs. Vinegar
¼ Cup Chopped Celery
¼ Cup Chopped Green Onions
¼ Cucumber, chopped
¼ Cup Chopped Bell Pepper
¼ Cup Chopped Carrots

In bowl, dissolve gelatine in boiling water.
Stir in spaghetti sauce and vinegar. Chill
till partially set, stirring occasionally. Mixture should be consistency of unbeaten egg
whites. Fold in vegetables. Turn into a
6½-cup ring mold. Chill until firm.

Note: Vegetables can be grated instead
of chopped.

CUCUMBER CREAM SALAD

1 - 3 Oz. Pkg. Lime Jello
1 Cup Hot Water
1 Tsp. Grated Onion
1 Tbs. Cider Vinegar
1 Cup Drained Chopped Cucumber
¼ Cup Mayonnaise
1 Cup Sour Cream

Chop cucumber fine and set aside to drain.
Dissolve jello in 1 cup hot water and add
grated onion, vinegar and salt. Stir and set
in refrigerator to cool. Let stand until syrupy. When jello mix is rather syrupy, drain
juice from cucumbers. Mix mayonnaise well
into jello, then stir in sour cream and drained
cucumber mix. Chill until firm. Serves 6 &
is a very nice combination to serve with sandwiches or other meat dishes.

AVOCADO SALAD

1 Pkg. Lime Jello
1 Cup Hot Water
1 Cup Mashed Avocado
1 Tsp. Salt
1 Cup Diced Celery
1 Tbs. Chopped Green Pepper
2 Tbs. Chopped Onion
½ Cup Chopped Walnuts
2 Tbs. Mayonnaise
2 Tbs. Lemon Juice
1 Cup Whipping Cream or Cool Whip

Dissolve jello in hot (boiling point) water. Add mashed, salted avocado and stir until well mixed. Add celery, green pepper, onion, walnuts and mayonnaise. Add the lemon juice; mix well. Fold in whipping cream; pour into a jello mold or pan and chill. Serves 8 to 10 people.

CRANBERRY—RASPBERRY MOLD

2 Pkgs. Cherry Jello
1½ Cups Hot Water
1 Can Crushed Pineapple, with juice
1 Can Whole Cranberries, with juice
1 Pint Sour Cream
2 Pkgs. Raspberry Jello
1½ Cups Hot Water
2 Pkgs. Frozen Raspberries

First Layer: Mix and let set till firm the 2 pkgs. cherry jello, 1½ cups hot water, 1 can crushed pineapple (with juice) and 1 can whole cranberries (with juice).

Second Layer: When above is set firm, spread with 1 pint sour cream.

Third Layer: Mix 2 pkgs. raspberry jello with 1½ cups hot water, and 2 pkgs. frozen raspberries. Let set until consistency of egg whites. Spread over top of sour cream. Let set till firm and cut into squares to serve.

DEEP DARK DELICIOUS SALAD

1 Small Pkg. Black Cherry Jello
1 Cup Boiling Water
1 Cup Juice from Cherries
1 Can Dark, Sweet Cherries, pitted
1 Small Can Crushed Pineapple
3 Bananas
¾ Cup Small Marshmallows
¾ Cup Chopped Pecans
½ Pint Whipping Cream

Dissolve 1 pkg. black cherry jello in 1 cup boiling water. Add 1 cup juice from canned dark, sweet cherries (supplement with water if necessary). Just before it congeals, add 1 can pitted cherries, 1 small can crushed pineapple (drained), 3 sliced bananas, ¾ cup small marshmallows and ¾ cup chopped pecans. Fold in one-half pint whipped cream; stir several times during setting to mix well.

ANTIPASTO

½ Head Cauliflower, in small pieces
2 Carrots, cut lengthwise
2 Celery Stalks, in 1" pieces
1 Green Pepper
1 Red Pepper
1 Can Black Olives
6 Small White Onions
¼ Lb. Fresh Green Beans
¾ Cup Water
¾ Cup Wine Vinegar
¼ Cup Vegetable Oil
1 Tbs. Olive Oil
2 Tbs. Sugar
1 Clove Garlic, pressed
1 Tsp. Oregano
Dash of Salt and Pepper

In a large frying pan, combine all ingredients and bring to a boil. Simmer, covered, for about 5 minutes. Cool and refrigerate, allowing a day or two to marinate before serving. Vegetables may be varied.

APRICOT SALAD

2 Pkgs. Orange Jello
3 Cups Boiling Water
1 Large Can Apricots, drained
  and mashed
1 Large Can Pineapple Chunks,
  drained and diced
About 40 Miniature Marshmallows
1 Cup Pineapple and Apricot Juice,
  mixed

Topping:
1 Cup Pineapple and Apricot Juice,
  mixed
½ Cup Sugar
1 Beaten Egg
2 Heaping Tbs. Flour
2 Tbs. Butter or Margarine

Dissolve jello in boiling water; add rest of ingredients. When firm top with the following topping.

Topping: Mix ingredients together & cook until thick. When cool, add 1 cup cream, whipped (can substitute 1 pkg. Dream Whip); spread over the firm gelatin.

Note: When you drain the cans of fruit, you get 2 cups of juice. These you combine and use 1 cup in each mixture.

CRANBERRY SALAD

1 Lb. Cranberries, Ground
2 Cups Sugar
1 - 9 Oz. Can Crushed Pineapple, drained
1 Cup Miniature Marshmallows
1 Cup Chopped Nuts
½ Pint Whipped Cream

Add sugar to ground cranberries, let stand 2 hours. Mix rest of the ingredients, whipped cream last, to cranberries. Refrigerate overnight.

FRESH SPINACH SALAD

1 or 2 Bunches Fresh Spinach
½ Can Bean Sprouts, or equivalent of
  Fresh Bean Sprouts
1 Small Can Water Chestnuts, sliced
2 Hard-boiled Eggs, chopped
¼ Lb. Bacon, fried and diced

Dressing:
1 Cup Oil
¼ Cup Wine Vinegar
1 Tbs. Worcestershire Sauce
1 Tbs. Salt
1/3 Cup Ketchup
1 Tbs. Minced Onion
½ Cup Sugar

Wash and cut up spinach; add all other ingredients and toss well. Shake dressing thoroughly and add to salad; salad should be mixed right before serving as spinach tends to lose zip quickly.

CHINESE CHICKEN SALAD

4 Oz. Mei Fun (Rice Sticks)
1 Large Head Lettuce
½ Lb. Cooked Chicken, chopped
6 Green Onions, chopped (optional)

Dressing:
2 Tbs. Sugar
2 Tsp. Salt
2 Tsp. MSG
½ Tsp. Black Pepper
1 Tsp. Sesame Oil
¼ Cup Salad Oil
¼ Cup White Wine Vinegar

Combine dressing ingredients and blend in blender.

1. Deep fry Mei Fun for just a second in very hot oil. Drain on paper towel.
2. Combine lettuce, chicken, onion; chill.
3. Just before serving, add Mei Fun and dressing. Mix well.

DELICIOUS FRUIT SALAD

3 Eggs
1 Cup White Sugar
2 Tbs. Flour
2 Tbs. Butter
1 Medium Can Pineapple Chunks or
   Slices
Pinch Salt
3 to 4 Apples
1 Orange
2 to 3 Bananas
1 Cup Walnuts
1 Cup Miniature Marshmallows
1 Cup Grapes, if desired
1 Cup Strawberries, if desired
1 Carton Whipping Cream

Beat eggs lightly. Add the sugar, flour and salt. Mix well. Boil pineapple juice and egg mixture. Stir over medium heat until thick. Take off stove, add the butter and let cool. While the mixture is cooling, mix in a bowl, the apples, oranges, pineapple bits, bananas, walnuts and marshmallows. When in season, you can add grapes and strawberries if you desire. When mixture is cool, fold into fruit and just before serving fold in whip cream which has already been whipped. Serves 6 to 8 people. Ideal for salad with dinner or just as a delicious dessert.

ITALIAN RICE SALAD

3 Cups Cooked Rice
2 Pimientos, cut in strips
1 Green Pepper, cut in strips
2/3 Cup Chopped Red Onion
1 Tsp. Dried Basil
18 Large, Stuffed Olives, sliced
1½ Cups Chicken, cut in strips
18 Anchovy Fillets, coarsely cut
Garlic Flavored French Dressing
Tomato Wedges
Hard-cooked Eggs

Combine the first 8 ingredients. Toss with dressing. Garnish with tomato wedges and quartered eggs. Serves 10 to 12.

MANDARIN ORANGE JELLO

2 - 3 Oz. Pkg. Orange Jello
1 Cup Hot Water
1 Cup Juice from Oranges & Pineapple
1 Large Can Crushed Pineapple, drained
1 Large + 1 Small Pkg. Cream Cheese
½ Pint Whipping Cream
2 Cans Mandarin Oranges, drained

Make jello, using 1 cup hot water and 1 cup juice. Let it start to jell. Whip cream; whip jello and cream cheese together. Add whipped cream. Stir in fruit and chill.

SHRIMP and CHICKEN SALAD

1½ Cups Elbow Macaroni
3 Cups Diced, Cooked Chicken
1 Cup Cleaned, Peeled, Cooked Shrimp
1 - 8¾ Oz. Can Peach Slices,
   drained and chopped
1 - 8¼ Oz. Can Pineapple Chunks,
   drained
1 Cup Chopped Celery
¼ Cup Sliced Green Onion
½ of 14 Oz. Can (2/3 Cup) Sweetened
   Condensed Milk
½ Cup Lemon Juice
2 Tbs. Salad Oil
2 Tbs. Prepared Mustard
¼ Tsp. Salt
Lettuce Cups
Optional: 1 Hard-cooked Egg,
   sieved

In a saucepan, cook macaroni in boiling, salted water according to package directions. Drain. In a large bowl, combine the drained macaroni, diced chicken, the shrimp, drained peaches, drained pineapple, celery and sliced green onion. In a bowl, stir together the sweetened condensed milk, lemon juice, salad oil, prepared mustard and salt. Blend into the macaroni-chicken mixture. Cover and chill several hours or overnight. To serve, spoon salad into lettuce cups. Garnish with sieved egg, if desired. Makes 6 to 8 servings.

MOLDED AVOCADO SALAD

1 Large Avocado or 2 Medium-size
  Avocados
1 Pkg. Lime Jello
1 Cup Boiling Water
1 Tsp. Lemon Juice
¾ Cup Celery, diced
½ Cup Mayonnaise
½ Cup Chopped Nuts
1 Cup Whipped Cream
1 Pinch Salt

1. Dissolve jello in water.
2. Add salt and lemon juice.
3. Chill jello, salt and lemon juice until syrupy.
4. Add mayonnaise, mashed avocado & whip until smooth.
5. Add celery and nuts.
6. Fold in whipped cream.
7. Pour into a 1-quart mold and refrigerate until firm.

Serve with grapefruit sections.

24—HOUR SALAD

6 Cups Chopped Lettuce
1 Tsp. Salt
½ Tsp. Pepper
1 Tsp. Sugar
6 Hard-cooked Eggs
1 - 10 Oz. Pkg. Frozen Peas
1 Lb. Bacon
2 Cups Shredded Swiss Cheese
1 Cup Mayonnaise
¼ Cup Green Onion
¼ Tsp. Paprika

Cook bacon and crumble in bits. Place 3 cups lettuce on bottom of covered bowl. Sprinkle with salt, pepper and sugar. Layer in order peas, bacon, onion, crumbled eggs, Swiss cheese. Add the last 3 cups of lettuce on top. Spread 1 cup mayonnaise on top of lettuce to seal edges. Cover tightly and chill for 24 hours. When ready to serve, sprinkle with paprika and toss.

GERMAN HERRING SALAD

¾ Cup Mayonnaise
1 - 16 Oz. Jar Sour Herring
1 Medium Onion
1 Big Apple
2 Medium Boiled Potatoes
2 Medium Sour Pickles
1 - 16 Oz. Can Beets
2 Hard-boiled Eggs
¼ Tsp. Pepper
1/8 Tsp. Salt
1 Cup Boiled Veal or Roast Beef
  (optional)

Dice apple, potatoes, pickles, beets, onion, sour herring and 1 egg. Mix all ingredients together with mayonnaise, salt and pepper. Garnish with sliced egg. Add diced veal or roast beef if desired.

SCANDINAVIAN SALAD

2 Cans Peas with Onions
1 Can Whole Kernel Corn
1 Can French-cut Beans
1 Jar Pimentos
1 Large, Chopped Onion
1 Stalk Celery, chopped

1 Cup Vinegar
¼ Cup Oil
1½ Cups Sugar
2 Tbs. Water
1 Tbs. Paprika

Drain well and mix together the peas with onions, whole kernel corn, French-cut beans, pimentos, chopped onion and chopped celery. Mix together and pour over the vegetables the vinegar, oil, sugar, water and paprika.

Let stand 24 hours or more in covered container. Keeps well up to six weeks in the refrigerator. The drained vegetable juice may be used for soups, stews, etc.

KIELBASA with GERMAN POTATO SALAD

6 Medium Potatoes, peeled (about
  2 lbs.)
Salt
5 Slices Bacon
½ Cup Chopped Onion
1 Tbs. Sugar
1 Tbs. Flour
1/8 Tsp. Pepper
1 Chicken Bouillon Cube, crumbled
1/3 Cup Vinegar
1 Lb. Kielbasa or Polish Sausage,
  scored at 1" intervals
Parsley, for garnish

In large saucepan, heat 1 quart water to boiling. Add potatoes and 1 tsp. salt and cook 20 to 25 minutes until potatoes are tender; drain. Cut into ¼" slices.

Meanwhile, in large skillet, cook bacon until crisp; drain on paper towels and crumble. To drippings in skillet, add onion and saute' until tender. Stir in sugar, flour, pepper & 1 tsp. salt until evenly blended; then add crumbled bouillon cube, ½ cup water and vinegar. Cook over medium heat until bouillon cube dissolves and sauce thickens and comes to a boil. Cook 1 minute. Add hot potatoes and toss lightly. Add Kielbasa and cook until potatoes and sausage are heated through. Sprinkle on bacon bits & garnish with parsley flakes.

You can bake in the oven at 325 degrees, covered, for approximately ½ hour, after potatoes are tossed and Kielbasa is added, rather than on stove top. Makes 4 to 6 servings.

HOT SEA FOOD SALAD

1 Cup Cooked Shrimp
1 Cup Cooked Crab
1 Cup Chopped Celery
½ Cup Green Pepper
¼ Cup Grated Onion
1 Cup Mayonnaise
3 Hard-boiled Eggs
1 Tsp. Worcestershire Sauce
½ Tsp. Salt
¼ Tsp. Pepper

Mix all ingredients together well. Top with buttered bread crumbs and slivered almonds. Bake at 350 degrees for 35 minutes.

CRANBERRY RING

1 - 3 Oz. Pkg. Strawberry-flavored
  Gelatin
1 Cup Hot Water
1 Cup OR 10½ Oz. Can Frozen Cranberry
  Relish (whole berries)
1 - 13½ Oz. Can Crushed Pineapple
1 - 3 Oz. Pkg. Lemon-flavored Gelatin
1¼ Cups Boiling Water
2 Cups Tiny Marshmallows
1 - 3 Oz. Pkg. Cream Cheese, softened
½ Cup Mayonnaise or Salad Dressing
½ Cup Heavy Cream, whipped

First Layer: Dissolve strawberry-flavored gelatin in hot water. Add cranberry relish and dash of salt. Pour into a 6½-cup ring mold. Chill till firm.

Second Layer: Drain pineapple, reserving syrup. Dissolve lemon-flavored gelatin in boiling water; add marshmallows and stir till melted; add reserved syrup. Chill till partially set. Blend cream cheese, mayonnaise and dash of salt; add to marshmallow mixture. Stir in pineapple. If mixture is thin, chill till it mounds slightly when spooned. Fold in whipped cream; pour over first layer; chill till firm. Unmold onto bed of lettuce. Serves 10 to 12.

SUPER SIX SPROUT SALAD

2 Cups Lentil Sprouts
2 Cups Alfalfa Sprouts
2 Cups Mung Bean Sprouts
½ Cup Radish Sprouts
½ Cup Cabbage Sprouts
½ Cup Wheat Sprouts (less than
   3 days old)

Toss gently, saving the wheat sprouts
to sprinkle on top. This makes four
hearty servings. Top with favorite
dressing.

CORNED BEEF SALAD

1 Can Corned Beef Hash
1 Large Green Pepper
1 Large Onion
1 Cup Celery
1 Cup Peas (small can)
2 Hard-boiled Eggs
1 Pkg. Lemon or Lime Jello
1 Cup Salad Dressing

Cut up green pepper, onion, celery, hard-
boiled eggs. Drain can of peas and put
peas in with other ingredients in jello. When
it begins to set, stir in salad dressing. Put in
molds and put in refrigerator.

CHICKEN SALAD DELIGHT

3 Cups Chicken Meat, cooked & shredded
6 Cups Shredded Lettuce
1 Can Sliced Water Chestnuts
1 Cup Diagonally Sliced Celery
6 Green Onions, sliced (include green part)
4 Sweet Gherkins, sliced
1 Can (3 Oz.) Chow Mein Noodles

Dressing:
½ Cup Mayonnaise
2 Tbs. Sesame Oil
2 Tbs. Red or White Vinegar
2 Tbs. White Corn Syrup
1 Tbs. Soy Sauce
½ Tsp. Ground Ginger
3 Tbs. Sesame Seeds

Combine all salad ingredients in large bowl.
Combine dressing ingredients and pour over
salad. Add sesame seeds. Serves 4.

PRETZEL SALAD

2 2/3 Cups Coarsely Chopped Pretzels
1½ Cubes Butter
12 Oz. Pkg. Cream Cheese
1¼ Cups Sugar
1 Large Pkg. Frozen Strawberries
¾ Carton (lg.) Cool Whip
1 Large Pkg. Strawberry Jello
2 Cups Pineapple Juice

Cream cheese and sugar; set aside. Mix
pretzels and butter or oleo; press into a
9" x 13" dish. Bake at 400 degrees for
10 min. Spread cheese mix over pretzels;
spread Cool Whip over cheese. Chill. Dissolve jello in hot pineapple juice; add the
strawberries. Allow to set. Pour over top
and refrigerate. Most unusual and delicious.

FROZEN CRANBERRY SALAD
(or Dessert)

1½ Pkgs. Cream Cheese (12 Oz.)
3 Tbs. Sugar
2 Cans Whole Cranberry Sauce
1 Large Can Crushed Pineapple
½ to 1 Cup Chopped Walnuts
1/3 Pkg. Small Marshmallows
1 Cup Whipping Cream

Cream cream cheese with sugar; add cranberries, pineapple, walnuts. Mix together
thoroughly. Fold in whipped cream and
marshmallows. Pour into a large pyrex
dish (9" x 13") or salad mold. Freeze
about 8 hours. Let sit at room temperature a few minutes before serving.

EGG SALAD MOLD

14 Hard Cooked Eggs
1 Qt. Mayonnaise
2 Envelopes Knox Gelatine
1 Cup Water
½ Cup Sweet Pickle Relish
½ Cup Diced Celery
½ Cup Diced Bell Pepper
½ Cup Diced Onion Greens
2 Tsp. Salt
¼ Tsp. Pepper

Dissolve gelatine in water. Mash or dice peeled eggs. Add mayonnaise, gelatine, salt and pepper. Mix well. Add remaining ingredients. Stir and pour into a greased angel cake pan or jello mold. Refrigerate for 1 hour or more. Serves 15 to 20 people.

CORIANDER CHICKEN SALAD

2 Lbs. Chicken Parts
Chicken Marinade:
2 Tbs. Light Soy Sauce
1 Tbs. Sherry
1 Tsp. Sugar
Dashes of Garlic Powder, Salt & Pepper
2 Tsp. Fresh Ginger, minced

12 Oz. Pkg. Bean Thread (also known as
   long rice)
2 Stalks Green Onions
1 Medium Head Iceberg Lettuce
1 Bunch Coriander (also known as
   cilentro or Chinese parsley)
½ Tsp. Dry Mustard
½ Tsp. Each Salt and Pepper
1 Tbs. Salad Oil
2 Tbs. Sesame Oil
2 Tbs. Light Soy Sauce
1-2 Tbs. Vinegar
3 Tbs. Toasted Sesame Seeds

Place chicken in marinade for several hours. Bake, skin side up, in 350 degree oven for 45 minutes. Cool and shred chicken by hand into small pieces. Deep fry bean threads by small batches in 2 cups of oil. The bean threads will puff up immediately. Take out and drain. Shred green onions and lettuce. Wash and cut coriander into 1-inch lengths. Assembling: Place chicken, lettuce, green onions and coriander in large salad bowl or pot and mix with dry mustard, salt and pepper. Toss to mix well. Add sesame oil, salad oil, soy sauce, vinegar, toasted sesame seeds and ¾ of the fried bean thread. Mix again. Transfer salad to a large serving tray and top with remaining bean threads.

Do-Ahead Notes: Bake and shred chicken and deep fry bean thread the day before. Store bean thread in an air-tight container. Shred the greens early in the day and keep in plastic bags. Toss salad just before serving.

Comments: You must use fresh oil to fry the bean thread so the noodles puff up better. The oil must be very hot. Otherwise, the noodles will be only partially puffed and will have hard interiors. You may substitute fresh watercress if coriander is unavailable.

COPPER PENNY SALAD

2 Lbs. Carrots, sliced
1 Can Tomato Soup
2/3 Cup Sugar
1 Cup Oil
¾ Cup Vinegar
1 Tsp. Dry Mustard
½ Tsp. Pepper
1 Tsp. Salt
1 Medium Chopped Onion
1 Bell Pepper, cut up in pieces
1 Lb. Mushrooms, cut in half

Cook carrots until just tender and cool. Mix soup, sugar, oil, vinegar, mustard, pepper and salt. Place carrots and soup mixture in large bowl. Add onions, bell pepper and mushrooms. You may add other vegetables such as celery, zucchini, if desired. Refrigerate at least 4 hours. It's better if left overnight. Will keep 2 weeks if kept refrigerated.

POTATO SALAD

5 Medium Potatoes
5 Tbs. Mayonnaise
1½ Tbs. Mustard
1 Tsp. Vinegar
1 Tsp. Sugar
2 Tbs. Milk
1 Medium Onion, chopped
1 Green Pepper, chopped
½ Cup Sweet Pickle Relish
2 Hard-Boiled Eggs, chopped
Paprika for color
Parsley to garnish
Salt to taste

Boil potatoes and eggs. Remove skins.
Cool. Heat mayonnaise, mustard, vinegar,
sugar and milk in saucepan until smooth.
Cool. Chop onions and potatoes, add
green pepper and relish, add eggs. Pour
on sauce and mix. Salt to taste. Garnish
with paprika and parsley. Serves 5.

SAVORY CORNED BEEF LOAF

1 Envelope Knox Gelatine
¼ Cup Cold Water
1½ Cups Tomato Juice
½ Tsp. Salt
1 Tsp. Grated Onion Juice
2 Tbs. Lemon Juice
1 Tsp. Worcestershire Sauce
1½ Cups Corned Beef, cut into
    small pieces
¾ Cup Chopped Celery
3 Hard-cooked Eggs, sliced
¼ Cup Chopped Pickle Relish

Soften gelatine in cold water and dissolve
in hot tomato juice. Add salt, onion
juice, lemon juice and Worcestershire
sauce. Stir well. Rinse loaf pan with
cold water; garnish bottom with slices
of hard-cooked egg and cover with a little of the gelatin liquid. Chill in refrigerator until set. Cool remaining liquid
until mixture begins to thicken; fold in
corned beef, celery and relish. Line
sides of loaf pan with sliced eggs and
fill with meat mixture. Chill until firm.
Unmold on platter and garnish with
watercress, lettuce or desired greens.
Serve with mayonnaise. Serves 6.

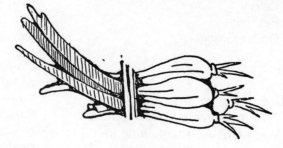

FROSTY CHERRY CRANBERRY MOLD

8 Oz. Jar Red Maraschino Cherries
1 Small Pkg. Cherry Flavored Gelatin
1 Lb. Can Jellied Cranberry Sauce
4 Tbs. Lemon Juice
1 Cup Heavy Cream
3 Tbs. Sugar
¼ Tsp. Grated Lemon Peel
1/3 Cup Salad Dressing or
    Mayonnaise
1/3 Cup Chopped Walnuts
Water

Drain cherries, reserving syrup; chop the
cherries & set aside. Add enough water
to cherry syrup to measure 1½ cups.
Heat to boiling. Remove from heat and
immediately dissolve gelatin in hot mixture. Add cranberry sauce and 3 tbs.
lemon juice. Beat slowly with rotary
beater until well blended. Chill until
slightly thickened. Fold in chopped cherries. Turn into lightly-oiled 6-cup mold.
Freeze until firm. Whip cream with sugar and lemon peel until stiff. Fold in
remaining 1 tbs. lemon juice, salad dressing or mayonnaise and walnuts. Spread
over frozen cherry layer, freeze until
firm. Unmold onto salad greens, garnish
with fresh mint and additional cherries,
if desired. This is great with Thanks-
giving dinner! Serves 12.

7 LAYER SALAD

½ Bowl Shredded Lettuce
¼ - ½ Cup Chopped Celery
1 Green Pepper, chopped
1 Spanish Onion, chopped
1 Pkg. Frozen Peas, cooked
1 Pt. Mayonnaise
3 Tbs. Sugar
½ Lb. Bacon, crisply-fried, or Bacos
Parmesan Cheese

Fill bowl ½ full of shredded lettuce. Make a layer of each of the next 4 ingredients. Mix sugar with mayonnaise. Spread on top. Sprinkle with Parmesan cheese. Crumble bacon on top (or Bacos). DO NOT STIR. Cover with plastic wrap and let stand overnight. Serve without stirring.

ARTICHOKE RICE SALAD

1 Small Pkg. Chicken-flavored Rice
2 - 6 Oz. Jars Marinated Artichoke
  Hearts
1 Large Green Pepper, chopped
½ Cup Mayonnaise
2 Green Onions, minced
8 Pimento-stuffed Olives, sliced
¼ Tsp. Curry Powder
3-4 Chicken Breasts, cooked and
  chopped

Cook rice; omit butter. Remove from heat and turn into a bowl; let stand until room temperature. Add onion, pepper & olives. Drain artichoke hearts, reserving half of the liquid. Combine curry with mayonnaise and liquid from artichoke hearts; mix until well blended. Add to rice along with artichoke hearts and chicken; mix well and chill, covered. Serve on beds of lettuce. Serves 6.

LIME & COTTAGE CHEESE SALAD

1 - 3 Oz. Pkg. Lemon Jello
1 Cup Boiling Water
1 Cup Whipping Cream
1 Pint Cottage Cheese

1 - 3 Oz. Pkg. Lime Jello
1 No. 2 Can Crushed Pineapple
1/3 Cup Chopped Walnuts
1 Cup Boiling Water

Dissolve lemon jello in hot water. Let cool. Whip in mixer briefly. Add whipping cream and beat until thickened. Stir in cottage cheese until well mixed. Pour into mold & set in refrigerator.

Dissolve lime jello in hot water. Let cool. Add crushed pineapple and nuts; stir well. Pour on top of lemon and cottage cheese mixture in mold; return to refrigerator to set.

WILTED LETTUCE SALAD

4 Slices Bacon, cut up
¼ Cup Vinegar
2 Bunches Leaf Lettuce, shredded
  (about 4 cups)
1/3 Cup Chopped Green Onions
2 Tsp. Sugar
¼ Tsp. Salt
1/8 Tsp. Pepper
3 Eggs

Fry bacon until crisp in a 10" skillet. Mix eggs with vinegar, sugar, salt and pepper. Add to skillet and heat until hot. Remove the skillet from the fire; add lettuce and onions. Toss 1 to 2 minutes, until lettuce is wilted. Makes 4 servings.

Dill Wilted Lettuce: Add ½ tsp. dried dill weed.

APRICOT—PINEAPPLE GELATIN SALAD

Salad:
2 Pkgs. Lemon or Orange Jello
  (regular size)
1 Cup Miniature Marshmallows
1 No. 2½ Can Apricots
1 No. 2 Can Crushed Pineapple
2 Cups Boiling Water

Topping:
1 Cup Pineapple Juice
1 Egg
½ Cup Sugar
3 Tbs. Flour
2 Tbs. Butter or Margarine
1 Pkg. Dream Whip

Salad:
1. Dissolve jello and marshmallows in 2 cups boiling water.

2. Drain juice from apricots, adding enough water to make 2 cups. Add to above mixture and chill until shaky.

3. Drain pineapple - reserve juice for topping.

4. Dice apricots and add apricots and drained pineapple to jello.

5. Chill until firm in a 9" x 13" dish.

6. Spread with topping; garnish with chopped nuts or grated cheese.

Topping:
1. Combine sugar, flour and beaten egg in saucepan. Add pineapple juice.

2. Cook over low heat until mixture thickens, stirring constantly.

3. Add butter; stir until it melts.

4. Fold in beaten Dream Whip.

5. Cool topping before spreading on jello.

FOURTH OF JULY SALAD
(Also Christmas)

2 Boxes Lime Jello
16 Marshmallows
2 - 3 Oz. Pkgs. Cream Cheese
1 Pkg. Orange Jello
1 Pint Whipping Cream
1 Small Can Crushed Pineapple

Mix lime jello and chill only until congealed. Mix together in top of double boiler the marshmallows, cream cheese, and orange jello (dry). Heat until all has melted and is creamy. Set aside.

Whip whipping cream; add pineapple (liquid and all). Add this to melted mixture in double boiler. Put in large pyrex dish; pour congealed lime jello over this. Put in refrigerator; chill until served.

CABBAGE SALAD

2 Carrots
1 Medium Onion
1 Large Cabbage
1 Large Green Pepper
4 Stalks Celery

Grate cabbage and carrots. Dice celery, pepper and onion. Mix all together.

Dressing:
1 Tsp. Mustard Seed
¾ Cup Salad Oil
¾ Cup Vinegar
1¼ Cups Sugar
1 Tsp. Salt

Boil all ingredients for dressing. Pour over vegetables while hot, stirring well. Pack in jars to chill. Refrigerate. This will keep for 2 weeks. Good for company.

FRENCH POTATO SALAD

6 Medium Potatoes
1/3 Cup French Dressing
½ Cup Blanched Almonds
2 Tbs. Finely Chopped Onions
2 Tbs. Finely Chopped Green Peppers
1 Cup Chilled Best Foods Mayonnaise
1 Tbs. Finely Chopped Parsley
3 or 4 Hard-boiled Eggs

French Dressing:
2 Tsp. Salt
1 Tsp. Fresh Ground Pepper
1 Tsp. Paprika
½ Tsp. Powdered Mustard
Few Grains Cayenne
1 Cup Olive Oil
¼ Cup Vinegar

Boil the potatoes, with jackets on, till tender; peel them quickly and put them in a bowl. Dive into them with a couple of big forks, stabbing and pulling crosswise until they are all broken up coarse and grainy. Give them our special family French dressing to drink, in proportions of a third of a cup to six medium potatoes and let them marinate. When the French dressing has permeated every atom, throw in a half cup of blanched almonds, sliced very thin, a couple of tbs. of finely chopped onion, a couple of tbs. of finely chopped green peppers. Mix it thoroughly and chill it off in the refrigerator. Just before serving, mix in a whole cup of mayonnaise (chilled) and a tbs. of finely chopped parsley; serve on lettuce, with paprika sprinkled here and there for garnish. If you like eggs (we do), three or four hard-boiled specimens cut into businesslike chunks introduced along with the onions add both color and flavor. Mutilating your potatoes while they are still hot and "floury" gets rid of that appalling toughness to which the cold boiled potato is generally subject when sliced with a knife.

French Dressing: Rub salt, fresh ground pepper, paprika, powdered mustard, good & fresh, and a few grains of cayenne all together in the bottom of a bowl. Then slowly drip in a cup of olive oil, stirring briskly all the time until the dry stuff is thoroughly emulsified. Into that drip a quarter cup of vinegar (French insists on red wine vinegar), also stirred and beaten vigorously. Then taste it, making sure your sample is thoroughly mixed.

CHILLED BEAN SALAD

1 Can Red Kidney Beans
1 Can Green Beans
1 Can Garbanzo Beans
½ Cup Chopped Green Pepper
½ Cup Chopped Celery
½ Cup Chopped Onion
½ Cup Sugar
1 Tsp. Salt
½ Cup Vinegar (wine vinegar with
  garlic)
½ Cup Salad Oil

Drain beans well. Mix with green pepper, celery and onion. Combine sugar, salt, vinegar and salad oil; pour over beans & mix well. Refrigerate for several hours before serving. Yield: 8 servings.

SUPER CARROT-RAISIN SALAD

7 or 8 Large Carrots
1 Cup Raisins
1¼ Cups Mayonnaise
3 Tbs. Honey
3 Tsp. Vinegar
1 Tsp. Cinnamon

Peel or scrape carrots and grate coarsely. Add raisins and mix. Mix mayonnaise, honey and vinegar. Thoroughly add cinnamon to the mayonnaise and mix. Pour over carrots and toss. Let marinate at least 2 hours or longer if possible before serving. This makes a large salad for a gathering. It can be divided for a smaller salad. Will keep good for 1 week.

DORITO SALAD

1 Head Lettuce, broken up
1 Avocado, cubed
8 Oz. Cheddar Cheese, grated
1 Med. Size Pkg. Doritos, regular
  flavor
2 or 3 Med. Tomatoes, chopped
1 Lb. Lean Hamburger
4 Green Onions, chopped
Salt and Pepper to taste
1 Pkg. Good Seasons Italian
  Dressing Mix

Fry hamburger; drain and let cool. Chop lettuce into bite-size pieces; chop the tomatoes, avocado and green onions. Grate the cheese. Add all ingredients, except the hamburger and Doritos, to lettuce. Just before serving, add hamburger and Doritos, slightly crushed, to salad mixture. Use 1 package Good Seasons' Italian Dressing, prepared by directions on the package. Toss lightly before serving.

Note: More of each ingredients may be added to suit one's own taste.

TACO SALAD

2 Lbs. Ground Beef
1 Can Chopped Olives
2 Cups Shredded Cheese
1 Head Lettuce
2 Tomatoes
1 Pkg. Dry Taco Seasoning
1 Med. Bag Dorito "Nacho Chips"
1 Med. Onion

Brown meat and mix in dry taco seasoning in skillet. In bowl, mix olives, cheese, lettuce, tomatoes and onions. Drain meat and mix in with salad, then break up the chips and mix all together. Top with taco sauce and favorite salad dressing.

LAYERED VEGETABLE SALAD

1 Head Lettuce; shredded
½ Cup Celery, chopped
½ Cup Onion, chopped
1 Pkg. Frozen Peas, partially
  cooked and cooled
1½ to 2 Cups Mayonnaise
2 Tbs. Sugar
4 Oz. Grated Cheddar Cheese
¼ Cup Bacon Bits

Starting with lettuce, put each ingredient in a 9" x 13" pan in separate layer in order given. Chill several hours or overnight. Add bacon bits just before serving.

ST. NICK'S SALAD

2 - 3 Oz. Pkgs. Red Raspberry Gelatin
2 Pkgs. Frozen Red Raspberries, partially
  defrosted
2 Cups Hot Water
1 Cup Whipping Cream
12 Large Marshmallows
2 - 3 Oz. Pkgs. Philadelphia Cream Cheese

Dissolve gelatin in boiling water; add the partially defrosted raspberries - also juice that is on the raspberries. Pour into an 8" pan or mold and chill in refrigerator until firm.

Combine marshmallows and cream cheese and mix together; add whipping cream and beat with beater until thick or stiff. Spread over gelatin mixture. Chill thoroughly. Serves about 10 to 12.

Note: This is a Christmas salad; decorate top with candies or a different gelatin cut into different shapes.

PIMIENTO CHEESE SALAD

1 No. 2 Can Crushed Pineapple
1 Pkg. Lemon-flavored Gelatin
2 - 3 Oz. Pkgs. Cream Cheese
½ Cup Chopped Pimiento (or 1 small jar)
½ Cup Chopped Celery
2/3 Cup Chopped Nuts
1/8 Tsp. Salt
1 Cup Heavy Cream, whipped

Drain crushed pineapple. Heat pineapple juice to boiling; add gelatin and stir until gelatin is dissolved. Cool until slightly thickened. Add softened cream cheese & pineapple to gelatin and beat with electric mixer until cheese is in small lumps. Add pimiento, celery, nuts and salt. Fold in whipped cream; chill until firm. Keeps in refrigerator or freezer.

LAYERED SALAD

2 Cups Chopped Lettuce
1 Cup Chopped Celery
1 Cup Chopped Green Pepper
1 Onion, chopped fine
1 Cup Frozen Peas
1½ Cups Salad Dressing or Mayonnaise
1 Cup Shredded Cheese
Baco Chips

Put each item in bowl in order given. Do not cook peas, put in frozen. Chill overnight or several hours before serving.

ICE—CREAM JELLO SALAD

2 Small Pkgs. Jello (Strawberry)
3 Apples
1 Large Can Crushed Pineapple
3 Tangerines
2 Tbs. Small Curd Cottage Cheese
3 Tbs. Ice Cream (Vanilla)
½ Cup Chopped Walnuts
1 Small Pkg. Cool Whip

Melt jello in hot water as directed on back of jello box. Add cottage cheese, ice cream. Peel apples and tangerines; cut into small pieces and add to jello. Add pineapple, including juice; add nuts. Place in jello mold and refrigerate. When ready to serve, unmold and top with Cool Whip.

MEXICAN CHEF SALAD

1 Lb. Hamburger
1 Onion
1 - 15 Oz. Can Red Kidney Beans
4 Tomatoes
1 Head Lettuce
1 Avocado
4 Oz. Shredded Cheese
1 Bag Taco-flavored Dorito Chips (small bag)
1 Small Bottle Kraft Thousand Island Salad Dressing

Brown hamburger and then add beans (drain well); simmer together for 10 minutes. Cool. While meat is cooling, in a large bowl, shred lettuce. Add 1 chopped onion, 4 tomatoes, 4 oz. cheese, 1 avocado (chunked). Add crushed taco chips and then bean and meat mixture. Good to make ahead of time.

CUCUMBER JELLO

1 Small Pkg. Lime Jello
1 Envelope Plain Gelatin
2 Tbs. White Cider Vinegar
1 Cup Water
1 Large Cucumber, peeled and coarsely chopped
1 Small Piece Shallot, finely chopped
1 Cup Sour Cream
½ Cup Mayonnaise

Mix lime jello and plain gelatin in the water and vinegar over heat until dissolved. Put all other ingredients into blender. Pour heated jello mixture into the blender and blend a few minutes. More blending makes it lighter. Pour into mold and chill until firm.

MISCELLANEOUS

COFFEE AND CREAM DE CACAO DELIGHT

1 Cup Chopped Walnuts
1 Cup Milk
8 Oz. Marshmallows
1 Pt. (2 cups) Whipping Cream
½ Cup Creme De Cacao
1 Tbs. Instant Coffee
Walnut Halves

Butter a 9 inch square pan and sprinkle with chopped walnuts. Melt marshmallows in milk over hot water; cool. Whip cream and fold into marshmallow mixture. Fold in creme de cacao and instant coffee. Pour into pan, decorate with walnut halves. Chill overnight. Cut into squares to serve. Makes 8 servings.

TIPSIGS or BOURBON BALLS (Candy)

1 - 6 Oz. Pkg. Semi-sweet Chocolate
   Pieces
3 Tbs. White Corn Syrup
½ Cup Bourbon
1 Box, or 2½ Cups, Crushed
   Vanilla Wafers
½ Cup Powdered Sugar
1 Cup Nuts, finely chopped

Melt semi-sweet chocolate over hot, not boiling, water. Add corn syrup and bourbon. Combine crushed wafers, powdered sugar and nuts. Add to chocolate mixture and mix well. Let stand 30 min. Form 1" balls and roll in powdered or granulated sugar. Let ripen in covered container at least several days. The longer, the better. Great for the holidays.

FOOL-PROOF PIE CRUST

4 Cups Flour
1 Tbs. Salt
1¾ Cups Shortening
½ Cup Water
1 Tbs. Vinegar
1 Large Egg
1 Tbs. Sugar

In a large bowl, stir with fork the flour, sugar and salt. Cut in shortening until crumbly. In small bowl, beat together water, egg and vinegar. Add to flour mixture until well moistened. Divide dough into 5 portions and shape each in a flat round patty, ready for rolling. Wrap each in plastic or waxed paper and chill at least 30 minutes.

Hint: Add more flour for rolling, handling too much will not effect this dough. It will also keep in the refrigerator for 3 to 5 days.

GREEN TOMATO MINCEMEAT

1½ Pints Apples
1 Pint Green Tomatoes, ground
2 Tsp. Cinnamon
1 Tsp. Salt
1 Tsp. Allspice
1 Tsp. Cloves
3 Cups Sugar
1 Lb. Raisins
1 Cup Suet
¼ Cup Vinegar

Mix together the ground apples, green tomatoes, cinnamon, salt, allspice, cloves, raisins, suet and vinegar. Cook for 10 to 15 minutes, stirring occasionally to avoid sticking. Makes 3 to 4 quarts. Use in double crust pie (top and bottom crust).

HOT CURRIED FRUIT

1/3 Cup Margarine
¾ Cup Brown Sugar
3 Tsp. Curry Powder
2 Tbs. Pineapple Juice
1 Can Pineapple Chunks
1 Can Pear Slices
1 Can Peach Slices
1 Can Apricot Halves
10 Maraschino Cherries

Mix margarine, brown sugar, curry powder and pineapple juice. Add fruit. Bake at 350 degrees for 45 minutes. Serves 12. Note: If 16 oz. cans of fruit are used, use only 2½ tsp. curry powder. Serve with fish or a ham dinner.

MINCEMEAT

2 Lbs. Tender Beef, cooked
1½ Lbs. Suet
4 Lbs. Apples, chopped
½ Lb. Currants
½ Lb. Raisins
3 Lbs. Sugar, white or brown
1 Lb. Citron, or any mixed dried fruit
1 Orange, grated, juice and pulp
2 Lemons, grated, juice and pulp
1 Oz. Cinnamon
¼ Oz. Cloves
¼ Oz. Mace
¼ Oz. Allspice
¼ Oz. Nutmeg
½ Cup Berry Jam, any kind
1 Quart Apple Cider
½ Cup Vinegar
1 Cup Burgundy Wine

Grind meat, suet, raisins, citron (or dried fruit) and currants. Add rest of ingredients. Usually I remove seeds and membrane from oranges and lemons & grind with rest of ingredients. Also, suet should be separated from thin tissue surrounding it. Make about 2 weeks ahead of time and keep refrigerated until ready to use. Pies may then be made and kept in freezer until needed. This recipe makes about 12 pies. Bake at 400 degrees for about 45 minutes.

SWISS APPLE RINGS

3 Apples
3 Tbs. Flour
3 Eggs
½ Tsp. Baking Powder
½ Cup Warm Milk
½ Tsp. Salt
1 Tsp. Sugar & Cinnamon Mix

Blend flour and milk in a bowl, sprinkle with salt, add baking powder & stir. Add yolks of 3 eggs. Beat egg whites stiff & add to first mixture. Core 3 ripe apples through the center. Slice into rings ¼" thick. Dip rings into batter until covered on both sides. Fry in hot deep fat. Remove and sprinkle with sugar-cinnamon.

IRISH COFFEE en GELEE

1 ½ Tbs. Good Instant Coffee
1 Envelope Unflavored Gelatin
4 Tbs. Sugar
2 Cups Water
2 Ozs. Irish Whiskey

Put ½ cup of cold water in a sauce pan. Sprinkle with gelatin. Add 1½ cups hot water. Stir to dissolve gelatin over heat. Add sugar and Irish Whiskey. Stir until blended. Pour into small serving dishes. Chill until firm. Serve with whipped cream. This is an excellent light dessert.

BRANDIED APPLE SAUCE

6 Tart Green Apples
2 Cups Water
1 Cup Powdered Sugar
1 Tsp. Cinnamon
½ Cup Fruit-flavored Brandy,
  any fruit flavor of your choice

Peel, core and quarter the apples. Place in water and cook over low heat until apples soften. Stir occasionally. Take from fire, add powdered sugar, cinnamon and brandy. Simmer 5 minutes. Serve hot or cold. Excellent with pork chops, chicken or potato pancakes.

TOMATO SAUCE

10 Lbs. Ripe Tomatoes
4 Large Onions
2 Green Peppers
2 Cloves Garlic
4 Tbs. Salad Oil
1 Tbs. Salt
1 Tsp. Pepper
4 Tsp. Monosodium Glutamate
1 Tsp. Dried Basil
2 Tsp. Paprika
2 Tbs. Celery Salt

Scald tomatoes; peel, cut into small pieces and put into large kettle. Finely chop the onions, green peppers and garlic. Lightly brown in the oil in frying pan, stirring occasionally. Add to the tomatoes along with salt, pepper, monosodium glutamate, basil, paprika and celery salt. Cook, uncovered, until mixture is reduced to about three-fourths the original amount, about 1 hour. Stir occasionally to prevent sticking. Remove from heat and when cool, blend with an electric beater to break up large pieces of tomato. Package, label and freeze. Makes 8 pints.

Uses of tomato sauce recipe:

1. Combine 1 pint of thawed sauce with 1 lb. crab meat or shrimp for a creole-style dish.

2. Simmer 1 pint of sauce with 1 lb. hamburger (browned first) for a spaghetti or ravioli sauce; add 1 tsp. oregano, if desired.

3. To 1 pint of sauce add 1 can consomme, diluted according to directions. Simmer with a handful of shell macaroni or other pasta for a version of minestrone.

4. Heat 1 pint tomato sauce with 1 can of consomme and 1 can water; add 2 envelopes (2 tbs.) unflavored gelatin, soaked for a few minutes in ½ cup water. Chill until syrupy; pour into a mold. If desired, stir in crab meat, celery, cubes of chicken, olives or any other foods you like. Chill until set.

5. Pour thawed sauce over pork chops and bake at 350 degrees until meat is well done. Also use in the same way on swiss steaks.

GOLDEN LEMON MARMALADE

1 Lb. Carrots
2 Medium Lemons
3¾ Cups Sugar
½ Tsp. Salt
½ Cup Water
1/3 Cup Maraschino Cherries

Clean carrots and quarter and seed the lemons. Put through fine blade of grinder. Should be about 3 cups of chopped carrots to ¾ cup of lemon. In a large kettle or Dutch oven, put carrots, lemon, sugar, salt and water. Bring to a rolling boil. Cook over medium heat for 10 to 15 minutes. Add sliced cherries, cook 5 minutes more or until thickened. Pour into hot sterilized jelly glasses and seal at once. Makes about 4 - ½ pints. Good way to use up lots of carrots.

CREAM CHEESE FUDGE

2 - 3 Oz. Pkgs. Cream Cheese, softened
2 Tbs. Cream or Milk
4 Cups Confectioner's Sugar
4 Squares Unsweetened Chocolate, melted
1 Tsp. Vanilla
1 Tsp. Rum (optional)
Dash of Salt
1½ Cups Chopped Nuts, divided

Beat cheese and cream until smooth. Gradually beat in sugar, then blend in chocolate. Stir in vanilla, rum, salt and 1 cup nuts. Press into lightly-buttered square pan and cover with remaining nuts. Mark in 64 pieces about 1" square and chill until firm enough to cut, about 15 minutes. Makes 1 lb.

CRANBERRY ICE

1 Quart Cranberries
1 Quart Water
2 Cups Sugar
2 Oranges, juice and grated
  rind

Wash and drain cranberries. Heat cranberries to boiling point and cook until soft. Run through a sieve. Add 2 cups of sugar, juice and grated rind of 2 oranges to pulp. Heat until sugar dissolves. Pour into ice-cream tray and slightly freeze. Take out and beat until very light. Return to tray and finish freezing. Serve with main course of meal as a side dish. Serves 12.

ZUCCHINI CHOW CHOW

10 Cups Ground Zucchini
4 Cups Ground Onions
2 Bell Peppers, green
5 Tbs. Salt
1 Qt. Vinegar
7 Cups Sugar
1 Tsp. Nutmeg
1 Tsp. Turmeric
1 Tsp. Dry Mustard
1 Tsp. Cornstarch
2 Tsp. Celery Seed

This is fabulous! Combine zucchini, onions, peppers and salt. Let set overnight, covered. Rinse with cold water and drain extremely well; press firmly to get water out (this is important).

The next day, add vinegar, sugar, nutmeg, turmeric, dry mustard, cornstarch, and celery seed. Bring to a boil. Simmer 30 minutes. Put in prepared jars and seal. Yields approximately 14 pints.

CREPES SUPREME

Crepes:
2 Eggs, beaten
Dash of Salt
2 Tbs. Melted Butter
2/3 Cup Flour
1-1/3 Cups Milk

Filling:
5 Oz. Italian Sausage
1 Clove Garlic
1½ Pkgs. Frozen Spinach
1 Cup Chopped Chicken
¾ Cup Parmesan Cheese
1 Tsp. Onion Salt

Sauce:
6 Tbs. Butter
6 Tbs. Flour
3 Cups Cream
2 Cups Parmesan Cheese
1 Tsp. Onion Juice
¼ Tsp. Curry Powder

Crepes: Beat 2 eggs till light; add salt and 2 tbs. melted butter. Mix and add 2/3 cup flour with 1-1/3 cups milk. Beat. Cook in crepe pan till bubbles show, then turn till lightly browned. You may freeze these by putting wax paper between the crepes then wrapping well in foil.

Filling: Saute' meat from 5 oz. Italian sausage; break up and drain off fat. Stir in smashed clove of garlic. Cook 1½ pkgs. frozen spinach; drain liquid off and add to sausage. Then add 1 cup cooked, chopped chicken, ¾ cup Parmesan cheese and 1 tsp. onion salt. Put this mixture in each crepe and roll up, securing with toothpick and put in baking dish. Cook for 20 minutes in oven at 350 degrees, after pouring sauce over the crepes. Reserve a small amount of sauce for serving.

Sauce: Melt 6 tbs. butter and blend with 6 tbs. flour. Add 3 cups cream and stir, then add 2 cups Parmesan cheese, 1 tsp. onion juice and ¼ tsp. curry powder. Mushrooms may be added to sauce also.

PEANUT BRITTLE

3 Cups Sugar
1 Cup White Karo
½ Cup Water
3 Cups Raw Peanuts
1/3 Cube Butter
2 Level Tsp. Baking Soda
1 Tsp. Salt

Prepare in a 3-quart saucepan: Sugar, white Karo, water; set aside. Measure into a small dish the baking soda, salt and butter.

With heavy-duty aluminum foil, make a tray about 25 inches long, turn up about 1 inch on each side and butter the bottom of the tray.

Cook all ingredients in saucepan to a boil that can't be stirred down; add 3 cups raw peanuts and cook till peanuts are a golden brown - about 10 minutes, stirring constantly. When peanuts are golden brown, add baking soda, salt and butter. The mixture will foam up a little and when it gets golden brown, pour FAST on buttered foil. Don't touch for 30 minutes. Let cool and break into pieces. For best results, use a wooden spoon for stirring.

SWEET POTATO STUFFING

1¼ Cups Mashed Sweet Potatoes
4 Cups Toasted Bread Cubes
4 Cups Finely Chopped Celery
1/3 Cup Chopped Onion
6 Link Sausages
¼ Tsp. Pepper
¼ Tsp. Salt
¼ Tsp. Rubbed Sage
¼ Tsp. Crumbled Marjoram Leaves
½ Tsp. Ground Thyme
2 Tbs. Butter

Combine the first 4 ingredients in bowl. Cut sausage links into ½ inch pieces and brown; discard grease. Add sausage to the mixture. Blend in remaining ingredients. Mix well and spoon into cavity of chicken or turkey.

MARINATED SHRIMP (Appetizer)

1 Lb. Fresh or Frozen Medium-size
  Shrimp
2 Tsp. Sugar
1 Tsp. Salt
½ Tsp. Mustard
Dash Tabasco Sauce
1 Crushed Bay Leaf
2 Tbs. Worcestershire Sauce
1/3 Cup Vinegar
1/3 Cup Catsup
1 Cup Salad Oil
1 Medium Onion, thinly sliced

Combine all ingredients, except shrimp, in a bowl with a tight-fitting lid (Tupperware). Mix thoroughly and then gently blend in shrimp. Refrigerate for at least 12 hours before serving.

ITALIAN PEPPERS

2 Lbs. Green Peppers, cut into
  ½" wide strips
12 Cloves Garlic, minced
2 Tbs. Fresh Mint Leaves
6 Tbs. Oil
2 Tsp. Cider Vinegar
Salt to taste

Heat half of the oil in a large, cast-iron or heavy pan at medium-high heat. Add half of peppers and keep moving at all times until all bright green color is gone, but peppers are not soft. Turn into large bowl and add half of garlic, half of mint, half of vinegar and salt to taste. Mix well and spoon into clean jars. Repeat same steps for second half of peppers; refrigerate. Will keep for 2 or 3 months.

This is a delicacy with fried egg sandwich, or any other kind of sandwich. Great addition to any meal.

SPICY CHEESE CREPE APPETIZER

1 Cup Grated Cheddar Cheese
½ Cup Sour Cream
3 Oz. Creamed Cheese
1 Lb. Bacon
1 Pkg. Thinly-sliced Spicy Beef
3 Tbs. Mayonnaise
¼ Cup Chopped Celery
2 Tbs. Chopped Parsley
8 Drops Tabasco Sauce
1/3 Tsp. Worcestershire Sauce
¼ Tsp. Dry Mustard
3 Fresh Scallions, sliced thin
½ Cup Chopped Pimento

Slice bacon in thin strips and fry until crisp. Crumble and add to all ingredients in large mixing bowl. Place in Beer Batter Crepes, fold over and cut in half. Garnish each half with sliced green pimento olive. Put remaining parsley around dish. Makes approximately 40 halves.

Beer Batter Crepes:
2 Eggs
2 Egg Yolks
1 Tsp. Salt
1 Cup Flour
1 Cup Beer
1 Tbs. Sour Cream
1 Tbs. Melted Butter

In medium mixing bowl, beat eggs and egg yolks with salt. Gradually add flour alternately with beer. Beat with electric mixer or whisk until smooth. Stir in sour cream and butter. Refrigerate batter about 1 hour. Cook on upside down crepe griddle or in traditional pan. Makes 18 to 22 crepes.

CRANBERRY COCKTAIL

1 Quart Apple Cider
3 Whole Cloves
2 Sticks Cinnamon
2 Whole Allspice
1 Quart Cranberry Juice
1/3 Cup Brown Sugar
Brandy (optional)

To the 1 quart apple cider add cloves, cinnamon and allspice; simmer for 5 minutes in covered container. Add the brown sugar; simmer another 5 minutes. Add cranberry juice. Can be laced with brandy as each cup is served.

CRAB MEAT PUFFS
(Hors d'oeuvres)

Filling:
1 - 7 to 8 Oz. Can Crab Meat, drained and flaked (I prefer King crab)
1 Stalk Celery, chopped fine
½ Small Onion, minced
¼ to ½ Cup Mayonnaise (just enough to make it creamy)
Salt and Pepper to taste
Lemon Juice to taste (1 tsp. to 1 tbs.)
Dash of Worcestershire Sauce, or to taste

Mix all ingredients together and fill miniature cream puffs with crab filling and refrigerate.

Puffs (miniature cream puffs):
½ Cup Butter
¼ Tsp. Salt
1 Cup Boiling Water
1 Cup Sifted Flour
3 Eggs, unbeaten

Add butter and salt to boiling water and stir over medium heat until mixture boils. Lower heat; add flour all at once & beat vigorously until mixture leaves sides of the pan. Add one egg at a time, beating thoroughly after each addition. Shape on greased cookie sheet using 1 tsp. of pastry for 1 puff, depending upon size desired. Bake in a hot oven, 400 degrees, for 10 minutes. Reduce heat to moderate, 350 degrees, and let bake about 30 minutes longer. Remove from oven and place on wire rack to cool. When cold, make slits on side. If there is any soft or spongy dough inside of puff, scoop out. This makes about 4 dozen small puffs. If you have extra puffs after filling with crab filling, you can freeze them.

APPLE—SAUSAGE STUFFING

1 Lb. Sausage
1 Cup Diced Bacon
1 Large Onion, chopped
½ Cup Chopped Celery
½ Lb. Mushrooms, sliced
2 Apples, cored and cut
  into ½" pieces
1 Cup Chopped Parsley
1 Tsp. Sage
1 Tsp. Thyme
1 Loaf Firm White Bread, cut into
  1" cubes
2 Cups Chicken Broth
Salt and Pepper

In large skillet, fry bacon and sausage until crisp and brown. Remove sausage and cut into 1" pieces. Replace in skillet; add onion, celery, mushrooms, apples, parsley & herbs. Saute' for 5 minutes. Stir in bread cubes and broth. Season with salt & pepper to taste. Pour into a bowl; cover and cool. Will stuff a 10 to 12 lb. turkey or bake in a 2-quart casserole for 1 hour at 350 degrees.

TOM AND JERRY BATTER

12 Eggs, separated
½ Tsp. Salt
1 Lb. Butter or Margarine, at room temp.
3 Lbs. Powdered Sugar
1 Tsp. Each Vanilla and Rum Flavoring (also
  may use Brandy Flavoring)
1 Tsp. Mace
1 Tsp. Nutmeg
1 Tsp. Cloves
1 Tsp. Allspice

Beat egg whites until stiff, add salt. Beat egg yolks until light. Cream butter with powdered sugar and mix until crumbly. Add egg yolks and flavorings, mix well. Add spices and egg whites. Beat until well mixed. Batter will keep for several weeks in refrigerator. May be frozen, covered for several months. Use 1 heaping tablespoon of batter for each Tom & Jerry serving. Into a hot mug pour one jigger of rum or brandy and boiling hot water. Place batter in first. Sprinkle with nutmeg. The best ever!

SWEET PICKLES - 14 DAYS

2 Gallons Sliced Cucumbers
2 Cups Salt
1 Gallon Boiling Water
1 Tbs. Alum
5 Pints Boiling Vinegar
6 Cups Sugar
½ Oz. Celery Seed
1 Oz. Cinnamon Stick
3 Cups Sugar
Sterilized Jars

Into sterilized stone jar, put 2 gallons of cucumbers, washed and sliced lengthwise. Regardless of size, they must be sliced or they will shrivel. Dissolve 2 cups salt in 1 gallon boiling water and pour, while hot, over pickles. Cover and weight down the pickles and let stand one week. On the eighth day, drain then pour 1 gallon boiling water over pickles; let them stand 24 hours. On the 9th day, drain. Pour 1 gallon of boiling water with 1 tbs. powdered alum over the pickles; let stand 24 hours. On the following day (10th day), drain again and pour 1 gallon boiling water over them. Let stand 24 hours, then drain.

For the pickling mixture, combine 5 pints vinegar, boiling hot, with 6 cups sugar, the celery seed, cinnamon stick; pour this over the pickles. Drain off for 3 mornings; reheat it and add 1 cup sugar each morning. With the third and last heating, pack the pickles into sterilized glass jars, pour the heated liquid over the pickles and seal. Very good.

EGG-OLIVE SPREAD

3 Hard-Boiled Eggs, chopped
1 - 8 Oz. Pkg. Cream Cheese, softened
½ Small Jar Stuffed Olives, chopped
Garlic Powder
1 to 2 Tbs. Mayonnaise

Sprinkle garlic powder on cream cheese to cover. Mix all other ingredients together. More mayonnaise may be added for spreadability. Spread on crackers and enjoy!

KANSAS WATERMELON PICKLES

3-½ Quarts Watermelon Rind
8 Tsp. Powdered Alum
1 Quart Vinegar
8 Cups Sugar
1 Tbs. Whole Cloves
2 Sticks Cinnamon
Whole Cloves, 2 for each jar
Food Coloring, optional

Trim green and pink from rind and cube.
First day: Cover with water and cook until just tender, about 20 minutes. Add powdered alum to the water and let stand overnight.

Second day: Drain, rinse thoroughly twice. Add to the rind the vinegar, sugar and spices tied in a cloth bag. Bring the syrup to a boil. Stir until sugar is dissolved. Remove from heat. Let stand overnight.

Third day: Again bring to a boil and remove from heat. This time let it stand for 5 days.

Eighth day: At the end of 5 days, remove the bag of spices that have been tied with a string and place cold pickles in jars. Cover with cold syrup. Add 2 cloves to each jar and seal. Yellow, green or red food coloring may be added, if desired. The recipe can be doubled or tripled according to the size of the watermelon it contains.

PEANUT BUTTER FUDGE

2/3 Cup Canned Milk
2 Cups Granulated Sugar
½ Pint Jar of Marshmallow Creme
1 Cup Chunk Style Peanut Butter
1 Tsp. Vanilla

Grease sides of a heavy 2 quart saucepan. Combine sugar and milk in it. Stir over medium heat until sugar dissolves and mixture boils. Cook to soft ball stage (234 degrees on candy thermometer). Remove from heat and add peanut butter and marshmallow cream and vanilla. Stir until well blended. Pour into greased 9x9x2" pan. Cut when firm.

BEEF JERKY

3 Lbs. Flank Steak or Round Steak,
 cut ½" thick
1½ Tbs. Salt
½ Cup Warm Water
½ Cup Soya Sauce
½ Cup Worcestershire Sauce
1 Tsp. Coarse-ground Pepper
Garlic Powder to taste

Cut meat in ¾" wide strips with grain. Dissolve salt in warm water and then add remaining ingredients. Soak meat in above mixture about 2 hours, turning strips of meat frequently so that each piece is drenched with mixture. Place strips of meat on paper towels for a few minutes. Then place strips of meat on oven rack. Turn heat on to 120 to 130 degrees and cook at this temperature for 8 to 9 hours with oven door slightly cracked open. After cooking, turn off heat, open oven door and let air dry for 8 hours more. Package jerky in bags or jars.

BEER BATTER for DEEP—FRIED FISH

1½ to 2 Lbs. Cob, Jumbo Shrimp, etc.
1 Pkg. Dry Yeast
1 Cup Beer, warm
1 Cup Flour
Pinch of Salt
1 Egg White

In warm bowl, dissolve 1 pkg. of dry yeast in ½ cup of warm beer. Add 1 cup flour sifted with pinch of salt (do not need to sift Wondra flour) and stir. Add more beer (about ½ cup) as needed for "sticky-run" dough. Cover with cloth and let stand in a warm place for ½ hour or more. Fold in egg white and use immediately. Serves 6.

CRISP-COATED HAM BALLS (Appetizer)

3 Tbs. Butter or Margarine
2 Cups Ground Cooked Ham
½ Tsp. Worcestershire Sauce
1 Medium Onion, finely chopped
1 Egg, slightly beaten
1 Tbs. Parsley, chopped
6 Tbs. Flour
1 - 1 Lb. Can Sauerkraut
Salad Oil (for frying)

Batter:
1-1/3 Cups Flour
½ Tsp. Paprika
1 Cup Water

In a large frying pan, melt butter, add onion and saute' for 5 minutes. Add flour and cook 3 minutes longer. Remove from heat and stir in ham, egg, well-drained and finely-chopped sauerkraut, Worcestershire sauce and parsley. Blend well. Cool, cover and chill thoroughly. Combine flour, paprika and water for batter and beat until smooth. In deep pan, heat 1½ to 2 inches of oil to 375 degrees. Shape chilled ham mixture into walnut-sized balls. Dip each ball into batter, drain briefly and fry a few at a time in hot oil until golden, about 2 minutes. Remove with a slotted spoon and let drain. Arrange cooked balls on a cookie sheet in a single layer and freeze. Then package air-tight. To serve, heat frozen balls, uncovered, in a 400 degree oven for 15 minutes or until heated through. Makes 4 to 5 appetizers.

COFFEE LIQUEUR

2 Cups Sugar
2 Cups Water
¼ Cup Instant Coffee (not freeze dried)
½ Cup Water
1 Fifth Vodka or Brandy
½ of a Vanilla Bean

Boil 2 cups sugar and water for 5 minutes. Then add coffee and ½ cup water.

Let cool; add vodka or brandy and the vanilla bean. Let stand at least 6 days.

SUPER LOW—CAL TOMATO DRESSING

1 Cup Tomato Juice
2 Tbs. Lemon Juice
1 Thin Slice Onion
1 Tsp. Prepared Mustard
¼ Tsp. Salt
½ Tsp. Celery Seed
Dash Hot Pepper Sauce
2 Tsp. Worcestershire Sauce

Combine tomato juice, lemon juice, onion, mustard, salt, celery seed, pepper sauce & Worcestershire in blender container; blend until onion is puréed. Makes 1 cup, with about 3 calories per tablespoon.

QUESADILLAS
(A Great Afternoon Snack)

Flour Tortillas
Monterey Jack Cheese (as needed)
1 Green Onion, chopped
1 Tbs. Sour Cream
Hot Sauce
Tomatoes
Lettuce
Cheddar Cheese

Slice cheese so that ½ of the tortilla is covered. Sprinkle onions on top of cheese. Spread as much or as little sour cream on the other half of the tortilla. Fold the tortilla in half so that all the ingredients are inside with the sour cream on top. Place in a 350 degree oven for about 5 minutes or until the cheese has melted. Then devour & enjoy.

PIQUANT COCKTAIL MEAT BALLS

2 Lbs. Ground Beef Round
1 Cup Packaged Corn Flake Crumbs
1/3 Cup Dried Parsley Flakes
2 Eggs
2 Tbs. Soy Sauce
¼ Tsp. Pepper
½ Tsp. Garlic Powder
1/3 Cup Catsup
2 Tbs. Instant Minced Onion
1 - 1 Lb. Can Jellied Cranberry Sauce
1 - 12 Oz. Bottle Chili Sauce
2 Tbs. Firmly-packed Brown Sugar
1 Tbs. Bottled Lemon Juice

Heat oven to 350 degrees. In a large bowl combine beef, corn flake crumbs, parsley flakes, eggs, soy sauce, pepper, garlic powder, catsup and minced onion; blend well. Form mixture into small meat balls about the size of walnuts. Arrange meat balls in a 15½" x 10½" x 1" pan. In a medium-size saucepan, combine cranberry sauce, chili sauce, brown sugar and lemon juice. Cook over moderate heat (about 250° F), stirring occasionally until mixture is smooth and cranberry sauce is melted. Pour over meat balls.

Bake, uncovered, 30 minutes. Serve in a chafing dish with toothpicks. Makes about 60 meat balls. Your time: 15 minutes. Baking time: 30 minutes.

AVOCADO - ORTEGA DIP

1 - 7 Oz. Can Ortega Diced Green Chilies
1 Bunch Green Onions
1 Ripe Avocado
1 - No. 303 Can Stewed Tomatoes
¼ Tsp. Garlic Salt
Sliced & Drained Olives
Salt to taste

Chop the onions and tomatoes. Do not drain the tomatoes. Dice the avocado. Mix these and all remaining ingredients togetner in a large air tight bowl. Refrigerate for 5 to 6 hours before serving. Serve with dip size corn chips. Makes 4 cups.

CHIHUAHUA CHEESE DIP

1 - 8 Oz. Pkg. Grated Sharp Cheddar Cheese
1 - 8 Oz. Pkg. Grated Velveeta Cheese
1 - 8 Oz. Pkg. Cream Cheese
1½ Pints Sour Cream
1 - 7 Oz. Can La Victoria Chili Salsa
1 - 4 Oz. Can Ortega Diced Chilies
2 Oz. Chopped Ripe Olives
2 Oz. Chopped Pimentos
1 Med. Onion, minced
¼ Tsp. Garlic Powder
½ Tsp. Chili Powder
Salt and Pepper to taste

Soften cream cheese and mix well with sour cream. Add all other ingredients & stir until well blended. Serve with tortilla chips or Fritos.

HOMEMADE "CRACKER JACKS"

10 Cups Popped Corn
1½ Cups Cocktail Peanuts
½ Cup Margarine
1 Cup Firmly Packed Light Brown Sugar
¼ Cup Dark Corn Syrup
¼ Tsp. Salt
¼ Tsp. Baking Soda
½ Tsp. Vanilla

Mix together the popped corn and the peanuts in a very large bowl or a roast pan. Keep warm in a 250 degree oven. Melt butter in a heavy 2 quart saucepan. Stir in the brown sugar, corn syrup and salt. Bring to a rolling boil, stirring constantly. Boil without stirring for 5 minutes. Remove from the heat. Stir in baking soda and vanilla. Quickly pour over warm popcorn and peanut mixture while tossing until popcorn and nuts are well coated. Spread out in a shallow baking pan or cookie sheet. Bake at 250 deg. for 45 minutes. Stir about every 15 min. Make sure every piece of popcorn has been moved around on the bottom. Remove from the oven. Turn out on aluminum foil to let 't cool. Store in a tightly covered container. Makes 2 quarts.

YOGURT

1 Cup Tepid Water
1½ Cups Powdered Skim Milk
3 Tbs. Yogurt Culture
1 Qt. Tepid Water
1 Large Can Evaporated Milk

Mix the 1½ cups of powdered milk into the 1 cup of tepid water. Dissolve all milk well. Buy a small carton of plain yogurt to obtain the 3 tbs. yogurt culture. Mix the powdered milk mixture, the yogurt culture, the quart of water and the evaporated milk. Pour into eight 8 oz. glasses. Set them in a pan of warm water (105 to 120 degrees). Put into the oven with only the pilot light on. Leave in oven overnight until it thickens. When set, put into refrigerator. Serve with fruit. You can also make a salad dressing with it. But be sure to save enough for your own starter next time.

HOMEMADE MINCEMEAT

1 Lb. Lean, Boneless Stew Meat
6 Tbs. Beef Suet
2 Lbs. Green Cooking Apples
½ Lb. Seedless Raisins
1 Tsp. Salt
1 Tsp. Chopped, Candied Orange Peel
1 Tsp. Chopped, Candied Lemon Peel
2 Cups Brown Sugar
½ Tsp. Grated Nutmeg
1½ Tsp. Ground Cinnamon
½ Tsp. Ground Cloves
½ Tsp. Ground Ginger
2 Cups Apple Cider

Cut meat in very small pieces. Chop the apples in small pieces. Cut suet in small pieces. Combine ingredients in the order given and simmer very gently for two hours. Very low heat should be used. If you have an asbestos pad, put it under the kettle to prevent scorching. Keep in tightly-covered jars in a cool place until needed. This mincemeat will keep six months.

JALAPENO PEPPER JELLY

1½ Cups Seeded & Finely-Chopped
  Green Bell Pepper
¼ Cup Seeded & Chopped Fresh Jalapeno
  Peppers
1½ Cups Apple Cider Vinegar
6 Cups Sugar
1 Bottle Certo Liquid
8 Drops Green Food Coloring

Blend green peppers and ½ cup vinegar in blender. Add sugar and remainder of vinegar. Bring to a boil. When you can't stir down the boil, remove from heat and let stand 5 minutes. Skim, then add Certo and coloring. Stir until liquid starts to thicken; pour into sterilized jars.

ZUCCHINI—CAULIFLOWER SWEET RELISH

10 Cups Zucchini, ground
4 Cups Cucumber, ground
4 Medium Onions, ground
2 Small Heads Cauliflower, ground
1½ Cups Water
3 Tsp. Salt
3 Cups Vinegar
5¾ Cups Sugar
1-1/3 Tbs. Dry Mustard
1-1/3 Tbs. Turmeric
1 Tbs. Pepper
2-2/3 Tbs. Celery Seed
1-1/3 Tbs. Nutmeg

1. Grind the above vegetables. If using large zucchini, remove seed before grinding.
2. After you have ground everything, put in large container, add salt and water. Cover and let stand overnight.
3. Next morning drain, and add ALL spices and vinegar and sugar.
4. Bring to a light boil and cook 30 minutes. Pour into hot sterile jars. Makes 9½ pints.

KISSES

2 Egg Whites
¾ Cup Sugar
1 Small Pkg. Chocolate or Butterscotch,
  or Mint Chocolate Chips
Few Grains of Salt

Turn oven to 350 degrees. Beat egg whites
with salt. Add sugar gradually. Beat until
very stiff. Fold in chips. Mix well. Drop
by teaspoons on ungreased cookie sheet.
These stay in the shape you put them in.
By this time, the oven should be heated to
350 degrees. Put kisses in oven. Turn the
oven off and leave in overnight. For variations, color the meringues. When using
mint chocolate chips, color meringues green
(3 drops). Butterscotch chips go well with
meringues colored pink (3 drops).

TV SNACK

¼ Cup Butter or Margarine
1 Tbs. Worcestershire Sauce
½ Tsp. Salt (scant)
½ Tsp. Garlic Salt
½ Tsp. Onion Salt
½ Tsp. Celery Salt
1-½ Cups Cheerios
1 Cup Wheat Chex
1 Cup Rice Chex
1½ Cups Thin Pretzels
1 Cup Spanish Peanuts
½ Cup Mixed Nuts, or family favorite

The above proportions can be increased
or decreased according to family prefer-
ences.

Melt butter and add flavoring. Place
mixture of cereals, pretzels and nuts in
large shallow pan. Pour butter mixture
over cereal, pretzels and nuts. Place in
slow oven, 250 degrees, and heat for
1½ hours, mixing occasionally.

FILLED OVEN PANCAKE

Italian Sausage Filling:
½ Lb. Italian Sausage, casings removed
½ Cup Chopped Green Pepper
1 Onion, chopped (small onion)
1 Clove Garlic, minced or pressed
½ Tsp. Dry Basil
½ Tsp. Thyme Leaves
4 Tbs. Butter or Margarine (approximate)
1 Cup Shredded Cheddar Cheese

Pancake:
1 Cup Milk
1 Cup Flour
4 Eggs

Topping:
Canned Pizza Sauce, heated, to pass
  around as topping,

Crumble the Italian sausage, casings removed,
into a frying pan and stir over medium heat
for 2 to 3 minutes. Add the chopped green
pepper, chopped onion, garlic, dry basil and
thyme. Cook until lightly browned; remove
from heat. Tip pan to estimate drippings,
then add butter to make about 5 tbs. fat.
Also shred and measure cheese (to be used
later).

Transfer sausage filling to a 9" x 13" baking
pan. Place the pan with filling in a 425 degree oven until butter melts and bubbles.
Meanwhile, quickly mix pancake batter. In
a blender, break eggs into container and
whirl at high speed for 1 minute. With the
motor running, gradually pour in milk, then
slowly add flour; whirl for 30 seconds (or
with a rotary beater, beat eggs until light,
then gradually beat in milk and then flour).
Remove pan from oven; quickly pour in the
batter; sprinkle with cheese and return to
oven. Bake until puffy and browned, about
20 to 25 minutes. Serve immediately with
pizza sauce, heated, to pass around as topping. Serves about 4. Serve for brunch or
supper.

BUTTERCRUNCH

1 Cup Broken Almonds
1 Cup White Sugar
¼ Cup Butter
¼ Cup Margarine
2 Cups Almond Meal

Melt butter and margarine at low temperature, below 250 degrees. Add sugar, when butter and sugar are well blended, add broke almonds and increase heat to 325 degrees within 7 minutes. The sugar mixture will first take on a creamy color and will not cling to the nuts and oil may separate from the mixture. As the heat is increased, the mixture will turn slightly tan. The heat is further increased to 350 degrees and held at that temperature for a few minutes, stirring constantly. More tan color will appear, the almonds will begin to crack with an audible popping sound and will turn very slightly tan. The mixture will become more fluid, will cling to the nuts and there will be a slight burned smell with some smoking. It is now time to remove from the heat. Total time 10 minutes from adding broken almonds. Before starting, spread the almond meal on a large sheet cake pan to a ¼" thickness. Upon removing mixture from heat, allow to cool slightly to avoid scorching, then pour mixture onto the prepared pan. Additional almond meal should be added to the top of the mixture and the candy pressed down to a thickness of 3/8 inch or less. Allow to cool, then break into desired size for serving. Surplus almond meal which does not cling to the candy may be reused. When cool the candy should be brittle and should shatter when struck. If it is sugary and not brittle, it is not cooked long enough or hot enough. If it is too dark and has too much burnt flavor it was too hot or cooked too long. For broken almonds use food chopper with coarse blade, for meal, use fine blade.

AMBER PEAR PRESERVES

4 Cups Under-Ripe Pears
3 Cups Sugar
1-½ Tbs. Lemon Juice

This recipe is about 75 years old. Peel and chop under-ripe pears. Let stand overnight with sugar and lemon juice. Stir then put on low fire and let simmer until pears have turned amber color, about 2 hours. Go by color. Stir to be sure it isn't sticking. Pour in prepared jars and seal. Use all juice. You are really in for a treat.

HAM-CHEESE LOGS

4 Oz. Sharp Cheddar Cheese, shredded
   (1 cup)
1 - 8 Oz. Pkg. Cream Cheese, softened
1 - 4½ Oz. Can Deviled Ham
½ Cup Pitted, Chopped Ripe Olives
½ Cup Finely Chopped Pecans

Have cheddar cheese at room temperature. In small mixer bowl, beat together cheddar cheese and cream cheese until blended. Beat in deviled ham; stir in olives and chill. Shape into two 8 inch long logs. Roll in pecans. Serve with crackers.

BOURBON BALLS

1 Small Pkg. Vanilla Wafers
1 Cup Chopped Pecans
1 Cup Powdered Sugar
2 Tbs. Cocoa
1½ Tbs. White Corn Syrup
2 Jiggers Bourbon Whiskey

Roll vanilla wafers until they are in fine crumbs. Mix crumbs with sugar, cocoa and nuts. Dissolve corn syrup in whiskey and add to the dry ingredients. Mix well to blend. The mixture must be moist enough to hold together. Form into small balls and roll in powdered sugar.

SALT CANDY

2 Cups Sugar
¾ Cup Sweet Milk
½ Tsp. Soda
1-½ Tsp. Vanilla
1 Tbs. Butter
1-½ Cups Pecans or Walnuts

Put sugar, milk, and soda in large saucepan and cook until a few drops in cold water form a soft ball. Remove from heat and add butter, vanilla, and nuts. Beat until creamy and drop to form patties on wax paper over which salt has been sprinkled. As candy cooks, it will turn golden brown. The finished candy is similar to pralines in appearance but different in flavor.

FROSTED SANDWICHES

2 Loaves Sandwich Bread
4 Cups Turkey or Chicken
8 Sieved Hard Boiled Eggs
1 Cup Chopped Ripe Olives
1½ Cups Mayonnaise (approx.)
1 Tbs. Instant Minced Onion

Frosting:
4 - 6 Oz. Pkgs. Sharp Cheese (Squeeze-
   A-Snack)
1 Cup Margarine or Butter
2 Eggs

Cut large rounds from 72 slices of bread with large doughnut or cookie cutter. Butter each slice lightly on both sides. Mix above filling ingredients well. Spread filling on bread rounds, top with another slice, spread again with filling and top with another round, making 3 slices to each sandwich and 24 sandwiches in all. Beat frosting ingredients until creamy and fluffy. Spread each sandwich with above frosting on both sides and top. Put on cookie sheet, not touching for at least 24 hours. When ready to serve, bake in a 350 degree oven for 15 minutes. These can be made a day or two ahead and make a delightful luncheon with a gelatin salad and some relishes. If any are left, they can be frozen for a short time. Leftover bread scraps may be used for dressing, pudding, etc.

CAVIAR MOUSSE

6 Hard-boiled Eggs, chopped fine
1 Cup Mayonnaise
2 Tbs. Lemon Juice
1 Tbs. Water
1 Pkg. Knox Gelatine
1 Tsp. Worcestershire Sauce
1 Tsp. Freshly Grated Onion
Salt & Pepper to taste
5 or 6 Oz. Caviar (lumpfish)

In a small saucepan, heat the gelatine, lemon juice and water to liquid consistency, do not boil. Add mayonnaise, chopped eggs, onion, Worcestershire sauce, salt and pepper to the gelatine mixture. Mix together and then carefully fold in the caviar. Pour mousse into an oiled mold and then refrigerate. Since the mixture sets up very quickly, it can be made the day it is to be used. It is particularly effective when molded into a fish and garnished accordingly after it has been turned out onto a serving dish. Serve with Melba toast or crackers.

Note: The combination of ingredients causes the mousse to turn green upon standing. However, it is perfectly edible and will keep for several days under refrigeration.

LITTLE PIZZAS (Appetizers)

1 Lb. Longhorn Cheese
1 Bunch Green Onions
1 Small Can Chopped Olives
¼ Cup Wesson Oil
1 Can Tomato Sauce
2 Tbs. Catsup
1 Tbs. Worcestershire Sauce
1½ Tsp. Oregano
Dash Tabasco
1 Pkg. English Muffins

Combine all ingredients. Spread over muffins; broil until bubbly and slightly brown. Cut into bite-size pieces. Delicious! P.S. Place in middle of oven when broiling.

NO—COOKING DILL PICKLES

1 Gallon Whole Cucumbers, small
   to medium
8 or 10 Dill Sprigs, about a foot long,
   with flower heads
6 Medium Cloves Garlic
6 or 8 Large Fresh Grape Leaves, if
   available (they make the pickles
   stay crisp)
One-half Pod Fresh Jalapeno Pepper
   OR 1 Long Green Chili OR 2 Tsp.
   Hot Pepper Sauce
6 Tbs. Salt (or 5 Tbs. Salt Substitute
   made of potassium chloride etc.,
   for low-sodium diet, if approved by
   your physician)
4 Tbs. Prepared Horseradish (OR, better,
   the equivalent of fresh horseradish root
   cut into thin strips)
3 Pints (approximate) White Vinegar
2 Pints (approximate) Water
4 Bay Leaves (OR 2 Calif. Bay, split in
   half)

Line bottom of gallon jar with 3 or 4 grape
leaves, if using them. Add to bottom of jar
2 or 3 sprigs of dill & pack in cucumbers
vertically, as many as will stand up on bottom of jar. Having peeled and cut up the
garlic (about 6 pieces each clove), drop one-
half of it among the cucumbers and add one-
half the horseradish, 2 bay leaves and one-
half the shredded, seeded chili pepper or 1
tsp. pepper sauce, whichever you are using.
Add a few more sprigs of dill, flower heads
on top and poking the stems down among
the cucumbers. Add one-half the salt, or
substitute. Finish packing the jar with cucumbers, putting the remaining garlic, bay
leaves, horseradish and chili pepper among
it, and the dill, with its heads toward the
top of the jar. Do not pack the jar full
above its "shoulder." Tuck the remaining
grape leaves over the top of the pack, after
having added the remaining salt, or salt
substitute.

Pour in 3 cups of vinegar, then 2 cups of
water. Add additional liquid in the propor-
tion of 3 parts vinegar plus 2 parts water,
to fill jar so as to cover the packed vegetables. Tuck a plastic lid between the shoulder
and the neck of the jar, to hold the pickles
about half an inch below the surface of the
liquid. Note: If using a straight-sided crock
or a glass or enamel container (NEVER A
METAL ONE), weight pickles down with a
small glass or china plate or two. Cover
loosely.

In a few days, when set in a cool cupboard
or anywhere out of the direct sunlight, the
pickles will turn from bright green to a dull-
yellowish "pickle green." They are then
ready to eat. They will, if not eaten, keep
a month or two in the jar.

For longer storage, drain off juice, bring it
to a boil and pour it over the pickles in the
strainer. Then pack the pickles into sterilized canning jars (sliced, if you wish), re-
boil the juice and pour it HOT over the
pickles and seal the jars. If not enough
juice, add 3 parts vinegar plus 2 parts water, boiling hot, to fill jars.

Note: This method also works for dill-
pickled green beans, zucchini or okra, or
whole green tomatoes. A few sticks of
celery or slices of onion are a good addition to these vegetables, but not to cucumbers. Herbs and spices may be added or
omitted to taste, so long as you use dill,
salt, garlic, vinegar and water as above.
Pack smaller vegetables in quarts.

PIE DOUGH FOR SIX

5 Lbs. (less 1 Cup) Flour
3 Lbs. Crisco
2 Cups Sugar
3 Cups Boiling Water
1/3 Cup Salt

Mix all ingredients well. Put in boiling
water; mix with wooden spoon or paddle.
Knead with hand till nice and round; put
into balls large enough for one pie, either
for top and bottom crusts, or just bottom
crust. Freeze till ready to make pies.
Keeps well. Should make 5 or 6 pies,
top and bottom. Put into Ziploc bags
(these can be used again).

COFFEE CRUNCH FROSTING

1½ Cups Sugar
¼ Tsp. Instant Coffee
¼ Cup Light Corn Syrup
¼ Cup Hot Water
1 Tbs. Baking Soda
½ Pt. Whipping Cream

Mix the first 4 ingredients and cook together to 290 degrees (hard-crack). Remove from heat and add baking soda. Stir vigorously until mixture pulls from sides of pan. Pour into a 9 inch ungreased pan. Do not spread or stir, cool. Knock out of pan and crush candy into coarse crumbs between layers of waxed paper. This may be done with a rolling pin. Cover cake with sweetened whipped cream and then with crumbs.

LIVERWURST SPREAD

1 - 10 Oz. Pkg. Liverwurst (Braunschweiger)
1 Can Consomme
1 Tbs. Horseradish
1 Envelope Knox Gelatine
6 Oz. Cream Cheese
½ Tsp. Onion Juice
1 Clove Garlic, crushed
Pinch of Dry Mustard
Salt to taste

Heat soup to boiling; add gelatine which has been dissolved in warm water. Put a thin layer of soup in mold and put in refrigerator to set. Add remaining soup to other ingredients and whip. When well mixed, pour into mold over the already-set soup. Two tablespoons of bourbon may be added. Makes about 2½ cups.

Note: It is well to spray your mold with Pam, then it will not be necessary to set the pan in hot water to unmold; just slip a knife blade to let a little air get under the pate', hold the pan upside down and it it will fall right out.

CHICKEN YUM—STICKS

20 to 25 Chicken Fryer Wings
1 Cup Water
1 Cup Soya Sauce
¼ Cup Pineapple Juice
¼ Cup Salad Oil
1 Tsp. Garlic Powder
1 Tsp. Ginger

Break apart chicken wings at first and second joints. Cook the tips separately with onion, salt and celery for chicken broth. Mix all ingredients above and pour over chicken in large, shallow dish and cover. Refrigerate overnight. Bake, uncovered, on a flat cookie sheet, 10" x 15" x 1". Bake at 350 degrees for 45 minutes, or until tender and brown. Makes 4 to 6 servings, or may be used as hors d'oeuvres.

SPINACH DRESSING (Best Ever)

½ Lb. Spinach
4 Cups Coarse Bread Crumbs
¾ Lb. Pork Sausage
2 Medium Onions
3 Oz. Cream Cheese
Salt and Pepper
1 Egg, beaten
½ Tsp. Dried Thyme

Wash spinach and cook in saucepan with small amount of water for 10 minutes; remove from liquid and chop. Sprinkle some of liquid over bread crumbs. Cook sausage in heavy skillet, covered, for 10 minutes. Remove sausage and add onions to fat in skillet; cook till golden brown. Mash sausage with fork and add to the spinach; combine with onions. Blend cream cheese with mixture; add egg to bread crumbs and blend well with spinach mixture in skillet. Heat but do not brown. Add seasonings. Should be light, not too moist. Mix and use for stuffing a 16 lb. turkey, or cool & store in refrigerator till ready to use.

PINEAPPLE FUDGE

3 Cups Sugar
1 Small Can Crushed Pineapple
1 Cup Canned Milk
Butter (the size of an egg)
1 Cup Chopped Nuts
¼ Cup White Karo Syrup
¼ Tsp. Cream of Tartar

Combine sugar, pineapple, milk, karo
and cream of tartar in a 3 quart saucepan;
stir well over fire. Cook over medium heat;
stir occasionally to keep from sticking.
Test with drop in cold water to form ball.
After a good soft ball forms, remove from
heat and add butter and nuts. Let stand
for 5 minutes. Then beat and pour into
a buttered pan. Cut when firm.

CHI CHI

1¼ Oz. Sweet & Sour Mix
1¼ Oz. Vodka
2 Oz. Pineapple Juice
1/3 Oz. Coconut Syrup

Mix with ice in blender; garnish with
pineapple spear.

EGG NOG

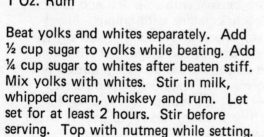

6 Eggs
¾ Cup Sugar
1 Pint Cream, whipped
1 Pint Milk
1 Pint Whiskey, optional
1 Oz. Rum

Beat yolks and whites separately. Add
½ cup sugar to yolks while beating. Add
¼ cup sugar to whites after beaten stiff.
Mix yolks with whites. Stir in milk,
whipped cream, whiskey and rum. Let
set for at least 2 hours. Stir before
serving. Top with nutmeg while setting.

SPECK KNÖDEL (Dumpling with Bacon)

16 to 18 Slices Stale Bread, cubed
¼ Lb. Bacon, cubed
1 Large Onion, chopped
2 Tbs. Chopped Parsley
4 Eggs
¾ Cup Milk
¾ Cup Flour

Place cubed bread into a bowl. Fry out
cubed bacon. Add onion and parsley &
saute' for 5 minutes over low heat. Pour
over the bread cubes and bacon mixture
and add the eggs and milk. Mix and let
stand for ½ hour. When ready to cook,
add flour and blend well. Shape into
dumplings. Dip hands into flour & round
out dumplings by hand. Cook in a large
pot of boiling, salted water. As soon as
they rise to the top of the water, reduce
heat and cook 2 or 3 minutes longer so
the center will be cooked. Lift out with
a slotted spoon; drain well on paper
towels. Serve with roast and gravy.

MONTEREY FONDUE

5 Slices (round loaf) Sourdough
  Bread, crusts removed
1 Lb. Sharp Cheddar Cheese
1 Can Niblet Corn
1 - 7 Oz. Can Green Chilies, seeds
  removed and chilies sliced
4 Eggs
2½ Cups Milk
1 Tsp. Dry Mustard
Salt and Pepper to taste

Butter both sides of bread slices and cut
into cubes. Grate the cheese. Arrange
half of bread in bottom of a 9" x 13"
casserole; cover with one-half can of corn.
Put half of sliced chilies over corn; sprinkle half of cheese on and repeat layers.

Combine eggs with milk, mustard, salt
and pepper; beat and pour over all. Refrigerate overnight. Bake in pan of water,
at 350 degrees, 45 to 50 minutes.

MAIN DISHES

MAIN DISHES (Cont.)

CAKES - BREADS

CAKES & BREADS (Cont.)

CAKES & BREADS (Cont.)

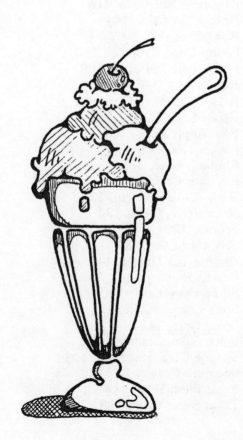

DESSERTS

DESSERTS (Cont.)

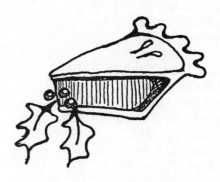

AN INFALLIBLE RECIPE FOR PRESERVING CHILDREN

Take:
1 Large Grassy Field
½ Doz. Children
2 or 3 Small Dogs
A Pinch of Brook & Some Pebbles

Mix the children and the dogs together well and put them in the field, stirring constantly. Pour the brook over the pebbles. Sprinkle this field with flowers.

Spread Over All: A deep blue sky. Bake in the hot sun. When brown, remove and set away to cool in a bathtub.

COOKIES

SALADS

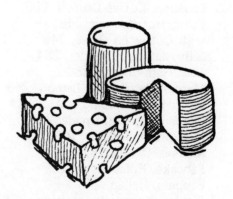

MISCELLANEOUS

GOD BLESS MY KITCHEN

God bless my little kitchen
I love its every nook
And bless me as I do my work,
Wash pots and pans and cook.

And the meals that I prepare
Be seasoned from above
With Thy blessing and Thy grace,
But most of all Thy love.

As we partake of earthly food,
Thy table for us spread,
We'll not forget to thank Thee Lord,
Who gives us daily bread.

So bless my little kitchen, God,
And those who enter in,
May they find naught but joy and peace
And happiness therein.